Deep Refrains

Deep Refrains

MUSIC, PHILOSOPHY,
AND THE INEFFABLE

Michael Gallope

The University of Chicago Press   CHICAGO & LONDON

The University of Chicago Press, Chicago 60637
The University of Chicago Press, Ltd., London
© 2017 by The University of Chicago
All rights reserved. No part of this book may be used or reproduced in any manner whatsoever without written permission, except in the case of brief quotations in critical articles and reviews. For more information, contact the University of Chicago Press, 1427 E. 60th St., Chicago, IL 60637.
Published 2017

26 25 24 23 22 21 20 19 18   2 3 4 5

ISBN-13: 978-0-226-48355-9 (cloth)
ISBN-13: 978-0-226-48369-6 (paper)
ISBN-13: 978-0-226-48372-6 (e-book)
DOI: 10.7208/chicago/9780226483726.001.0001

LIBRARY OF CONGRESS CATALOGING-IN-PUBLICATION DATA
Names: Gallope, Michael, author.
Title: Deep refrains : music, philosophy, and the ineffable / Michael Gallope.
Description: Chicago : The University of Chicago Press, 2017. | Includes bibliographical references and index.
Identifiers: LCCN 2017021802| ISBN 9780226483559(cloth : alk. paper) | ISBN 9780226483696 (pbk. : alk. paper) | ISBN 9780226483726 (e-book)
Subjects: LCSH: Music—Philosophy and aesthetics. | Bloch, Ernst, 1885-1977—Criticism and interpretation. | Adorno, Theodor W., 1903-1969—Criticism and interpretation. | Jankélévitch, Vladimir, 1903-1985—Criticism and interpretation. | Deleuze, Gilles, 1925-1995—Criticism and interpretation. | Guattari, Félix, 1930-1992—Criticism and interpretation.
Classification: LCC ML3800 .G18 2017 | DDC 781.1/7—dc23
LC record available at https://lccn.loc.gov/2017021802

Publication of this book has been supported by the AMS 75 Pays Endowment of the American Musicological Society, funded in part by the National Endowment for the Humanities and the Andrew W. Mellon Foundation.

CONTENTS

Musical Examples vii
Figures ix

Introduction   1

PRELUDE   A Paradox of the Ineffable   33

   0.1 *Schopenhauer's Deep Copy*   34
   0.2 *The Platonic Solutions*   42
   0.3 *Four Dialectical Solutions (after Nietzsche)*   49

1   Bloch's Tone   63
   1.1 *The Tone*   69
   1.2 *The Natural Klang*   77
   1.3 *The Expressive Tone*   79
   1.4 *Bloch's Magic Rattle*   81
   1.5 *The Tone's Ineffable Utopia*   84
   1.6 *The Event-Forms*   91
   1.7 *A Dialectical Account of Music History*   95
   1.8 *Utopian Musical Speech*   98

2   Adorno's Musical Fracture   107
   2.1 *Adorno's Tone*   111
   2.2 *Adorno's Conception of History*   118
   2.3 *Tendenz des Materials*   122
   2.4 *Music's Language-Like Ineffability*   127
   2.5 *The Immanent Critique*   136
   2.6 *The Paradox of Mahler's Vernacular*   145
   2.7 *The Curve of Inconsistency*   155

INTERLUDE Wittgenstein's Silence 160

3 Jankélévitch's Inconsistency   165
   3.1 *Bergson and the Inconsistency of Time*   169
   3.2 *The Aporetic Source of Fidelity*   173
   3.3 *Charme*   181
   3.4 *Cosmic Silence*   192
   3.5 *Unwoven Dialectics*   199

4 Deleuze and Guattari's Rhythm   204
   4.1 *Deleuze's Rhythm*   207
   4.2 *The Rhythm of Sense*   211
   4.3 *A Structuralist Quadrivium*   215
   4.4 *The Rhythm of Life*   224
   4.5 *Sonorous Coextensions*   229

Conclusion: A Paradox of the Vernacular 243
Acknowledgments 259
Notes 261
Select Bibliography 301
Index 325

MUSICAL EXAMPLES

1.1. Wolfgang Amadeus Mozart, *Die Zauberflöte*, K. 620, act 2, "Der, welcher wandert diese Straße voll Beschwerden," mm. 15–25   100
1.2. Ludwig van Beethoven, Symphony no. 3 in E-flat major, "Eroica," op. 55, mvt. 2, mm. 114–21   101
2.1. Arnold Schoenberg, *Harmonielehre*, 53   129
2.2. Beethoven, Sonata no. 14 in C-sharp minor, "Quasi una fantasia," op. 27, no. 2, mm. 162–66   135
2.3. Schoenberg, *Herzgewächse*, op. 20, mm. 1–2, harmonium part (right hand)   139
2.4. Schoenberg, *Herzgewächse*, op. 20, mm. 1–4, soprano part   140
2.5. Schoenberg, *Herzgewächse*, op. 20, mm. 15–18, soprano part   140
2.6. Schoenberg, *Herzgewächse*, op. 20, m. 5, harmonium part   141
2.7. Schoenberg, *Herzgewächse*, op. 20, m. 5, harp part   141
2.8. Schoenberg, *Herzgewächse*, op. 20, m. 18   143
I.1. Robert Schumann, *Dichterliebe*, op. 48, mm. 4–12   162
3.1. Franz Schubert, *Die schöne Müllerin*, "Morgengruß," op. 25, mm. 12–15   172
3.2. Antonín Dvořák, Trio, "Dumky," op. 90, B. 166, mvt. 6, mm. 1–26   185
3.3. Erik Satie, *Vexations*, m. 1   187
3.4. Maurice Ravel, *Le tombeau de Couperin*, "Prélude," mm. 1–3   188
3.5. Claude Debussy, *Pelléas et Mélisande*, act 1, scene 1, rehearsal no. 2, mm. 1–12   196
4.1. Schumann, *Fantasiestücke*, "Warum?" op. 12, no. 3, mm. 1–16   236

FIGURES

0.1. Schopenhauer's metaphysics of music   47
1.1. Hegel's *Klang*   78
1.2. Bloch's tone   90
3.1. Quiddity versus quoddity   174
3.2. A page from the autograph manuscript of Jankélévitch, *La mort*   176
3.3. Quiddity's fidelity to quoddity   178
3.4. Music's speculative multiplicities   191
4.1. Deleuze's rhythm   209
4.2. The "Divine Monochord" from Robert Fludd, *Turiusque cosmi . . . historia* (1617), 1:90   222
4.3. Bowerbird photograph   226
4.4. Jakob von Uexküll, "Originaler Wirkkreis von Uexküll"   227
4.5. Paul Klee, *Die Zwitscher-Machine*   239

Introduction

In a famous passage in book 3 of Plato's *Republic*, Socrates banishes most music, and condemns various *harmoniai* (or modes) for their perniciously emotional and unpredictable effects upon the guardians of his ideal city-state. For the purposes of training his police force (recall the omnipresence of war and political struggle in Plato's time; control was a real concern), Socrates retained an "enforced" mode he claimed would inspire a warrior's courage in the face of death, and a second "voluntary" one that would render his police pliable for the purposes of education. All else was expunged.

I have taught this text many times to undergraduates, and a typical response is a desire to know exactly what kind of music Socrates had in mind. For the "enforced" mode, we discuss the equivalent of "walk-up" music before a pitcher goes out to the mound; we talk about Wagner, Slayer, and Metallica—music that has inspired members of the US military to have courage in a war zone.[1] For the "voluntary" mode, we discuss the marketing cliché of Mozart for the education of children. Invariably, a productive point of discussion is the difficulty one has in specifying exactly what music would imitate these various effects. And imitation is the key; Socrates held that the link between musical elements and social effects was mimetic, just as it was for poetry, theater, and visual art. His theory, known for centuries as the *ethos* doctrine, infused the musical thought of Christianity and Islam, as well as the Neoplatonism of the Renaissance and the eighteenth-century *Affektenlehre*. Even today the descendants of the *ethos* doctrine live on in the affective taxonomies, proposed by Pandora and Spotify, that classify music with a range of instrumental functions: relaxation, exercise, sleep, romance, and the like.

In the age of new media, crowdsourced data puts recordings into these boxes based on preferences, clicks, and votes. Plato, by contrast, claimed to discern formal similarities between musical elements and social behaviors, though he found that it was often difficult to make the connections. In the passage below, Socrates has just finished describing several modes that trigger social effects he finds dangerous for the purposes of training the guardians. He repeatedly defers to his interlocutor, Glaucon, when it comes to the details. Glaucon remarks:

> "But you seem to be left with just the Dorian and the Phrygian."
> "I do not know the *harmoniai*," [Socrates] said, "but leave the one that would appropriately imitate the sounds and cadences of a man who is brave in deeds of war. . . ."[2]

It is a plea of ignorance from Socrates, just one of many in a long line of philosophical befuddlements over the impact of music. Notice that his criteria for the banishment of various *harmoniai* are empirical, not musical: Socrates focuses his attention on the observed effects he finds dangerous, not formal properties of the modes themselves. In fact, the precise effects of the two he spared—the Dorian and Phrygian—are left ambiguous; Socrates seems uncertain as to exactly which of the two modes imitates which behavior.

Soon after, the conversation has shifted to the topic of appropriate rhythms for the training of guardians. Socrates's uncertainty continues. He states:

> "It is your job to say which these rhythms are, as it was with the *harmoniai*."

But this time, Glaucon is less sure.

> "But I can't tell you, I assure you," [Glaucon] said. "I have studied enough to say that there are just three kinds from which the movements are woven together, just as in notes there are four, from which come all the *harmoniai*: but which kinds are imitations of which sort of life I cannot say."[3]

One can imagine the panic in Socrates's voice. If both he and Glaucon are conversing in ignorance, it would seem that the dialectic itself is at risk of collapse. It is at this point that Socrates refers to Damon, a music theorist who has the answers (as we are told) but is unfortunately not here to clarify the relationship between different metrical feet and various social behaviors. Socrates responds as follows:

"Then on these points we shall take advice from Damon, [. . .] and ask him which movements are suitable for illiberality, conceit, madness and other vices, and what rhythms we must keep and assign for their opposites. I think I have heard him—though I didn't quite follow—mentioning by name a 'composite *enhoplos*' a 'dactyl' and a 'heroic,' organizing the rhythm in ways I don't understand, and making the rise and fall equal as it moved to the short and the long: and I think he named an 'iambus,' and called another a 'trochaeus,' and assigned them their long and short elements. And I believe that he criticized and applauded the tempo of the foot of each of them as much as he did the rhythms themselves—or it may have been both together: I can't say. But as I said, let us turn these matters over to Damon, for it would take no little discussion to decide them."[4]

Now Socrates has the opposite problem; he can recount formal features of various metrical feet, but has no real sense of their social effects. By the end, I picture Glaucon's eyes glazing over. Socrates himself seems to acknowledge that he is rambling, lost in a meandering swirl of technical references. He projects little authority on these matters, and somewhat compulsively hedges his claims. Perhaps his memory of Damon is failing him. Yet, even with a clear head, it was apparently difficult to understand the man who Socrates himself "didn't quite follow." With a slight tinge of resignation, Socrates finally pulls back and suggests to Glaucon that it would be better to allow Damon himself to weigh in on the matter.[5] The truth of the *ethos* doctrine would require a comprehensive book of musical knowledge that reflects an expertise in music that philosophy does not have.

Aristotle, too, defers to the specialists, who are again absent. In the *Politics* he remarks:

> Now since I believe that many excellent things have been said about these matters both by some contemporary musical experts and by those philosophers who have been well acquainted with education in music, I shall hand over to them the people who wish to pursue a precise account of every detail, and deal with the issues only in general terms for the present, stating no more than their outlines.[6]

The lack of expertise does not, however, call into question Aristotle's basic philosophical proposal that music is generally important for the purposes of educating the youth. It is the precise discussion—the rules of how it works— that never arrives. Thus, the prudent and safe course for language and reason would be to remain quiet, modest, or vague when a question eludes the scope of philosophy. Philosophy sticks to the outlines and leaves the technical matters to the specialists.

And yet perhaps this is not a mere insufficiency of empirical knowledge. Consider a counterfactual: if Aristotle were a virtuoso on the aulos or the kithara, would he have plunged confidently into a scientific treatise on the specific effects of particular melodies, harmonies, and rhythms? The musician in me suspects that he would have refrained. And perhaps refraining is a wise and even insightful course of action. Plato and Aristotle assume that someone else has the answer: a perpetually inaccessible translator who must know music inside and out. To the philosophers' eyes and ears, the effects of music seem precise; it is just an empirical problem that when it comes to the exact rules, everyone immediately accessible to them is an amateur.

But is not knowing what to say in the face of musical experience an honest, and in fact perfectly apt and philosophically rich, response to its notoriously inexact powers? Perhaps the inconvenience reveals something in the minimal words that are there on the page: a philosophical befuddlement that is nevertheless an explanatory and illuminating account of music's impact.

In the eleventh century, the Ikhwan Al-Safa, a priesthood of Islamic scholars who lived in what is current day Basra, Iraq, compiled their philosophy of music in epistle 5 of their encyclopedia, *Epistles of the Brethren of Purity*. Members of this priesthood were scholars of Plato and Aristotle's writings on music, among many other traditions of ancient thought. Chapter 16 is entitled "On the Wise Sayings of the Philosophers Concerning Music," and is organized in a manner redolent of a Greek symposium, in which a series of philosophers hold court with various and sometimes disagreeing declarations of wisdom. The very first philosopher speaks plainly of music's ineffability. He converts what was an ignorance plea in the hands of Plato and Aristotle into a rule in propositional form: "Music has a quality that speech cannot render, and words cannot express."[7]

Taken as a dictum, it would appear that even if an expert in music theory of the echelon of Damon—or a technically minded virtuoso player of the lyre, for that matter—were to be at this party, neither would have been able to adequately address the quality of music—what it does. This is because there is an insufficiency in the medium of language itself—its reasoning, its concepts, and its reliable powers of reference. Of course, this being a party of philosophers, the words keep coming. When the sixth philosopher chimes in with a few apt words, he proposes a theory of music's ineffability that is focused on the nonlinguistic powers of a musical instrument: "Although an instrument is inanimate, it gives clear expression, revealing the secrets of souls and the innermost recesses of the heart, but it is as if what it says is in a foreign tongue that needs an interpreter, because its utterances are simple, lacking dotted letters."[8]

Far from conveying a universal language, for this philosopher the sound of this instrument is stubbornly foreign, yet also simple and clear. Its sound does not simply enact a sensational flooding of our ears, or trigger any sense of collective assent. There are rules in there. To be sure, as with any metaphor, there are limits to this one: to find oneself enraptured at length by a foreign language that one does not know seems highly unlikely. Still, the comparison captures a certain contradiction that is specific to the medium: music attracts, at the same time that it resists, interpretive scrutiny. Detailed meanderings of musical form can be language-like in their conventionality and expressivity, but at the same time resistant to semantic decoding. What then is a transfixed interpreter to do? Instead of appealing to experts, this philosopher turns to the numinous words of the Persian poet, Rudaki (858–c. 941). We can imagine it bringing a hush to the party:

> The nocturnal lament of the lute string
> Is sweeter to my ear than [the cry of] 'God is great!'
> If the plaint of the lute string—and do not think this strange—
> Attracts its prey from the wild plains,
> With no arrow it yet from time to time
> Pierces its body, the dart transfixing the heart,
> Now weeping, now grief-stricken,
> From break of day through noon till dusk.
> Although bereft of a tongue, its eloquence
> Can interpret the lovers' story
> Now making the madman sane
> Now casting the sane under its spell.[9]

It would already be a transgressive move for a lute player to challenge the power of God. When it attracts and then strikes the prey, the music has no message to communicate—it is "bereft of a tongue"; it is not appreciated as an object or a work. It pierces its listener like a weapon—a linear impact—"the dart transfixing the heart." But of course there is no physical arrow; its impact is diffuse and immaterial. This is because the music does not sit there, as it would for Plato's *melos* doctrine, passively following the semantic boundaries of poetic language. The music has its own peculiar agency and effects, like a glass of wine that brings poetic words to life with a power that is quite ambiguous, even duplicitous. The effect is in fact an explicit violation of the reliable mimesis of the *ethos* doctrine: music cures insanity with its therapeutic powers while undoing the straitlaced listener into madness.

This is when philosophers often stop. The ones who insisted on controlling it (Plato) will dismiss certain kinds of music, or refer to authorities. Others loosely followed Aristotle and imagined harnessing it for its moral potential (Rousseau), or ended up marginalizing it as a disorderly flux of sensations (Kant), while many others simply ignored it.[10] More recently, particularly in the modern field of analytic philosophy, many have bracketed out music's complex and duplicitous effects and defended formalist views of it.[11] But very few, save a few high Romantics with a certain poetic sensibility, seek to explain the powers of its sensory impact in any detail, likely because music's ambiguous qualities seem so murky and inassimilable to the powers of reason.

But suppose a philosopher were to dwell upon the imprecision of music's impact as a particular locus of thought. From our perspective in late modernity, what is philosophically significant about music's stunning force? Does it harbor a distinct kind of critical potential?

This book focuses on the writings of four European philosophers of the twentieth century—Ernst Bloch, Theodor Adorno, Vladimir Jankélévitch, and Gilles Deleuze alongside his collaborator, psychoanalyst Félix Guattari—all of whom address the ineffability of music with an unprecedented level of precision. From the broadest perspective, they ask: What is this nonconceptual, intoxicating, often highly technical art form that bears the force of sonic impact? And what is its philosophical significance? What does it help us think that no other medium does in quite the same way? And finally, if music can allow us to think something—if it has philosophical significance—how might it embody an ethics that resists and even disrupts the norms and strictures of modern life?

These philosophers do not venerate the ineffable impact of music as a transcendent art of feeling in the manner of German Romantics like Wilhelm Heinrich Wackenroder, Ludwig Tieck, and E. T. A. Hoffmann. Rather, for these twentieth-century philosophers, the ineffability of music engenders a dialectically productive sense of perplexity. It helps them think through problems that seem to exceed the boundaries of conceptual reasoning: a utopian potentiality that inspires hope (Bloch), an ethical critique of modernity (Adorno), an exemplification of the ephemeral movement of lived time (Jankélévitch), and a sonic extension of the syncopated, contrapuntal rhythms of sense and social life (Deleuze and Guattari). Running parallel to their theories, these philosophers articulate distinct and not always commensurable views of what counts as musical material. For Bloch it is the tone, for Adorno it is music's ideological turn towards a tonal language or *Versprachlichung*, for Jankélévitch it is its temporal inconsistency, for Deleuze and Guattari its rhythm. By weaving together these theories for the purposes of analysis and comparison, this book argues that a philosophical engagement with music's ineffability rarely calls for silence or declarations of the unspeakable. Rather, it asks us to think through the ways in which the impact of music is made to address intricate philosophical problems specific to the modern world.

Thus, for all these intellectuals, music was an exceptionally powerful, even transformative experience. And yet, philosophers with expertise in music are rare enough in the twentieth century that few have had the chance to confer very much with one another. With the exception of Bloch's well-known (if rarely explored) influence on Adorno, historical encounters among these four philosophers are relatively few. The two Germans were forced into exile in the United States and returned to different sides of the Iron Curtain, and corresponded only occasionally. Jankélévitch actively avoided and resisted much German thought after the trauma of National Socialism, even as he wrestled with problems with a common intellectual ancestry. Within France, too, Jankélévitch described his position as isolated. He and Deleuze inhabited different cultural spheres. Jankélévitch, while generally supportive of the student movement, stayed on the sidelines during the events of May 1968, as Deleuze and Guattari became key figures of the French intellectual vanguard. Deleuze and Guattari, of a slightly later generation, were also more open in their adoption of German philosophy. In their last works, they even include a few references to writings by Bloch and Adorno. One reference to Adorno appears in Deleuze's books on cinema; and Bloch and Adorno each appear once in their final collaborative book, *What Is Philosophy?* (1994).

Though these intellectuals were not part of a shared scene, they had many common influences and points of reference. With the exception of Guattari, a practicing psychoanalyst, all were well versed in the history of European philosophy; they read, studied, and taught the history of philosophy from the ancient Greeks to the twentieth century. Kant, Hegel, Schopenhauer, Nietzsche, and some version of Bergson were important in varying amounts for each of them, either directly or indirectly. Marx and Freud were important for Bloch, Adorno, Deleuze, and Guattari, all of whom considered themselves committed leftists and critics of ideology. Jankélévitch was an exception in this regard, as he was inclined more towards the moral and ethical dimensions of politics than its structural problems.[12] For all but Guattari, Schelling and Kierkegaard could be said to play interesting if subterranean roles. When it came to music, all of them predictably recognized the power and historical weight of

Beethoven and Wagner, though the French thinkers tended to privilege non-Germanic musical lineages. Adorno, Deleuze, and Guattari all expressed a notable admiration for Schumann (something they incidentally shared with Wittgenstein and Barthes). All devoted particular attention to how best to practice modern music, but none were entirely comfortable with Schoenberg's twelve-tone system or its midcentury development into integral serialism. All except Deleuze played the piano as amateurs, yet all were also curiously ambivalent about (and sometimes even hostile towards) the impact of mass media and mechanical reproduction on music. Though they were occasionally interested in the problem of vernacular creativity, none thought popular music was of particular value to philosophy, and at least one—Adorno—famously subjected it to withering critique. (The French thinkers simply expressed little interest or desire to take it seriously.)[13]

While this rich tapestry of alliances and differences makes for a compelling set of comparisons, given the rugged, even fragmentary, nature of the empirical terrain, this book is not an intellectual history. It focuses squarely on the thinking of these philosophers, rather than chasing after scant empirical connections. It is, in this way, a synoptic analysis that weaves together a constellation of interlocking arguments. Its aim is to stage a conversation between four philosophers who have been summoned for the central purpose of making explicit a great number of unacknowledged philosophical relations, affinities, and disagreements among them. This book might be said to have methodological parallels with a conceptual history insofar as it proposes a panoptic view of an intellectual group. But it comes with a significant twist: this book is not based in the lineage of a circulating concept, or in the history of an idea. Rather, it explains how, among these intellectuals, philosophical thinking was destabilized, distorted, inspired, and enraptured by a common experience: the sensory impact of music.

What exactly is the significance, then, of this link between music and philosophy? In the professional subdiscipline of analytic aesthetics, philosophy is taken as the method and music the object. With a sophisticated degree of intellectual detail, analytic philosophers pose and answer questions about what music is. They debate how it works; its relationship to emotions, consciousness and cognition, and entrainment; questions of authenticity and ontology; the status of its various formal parameters; and so on. This book, by contrast, examines a two-way street between music and philosophy. It takes the perspective that, given the somewhat independent existence of two practices—music and philosophy—the two may dialectically impinge upon one another, often quite unpredictably. Or, given their relative autonomy, they have ways of commenting upon one another, often surreptitiously and shyly acknowledging one another's existence. In this way, the book aims to bridge the separate fields of music and philosophy, under the assumption that there need not be any single positive or rigorous method linking the two. What lies between the two are explanatory and comparative links between the specificity of musical impact and the details of philosophical problems.

If there is a dialectic between philosophy and music, it has an irregular pulse—contrapuntal, yet rhythmic and stuttering, since the conversation is rife with losses in transmission—the two disciplines are highly professionalized, usually independently. It is nearly impossible to find someone with equal expertise in both. Adorno may have been unique in this regard, and even his knowledge of music was not deeply technical in a way that would match new disciplinary standards: the mathematical intricacy of neo-Riemannian approaches to musical analysis, the sophisticated historiography of today's musicology, the reflexive and highly theorized ethnographies of the twenty-first century, or the virtuoso performers, composers, and producers of today's conservatories and vernacular creative scenes. Bloch was an amateur pianist and something of a musical enthusiast. Even Jankélévitch, who published widely as a music scholar, thought of himself as little more than an amateur at the keyboard.[14] The same holds for Guattari, an amateur pianist, who was uncomfortable with any music outside the tradition of Western art music.[15] Deleuze's own knowledge of music came largely from colleagues and seminar participants, and typically unfolded only with the vaguest of outlines, leaving a tempting opening for scholars to complete the links themselves.[16]

But vagueness can nonetheless be explanatory in its own right. For one, these philosophers often explain the experience of music in ways that are vividly attentive to the specificity of the medium, even when only a minimum of technical detail is at hand. More significantly, technical vagueness may be symptomatic of an exact position regarding the way the powers of music affect the course of philosophical reasoning. As with the opening examples of Plato and Aristotle, a lack of attention to technical detail can be read paradoxically as a mode of rigorous attention to the perplexity of music's sensory impact. Along these lines, as philosophers approach the ineffability of musical experience, this book seeks to maintain the integrity of what certain thinkers are willing to specify (as well as what they do not specify) in order to diagnose, accurately, an index of music's impact on philosophy, and to get a fair sense of the philosophical work the music is actually presumed to be able to do. For the value of these philosophers' writings lies not in their ability to practice musical analysis. It lies in their ability to explain music's significance in philosophical terms.

In a relatively concise form, then, consider the following thesis: for Bloch, Adorno, Jankélévitch, and Deleuze and Guattari, music requires form amid the material force of its gestures. Yet these forms do not mean anything in particular; none of these intellectuals claim that music is made of signs. They describe in more or less general terms what musical forms do to our senses as a sonic art, and they account for what that experience might mean for philosophy. In line with the claim forwarded by the Ikhwan Al-Safa, for each of the philosophers, music is somewhat akin to a foreign tongue. Yet it never "speaks" like a language, nor is it entirely nonlinguistic; the specificity of its vague impact, in its forms, invites perpetual explanation and thought. In this way, music and language are not completely separate, yet neither are they the same—they are insoluble *and* deeply intertwined. This leads us to what I will call the paradox of the ineffable: music appears as a sensuous immediacy at the same time that it always remains mediated by forms and techniques. It is this paradoxical structure that allows music to serve as a magnet for philosophical conundrums. For music attracts meanings in fluid and unpredictable ways; as Adorno says, "intentions stream into it." When a particular question—say of utopia, or lived rhythm—presents problems for philosophy, what Jankélévitch refers to as music's "broad shoulders" supports dense metaphysical traffic.

Which brings us to the question of ethics. Each of these philosophers venture ethical prescriptions about what kind of music best exemplifies their positions on the nature and significance of music's ineffability. If they often hold overlapping perspectives on the general question of music's ineffability, this ethical question of how and what kind of music each thinker prizes is one place where instructive differences come into relief. Each author's approach to this question spawns contrasting guidelines and criteria for modern music. In a similar fashion, what counts as musical form remains something of a moving target over the course of this book. When Bloch's tones take shape as ethical compositions, they acquire significance through the forms of *fugatos* and *adagios*, secular choruses, revolutionary trumpet calls, and exemplary works and composers of the eighteenth and nineteenth centuries. If, for Adorno, musical form is tightly wound around the axis of historical inheritance, the criteria he maintains for ethical resistance are comparatively technical, specified down to the contrapuntal workings of atonality in the Second Viennese School or vernacular musical references in Mahler's symphonies. For Jankélévitch, music is an open and inconsistent medium, so correspondingly his ethical modernism entails a wide multiplicity; it ranges from mimetic treatments of bird song to Liszt's improvisatory style of composition, to mechanical and neoclassical tropes in Ravel, to Wagnerian tapestries of intertwined emotions in Debussy's *Pelléas et Mélisande*. For Deleuze and Guattari's rhythm, form is still more loosely specified, with references to ethical musical works ranging from Schumann's character pieces to Boulez's high modernism and the open gesture whereby "one launches forth, hazards an improvisation."[17]

Jankélévitch described this multiplicity in the form of a question: "But exactly *where* in the end, is music? Is it in the piano, or on the level of the vibrating string? Does it slumber within the score? Or maybe it sleeps in the grooves of the record? Is it to be found on the tip of the conductor's baton?"[18]

Amidst these multiple material supports, we may ask: What would these philosophers say about the "grooves of the record?" Indeed, this is an essential question, because music's ineffability does not simply concern music's mediation by language. If music's ineffability is always mediated by form, in the context of the twentieth century it is imperative for us to consider the significance of mechanical reproduction as a form of mediation. Michael Denning has recently argued that sound recording ushered in a revolution within the politics of musical expression and literacy in the 1920s and '30s.[19] Media theorist Friedrich Kittler likewise theorized the shift in the era of mechanical reproduction as epochal and irreversible.[20] In his view, the phonograph enabled musicians to supersede the cognitive selection of ordered intervals and ratios; recorded music after 1900 could readily make use of the entire frequency spectrum and harness the unconscious noise of the real. It is certainly undeniable that, over the course of the twentieth century, what was played, heard, and sensed as music expanded dramatically, in a reflection of what Jacques Rancière has called an ever-widening "distribution of the sensible" in the modern politics of the arts.[21] This revolutionary expansion, which has only accelerated in the last thirty years of new media, led Richard Taruskin to forecast the eventual demise of musical literacy in the traditional sense.[22]

It is significant, however, that, pace Denning's affirmation of music's widening modes of inscription, in their ethics of modern music, none of these philosophers really embraced popular music or any oral musical traditions—musical practices that were both recorded and powerfully industrialized in the era of mechanical reproduction. As I will argue at the conclusion of this book, one can nonetheless understand their philosophical engagement with the widening scope of the sensible to yield a specifically modern ethical paradox: that of the vernacular.

Though I will more fully explain this paradox in section 2.6, let us consider here a brief précis. In the modern paradox of the vernacular, resistance and creativity comes not from the fragmentation of established musical techniques, but instead from a peripheral space that operates at a remove from the legitimating order of centralized institutions. A vernacular music may unpredictably affirm and reject what is taken by institutions to count as musical form, and because of the vernacular origin of the challenge, a normative formalism may not know and understand the rules in play.

The paradoxical nature of this situation becomes explicit in Adorno's discussion of Mahler. In Mahler's music, references to vernacular songs, narratives, and other extramusical forms are prevalent, but are often opaque to Adorno's ears. In one sentence Adorno seems sure that resistance is embodied by a single detail in one of Mahler's symphonies. Yet in the next, he swerves outward to associations and metaphors, as if he is unsure of the criteria for resistance. On an ontological level, this instability reflects the general openness of music's ineffability. But, as a historical symptom, it more vividly mirrors a modern predicament: a multiplicity of vernacular idioms newly inscribed within an expanded sphere of the sensible.

In my view, the instability of Adorno's approach to Mahler is symptomatic of an underlying tension in his method. On the one hand, Adorno maintains a normative and universalizing commitment to the centrality of form as the basis for resistance. And according to Adorno's diagnosis, formalism is ever expanding, more powerful, and more detailed in the rationalized age of late modernity. Yet on the other, Adorno contends that Mahler's music is ethical and resistant in its apparently naive use of tonal materials and other traditional compositional techniques. This leads Adorno to a paradox. A knowable and specific fracture of a normative musical technique would seem to require a basis in clear criteria. But the multiplicity of vernacular idioms in Mahler's music seems to harness resistance at a larger, less consistent, and more vague level of assembly. As a result, in Adorno's prose, the possibility of a vernacular formalism—a detailed method for what he will call an "immanent critique"—becomes productively withdrawn, loosely defined, and only intuitively accessible.

Even though it is Adorno who brings to life this paradox most vividly, and as fruitful as I find it, it is not then my view that his philosophy wins out among the four. In fact, I will ultimately argue that this paradox emerges at a moment when Adorno appears to be at his most Jankélévitchian, his most affirmative of multiplicities and inconsistency. Nonetheless, I do find that the paradox of the vernacular is a productive way to end this comparative study of the four philosophers. It points directly to enduring problems of the medium, and provides insights about resistant musical practices that seem to elude these philosophers' conservative aesthetic preferences. In my conclusion I will argue that, delightfully, neither paradox—neither the ineffable nor the vernacular—can be resolved with any sense of finality, even as one can still ethically navigate one's way toward a vernacular horizon of the insensible, the excluded, and the peripheral. In this book the persistent qualities of these paradoxes are not signs of refusal, emptiness, or silence. Quite the opposite: with music's paradoxes of the ineffable and the vernacular working in tandem, one can productively understand how a peripheral musical poetics can exploit, with an exceptional ingenuity, the general instability of the medium.

*

While *Deep Refrains* is the first comparative study of these thinkers, it is certainly far from the first book to address these philosophers' writings on music. The secondary literature on Adorno and Deleuze has grown to astounding proportions in the past two decades. In the Anglo-American world of music scholarship, the writings on Adorno and music are equally extensive, and stretch back to Rose Rosengard Subotnik's pioneering work in the 1970s.[23] The work on Deleuze and music is more recent—largely of the past ten years.[24] While Bloch and Jankélévitch have garnered some attention from scholars in literary studies, philosophy, and theology, their writings on music are only now gradually receiving the attention of music scholars.[25] As the scholarship on these philosophers as individuals grows at a steady pace, this book aims to use the cooling effects of comparison and contrast to ease prejudices and biases that may have accrued over time. In the process, I hope it yields a rejuvenated and deepened understanding of their commonalities and differences.

In particular, this comparative approach aims to redress a tendency in music studies. Over time, these philosophers have been subject to a certain amount of caricaturing. Some of this has been done in order to celebrate particular strains of modernism. Other scholars, like Taruskin, have positioned one—Adorno—polemically as an enemy in order to defend denigrated musical territory. It is the readiness with which he labeled Jankélévitch the "anti-Adorno" on the dust jacket of the English translation of *Music and the Ineffable* that has served as a steady reminder of why this book should attempt to give equal voice to a contrasting array of intellectual points of view. Taruskin, of course, is not alone in having strong opinions. Yet this book aims to modulate polarized views of these intellectuals by understanding how their work might be mutually illuminating. Such is the ethic of this book: its central aim is to cool the polemical fire of nationalist divides with the steady hand of comparison.

I harbor no illusions that it is possible to write about any of these philosophers without some degree of sympathy. Still, I have tried to forgo elaborate reconstructions that would extend the technical expertise or philosophical insights of these thinkers far beyond what they present in their writings. Though recourse to gestures of reconstruction are inseparable from the work of exegesis, any sustained application of these philosophers ideas I feared would run the risk of advocacy that would muddy the already challenging prospect of a comparative study. This, of course, is not to propose that my book is free of any reconstruction, or to oppose others' applications of philosophy. I have sought to maintain a certain ethical sobriety, a strategic agnosticism that aims to consider the work of philosophers in slow and methodical terms without any immediate aim of musical application in mind. Given the comparative scope of the terrain, this book can make no claim to philosophical comprehensiveness, nor can it engage fully with the vast world of secondary literature on these intellectuals in the way that a study of a single philosopher could. What structures the book's comparative axis is the common philosophical response to music. In the end, I hope I have struck a balance between philosophical details and synoptic comparisons appropriate to the interdisciplinary aims of the project.

*

With respect to broader questions of methodology, a closer look at these intellectuals may be instructive and helpful to music scholars. In line with a broad material turn in the humanities, music scholars like Georgina Born, Benjamin Piekut, and Emily Dolan have increasingly oriented their research away from the "great works" of music history to the details of social and cultural networks as well as media apparatuses.[26] A new kind of empiricism is afoot that foregrounds material cultures that operate beneath the realm of human agency: histories and sociologies of print, recording, science, medicine, and the body, as well as a new organology, some of which has been carried beneath the banner of the egalitarian flatness of actor network theory. The upshot of this work has been a decentering of the human from our understanding of historical processes, and an increased attention to the agency of material circumstances. At their best, these methodologies can serve as a form of bottom-up ideology critique. The grand narratives, geniuses, and dominant genres of an idealized conception of music history are exposed to material and technical determinants—grey areas—and rhizomatic framings.

But amid this network of material determinants, what is to be made of the power of ideas in shaping the significance of music as a practice, an experience, and an object of study? In 2009, James Currie staged a trenchant critique of what he took to be an a priori pluralism at work in musicology's collective turn to cultural history.[27] He took aim at the false politics of relativism that, in his view, had overlooked the negative potentiality of the musical object, and its latent and functionless autonomy. In his study *Music and the Politics of Negation* (2012), the musical objects he takes to have negative potentiality are of the highest canonical sort, straight from late eighteenth-century Vienna when the phenomenon of aesthetic autonomy gathered steam in the West (Haydn, Mozart, and Beethoven). Many have found this intellectual move inspiring, a revival of Marxist speculative theories that posit autonomous music as secretly critical of the society it reflects. At least one historian of music, Nicholas Mathew, has responded with skepticism, claiming that political resistance is not so easily dreamed up or enacted from within the sonic boundaries of a musical work.[28]

And yet even if one does not endorse Currie's polemical return to aesthetic autonomy, does not the ascription of such powerful and diffuse meanings (for Adorno: "Intentions stream into it") remain testimony to the fact that music *can* and *does* have extraordinarily complex significance, which is often not exhausted by historical and material evidence? This is what, I would propose, at a broader methodological level can be understood as a question lying at the nexus of music and philosophy. The simultaneity of music's slipperiness and our sense that it *could* mean something is part of what it is; and it asks us not simply to agree or disagree with this or that interpretation, or to subscribe to any particular conception of musical autonomy, but to understand the complex and paradoxical form of its sonic impact—what Currie describes beautifully as an exact perplexity "at the moment we fall into the blank transformative hole it opens up."[29] For philosophy, I would argue, is perhaps best suited not to interpret this or that particular meaning of a given composition, but to explain the general form of its sensory specificity.

I recognize that allied proposals of this sort have been met with skepticism. In 2004, Carolyn Abbate used the pages of *Critical Inquiry* to propose a "drastic" musicology that would be attentive towards the vicissitudes of real-time performance, and critiqued the explanatory power of music scholarship's two main methods: formalism and historicism.[30] Many scholars in the nascent interdisciplinary field of sound studies have argued along similar lines in developing ontologies of sound; they have drawn on philosophers like Martin Heidegger, Maurice Merleau-Ponty, Jean-Luc Nancy, and Adriana Caverero in order to show how sound is uniquely immersive and embodied, and bears the sensation of presence. Some have responded to such experiential injunctions by claiming that we cannot do without interpretation, that "gnostic" discourse is inescapable.[31] Hans Ulrich Gumbrecht has posited an "oscillation" effect between gnostic meaning and drastic presence.[32] Others, such as James

Hepokoski, have critiqued the ineffable by claiming that such an orientation is uncomfortably close to a romanticized and theological call to silence.[33]

This book maintains that the ineffability of music need not be taken as a challenge to any methodology in particular, nor as a call to silence. It can instead be taken as an impetus to find ways to address and explain the befuddling, vague, and untranslatable specificity of musical experience at a certain register of philosophical precision. In this book, the converse holds equally. Insofar as music can stun and perplex us with its opacity, this book describes how music in turn can impact the course of philosophical thinking.

With respect to music scholarship, it is my view that philosophy and cultural history need not be cast as mutually exclusive approaches to the study of music (or any art form, for that matter), even if, as I have argued elsewhere, they can occasionally and quite instructively turn out conflicting results.[34] A philosophical account of music can be rendered consonant with, explanatory of, and integral to music studies' methods of cultural history, ethnography, and musical analysis. In fact, it may be that philosophy helps us understand how it is possible to confront the ineffability of music head-on—not as a romantic conceit or as a vitalist immediacy, but as a phenomenon saturated with potential significance that is mediated by form while remaining inexact in its meaning. In this way, the impact of the musical object remains integrated with but not reducible to the fabric of cultural history, to multiple forms of technical mediation, and to the linguistic coordinates of representation.

*

In his famous 1940 essay "Towards a Newer Laocoön," Clement Greenberg proposed that music itself was an agent for the mid-century explosion of interest in abstraction across the arts.[35] The reasons, in his view, were twofold. On the one hand, Greenberg claimed that music was "the art of immediate sensation" and could thus forecast the emergence of modern painting as a medium of coordinated color, sensations, and vibrations that was equally forceful in acting directly on the sensorium. On the other, Greenberg held that music's abstraction modeled the formalized abstraction of a composition that could exist independently of any imitation or "literary" illusion.

With Greenberg in mind, one can think of music's ineffability as a dialectical linkage of sensory immediacy and formal coherence. Such a dialectical view of music allows us to foreground the specificity of music's material impact without reifying this experience into a vitalism, an appeal to the real, or a conceptualization of the body that is absent of form, structure, ideas, technique, historicity, and ethical skill. For dialectics emphasizes the necessity of mediation, even in cases where the mediation is not conceptual, as is the case for Deleuze and Guattari's syncopated "dialectic of difference and repetition."[36] In my view, an analysis of music's ineffability needs both sides of this duality—what Deleuze and Guattari called the rhythm of "the smooth and the striated"—in order to grasp the philosophical structure and significance of an inconsistent impact.

This dialectical conception of music, which is, as I shall argue shortly, exemplified by Bloch's conception of the musical tone, foregrounds the indeterminacy of music's referential powers, its distance from language. Certainly, for these intellectuals music might carry a wide range of associations depending on its context, but its philosophical significance is predicated upon a distinct blankness; there is no exact referent to a musical element. In fact, with the exception of the intermedial aesthetics of Deleuze and Guattari, these thinkers are very careful to theorize music and language as distinct arts. They do this to make explicit the nonlinguistic character of music, and to allow us to better understand the distinct interchange between the two. Of all the views expressed here, Adorno's method of immanent critique was perhaps the most explicit in its conception of such a dialectic, but also in some ways the most narrow: he conceives of form as a product of a universal ideological history to the point that a musical form of resistance can only acknowledge a negative fracture. By comparison, the other philosophers adopt dialectical thinking with more flexible conceptions of form, discipline, and ideology, while they can be frustratingly (or illustratively) vague when it comes to specifying criteria for their ethics.

The term "dialectics" is admittedly not one that all these thinkers equally espouse, for reasons that are noteworthy but not insurmountable. Certainly the Hegelian meaning of the term is central for Bloch and Adorno. Notwithstanding the profound impact of Jean Wahl, Alexandre Kojève, and Jean Hyppolite on the French reception of Hegel, Jankélévitch and Deleuze alike single the term "dialectics" out for critique, frequently pinning it to some aspect of Hegelianism they choose to reject. In Jankélévitch's 1933 doctoral thesis on Schelling, Jankélévitch associates the term with Hegel's excessive idealism, which in his view seems to have overcome all dissonance with an idealized "logo-logic," a formalist "poem about poetry" that unfolds "without matter and without content." Similar gestures abound in his 1931 book on Bergson. Deleuze's *Nietzsche & Philosophy* (1962) contains an entire chapter, called "Against the Dialectic," which attacks the Hegelian theory of a pliant guilty conscience that lacks the Nietzschean affirmation of risk and chance.

And Deleuze frames many pages of the opening of *Difference and Repetition* (1968) as an anti-Hegelian project.

If the term dialectics were intrinsically linked to Hegel's reconciliation of internal contradictions—that is, if it always referred to the teleological power of ideas—it would indeed be an anachronism. But it need not be taken so narrowly. The term was also central to Gaston Bachelard's widely read *Dialectique de la durée* (1938), which held that lived time was inaccessible without complex forms of structural (but not necessarily idealized or hierarchical) mediations and punctuations. In 1953, Jankélévitch likewise retains the term "dialectic" in his *Philosophie première* as he attempts to reconcile the metaphysical flux of Bergsonian creativity with his consonant view that mediation is always necessary and constitutive of the emergence of the conscious intellect.[37] And by the 1960s, even as Deleuze is explicitly polemicizing against Hegelian dialectics on behalf of Nietzsche, in *Difference and Repetition* (1968) he is also exploring the possibility of a post-Hegelian conception of the dialectic based in the multiplicities unleashed by differential calculus.[38] Perhaps symptomatic of this now forgotten strain of French dialectical thinking, there has recently emerged a small but growing cottage industry of readers of Deleuze who have discerned latent continuities between Hegel and Deleuze concerning the question of identity and difference.[39]

More to the point, Hyppolite conceptualized a dialectical framework around the ineffable that is an apt point of departure for the argument of this book. In his book *Logic and Existence* (1953), Hyppolite contended that Hegel's account of sense-certainty is based in the starting point of an ineffability of sense that is overcome and assimilated by the dialectical movement of language, reason, and logic. In his view, language and concepts as mediations of sensuous particularity become central to the production of any kind of meaning. Hyppolite's reading of Hegel can be taken as an early exemplar of the linguistic turn in French structuralism, later epitomized by dicta like Jacques Derrida's famous line from *Of Grammatology* (1967): "Il n'y a pas de hors-texte."[40]

I find it instructive to revisit Hyppolite's argument, yet without following through on Hegel's conviction that the ineffability of sense can only be presented through the medium of language, concepts, and its community of self-conscious actors. That is, we might say that for these philosophers, music presents some kind of problem for Hyppolite's dialectic, whereby a sensuous particularity—an impact that is ineffable—remains as a stubborn reminder of what might not be adequately subsumed by the movement of the concept. Of course, within philosophy, the work of the concept still remains essential to describing and explaining its intellectual significance. But these philosophers sustain the paradoxes, contradictions, and incommensurabilities of music's dialectic to an unprecedented degree: the irrational flux of muscular sound and gesture continually resists wholesale conceptual mediation, even as it continues to require mediation in some form. The ineffable does not lapse into an idealized flux of the body's agency, nor do these intellectuals take the ineffable for granted, as if it were a normative or reliable proposition on its own. This would hold true of Deleuze and Guattari's approach to music as well. Even though they aim at an aesthetics of "sensation in itself" unregulated by concepts, they still describe music as coextensive with what I will call a "contrapuntal dialectic" of lived rhythm that requires the mediation of formal elements, individuations, and techniques. Art, after all, for Deleuze and Guattari, acquires significance by producing a practical occasion for philosophy to create new concepts.

It is with this in mind that I propose to think of the dialectic between philosophy and music as a productive exchange between two entities, whose interaction is not always strictly contradictory and discursive in the Hegelian sense, nor simply relational, as if it operated without boundaries or rules. Rather, the dialectic in play for these philosophers is co-constitutive and sometimes incommensurable; it is still based in a codependent dyad, a stubborn amalgam of form and sensation. But the interaction of the two halves is irresolvable by one side or the other. Consider three ways in which such an inclusive conception of the dialectic applies to philosophical accounts of music. One simply regards what Greenberg claims music is: a linkage between sonic sensation and abstract form. Another dialectic straddles the disciplinary divide and regards what music does for philosophy—what philosophical problems it inspires one to think. A third regards what music should be: an ethical modernism that draws conclusions about what kind of music might follow from a distinct philosophical position. As a trio, these three dialectics would argue together that (1) the dialectical material of music is (2) summoned to do a certain kind of philosophical work that no other medium can do in quite the same way in (3) an exemplary modernist form. All the philosophers conclude that music is specifically ineffable—special, in a way that is nonconceptual—even if what it does to philosophy, as well as the exact way it is worked out in an ethics of modernism, is something subject to disagreement.

Though the comparative effort here confronts what for many appears to be a significant intellectual divide regarding the consequences of Hegel's idealism—to critique the ideological powers of reason from within by surfacing contradictions in the dialectic (Bloch and Adorno), or to circumvent them altogether by positing and developing a materialist ethics of creativity focused on the inconsistency of time (Jankélévitch) or the dynamics of rhythm and differentiation (Deleuze and Guattari)—this book cannot claim to resolve (or even properly stage) such grand disagreements. It can only propose suggestive points of comparison between these two intellectual spheres: a German tradition of critical theory that emphasizes the weight of expression, history, ideology, the historical fact of Romanticism, the breakdown of a universal musical language, and so on versus a French tradition that emphasizes Bergson, empiricism, the axis of temporality, the eventlike character of experience, and an aesthetic sphere of neoclassicism, innocence, irony, impersonality, and emotional distance. No doubt certain intellectual and aesthetic differences are undeniable and will surface in the course of this study. If I ultimately read the Francophone thinkers in dialectical terms, and the Germans as aporetic thinkers of the ineffable, it is in order to deliberately allow hidden continuities to come to the surface.

*

To return full circle to the early history of Western musical thought, philosophy's take on music, from Plato, was a paranoid one; music was an object of practical control, one that was classified according to its effects. We may recall that Greek *mousikē* was taken to be a deeply mimetic practice that linked together poetry, dance, and song.[41] Yet as discussed in the outset of this introduction, the only two harmonic modes Socrates left in the *Republic* were two that triggered the guardians to be pliable for the purposes of learning, and courageous in battle. In *kallipolis*, his imaginary city, intoxicating rhythms or emotional outpourings, even multistringed instruments, would be strictly forbidden.

Aristotle expanded upon Plato's mimetic view, though without the same level of interest in control; he was a great admirer of leisure and pleasure, and his more empirical, observational, and reflective theory of music still assumed that there were various effects to be had on the soul (the foundation of the *ethos* doctrine), but the author of the *Poetics* was not about to cast out his beloved poets. In the *Politics* he distinguished two types of music (both of which were accompanied with poetic recitation), *paidia* and *diagōgē*—a distinction one might compare to the modern distinction between low art and high art. *Paidia* was playful entertainment, akin to the medicinal functionality of unwinding after work, whereas Aristotle's *diagōgē* was an intellectual divertissement, a true liberal art associated with Homeric poetry, which was understood to be an end in itself.[42] Aristotle further credited music for helping trigger catharsis in the context of a narrative tragedy, one that produced that peculiar mixture of pity and fear for a character's predicament. This was a feeling that, for some interpreters, came with a certain intellectual distance, and which, for that reason, has been celebrated for centuries. We fantasize and identify with characters, but we do so at a remove, and that is both the pleasure as well as the ethical and intellectual potential of *mimesis*. The powers of music, despite their wild ambiguity, were essential to the operations of this effect.

Alongside these mimetic accounts of music, there was another related, but in many ways distinct, philosophical account that emanated from ancient Greece, one that rendered music exceptional among the arts. The Pythagorean tradition claimed that music was abstract and universal, and posited a link of co-extension between the physical properties of whole number ratios and metaphysical principles of cosmic harmony. Its key surviving source text is Plato's *Timaeus*, which offers a philosophical explanation of how a demiurge (a divine cause) created the ephemeral physical universe by drawing on eternal forms that were embodied in the whole number ratios of the diatonic scale.

This cosmology, commonly attributed to Pythagoras but disseminated and received in the form of Plato's text, became a cornerstone of musical metaphysics in Western thought. For centuries, innumerable treatises recapitulated it, or quietly relied upon it as some kind of vague metaphysical backbone. Texts by Cicero, Ptolemy, Boethius (who gave it the Latin name of *musica mundana*), and Thomas Aquinas are a few early exemplars. In the medieval disciplines of the liberal arts, Boethius placed music in the quadrivium alongside mathematics, geometry, and astronomy because he considered it to be exceptionally close to the eternity of truth. Others applied Pythagorean metaphysics to practical and compositional questions in actual pieces of music. Though the prominence of such a numerical metaphysics eventually declined as it struggled to be reconciled with the rising tide of scientific reasoning, empiricism, aesthetics, and the like, the mystical abstractions linking music and number have persisted into the modern day as minoritarian undercurrents.[43]

This Pythagorean view of music spawned an early and influential conception of the ineffable. The reason logically follows: when music is taken, by virtue of its proximity to number and eternal truth, to be in some sense separate from the finite world of human understanding, how could language ever name or describe its structural perfection? Like God or the ideal forms, how does one speak about something that defies all segmentation and mediation? A crucial formulation of this metaphysical problem of the ineffable appears in the work of Plotinus (c. 204/5–270), for whom the One (a formless and self-defining Unity beyond Being) was strictly ineffable. In *The Enneads*, Plotinus remarks:

> Thus The One is in truth beyond all statement . . . we can but try to indicate, in our own feeble way, something concerning it. . . . We do not, it is true, grasp it by knowledge, but that does not mean that we are utterly void of it; we hold it not so as to state it, but so as to be able to speak about it. And we can and do state what it is not, while we are silent as to what it is: we are, in fact, speaking of it in the light of its sequels; unable to state it, we may still possess it.[44]

Notice that the points Plotinus makes here will continue to inform the dialectal methods of the modern philosophers in this book. One is that, for Plotinus, the ineffable may be "beyond all statement," but it does not call for silence. One can (and should) still give it a shot. Moreover, this effort enjoins us to dialectical thinking. One's means of indicating the ineffable are negative, but we can still use language to thus develop a virtuous path of metaphysical "possession" by speaking "about it."

Plotinus's dialectic had a profound effect on the intellectual formation of the early Christian church. At the hands of a musically inclined thinker like St. Augustine, Plotinus's conception of the ineffable could acquire musical significance because music, properly sung and heard, was similarly taken to be an exemplary vehicle of the divine. Augustine wrote about singing in jubilation:

> Sing in jubilation: That is to say, to sing well for God is to sing in jubilation. What is it to sing in jubilation? It is not possible to understand, to explicate in words that which is sung in the heart. Indeed those who sing, whether in the harvest or in the vineyard or in some heated work, when they have begun in the words of their songs to exult with joy, as if filled with such great joy that they are not able to explicate it [the joy] in words, turn themselves aside from the syllables of words and go into a sound of jubilation. For *jubilum* is a certain sound signifying that the heart is giving birth to what cannot be spoken. And who deserves this jubilation except ineffable God? For he is ineffable whom you are not able to utter. And if you are unable to utter him, and you may not be silent, what remains except that you should jubilate, in order that your heart may rejoice without words and that an immense breadth of joys should not be bounded by syllables? Sing well to Him in jubilation.[45]

Lewis and Short define *jubilum* as "a wild cry, shout, shepherd's song."[46] Oliver Nicholson has remarked that Augustine's use of the term *jubilum* likely denoted work shanties in which laborers were so absorbed in the rhythm of work that they would have not bothered singing specific words.[47] A dialectic of the ineffable that was intellectually rarefied in Plotinus's *Enneads* is here, in Augustine's hands, rendered more widely accessible. Shorn from the complex workings of reason in Plotinus's dialectic, for Augustine the ecstatic song of the common vineyard worker could name the unnameable with sensory means, and convey a transcendent joy that exceeded the rigid segmentation of specific words.

There is something strikingly modern about Augustine's formulation, notwithstanding its context in late antiquity. It entails an affirmative recognition of music's sensuous inconsistency. Though it lies far beyond the scope of this book to recount a detailed intellectual history of music's ineffability that lies between Augustine and modern Europe, the nexus of influences surrounding the onset of German Romanticism at the end of the eighteenth century represents an instructive parallel to Augustine's view of music's ineffability, and stands as a modern turning point for the philosophers in this book. Thus, let us consider below a brief sketch of the ways in which a few significant figures in German Romanticism—Johann Gottfried Herder, Wackenroder, and Hoffmann—approached music's ineffability.

Herder, Wackenroder, and Hoffmann shared Augustine's interest in the ineffability of music's sensuous inconsistency. But they would differ from dominant strains of late antiquity on two counts. One is in positive terms: by 1800, the terrain of what the unique medium of music was had shifted away markedly from the metaphysics of number, which had still preoccupied Augustine in his Pythagorean text on music, *De musica*.[48] Though undercurrents of Pythagoreanism had by no means disappeared by the nineteenth century, Mark Evan Bonds and Holly Watkins have shown in historical and rhetorical detail how the German Romantics tended to cast music's ineffability as an aesthetic abstraction exemplified not by number, but by a metaphorical sense of depth and an exceptional feeling of emotional intensity.[49]

Two, in negative terms, these Romantic writers often positioned music's ineffability not against the limits of finite syllables uttered by God (as Augustine had), but instead against the baroque fashion for musical imitation and the attendant theory that music was amenable to the language-like representation of emotions, a trend that would later be dubbed the *Affektenlehre* by German musicologists.[50] In a modern echo of Socrates' ignorance plea, M. H. Abrams elegantly described this epochal shift: "Music, by its nature the weak spot in the theory of imitation, as this theory was usually interpreted in the eighteenth century, was thus the first of the arts to be severed from the mimetic principle by a critical nexus."[51] In other words, for the Romantics, music's inconsistency could not be contained by the orders of imitation and representation. Rather, in their view, music was ineffable because it overwhelmed such quasi-linguistic correspondences with a singular force of affective sensation.

In 1778, Johann Nikolaus Forkel, the early biographer of J. S. Bach, presaged many of the theories of the Romantics when he described music as an infinitely graded ineffability beyond the limits of a language of emotions.[52] Likely influenced by elements of British empiricism, Forkel wrote: "[Music] only becomes the real language of the infinite gradations of the feelings at that point where other languages can no longer reach, and when their ability to express ends."[53] For Forkel, music's ineffability was deeply linked to sensuous particularity, and its exceptional powers followed from the way it confounds the exacting pretense of a language of the emotions.[54] In a similar vein, Wilhelm Heinrich Wackenroder turned to Heraclitan imagery to make music's ineffability expressible in the form of a poetic image. In his 1779 essay "The Characteristic Inner Nature of the Musical Art and the Psychology of Today's Instrumental Music," Wackenroder claimed that the inconsistent multiplicity of music resisted the reasoned containers of language. And in an echo of a frequent refrain in the eighteenth and nineteenth centuries, he suggested that music's unspeakable power reflected a "secret" language of the soul:

> A rushing river shall serve as my image. No human art is capable of sketching for the *eye* with *words* the flowing of an immense river, following all the thousands of individual smooth and mountainous, plunging and foaming waves. — Language can only inadequately *count* and *name* the changes, not visibly portray for us the interdependent transformations of the drops. And so it is also with the secret river in the depths of the human soul. Language counts and names and describes its transformations, in a foreign medium; — the musical art causes it to flow past us ourselves. It reaches spiritedly into the mysterious harp, it strikes certain obscure, marvelous signals in the dark world in a definite succession, — and the strings of our hearts resound and we understand their ringing.[55]

It was Wackenroder's writings on music, alongside similar musings from his friend Ludwig Tieck, that would turn out to be such a profound influence on E. T. A. Hoffmann in his celebrated 1810 review of Beethoven's Symphony no. 5. For Hoffmann, instrumental music would convey the infinite quality of a longing separate from any particular emotions: "Music reveals to man an unknown realm, a world quite separate from the outer sensual world surrounding him, a world in which he leaves behind all precise feelings in order to embrace an expressible longing."[56] Herder's writings on music are likewise exemplary.

For him, music harnesses interior and invisible forces of feeling that befuddle and transfix. When speculating about ancient views of music, Herder suggests that the Greeks' recourse to the immaterial science of Pythagorean metaphysics was, in actual fact, directly due to the sensory impact of music's ineffability:

> But what poetic language did they use when they wished to intimate the *inwardness of music as such?* The inner shudder, the all-powerful feeling that seized them they were unable to explain; they knew of nothing in all of visible Nature that could affect them so inwardly and profoundly. So they believed that spirits, spirits of heaven and earth, had been drawn toward them by the chains of music, had descended from celestial spheres and risen from tombs, and floated all about them, invisibly to be sure, yet all the more sensibly.[57]

The axis of ineffability allowed Herder to reimagine the numerical coordinates of cosmic harmonics as an inner sensuous particularity that was tightly woven with emotions and affects. For Herder, as for his Romantic compatriots, music's ineffability was wedded to concrete worldly knowledge, but unfolded in excess of it—as a metaphorical sense of depth or an idealized absolute. Significant here is its nonconceptual character; music seemed to articulate an affective intensity and spiritual depth beyond one's capacity to represent it. In the domain of aesthetics, this idea helped secure music as an art form that stood at the top of the hierarchy of the arts. Many critical and philosophical accounts of music's ineffability relied upon a Kantian philosophical vocabulary: music was intrinsically linked to a noumenal thing-in-itself that could not be presented to conscious experience through concepts.

It is around the philosophical tensions of such a sensuous interiority that the story of this book begins. In 1818, Arthur Schopenhauer first described a paradox around music's proximity to Kant's noumenal: if it copied the blind force of the unconscious will of all life, it could only do so by becoming mediated. The opening prelude of the book argues that Schopenhauer, as well as Nietzsche, made a significant break with the Romantic tradition known for venerating music's metaphysical depths—as transcendent tones, nature, the essence of life, an affective longing, or the thing-in-itself—by giving its ineffability a distinct form: that of the unmediated copy.

That is, for Schopenhauer, music copies the will—it creates a copy of it—but the copy remains somehow immediate to the will. As I have argued, this strange liminality of being formed and mediated by style, idiom, genre, and intellect, while also hitting us in the gut with the sensuous appearance of immediacy, is key to music's specificity. It describes the paradoxical structure of music's ineffability rather than a Romanticized assertion of its unspeakable or sublime properties.[58] It is based in the theory that music's impact copies something beyond experience—the noumenon, the thing-in-itself—something real that resists, while remaining mediated by, the conceptual framing of the intellectual order.[59] In the terms Nietzsche adopted from a long-standing tension in German aesthetics, music copies the flux of Dionysian forces into the self-conscious intellectual framework of Apollonian forms, while maintaining the two artistic drives in a co-constitutive structure.

For modern philosophers who read Schopenhauer's account of music, and considered this paradoxical tension to be significant, it was hard not to find fault with the conclusions of the philosopher's account. As I will detail in section 0.2, Schopenhauer ultimately turns to an array of Platonisms that circumvent the richness of the very paradoxes he had discovered. By contrast, Bloch, Adorno, Jankélévitch, and Deleuze show how the paradoxical tensions of Schopenhauer's unmediated copy deserve sustained philosophical attention. By repositioning what Schopenhauer disavowed as the central axis of a philosophical inquiry, all four of these philosophers demonstrate that the paradox of music's ineffability might be productively developed through an array of sophisticated and in many ways contrasting dialectical methods.

Chapter 1 turns to the first of the philosophers—Ernst Bloch—and argues that he adopts Schopenhauer's conception of the unmediated copy and transforms it into a dialectical theory of the tone, in a way that is substantially indebted to the influence of Hegel. In my analysis, Bloch in turn develops a range of motifs around this concept of the tone: a speculative theory and history of music, a dialectical conception of the tone that foregrounds unresolved contradictions, and a nonsynchronous method of immanent critique whereby uncanny uses of past technical procedures give us the glimpse of something unforeseen, something utopian. For Bloch, the ineffability of the tone is based in its "delicate translucent body," one that is "a metaphysical word"—both formally precise and semantically vague. Nested within the chapter are an account of Bloch's inheritance of the concept of the tone in the climate of nineteenth-century German thought, a discussion of the importance of Hegel's distinction between *Klang* and *Ton* for Bloch, and an account of the ways in which elements of Bloch's social thought were foundational for Adorno's dialectic. The chapter concludes by discussing several aspects of musical compositions by Mozart, Beethoven, and Mahler that exemplify the ethical and utopian compositions Bloch calls event-forms (*Ereignisformen*).

If Bloch in many ways remained a Romantic, Adorno's musical thought more explicitly reflects the professionalized humanities of the twentieth century—in which abstraction was accorded more prestige, autonomy, and resistant potentiality. In the context of such modern disciplinary formalisms, music's stock rose higher. Kant had first described this modern aesthetic in the *Critique of Judgment* (1791) as a "purposiveness without purpose"—an indeterminate orderliness of the art object that was wedded to no particular function or interest in the world. Kant's formalism, as many scholars have noted, served as the foundation for Eduard Hanslick's conception of "tonally moving forms [*tönend bewegte Formen*]" in *Vom Musikalisch-schönen* (1854), a text that would in turn be intellectually foundational for the emergence of "absolute music."[60] In this vein, Walter Pater's oft-quoted 1877 dictum about the exceptional "condition of music" would become increasingly emblematic of music's privileged relationship to aesthetic abstraction, and foundational for seminal texts of twentieth-century modernism. Wassily Kandinsky, Hans Hofmann, Victor Shklovsky, Boris Eikhenbaum, T. S. Eliot, Susanne Langer, and the aforementioned Clement Greenberg all positioned music as exceptional among the arts for its nonreferential properties. What distinguished the twentieth-century modernist exceptionalism of music from the Romantic one a century earlier was a conviction that music's ineffability was no longer based in an aesthetics of feeling. While retaining its sensuous character, in late modernity it would be linked to a sui generis abstraction, a formalist difficulty, a slowness of thinking, a strategy of close reading and immanent critique that resisted ideology and normative modes of social life.

Chapter 2 takes up this modernist critical practice where chapter 1 leaves off: a conversation between Bloch and Adorno during a radio interview in 1964. It argues that the principal innovation in Adorno's philosophy of music is the remaking of Hegel and Bloch's conception of the tone into a teleology toward the ideological language of tonality (or *Versprachlichung*). I then discuss both historical and methodological foundations for Adorno's approach to music. As I contend, Adorno's conception of music's ineffability is based in the way it approximates the structures of language while not saying anything in particular. To make this theory concrete, two contrasting case studies of Adorno's immanent critique are offered: that of Schoenberg's early turn to atonality (exemplified by *Herzgewächse*), and the more open-ended themes at play in his monograph on Mahler. As mentioned earlier, it is here that I locate the paradox of the vernacular that I shall return to in the conclusion. In the final section of the chapter, I turn to Adorno's speculative writings on the inconsistency of the radio and of phonograph grooves in order to argue that it is an aporia that could not be reconciled within the central theory of musical technique that Adorno had developed and deployed in his practice of immanent critique. By way of transition, I point out that it is precisely the temporal inconsistency of music that Adorno saw in the "curves of the needle" that would become the foundation for the French philosophers' views of music.

If the German thinkers emphasize the weight of abstraction and ideology in assessing the experience of music, the French focus on music's proximity to temporality and experience. Between chapters 2 and 3, a brief interlude describes Wittgenstein's parallel intuition that music was language-like, even as its sensuous inconsistency was met largely with an injunction to silence. Taking this "silence" as a point of departure, chapter 3 explores the principal theme of Jankélévitch's philosophy of music: a fidelity to music's inconsistency based in the a priori rejection of any kind of *Versprachlichung* (Wittgensteinian, Adornian, or otherwise). That is, if Bloch's and Adorno's conceptions of music's ineffability were based in its vague shadowing of linguistic structure, Jankélévitch's is based in its qualitative refusal of it. The first half of chapter 3 links Jankélévitch's views of music with his enduring philosophical commitments: to Bergson, to the aporetic experience of the vanishing now, to key aspects of his moral philosophy, and to the metaphysical dynamism of the instant. The second half explains how Jankélévitch develops what I call a "speculative multiplicity" of philosophies of music that are united by their deliberate refusal of any kind of language-like character in music. It concludes by arguing that Jankélévitch's philosophy is best described not as "antidialectical" but rather as practicing an "unwoven" dialectic that retains an attentive ethics to musical forms while dramatically slackening the criteria one would use to specify them.

The fourth and final chapter focuses on the writings of Deleuze and Guattari. In my view, these thinkers show themselves to be as Bergsonian as Jankélévitch in conceiving of music and sound as containing an intimate link with the flow of lived time. But they develop this idea in a new direction by proposing that music is not simply an inconsistent flux but, rather, is in line with Bachelard's 1938 critique of Bergsonism, a punctuated flow that is coextensive with the cosmic powers of social and creaturely life. Moreover, due to their contention that "being is univocal" and that an artwork is a pure presence, or a "sensation in itself," they would contend that music is part of the same pluralized substance as language. Crucially, they nod to the ineffable in practical terms when they state that it is "hard to say" what music does in relationship to language. But on a philosophical level, their ontological joining of music and language in something of a Mobius strip represents a remarkable shift that sets Bloch, Adorno, and Jankélévitch powerfully into relief. For Deleuze and Guattari, there is no mysterious depth or "unrepresentable" aspect to music's sensuous power by comparison with language; music is merely a sonic extension of a cosmic rhythm of lived forces.

To forge a link of coextension between music and the cosmos returns us, quite surprisingly, to ancient themes in Pythagorean cosmology, though under late modern historical conditions. The second half of the chapter argues that Guattari's famous concept of the *"ritournelle"* amounts to a post-structuralist revival of Pythagoreanism; in *A Thousand Plateaus* (1980), music bears a structural link of coextension with the cosmos, though by way of mobile counterpoints of varying rhythms rather than the eternal stasis of ancient harmonics. It concludes with a discussion of Deleuze's intermedial aesthetics, developed in his late works, and features interpretations of Schumann's "Warum?" (1837), Paul Klee's *Twittering Machine* (1922), and a discussion of sound in Deleuze's cinema books. I finally argue that, notwithstanding the elimination of the power of ideas or "the image of thought," their writings still parallel many aspects of Bloch's, Adorno's, and Jankélévitch's thinking.[61] Deleuze and Guattari still maintain the necessity of music's formal and technical mediation (echoing Schopenhauer's paradox of the immediate copy) as they go about developing their own prescriptive ethics of modern music.

In the conclusion of this book, I argue that Adorno's commitment to form yields us a significant lesson, even if we are ultimately hampered by the narrowness of his preferences. That is, when we line up the narrowness of Adorno's immanent critique against the others (Bloch, Jankélévitch, Deleuze, and Guattari), one finds far looser dialectics at work in the other thinkers, for the other intellectuals have less exacting conceptions of ideology and history. They are also interested in an ethical practice of musical creativity and resistance; they just don't have the same precise formal criteria. While Adorno's conservative teleology of musical material is often maligned as elitist, in my view the comparatively open-ended views forwarded by Bloch, Jankélévitch, Deleuze, and Guattari loosen the link between music and language without doing away with Adorno's overarching preoccupations—of formal criteria, of historical weight and influence, and of normative grammars and modes of inscription. This of course means not that Adorno was "right," but rather that a musical modernism that accords music philosophical significance seems to require some kind of self-reflexive account of musical form, no matter how negative, inconsistent, or ambiguous.

At the same time, I insist on heeding a crucial lesson from Jankélévitch: music withdraws from meaning as often as it seems to want to disclose it. He models a certain cool indifference to its outwardly expressive dimensions. And as a virtue ethicist, he practices a courageous gesture of caution against reinscribing the impact of music into an exacting dialectics of latent secrets. Even as musical forms develop into complex quasi-syntactical works, Jankélévitch's attention to music's temporal inconsistency reminds one that all music is also inexpressive wallpaper; its ability to do nothing or to withdraw is part of the medium. Yet his approach to music does not entail a pious silence, a worship of the irrational, or an undialectical realism of the body. Dialectics, as it does for Bloch and Adorno, still marks the necessity of mediation. Forms and technical supports of some sort are intrinsic to the formation of music's ineffable impact. It is just that the resultant significance of the forms is nonlinguistic, blank, or vague. Dialectics nonetheless ensures productivity and perplexity; it structures collisions with meaning. As a result, one can go on discerning, specifying, and explaining music's significance.

In the ethical terms of twentieth-century critique, the paradox of the ineffable is closely paralleled by the paradox of the vernacular. As discussed earlier, in the paradox of the vernacular, normative forms can be unpredictably espoused and critiqued to the point where the criteria for decoding the music's resistance is itself occluded. When one accepts, as Adorno does in his discussion of Mahler, that one does not know if a form is being negatively fractured or positively assembled, and one also accepts that *some* minimal grain of form, idiom, and history are never fully eliminated, one has sensed the complexity of the paradox of the vernacular. To eliminate the mediating axis of form in the veneration of a vernacular expression is to risk a collapse into a philosophical realism in which one has only bodies and authenticities, but no disciplines, influences, or systems; it is to risk idealizing a resistance or a proximity to the will, *durée*, or the real that knows no historical and cultural boundaries—that has no dialectical praxis. In my view, a desire to explain the resistance of musical vernaculars reflects a desire to respond adequately to an exemplary form of musical disunity, fragility, and inconsistency. This response is linked, as it was for the Ikhwan Al-Safa, to the structured vagueness of music's ontology, an ontology that resulted in a paradox of the ineffable so vividly expressed by Schopenhauer as one of an immediate copy.

A few final words about a frequent confusion. Music's ineffability and absolute music may overlap, but are by no means coextensive terms. As I suggest in the course of my chapter summaries, the concept of absolute music is a modern one. It develops in the mid-nineteenth century, in a polemical fight polarized by Wagner's radical intermedial theories of music drama. Since Hanslick, the term has been frequently linked to conservatism, formalism, and high abstraction. Confusion between the two terms stems from the fact that they are both often defined negatively against language, specific emotions, or narrative content, particularly if one draws their histories back to E. T. A. Hoffmann. But, in my view, music's ineffability is a far less circumscribed phenomenon. One is under no obligation to assume that music's ineffability is axiomatically linked to conservatism, abstraction, or apolitical autonomy. This book presumes that its life is multicultural, expansive, relational, porous, and often vernacular. It is relevant in music with text, in opera of all kinds, in film music, protest music, electronic dance music, hip-hop, and soul music; it is a generic quality of the medium. By contrast, absolute music typically denotes a narrow repertory subject to a strong autonomous criterion of abstraction. (Notwithstanding the logical affinity, at the hands of modern scholars, absolute music is often not ineffable anyway. Formalists in analytic philosophy and music theory would likely argue that absolute music is graspable with a combination of structural models, analytical language, and mathematics.)

By contrast, music's ineffability is sustained by dialectical recursion. It is only occasionally related to an absolute conception of musical form. Moreover, one could argue that, to have philosophical significance, one cannot remain autonomously musical; the music has to collide quite relentlessly with language. Thus, music's ineffability denotes a specific kind of metaphysical productivity, a puzzle engendered by the uniqueness of its sensory impact. Just as Plotinus spills many words over the ineffability of the One, or Plato develops an elaborate dialectical method to disseminate the ideal truth of being, one still has to speak of it. No ineffabilist is silent when faced with the unspeakable; they have all used the dialectic to maintain virtuous mediations. To face the ineffable is to face the weirdness and complexity of the medium head-on as a productive and inconsistent multiplicity.

*

There are a few other figures in twentieth-century French intellectual history who could have been included. Gabriel Marcel is a religious thinker of music's ineffability who has some proximity to Jankélévitch.[62] The same could be said for Clement Rosset, who is an unapologetic revivalist of Schopenhauer and Nietzsche, and who associates music's power directly with that of the real.[63] On the left, Roland Barthes and Catherine Clément make brief cameo appearances; they could conceivably have been given their own chapter.

In the Marxist tradition, Jacques Attali's *Noise* (1977) is unique in broaching the national divide; written by a French economist, it is something of a revival of Adorno under a less narrow conception of musical resistance (influenced in part by the writings of Roland Barthes), and a more all-encompassing and historically variagated base-superstructure correlation.[64] Attali's prized practice of "composition" features an ethical vision of modernism that is focused on the revival of collective improvisation (free jazz in particular, which famously made an impact in France during the 1960s and '70s) as a protest against the deadening effect of sound recording and the modern music industry. Also in a Marxist vein is Henri Lefebvre, a geographer by disciplinary training, who developed the musical concept of a "rhythmanalysis" that reflects a more spatialized approach to Deleuze and Guattari's metaphysics of rhythm.[65] While for some time I considered including their writings, from the perspective of organizing the argument and narrative of the book as a coherent whole, offering more than four case studies struck me as something that would have been unwieldy for the purposes of a comparative study.

*

Finally, a few words about my choice of title, *Deep Refrains*. By tackling the question of music's ineffability in the context of twentieth-century European philosophy, rather than in the ancient terms of a cosmic harmony or the Romantic metaphysics of the nineteenth century, I propose to revisit the "deep" nature of music's ineffability with a certain critical and philosophical rhythm, a dialectical refrain that surfaces paradoxes and tensions while finding, delimiting, and connecting the contours of various recurrent themes and motifs. The book's method, and my own fascination with reading, rethinking, and reteaching these philosophers again and again, reflects my passion for the recursive and ethical circulation of critical thought. It seeks out the question of the new, the resistant, and the vernacular via an intellectual act of reflection. But it also respects the blankness, inexpression, and coolness of an experience that is specific to music among the arts. The method opens itself repeatedly to the befuddling flux of sonic impact, reforms its speculations, finds itself without a concept, and maintains fidelity toward virtue, towards ethics, and toward the intellectual contours of a resistant novelty.

PRELUDE

A Paradox of the Ineffable

Does music speak to us independently of concepts and signs? Does it speak to us at a level of deep reality beyond our world of ordinary language? It is a challenge even to form such a question without engendering a paradox. For if music were to "speak" to us beyond language, by what criteria and idiom is it speaking, and does this speaking—now at a metaphorical level—still entail some process of signification? And how exactly would the "speaking" of a nonreferential medium like music get translated into a referential medium like language without sacrificing the specificity of one's musical experiences?

These questions have often haunted efforts to positively define the idea that music has no signification outside its own sonorous form. For to argue that music is entirely autonomous still seems to entail at least two realms of nonmusical scaffolding: (1) a linguistic argument and (2) an extramusical context of values and relationships in which such a claim is wagered and maintained. It is perhaps symptomatic that negative arguments defending the formal autonomy of absolute music are far more common than positive ones. Hanslick, easily the most influential formalist of music in European aesthetics, is a case in point. He spent much of *Vom Musikalisch-Schönen* (1854) critiquing all that should *not* be associated with music: namely emotions and various representational illusions. Musicological studies of absolute music have often expounded upon this negativity as a fruitful source of hermeneutic, genealogical, or deconstructive inquiry. Daniel Chua, Susan McClary, and Berthold Hoeckner, among many others, have sought to unearth the ironies, betrayals, and polyphonies of meaning that haunt the nineteenth-century conceit of absolute music's pure form.[1]

But, as has been stated in the introduction, absolute music is only one particular case of music's ineffability. Consider this opening question in broader philosophical terms: Can the experience of something boundless, infinite, or absolute ever be truly immediate? Or must it be mediated by something else, namely reason, the intellect, and language? In a short essay on the ineffable, Roger Scruton has described the routinely paradoxical situation that ensues for philosophers like Schopenhauer and Jankélévitch, who like Plotinus, posit an ineffable realm and then proceed to write about it for pages and pages.[2] Scruton himself acknowledges that certain things may be ineffable (ultimate causes, aesthetic experiences, and so on), and describes the ineffable as a realm that should be recognized rather than dismissed (as scientific positivism might claim). He also asserts, however, that loquacious accounts of the ineffable are temptations that may be best overcome by the virtue of silence, or otherwise disclosed through more indirect forms of meditation.

Adorno confronted this philosophical paradox several times over, and described it in processual terms, as if the absolute (unlimited, infinite, self-reproducing) quality of music was like soap or melting chocolate in our hands. Its discreetness fades, and eludes our precise grasp. Ephemerality haunts the experience of the absolute: "Music reaches the absolute immediately, but in the same instant it darkens, as when a strong light blinds the eye, which can no longer see things that are quite visible."[3] By way of a reference to a blinding light, Adorno alludes to Plato's allegory of the cave. The meaning is clear: for Adorno, as one seeks to apprehend knowledge of the absolute, one's eyes are pained and blinded as a paradox takes hold. Nothing essential—of being qua being in the Platonic sense—may be copied without distortion and falsification. Notice too that "the absolute" is a philosophical term here, not a formalist one (as it would be for "absolute music"). Adorno's question is: What happens when music reaches the absolute—*the* absolute? In other words, what if music is accorded a philosophical significance that is unbounded?

This is one way to characterize Schopenhauer's aspirations for music. In his philosophy, music's ineffability is not presumed to be absolute in a formalist sense, but is instead taken to "speak" in a way that is coextensive with the unbounded flux of one's inner emotional drives, or will. And Schopenhauer's will joins us to the universe. It is an absolute, inexhaustible, and self-determining force that operates as the foundation of all there is.

0.1 SCHOPENHAUER'S DEEP COPY

In order to make clearer the stakes of this claim, consider some of the basics of Schopenhauer's approach to music, as well as central aspects of his philosophy more broadly. In *The World as Will and Representation*, Schopenhauer contends that music is exceptional among the arts because of its unique intensity and nonrepresentational character. As he puts it: "Music's effect on us is on the whole of the same nature [as the other arts], but stronger, faster, effective and infallible [*nur starker, schneller, notwendiger, unfehlbarer ist*]."[4] In another passage, he refers to music as "that profound pleasure" that is capable of expressing "the deepest recesses of our nature."[5] In the modern vocabulary of the humanities, we might describe these remarks as an early version of music's medium specificity: among all the arts, music is stronger and faster in its effect upon us, and it has a way of tapping into an "inner" feeling, something Schopenhauer describes elsewhere as a "serious and profound significance that refers to the innermost being of the world and of our own self."[6]

The philosophical basis for Schopenhauer's contention that music is exceptional among the arts is a dualism between two capacities of the subject: reason (*Vernuft*) and feeling (*Gefühl*). Reason, in Schopenhauer's view, is mediated by the Kantian a priori of concepts, forms, individuations, and representations, and pertains to the world of space, time, and causality. Feeling, by contrast is a "wide and negative concept" linked to the affective dimension of moods, passions, and emotions. If for Kant, all knowledge was mediated by the form of the concept, Schopenhauer defended the existence and the value of nonconceptual and intuitive knowledge; for him, feeling and intuition had their own special precision, and were linked to a much greater natural force—something he called the will.[7]

In his early discussions of the will in *The World as Will and Representation*, Schopenhauer discusses the experience of one's own body. In his view, when we experience our own bodies in voluntary action, our body becomes a "double reference." A "double reference" means that one's body is framed by the Kantian orders of representation at the same time as it is accessible to us as part of a cosmic will of force and energy. For one ordinarily apprehends such an experience of a body's voluntary action as part of a world determined by space, time, and causality. Schopenhauer keenly reminds his readers that this experience is simultaneously undetermined by these factors; at some level, he insists, one has an absolutely immediate experience of one's own embodied volition. From these undetermined aspects of a voluntary action, he deduces the existence of a broader cosmic will, a thing-in-itself, all that Kant took to be inaccessible to a subject's cognitive powers. In Schopenhauer's view, one's volition is merely the apex of a vast fabric of blind striving, a world of natural forces devoid of rationality or intellect.

Schopenhauer offers his readers vivid examples of what he means by the term "will." If our voluntary, embodied movements provide direct evidence of the will, Schopenhauer claims that this experience of freedom is inseparable from a teeming universe of interior forces that courses through all levels of the cosmos. Birds and insects, for example, who are not guided by knowledge, nonetheless reflect the activity of the will: "The one-year-old bird has no notion of the eggs for which it builds a nest; the young spider has no idea of the prey for which it spins a web; the ant-lion has no notion of the ant for which it digs a cavity for the first time."[8] The many nonintentional systems of our body are likewise objectifications of the will: "Even in us the same will in many ways acts blindly; as in all those functions of our body which are not guided by knowledge, in all its vital and vegetative processes, digestion, circulation, secretion, growth, and reproduction."[9] Schopenhauer further adds that cosmic bodies, gravity, and light from the sun are facets of this all-encompassing will, which exists outside of space and time. From the simplest inert matter up through the conscious actions of man, there lies a metaphysical hierarchy that echoes a Neoplatonic chain of being: "There is a higher degree of this objectification [of the will] in the plant than in the stone, a higher degree in the animal than in the plant; indeed, the will's passage into visibility, its objectification, has gradations as endless as those between the feeblest twilight and the brightest sunlight, the loudest tone and the softest echo."[10]

Schopenhauer's recourse to sonic metaphors of tones and echoes in this sentence is not merely a flourish of figurative language. In his discussion of music, he argues more fully that the exceptional intensity of music gives us what he will call "an unmediated copy" of the will. This is the foundation of music's ability to "speak" its own specific language. Melody has a particularly expressive role in this regard:

> Melody, however, says more; it relates the most secret history of the intellectually enlightened will, portrays every agitation, every effort, every movement of the will, everything which the faculty of reason summarizes under the wide and negative concept of feeling, and which cannot be further taken up into the abstractions of reason. Hence it has always been said that music is the language of feeling and of passion, just as words are the language of reason.[11]

Things get complicated from here, because this thought is teeming with paradoxes. What does it mean to say that music is a language of feeling, when language by definition is made of words, and thus entails representations? And what does it mean that its history "of the intellectually enlightened will" is a secret, rather than something that is manifestly obvious? Finally, if melody "portrays" or "paints [*malt*]" every tiny "movement of the will" in a way that is inassimilable to reason, how can we say and understand this thought in language without corrupting it? Minimally, to return to the central thesis: We know that for Schopenhauer, music speaks in a way that language cannot. It speaks a language of feeling and passion; it speaks about things that do not get said in ordinary language.[12] In a particularly provocative (and prescient) turn of phrase, Schopenhauer even claims that music's secretive character emanates from the nocturnal depths of the unconscious, delivered to us in the manner of "a magnetic somnambulist" without the aid of any concepts: "Here, as everywhere in art, the concept is unproductive. The composer reveals the innermost nature of the world, and expresses the profoundest wisdom in a language that his reasoning faculty does not understand, just as a magnetic somnambulist gives information about things of which she has no conception when she is awake."[13]

If we take a step back, it would appear that we have at least two somewhat distinct conceptions of the will in play, both of which Schopenhauer understands to be central to the powers of music. One the one hand we have a Neoplatonic chain of being, a metaphysical hierarchy of energetic life that stretches from heavy matter up through plants, animals, and humans; and on the other, a Romantic stratum of inner feelings that is centered in human experience. For Schopenhauer, it is crucial to understand the intimacy with which the two are intertwined: the Platonic forms structure metaphysical access to the noumenal secrets of life. It is for this reason that Schopenhauer can claim that music's language of feeling—a profound wisdom in musical sound alone—has a certain exactitude that Schopenhauer claims is *more precise* than language. For Schopenhauer, music's exactitude even engenders a sense of universal assent: "[Music] creates such a powerful reaction in man's inmost depths, it is so thoroughly and profoundly understood by him as uniquely universal language, even exceeding in clarity that of the phenomenal world itself."[14] Music, as a precise language of feeling, is a pure epiphany, an undeniable infusion of musical truth. It communicates with us like "the silent sunbeam, cutting through the path of the storm, and quite unmoved by it."[15]

Schopenhauer derived his Platonic convictions about the clarity of music's universality from residues of Pythagorean metaphysics, which maintained that music's mathematical properties positioned it closer to the eternity of the cosmos. This influence was, to be sure, ready to hand. For centuries the medieval quadrivium associated music with mathematics, geometry, and astronomy. And even by the nineteenth century, Pythagorean thinking had never fully been cast away by the rising tide of the natural sciences; it could easily lurk in minor passages of otherwise cutting-edge philosophical accounts of music by Schelling and Hegel.[16] (Famously, even Hanslick indulged in Pythagorean speculations in the early editions of *Vom Musikalisch-Schönen*).[17] And beyond Pythagoreanism, it is noteworthy that Schopenhauer was a close reader of Plato. In fact, a certain current of Platonism inflects the way Schopenhauer thinks of music's exceptional precision.

Consider just a few examples. In one of his most Platonic statements about music, Schopenhauer understands music to have a distinct status as axiomatically transcendent and eternal; to even exist without the world. As he puts it: ". . . music, which bypasses ideas, is also totally independent of the phenomenal world; it simply ignores the world, and it could in some sense continue to exist even if the world did not, something that cannot be said of the other arts."[18] He also draws direct points of comparison between music and mathematics in order to underscore their proximity to a Platonic heaven of forms. For Schopenhauer, music's virtue, unlike that of mathematics, is the way it retains a powerful sense of sensuous particularity at the same time that it embodies a crystalline purity. He writes, music "is like geometrical figures and numbers, which are the universal forms of all possible objects of experience and are *a priori* applicable to them all, and yet are not abstract, but perceptible and thoroughly definite."[19] Finally, Schopenhauer understands music to be absolutely exceptional among the arts due to its sense of autonomy from the world. It is the most independent art form, a sui generis medium: "Far from being a mere aid to poetry, music is certainly an independent art; in fact, it is the most powerful of all the arts, and therefore attains its ends entirely from its own resources."[20] To be sure, the other arts embody the eternal transcendence and autonomy of Platonic ideals as well.[21] In his reworking of Kant's thesis that judgments of taste must remain disinterested and thus divorced from the particular charms and desires of the will, Schopenhauer insists repeatedly that the creation and appreciation of art in general is akin to a form of Platonic contemplation, in which an eternal model of the world is beheld: "For [art] plucks the object of its contemplation from the stream of the world's course, and holds it isolated before it. This particular thing, which in that stream was an infinitesimal part, becomes for art a representative of the whole, an equivalent of the infinitely many in space and time. It therefore pauses at this particular thing; it stops the wheel of time; for it the relations vanish; its object is only the essential, the Idea."[22]

Artists and their artworks wrest our perception from the ordinary demands of desire, lived action, and horizontal relationality; they invite us into a vertical, functionless mode of ideal contemplation. For Schopenhauer, an artist's "genius" lies precisely in her instinctive attachment to all that is not functional, predictable, or empirically knowable; artists are visionaries who point to essences that resist all forms of ordinary knowledge.

Given that Schopenhauer was a Romantic, of course, many important aspects of his philosophy were not compatible with Plato's actual views of art. Schopenhauer is resolutely affirmative of art rather than fearful of it. He openly celebrates all that Plato wanted to banish: expression, emotion, a sensory effect that was "stronger, faster, effective, and infallible," and so on—everything that makes music impactful and unique among the arts. Thus, when Schopenhauer alludes to the exceptional precision of music, he places as much emphasis on its expressive quality ("the innermost nature of the world and of ourselves") as he does on its numerical or formal properties. Again, the fact that the two sides are so fully imbricated with one another is extremely significant; it is what distinguishes Schopenhauer's philosophy of music from a simple Platonism on the one hand, and an emotion-laden Romanticism on the other. If, in the introduction to this book, I remarked that Pythagoreanism was generally in decline by Schopenhauer's time, here we have a peculiar counterexample in which ancient abstraction and sensuous Romanticism are delightfully mashed up. It is a strange fusion of unconscious depth and numerical rules, of noumenal ineffability and Platonic precision.[23]

In order to ensure that music sustains this paradox while remaining untainted by concepts and referents, Schopenhauer proposes a synthesis. He turns to a mimesis that is unorthodox to modern ears. It links noumenal passions with the loosely transcendental power of numbers, rather than elements that are sensibly similar or linguistically referential. Thus, when Schopenhauer forwards what he calls an "imitative connection [*nachbildliche Beziehung*]," it is thus not with the aim of simulating various affects or emotions, nor depicting anything extramusical, but with the aim of asserting the more abstract "infallibility [*Unfehlbarkeit*]" and universality of music's power: "Further, its imitative connection [*nachbildliche Beziehung*] to the world must be very profound [*sehr innige*], infinitely true, and really striking [*richtig treffende*], since it is instantly understood by everyone, and presents a certain infallibility [*Unfehlbarkeit*] by the fact that its form can be reduced to quite definite rules expressible in numbers, from which it cannot possibly depart without entirely ceasing to be music."[24]

The backbone of mathematics and a sui generis formalism guarantees the universal "infallibility" of music on a general, structural level. Shorn of any reference to a baroque *Affektenlehre*, Schopenhauer's mimesis is grounded in the eternity of number so that it can establish an "immediately and universally comprehensible" nature of music. In the long view of Western intellectual history, this idea remains Greek; it is as if the Pythagorean cosmology of Plato's *Timeaus* speaks obliquely through Schopenhauer. Animated in this way, Schopenhauer seems to ask his reader to marvel at the numerical integrity of music while he asserts, even insists with something of a hand-wavy conviction, that there must be some mimetic rules keeping its intensity unified and universal. Of course, this is not merely a nostalgic conservatism for an ancient metaphysics. For just decades old are the Romantic references to the depth and centrality of feeling to music—*sehr innige*. These echo similar positions held around 1800 by Wackenroder, Tieck, Hoffmann, and others who claimed that music should not aim to express specific emotions, but instead should unleash an emotional totality that is "infinitely true and really striking."

Schopenhauer expresses this tension between the purported universality of music's form and the emotional power of music's sensuous particularity vividly as a paradox. Music, for him, imitates the will—a valueless, blind flux based in the materiality of concrete life. And yet, music's imitation of this sensuous flux of the will must somehow remain immediate to both the music and the will—to fuse them without loss, something of an impossible proposition. In the passage below, Schopenhauer lets this paradox speak, and concludes that music has an enigmatic ontology; it is an immediate copy, an imitation of a will that remains coextensive with itself even after it has been actualized as music and has hit our ears.

> Thus music is as *immediate* an objectification and copy of the whole *Will* [*unmittelbare Objektivation und Abbild des ganzen Willens*] as the world itself is, indeed as the Ideas are, the multiplied appearance [*Erscheinung*] of which constitutes the world of individual things. Therefore music is by no means like the other arts, namely a copy of the Ideas, but *a copy of the will itself* [*Abbild des Willens selbst*], the objectivity of which are the Ideas.[25]

A paradox that is elsewhere staged as an elaborate counterpoint between Romanticism and Pythagoreanism is here compressed linguistically and conceptually. With just a few words, Schopenhauer states it as a plain contradiction: an "immediate objectification and copy of the whole will" and "a copy of the will itself." These formulae raise the opening question: How could something dependent on the mediation of copying nonetheless maintain immediacy? Schopenhauer addresses this question by arguing that music and Ideas imitate the will differently. Ideas are objectified and multiplied appearances of the will (resulting in a world of individuated things), whereas music is a *direct* copy of the will. If the nonmusical arts imitate Ideas, thus making their mediations explicit, music copies the will immediately—without being routed through Ideas. This comparison illustrates the way in which Schopenhauer imagines music's exceptionalism. He squares the circle of the infallible universality of the inner nocturnal will by adopting a version of Greek mimetic theory that is abstracted from any reference to particular ideas, emotions, or representations. It asserts music's mimesis in general form alone; for one cannot create a typology of the ways in which various effects are imitated and simulated when the only thing being imitated is the unity of the will itself. Or put otherwise, the particular emotions are less important than a loose metaphysics of the gestalt.

Various paradoxical tensions remain within the text, however. Schopenhauer uses several different words and phrases when describing the nature of this link. He calls the link an Objectivtion [*Objektivation*], Copy [*Abbild*], and a imitative connection (or "reference" in Payne's translation) [*nachbildliche Beziehung*] of the will. He uses the verbs *wiedergeben* (which can mean to echo, reproduce, recite, or mirror), *aufschließen* (which means to unlock, disclose, or open up), and elsewhere, when discussing emotion and feeling, *ausdrucken* (to express or give utterance). In a passage quoted earlier, he adds some intermedial texture and a sense of latency to his theory when he claims that melody "narrates the most secret history [*sie erzählt seine geheimste Geschichte*] of the intellectually enlightened will" and that it "portrays" or "paints [*malt*] every agitation, every effort, every movement of the will."[26]

There is, then, considerable extramusical play in Schopenhauer's word choices that aim to denote exactly how music imitates the will immediately. Music paints the will; it narrates its secrets, it expresses it, mirrors it, objectivizes it, and so on. How does one assume universal access to music when mimesis seems to entail such complex negotiations with the representational aspects of the world? No one medium or verb can adequately address the task Schopenhauer has set for music; only a nonlinguistic medium—mathematics— can metaphysically transduce the will into a music that copies it immediately. The catch is that a description of the way mathematics enables this relationship must itself be mediated by language; thus the polysemy, the shifting terminology, and the shimmering aporias.

At one point in the text, the paradox rears its head. If music is an immediate copy of the will, it also externalizes an impossibly deep copy of the essence and energies of life. By definition, since what it externalizes is what is already in us (the will), it would ostensibly be quite familiar; but its externalization as music is perplexing and intimidating. The emotions the music triggers can seem unreal, even simulacral, in their musical being: "The inexpressible depth of all music, by virtue of which it floats past us as a paradise quite familiar and yet eternally remote, and is so easy to understand and yet so inexplicable, is due to the fact that it echoes all the emotions of our innermost being [*daß sie alle Regungen unsers die innersten Wesens wiedergiebt*], but entirely without reality and remote from its pain."[27]

Tensions abound. The above sentence interests me in part because it is one of the few sentences in Schopenhauer's discussion of music where he seems to acknowledge the work of music's paradoxical status in explicit terms. The sentence discusses and performs the work of the ineffable by describing how music can embody serious contradictions: music can be readily understandable and yet so distant and confusing, familiar yet foreign ("inexpressible," "eternally remote") at the same time. Even a painful emotion triggered by music can seem strangely distant from the real thing—an experience of pain itself. The sentence expresses something of an enigma: like Socrates's ancient complaint against sophistry's mere appearances, music cannot imitate or objectify emotions without raising a question about music's authenticity and recognizability.[28] Even as Schopenhauer outwardly maintains that music is immediate and coextensive with the will, his observations about actual musical experience reveal that its sonic transmission and dissemination spawns puzzling aporias.

0.2 THE PLATONIC SOLUTIONS

Notwithstanding the striking originality and vivid linguistic formulation of this paradox (which I shall henceforth call **the paradoxical theory**), Schopenhauer ultimately proposes not to develop the paradox but to resolve it, a decision that will inspire critique from a subsequent generation of intellectuals. His solutions are twofold and, broadly speaking, Platonic. Though there are passages that undoubtedly overlap them, these solutions are separate enough in their claims that, for the sake of clarity, I will here break them out as **solution 1** and **solution 2**. In one solution (henceforth called **solution 1**), music embodies the abstracted essence of emotions rather than a contextually situated emotion. In the other (called **solution 2**), the way music copies the will is analogized to the way the Ideas in general objectify forms of the will. In **solution 2**, Schopenhauer follows elements of the Pythagorean tradition, and draws a metaphysical analogy between the Neoplatonic chain of being (which ranges from the matter of the earth to the form of human freedom) and the frequency spectrum (which ranges from the double bass to the flute).

Let us consider the first Platonic solution, **solution 1**. Its thesis, which has been much discussed in the secondary literature, is as follows: music exhibits the will's emotions in their Platonic form. As Schopenhauer puts it: "Therefore music does not express this or that particular and definite pleasure, this or that affliction, pain, sorrow, horror, gaiety, merriment, or peace of mind, but joy, pain, sorrow, horror, gaiety, merriment, peace of mind—*themselves* to a certain extent in the abstract [*in abstracto*], their essential nature [*das Wesentliche derselben*], without any accessories [*Beiwerk*], and so also without the motives [*Motive*] for them. Nevertheless, we understand them perfectly in this extracted quintessence."[29]

If music allows one to extract the Platonic essence of each individual emotion that is actualized by the will "*in abstracto*," then music can ostensibly imitate the will's affective charge without falsifying its essence into the realm of representation. One can likewise maintain some degree of intellectual distance from any specific mimetic effects; these emotions can be sensed at an abstracted, disinterested, and ideal remove from any secondary accessories or motives that might pertain to a specific, interested situation. In so doing, Schopenhauer shows how the universality, intensity, and expressive precision of music does not fully dispense with the conventional forms of mimesis that have dominated the discussion of art since the Greeks. It is just that music does not imitate anything in a traditional way: ". . . to the man who gives himself up entirely to the impression of a symphony, it is as if he saw all the possible events of life and of the world passing by within himself. Yet if he reflects, he cannot assert any likeness between that piece of music and the things that passed through his mind."[30]

Schopenhauer states that music is not mimetic in any recognizable way because there is no likeness between musical material and events in the world.[31] Rather, **solution 1** proposes something like a virtual space in which music imitates "all possible events of life and the world." Music mimics life with a certain mode of abstraction because what is being imitated is the will itself—a valueless striving or energy that, by definition, cannot be represented to us without corrupting the being of the thing-in-itself. Quite evocatively, Schopenhauer further claims that music, in something of a feedback loop, "acts directly on the will" to such an extent that it can artificially and theatrically manipulate emotions within the listener. "Because music does not, like all the other arts, exhibit the *Ideas* or grades of the will's objectification, but directly the *will itself*, we can also explain that it acts directly on the will, i.e., the feelings, passions, and emotions of the hearer, so that it quickly raises these or even alters them."[32]

But notwithstanding this space of virtual manipulation of abstracted emotions, at no point does any musical mimesis become concrete and simulate actual events.[33] Occasionally, Schopenhauer seems to tinker with the idea of a specific mimesis, as in, for example, the *Affektenlehre*, if only to dismiss it as something that does not warrant too close a focus. For example, when it comes to the discussion of specific musical resources, Schopenhauer marginally embraces the language-like character of tonality, but at the same time pushes back against any specific "language" of harmony by hinting at a subtle contradiction that loosens the specificity of individual emotions. Consider his words about the sound and effect of the minor mode: "But it is indeed amazing that there is a sign of pain, namely the minor, which is neither physically painful nor even conventional, yet is at once pleasing and unmistakable [*ansprechendes und unverkenbarres*]. From this we can estimate how deeply music is rooted in the real nature of things [*Wesen der Dinge*] and of man."[34]

Because it has been abstracted, the pain of the minor mode is universally "pleasing and unmistakable" rather than mimetically specific. With respect to the movement between consonance and dissonance, Schopenhauer claims that this horizontal motion reflects one's blind will as it strives for satisfaction, which is in turn reflected in a melody's "constant digression and deviation from a tonic in a thousand ways." In his discussion of tonal harmony, he describes a range of concrete mimetic accounts of certain musical effects in terms of what they capture emotionally and affectively.[35] But he pedals back with caution by reminding the reader that none of these should be taken too literally or instrumentally. The loose Pythagoreanism wins out.

Philosophically, these abstracted emotional "essences," in all their dynamism, reveal to us an ontology of life that is inaccessible to reason (which is fully mediated by concepts). Again, here, the intelligible universality of music serves as a noumenal backbone to its ineffability: "Music also answers [the question 'What is life?'], more profoundly indeed than do all the [other arts], since in a language intelligible with absolute directness, yet not capable of translation into that of our faculty of reason, it expresses the innermost nature of all life and existence."[36]

In **solution 2**, another Platonic solution to the paradox of the ineffable, Schopenhauer returns to the chain of being (the hierarchical or "graded" objectification of the Ideas of the will) in order to assert a range of "analogies" and "parallelisms" between elements of music and corresponding Ideas. If just earlier he had stated that the ideas and music objectify the will differently (but to a similar extent), he now laterally compares Ideas and music in order to discern similarities in how both objectify the will.[37] While Schopenhauer does not want to link music and the Ideas directly as an "absolutely direct likeness," he does claim that if one considers that both are somewhat independent objectifications of the will, one can discern a loose analogy or parallelism between them:

However, as it is the same will that objectifies itself both in the Ideas and in music, though in quite a different way in each, there must be, not indeed an absolutely direct likeness [*unmittelbare Ähnlichkeit*], but yet a parallel [*ein Parallelismus*], an analogy [*eine Analogie*], between music and the Ideas, the appearance [*Erscheinung*] of which in plurality and in incompleteness is the visible world.[38]

Though Schopenhauer uses a fair amount of prose space to discuss the analogies, they can be summarized in fairly short order. As mentioned above, the analogies follow the spectrum of frequencies from low to high, in the manner of a Pythagorean metaphysics.[39] At the bottom, one has the slow-moving ground bass, the lowest notes, which are analogized to "inorganic nature, the mass of the planet." In the middle range, one finds the *ripieno*, the frequencies of the accompanying band playing harmonies, counterpoint lines, and orchestral *tutti*. This range is analogous to the plant and animal world, and breaks down into scalar detail; he claims that intervals of the score are analogous to individual species in the chain of being, while the Pythagorean gap (a mathematical property that ensures that no tuning system can be perfectly consonant) is analogous to an intrinsic imperfection that ensures variation among life forms. Moreover, discontinuities in texture within the middle range parallel the imperfect and fixed nature of life at the unfree level of animal existence.

At the top of his metaphysical hierarchy, in the highest register, Schopenhauer hears a soaring melody, which to him is analogous to "the intellectual life and endeavor of man."[40] He further contends that since the upper partials of the overtone series are already present in most iterations of these low sounds, there is an interconnectedness of these frequency ranges, and likewise of these forms of life: "All the bodies and organizations of nature must be regarded as having come into existence through gradual development out of the mass of the planet."[41] It is here that we end up where we began; the passing melody at the apex of his analogized chain of being is a copy of the most interior secret emotional world. It is inexpressible because it externalizes the essence of what life is—a blind will that has no self-consciousness—and which cannot in principle be copied.

There are several moving parts to Schopenhauer's metaphysics of music, but figure 0.1 may help us conceptualize them as a group. In the bottom portion of this image I have represented the blind striving of Schopenhauer's cosmic will with an arrow that moves from left to right. The will is individuated in a hierarchy of beings, from matter up through plants and animals, to human life, which I have represented with a series of expanding circles from left to right. Above, we have the workings of music, which I have divided into three components. **The paradoxical theory**, on the far left, is the general thesis that music paints or narrates a secret history of the will. This is represented by a single dotted line that represents the will itself, and remains independent of any particular individuations. The dotted nature of the line indicates the internal tensions and paradoxes of the will. The second two components reflect what I have described as Schopenhauer's two Platonic solutions to such paradoxes. **Solution 1**, in the middle of the figure, represents the idea that music "extracts" the Platonic essence of individual emotions and separates them from any particular narrative or embodied context. I have selected just four emotions that Schopenhauer lists in his own description as representative of this phenomenon: joy, sorrow, pain, and peace of mind. But one should be reminded that for Schopenhauer these musical emotions are highly interconnected. For him, there is no precise *Affektenlehre*. Finally, on the far right, **solution 2** represents the grand Pythagorean parallelisms: the analogies between the frequency spectrum and Schopenhauer's Neoplatonic chain of being. Three basic registers of pitch (low, middle, and high) copy, in miniature, the actual chain of Being depicted in the lower portion of the diagram.

As mentioned earlier, unlike Bloch, Adorno, Jankélévitch, and Deleuze's collaborator, Félix Guattari, Schopenhauer was not an amateur pianist. He studied the flute, and in his leisure time he attended the opera and enjoyed playing transcriptions of compositions by his favorite composer, Gioachino Rossini.[42] He knew Mozart's music, but likely not Beethoven's. And his background as a musician bears an imprint on his musical thinking. Philosophers after him in the twentieth century puzzled over a wide range of musical topics: the stylistic frontiers of Romanticism, the breakdown of tonality, the dichotomy of outward expressionism and cool neoclassicism, the deadening repetition of kitsch, and the impact of radio and sound recording. By contrast, Schopenhauer said relatively little about modern compositional questions. His conception of musical form is largely based in general statements about the raw materials of music (pitch space, ensemble textures, scales, harmonies, and melodic lines). Schopenhauer likewise focused his "metaphysics of music" largely on generic registers of pitch, and attended far more to the basic phenomenon of melodic expressivity than to prescriptions about musical creativity. In fact, it is generally the case that, despite his noted influence on Wagner, Schopenhauer did not aim to prescribe or defend any particular kind of music. He sought only to explain the outlines of its metaphysical structure.

Charitably, saying less about music can also be a precise mode of speculating about the medium's significance at a certain level of generality. If Schopenhauer eschews specific works and detailed techniques in order to focus instead

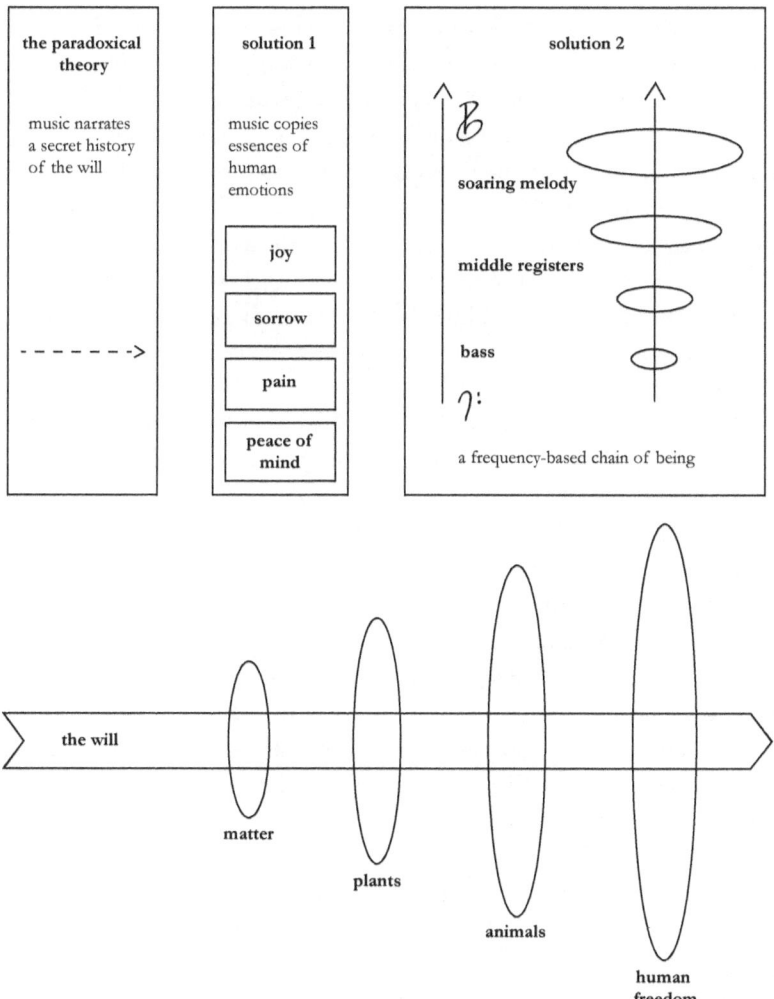

FIGURE 0.1. Schopenhauer's metaphysics of music. Drawing by the author.

on basic elements like pitch space and melodic expression, it is likely because these generalities give him the latitude and flexibility to speculate loosely about large-scale tensions that structure the paradoxical qualities of music.

At the same time, for an avowed metaphysician, the complications of praxis are typically instructive. And at some level, Schopenhauer seems to have been aware of potential problems that might attend the development of his metaphysics into a more systematic dialectic. It requires no major contortions on the part of the reader to notice, for example, that the philosopher himself remains somewhat unsure as to whether or not his analogies of **solution 2** adequately address the gravity of the paradox he has presented. His claim that the parallelisms are universal is plainly hedged with admissions of obscurity and difficulty. Early on in his discussion of music he acknowledges as much, by pointing out that most listeners do not fully comprehend the universality of music's significance: "Yet the point of comparison between music and the world, the regard in which it stands to the world in the relation of an imitation [*Nachahmung*] or a repetition [*Wiederholung*], *is* very obscure. Men have practiced music at all times without being able to give an account of this; content to understand it immediately, they renounce any abstract conception of this direct understanding itself."[43]

As Schopenhauer continues, however, his confidence increases. He forwards a rare claim of strong musical expertise by a philosopher:

> I have devoted my mind entirely to the impression of music [*Eindruck der Tonkunst*] in its many different forms; and then I have returned again to reflection and to the train of my thought expounded in the present work, and have arrived at an explanation of the inner essence of music, and the nature of its imitative relation [*nachbildlichen Verhältnisses*] to the world, necessarily to be presupposed from analogy. This explanation is quite sufficient for me, and satisfactory for my investigation, and will be just as illuminating also to the man who has followed me thus far, and has agreed with my view of the world.[44]

But anxiety about the universality of the analogies is palpable amidst this flourish of confidence. Like the philosopher-king who encounters misunderstanding and danger after re-entering the cave, Schopenhauer sets a high bar for assent; one has to agree with his overall view of the world and the will. A telling problem specific to the metaphysics of music is that Schopenhauer seems to be at a loss concerning how to defend the analogies *because* of the paradoxical nature of music's exceptional significance: "I recognize, however, that it is essentially impossible to demonstrate this explanation, for it assumes and establishes a relation of music as a representation to that which of its essence can never be representation, and claims to regard music as the copy of an original that can itself never be directly represented."[45]

This is Schopenhauer at his closest to the Ikhwan Al-Safa; here, he openly acknowledges the intransigence of the paradox of the ineffable. In light of the hedged claims regarding the comprehension of his metaphysics, it would appear that the paradox is ultimately insoluble within the medium of his philosophy. It can only be left to an empirical result, external to the argument of the text itself; he prefers to leave it to the reader to decide, and to take the contention along with the totality of his interlocking arguments. He insists: Listen to music with the injunction of "constant reflection on this." An injunction to constant reflection presupposes lots of performative felicitousness and a presumably high standard of education and expertise, both in the name of an axiom of Platonic universality. It is perhaps telling that in Plato's texts themselves, when discussing the dissemination of Being, Socrates could reveal a similar anxiety. After leaving the cave and becoming educated, the philosopher-king often struggled to communicate with those back inside the cave.[46]

0.3 FOUR DIALECTICAL SOLUTIONS (AFTER NIETZSCHE)

If Schopenhauer's Platonic analogies were not all that influential for subsequent philosophers as solutions to the paradox of the ineffable, it was the deliberately unresolved form of this paradox that turned out to be a rich resource for twentieth-century philosophical accounts of music. In fact, for the four philosophers at issue in this book—Bloch, Adorno, Jankélévitch, and Deleuze—it is my view that, far from resolving the paradox of music's ineffability as Schopenhauer has with the Platonic gestures of **solutions 1 and 2**, all four philosophers can be understood to develop **the paradoxical theory** into productive dialectical methods.

Consider a brief sketch of their responses. Bloch and Adorno, both close readers of Schopenhauer, accept his proposal that music is exceptional in its powers. But they side with Hegel on the question of mediation. Both claim that Hegel's concept of *Geist*—a "mind" or "spirit" that denotes forms of human self-consciousness that externalize themselves in the course of human history—cannot be eliminated from the experience of music. In Schopenhauer's terms, this means a musical copy of the will could not be immediate, universal, or infallible in any Pythagorean sense; the fallen realm of representation and its historically specific techniques and reifications would structure profoundly the possibility of any musical expression. At the center of their adoption of the dialectic is a contradiction between an enlightened claim to self-conscious freedom and a modern reality concerning the reification of society.

If the German thinkers stress the importance of history and the power of ideas, the French emphasize the weight of mediation in other ways. Jankélévitch maintains that language and the intellect structure and condition the apprehension of music, though his ethics is ultimately based in a certain fidelity to the real inconsistency of musical time. This inconsistency is associated not with an inner will, but with a Bergsonian flux of time that courses through all living things. What I call Jankélévitch's "unwoven dialectic" finds its basis in a fidelity to inconsistency that remains everywhere mediated by language, musical form, and the intellect. For Deleuze and Guattari, finally, the abyss of Schopenhauer's will would itself be structured by an internal difference that pluralizes it and prevents it from remaining unified and immediate to itself. In *Difference and Repetition* (1968), Deleuze develops this internal difference into a metaphysics of punctuated rhythm. What I call Deleuze and Guattari's "contrapuntal dialectic" sidesteps Hegelian contradictions, and argues that mediation structures immediacy at a material level beneath that of ideas, the human, the subject, and historical progress. Broadly speaking, the French intellectuals could be said to hear music in a way that is based in empirical structures of creaturely mediation that they take to operate at a level anterior to the historical power of ideas.

Before investigating how these intellectuals responded to Schopenhauer's paradox in greater detail, let us first consider Nietzsche's response to Schopenhauer in his first book, *The Birth of Tragedy* (1872), since it was a response generally familiar to all the philosophers featured in the subsequent chapters. With Nietzsche, one can begin to further tease out the paradoxical tensions of Schopenhauer's philosophy.

Nietzsche seems to know that Schopenhauer's Pythagorean analogies are a misguided and unsatisfactory answer to this paradox of the ineffable.[47] For the epistemological problems Schopenhauer confronts are formidable. If musical forms (melodies, harmonies, bass lines, etc.) reveal the Platonic essence of individual emotions (**solution 1**) or if they appear metaphysically analogous to a cosmic chain of being (**solution 2**), how can we be sure a given musical composition does not revert to a more concrete mimesis, such as one might find in Aristotle, Rousseau, or the *Affektenlehre*? How do we maintain Schopenhauer's strict (infalliable, fast, noumenal, unconscious, etc.) universality of the inexpressible nature of music without the help of a secondary language that helps one understand it? Would not such a language threaten to falsify music's immediate link to the will?

Nietzsche abdicates Schopenhauer's epistemological quandary altogether, and instead posits an encompassing explanation about art in general. Through an elaboration of a long-standing tension in European aesthetics, he extends Schopenhauer's distinction between representation and the will, and proposes that great art is a product of an oscillation between two corresponding artistic drives or "*Kunsttriebe*." One drive, based in the realm of representation, is the Apollonian tendency towards form (ideas, Platonic dreams, individuations, which are associated with Greek sculpture). The other, based in the will, is the chaotic energy of the Dionysian, associated with the lawless flux of sensation, emotion, pleasure, and the powers of music.

But rather than pin this dichotomy to Schopenhauer's parallel facets of the world—representation and the will—Nietzsche offloads the distinction onto different styles of art making. In so doing, he rewrites Schopenhauer's paradox of the ineffable as a topology: Dionysian intoxication is the essence of music, but in a world of intermedial arts, it always everywhere must be structured in dialogue with Apollonian forces. Nietzsche does not propose a resolution to the dichotomy, but rather seeks to show how each facet embodies an artistic drive entwined within a perennial conflict. And great art showcases this conflict. Namely, Greek tragedies by Aeschylus and Sophocles are exceptional in the history of art for maintaining these two forces in balance. In the nineteenth century, Wagner as well stands alone among composers for having recaptured an adequate sense of the balance between the Apollonian and the Dionysian drives.

Amid this conflict, music retains a certain privilege, a Romantic exceptionalism. After all, for Nietzsche, all the arts are born from the *Geist* of music. Thus, in Nietzsche's topology, music functions as an original excess that is captured or externalized in different ways by the nonmusical arts. Apollonian individuations are built out of the *Geist* of music in poetry, sculpture, and philosophy (after all, *The Birth of Tragedy* itself is written in language).[48] Consequently, we might say that Schopenhauer's paradox becomes Nietzsche's balancing act. Out of the Dionysian *Geist* of music, Nietzsche looks to the intermedial arts of Greek tragedy and Wagnerian music drama in order to explain how the Dionysian drive might be adequately and ethically substantiated as a sensuous appearance.

Notwithstanding the openness and variety in which the arts express the Dionysian drive of music—in a conflicting manner, of course, since the Dionysian force of music always requires Apollonian mediation—Nietzsche does not sustain much attention on it as a paradox. If for Schopenhauer it seemed like a contradiction to admit that an immediate copy actually echoed, painted, or narrated the will, for Nietzsche it is plainly obvious, in fact structurally central, that Apollonian forms have to serve as the ethical handlers of Dionysian forces. The question of whether or not the two are inherently contradictory does not function as the basis for any kind of fundamental aporia.

Yet, contra Schopenhauer, for Nietzsche the uniqueness of music should not merely be stated in abstract, metaphysical terms. As mentioned above, Nietzsche understands the purpose of art to be ethical. Not ethical in an applied sense, but in an abstract one: he wants to prescribe criteria for the production of excellent work, and in this case he is willing to name and celebrate Wagner. This starts a new trend in philosophical accounts of music; Bloch, Adorno, Jankélévitch, and Deleuze will link broad philosophical claims about music to some particular ethics of how to do it well, and they name composers and works that fulfill their criteria. In Nietzsche's view, Wagner taps into the vital forces of the will that unleash the *Geist* of the Dionysian, and restores excellence to the aesthetic sphere. With a measured distance, his music dramas give us an ethical way to experience the contradictory drives of the Apollonian and the Dionysian.

For Nietzsche, this aesthetic dichotomy structures the activity of philosophy as well. He names his two artistic drives with substantive adjectives: *das Apollinische* and *das Dionysische*. While the categories are dependent upon one another for their coherence, Nietzsche would not describe their codependence as dialectical, insofar as he associated the term dialectic squarely with the Apollonian technique of Socratic dialogue.[49]

Yet it would appear that Nietzsche also slyly sought to transform this dialectic with his grand opposition even as he pinned the technique to Socrates. For Nietzsche described his ideal philosopher (in ethical terms) as a "music-making Socrates"—an intellectual who could integrate what appeared to be a contradiction: the enlightening power of philosophy and the vernacular, disorderly bliss of music. Socrates was a master interrogator and practitioner of reason, but a musician he was not (until he was at death's door, we are told).[50] Yet an intoxicating infusion of immediacy (via music) is exactly what Nietzsche thought the science of philosophy needed. In this way, Nietzsche might be read as transfiguring Schopenhauer's paradox into a contradictory way of life: one that integrates as an ethics the aesthetic impact of musical sensation with the logical insights of Socratic wisdom.

*

If Nietzsche displaced Schopenhauer's paradox onto the figure of a contradictory philosopher—one who was both a purveyor of wisdom and a seeker of aesthetic excellence—Bloch, Adorno, Jankélévitch, and Deleuze can be understood to develop the paradox of music's ineffability—in particular, Schopenhauer's immediate copy—into a variety of dialectical methods.[51] In so doing, all four held that music is neither fully sensational (or Dionysian) nor fully formal (or Apollonian). It has an undecidable, vague ontology that leaves it stuck in a strange place between systematic abstraction and sensuous immediacy, at once an exceptionally malleable object of contemplation and a befuddling trigger of speculative thought.

One way to get a synoptic view of the dialectical productivity of this paradox is to survey their written responses to Schopenhauer. To bring this prelude to a close, then, let us turn to an encapsulated set of comparisons that traverse the range of the book's arguments by considering how all four philosophers responded to Schopenhauer's paradox of the immediate copy in their own words.

*

In *The Spirit of Utopia* (1917), Bloch summarizes Schopenhauer's philosophy of music in an extended passage. In so doing, he seems to share, in broad strokes, the philosopher's enthusiasm that music is an immediate copy of the will. Yet when he switches from summary to commentary, Bloch turns critical of Schopenhauer's Platonism, which in his view makes music complicit with fatalism (or the philosopher's infamous pessimism). For Bloch, the potentiality of true inwardness, a crucial "starting point" for Bloch's conception of utopia, is "disavowed" by the eternity of Platonic metaphysics. Schopenhauer's will, in Bloch's view, ultimately enacts a totalitarian control over life:

> Vainly Schopenhauer affirms—vainly according to precisely the deepest conclusions of his philosophy—that every music is at its destination, since its object really remains always just the Will. Equally futile remains the claim that music could exist to a certain extent even if the world did not, for the world could really only exist insofar as music here lets the world reappear with heightened significance, as in other words music represents an objectification of the total Will just as immediate as the world itself, so that consequently—far from being a panacea for all our suffering—it [music] more confirms and affirms than averts [*bestärkt und bejaht als wendet*] the universal Will whose cries it lets ring [*sie klingen läßt*]. . . . However much they are part of the illusion, human beings are consequently even less able than such parts to act independently. Rather, they are merely the scenes of the action, cheated, and ironized puppets in the hand of the solitary false idol and in his drama.[52]

In his earlier edition of *The Spirit of Utopia,* Bloch suggested that Schopenhauer, Hegel, and Marx alike were victims of this same kind of totalizing metaphysics. In his revised version for the *Werkausgabe* of 1964, Bloch, perhaps seeking to bolster connections to his dialectical forebears, cut the references to Hegel and Marx in order to focus his critique on Schopenhauer's bad immanence, one that, as he saw it, left no room for individual expressivity and social potentiality.[53] Bloch wrote of Wagner (who is taken here to be thoroughly Schopenhauerian) that his music "confirms" and "affirms" the will in a way that risks passing into a dark, unsubjective "automatism":

> Individuals and their particular, their not only compulsive will are nothing before the Will of the One, the alone real wave of the universal Will or perhaps universal *Geist*. Thus Wagner also found his philosophy here; much of *Wagner's music* as urge, delusion, the metaphor of the firefly, ocean swells, clouds of steam and the deep sleep of the unconscious expounds the same raging and forever static automatism, the same un-subjective nature legend.... As we wanted to say, a strangely un-subjective animal lyricism ensues, foremost in the *Ring*; these people are no *dramatis personae* advancing into the space of an encounter with each other and with their own profound destiny, but rather blossoms on a tree, indeed even just bobbing ships unresistingly obeying their subhuman ocean's sufferings, labors, love, and yearning for redemption; over whom, in every decisive moment, the universal wave of Schopenhauer's Will thus sweeps: of that craving for the thing-in-itself, in other words, and its tyranny, which is not only foreign to the moral will of Beethoven's music but which also diverts, envelops the specifically Wagnerian initiation of a fervent-spiritual *espressivo*.[54]

Schopenhauer's hypostatization of a blind will leads him to express a dark naturalism, morally salvageable only by a passive asceticism. In the face of such a Dionysian nightmare, Bloch's philosophy of music can be read as a recasting of Schopenhauer's paradox of the immediate copy in a way that takes far greater notice of music's mediations. Eschewing any kind of pessimistic abyss of Romantic depth, in *The Spirit of Utopia* Bloch transposes the paradox of the ineffable onto a positive Apollonian unit of the tone—a "delicate translucent body" that joins together noumenal multiplicity with an individuated ideality. The tone is built upon a dialectical balance that is exemplary of music's nonsemantic immediacy in its simplest form. As I will argue in chapter 1, the tone expresses, as a single unit, the paradox of the immediate copy. In its lack of positive meaning, and in the form of certain ethical musical configurations, the tone can potentially challenge the normative coordinates of reification and disclose unforeseen social potentialities. Its dynamism embodies the sensory power of one's inner potentiality at the same time that its well-ordered forms mirror the historical self-consciousness of *Geist*.

Similarly, in Adorno's view, a pure Dionysian art based in the powers of will would be a sign of pure hubris, a foolhardy primitivism. In order to create genuinely resistant art, one has to even more fully mediate one's artistic practice through reflection and self-consciousness—the historical objectivity of suffering. In Adorno's hands, even more explicitly than in Bloch's, the Apollonian objectification of Ideas is intrinsic to the possibility of accessing music within the matrix of modern experience. As a consequence, the ineffability of Schopenhauer's immediate copy becomes an agonistic, dialectical aporia, now associated with music's specificity as a medium. Its purchase on "ontological categories" like the will is consistently paradoxical, without any resolution in sight:

> . . . . the music is as clear [*deutlich*] as it is cryptic [*kryptisch*]. It can make the ontological categories of objective reality its own only insofar as it dims itself [*sich abblendet*] from objective immediacy; it would remove itself [*entfernte sich*] from the world if it tried to symbolize [*symbolisieren*] or even depict [*abbilden*] it. Schopenhauer and Romantic aesthetics discovered this when they pondered [*nachsannen*] the shadowy and dreamlike quality of music. But music does not so much paint [*malt*] shadowy and dreamlike states of the soul as, in terms of logic and appearance, it is itself related [*verwandt*] to the soul of dream and shadow. It takes on being [*Wesenhaft wird sie*], as a reality sui generis, through derealization [*Entwirklichung*].[55]

Like Schopenhauer, in his verb choices Adorno reveals a range of valuations and difficulties at the nexus of the immediate copy. Adorno replaces Schopenhauer's verbs—*malen* and *abbilden* with Marx's language of derealization [*Entwirklichung*]. Music is real—it speaks the will—only insofar as it becomes a "reality sui generis" that is no longer real, that dims itself, removes itself, and becomes de-realized at the moment it begins to speak the language of being, of the thing-in-itself. This paradox parallels the unrecognizability of particular emotions in Schopenhauer's metaphysics of music. But for Adorno, the meditations of logic, appearance, history, and *Geist,* make the appearance of music into a shimmering ephemerality that forever eludes one's grasp. The reality of life—figured as madness, inwardness, being, and the like—can never be adequately and permanently presented in musical experience.

In the passage below, Adorno's verb choices (*assimilieren, rauben, ergreifen*) emphasize the Apollonian role of mediation still further—music aggressively and formally "seizes" and "robs" the inner forces of the will. Or, music's inwardness passively "assimilates" the outward. But the inward and the outward do not neutrally equate, represent, or externalize one another:

The inwardness of music assimilates [*assimiliert*] the outward, instead of representing [*darzustellen*], externalizing [*zu veräußerlichen*], the inward.... If [music] were immediately identified with being—and after Schopenhauer's insight it is music that is being immediately—music would be madness.[56] All great music is robbed [*geraubt*] from madness; all music harbors the identification of inward and outward, but over the outcome madness has no power. Music sanctions the separation of being and object as its own boundary to the objective; thus it seizes [*ergreift*] being.[57]

When discussing musical examples, Adorno is no less attentive to the power of this paradox. In the following passage, Mahler's music exemplifies a self-conscious process of "reflecting" [*reflektiert*] on its own cry" that incorporates "laughter at its untruth." It is untrue because to know, to form, and to represent is to commit a barbaric falsehood; it is to unwittingly repeat an ideology. Rather than pave the way toward a transcendent copy of the world's interior forces, Mahler makes this impossibility of externalizing the emotional force of crying explicit as a dissonance. And in another fold of the dialectic, Mahler expresses laughter—a sign of vitality—within the false, Apollonian character of the result. On the whole, the ephemerality of emotional rapture bleeds in through the corners of Mahler's Apollonian tones and threatens the ideal vitality of its tonal and harmonic form. This happens even as the music hopelessly "aims at reconciliation":

When in a passage moving beyond all words the drunken man hears the voice of the bird, nature as an exhortation to the earth, he feels dreaming. In vain he would go back once more. His solitude oscillates violently in his intoxication between despair and the joy of absolute freedom, already within the zone of death. The *Geist* of this music converges with Nietzsche, whom Mahler admired in his youth. But where the Dionysus of the objectlessly inward set up his tablets with imperious impotence, Mahler's music escapes hubris by reflecting [*reflektiert*] on its own cry, including within the composition laughter at its untruth. The intoxication [*Rausch*] of self-destruction, the heart that cannot contain itself pours itself out to that from which it is separated. Its downfall aims at reconciliation. The adagio finale of the Ninth Symphony, in the last phrase of the first D-flat major paragraph, for example, has the same tone of the rapture of self-surrender. However, the drunken man's ecstasy, imitated by the music, lets in death through the gaps between tones and chords.[58]

Dionysian intoxication, in Mahler's hands, is infused with the Apollonian work of reflection. The result is a violent oscillation between joy and despair, ephemeral vitality and death. In Adorno's rendering, Schopenhauer's realm of representation, or Nietzsche's realm of the Apollonian, both of which governed the principle of all individuations, remain integral ontology of the work of art. Art could not be an Idea in sensuous form (as in Hegel), nor could it be a copy of the blind will (as music is for Schopenhauer), without somehow being mediated by the ideological violence of individuation—what Hegel defined as *Geist*. The result is an artwork that is by necessity "refracted" [*gebrochen*] because of its individuated character as appearance. In more philosophical and less figurative terms, the necessity of mediation reflects the necessity that all art be mediated by "real events in history." In *Aesthetic Theory*, Adorno writes:

> Schopenhauer's *principia individuationis*—space, time, and causality—appear in art, in the realm of what is extremely individuated, a second time; however fractured [*gebrochen*], and such refraction [*Brechung*], enforced through art's character-as-appearance [*Scheincharakter*], confers on art its aspect of freedom. It is through this freedom, through the intervention of *Geist*, that the sequence and nexus of events is established. In the undifferentiatedness of *Geist* and blind necessity, art's logic is reminiscent of the strict lawfulness that governs the succession of real events in history.[59]

Music's dialectical linkage with a historical *Geist* is what individuates, disciplines, and refracts the art of music. Among the arts, music remains exceptional for Adorno, but not because it is a copy of the will; rather, because it remains a nonsemantic and immediate sensuous appearance as much as it is exceptionally abstract, formalized, and disciplined. Its ineffability is still a mark of its exceptional power, though Adorno's dialectic gives far greater emphasis to the paradoxical weight of mediation.

Jankélévitch approaches Schopenhauer from a somewhat different angle. In contrast to Bloch and Adorno, he is more sympathetic to Schopenhauer's conception of the will; certainly, he expresses more sympathy than Adorno does in his dismissal of the hubris of the Dionysian. In his book on Liszt, Jankélévitch describes his own version of the "groundless" form of life as the origin of all improvisation, a "primordial mystery" and a "grand maternal disorder," akin to Schopenhauer's will:

> Philosophers and romantic musicians, passionately attentive to all problems of genesis, were in some way the metaphysicians and the practitioners

of improvisation. There is no longer an intellectual itinerary to browse, but an organic process, which is to say a vegetal outbreak of description. Or if one prefers other images: the form emerges of a primordial mystery—that this mystery is chaos, an original lack of grounding [*Ungrund*], or nothingness [*néant*]—like Venus Anadyomene arising from the foam of the sea; the form takes form incomprehensibly in the limbo of the formless and the deformed; order fumbles at length in the nebulosity of this grand maternal disorder [*ce grand désordre maternel*] that begins all. *Omou panta chremata en* [collectively everything is of nebulous chaotic origin].[60]

But Jankélévitch sides with Bergson against Schopenhauer about the nature of this void. Whereas Schopenhauer presumed that the void was a blind will outside space and time, for Jankélévitch the void is intrinsically temporal.[61] Hence, the key to music's exceptionalism among the arts lies precisely in its proximity to the passage of time: "Why should hearing, alone among all the senses, have the privilege of accessing the 'thing in itself' for us, and thus destroy the limits of our finitude? . . . We would understand this favoritism toward sounds if time were the essence of being and the most real reality: this is what Bergson says, but not what Schopenhauer says, not at all."[62]

Though Jankélévitch understands time to have ontological priority over space, he is no naive apologist for Bergsonian immediacy. The second point of contrast places Jankélévitch in proximity to Bloch and Adorno, and concerns the question of mediation. In his response to Schopenhauer, Jankélévitch urges modesty and caution by stressing the rhetorical and metaphorical nature of the mimesis that mediates any metaphysical statements about music. For Jankélévitch, an ethical relationship to musical experience entails a "vegetal outbreak of description." It is a plain fact for Jankélévitch that language has an extraordinary power to mediate the ephemerality of musical sound. What makes Schopenhauer's "metaphysics of music" problematic is that his approach to it is inattentive to its own dependence on metaphors, comparisons, and linguistic convention:

> The "metaphysics of music," like magic or arithmatology, always loses sight of the function of metaphors and the symbolic relativity of symbols. A sonata is like a précis of the human adventure that is bordered by death and birth—but is not *itself* this adventure. . . . Everything hangs upon the meaning of the verb *to be* and the adverb *like*, and just as sophisms and puns slip without warning from unilateral attribution to ontological identity—that is, make discontinuity disappear magically—so metaphysical-metaphorical

analogies about music slip furtively from figural meaning to correct and literal meaning. Thus, anthropomorphic and anthroposophic generalizations are shameless in ignoring the restrictive clause on images and take comparisons at face value. Being-in-itself ascends the five lines of the staff.[63]

In Jankélévitch's view, the key elision Schopenhauer commits is one between the immediacy of being—ontological and metaphysical—and the similitude or mimesis of "like" which stresses mediation. Is music coextensive and immediate to what is—the will, the void, and so on—or does it mimic it by making the mediating link of similitude explicit? Jankélévitch contests the mimesis at work in Schopenhauer's analogies because it seeks metaphysical solutions to a paradox that Jankélévitch takes to be irresolvable. For Jankélévitch, by contrast, one should be productively modest about what it means to be trapped within the mediations of language. In relation to musical experience, he contends that one should remain attentive to the asymptotic impossibility of exhausting music's inconsistency, while acknowledging the foolhardiness of claiming to decode it with any kind of meta-language. At the same time, however, he also states that one should press ahead with responsive linguistic accounts of it.

On a philosophical level, like Bloch and Adorno, Jankélévitch sustains the aporetic richness of these questions of music's ineffability as a dialectical source of philosophical perplexity.[64] And as I will argue in chapter 3, Jankélévitch's philosophy of music can similarly be understood as dialectical because music is taken to be insoluble with language even as music is nonetheless productive of philosophical reflection. This forms the basis for a philosophical riddle that is never quite resolved. In Schopenhauer's terms, the immediacy of music's inconsistency is incommensurable with the mediating filters (or "copy") of language. This incommensurability becomes discursively productive insofar as one maintains music's inconsistency as a virtuous locus of one's attention. The result is something I call an "unwoven dialectic," which is marked by a fidelity to inconsistency that specifies and points to sonic detail in musical works while remaining exceptionally open and responsive to music's nonlinguistic character.

Deleuze, like Jankélévitch, is sympathetic to the chaotic void of Schopenhauer's will. In fact, in *The Logic of Sense* (1969), he expresses admiration for the broad outlines of Schopenhauer's metaphysics—it is a language of the abyss, the beyond of representation: "Always extraordinary are the moments in which philosophy makes the Abyss [*sans-fond*] speak and finds the mystical language of its wrath, its formlessness, and its blindness: Boehme, Schelling, Schopenhauer."[65] Yet for Deleuze there are still complaints, and in this case the complaint is somewhat familiar: As Schopenhauer conceived of it, the will takes insufficient account of mediation. Yet, unlike Bloch, Adorno, and Jankélévitch, for Deleuze the necessity of individuation and mediation does not take the form of representation, history, language, rhetoric, or the intellect. For him, individuality is a pre-personal "event" of individuation that, in Schopenhauer's terms, inhabits the will itself. In other words, if there is a will in Deleuze's philosophy, it is a virtual realm of forces (or "Ideas") that must itself contain difference, mediation, and individuations. Deleuze explains this when he is describing his view of the self and the subject in *Difference and Repetition*:

> ... the self in the form of passive self is only an event which takes place in preexisting fields of individuation: it contemplates and contracts the individuating factors of such fields, and constitutes itself at the points of resonance of their series. Similarly, the I in the form of a fractured I allows to pass all the Ideas defined by their singularities, themselves prior to fields of individuation. Just as singularity as differential determination is pre-individual, so is individuation as individuating difference an ante-I or ante-self. The world of "one" or "they" is a world of *impersonal individuations* and *pre-individual singularities*; a world which cannot be assimilated to everyday banality but one in which, on the contrary, we encounter the final face of Dionysus, and in which resonates the true nature of that depth and groundlessness which surrounds representation, and from which simulacra emerge....[66]

Instead of a unitary will of groundless striving, behind the self or subject one finds a dynamic and variegated field of singularities and mediating individuations. In Deleuze's view, Schopenhauer erroneously conceives of the will as unified, prior to all individuation, thus mistakenly suggesting that the will "should lack differences, when in fact it swarms with them."[67] For Deleuze, the form of an individuation cannot be understood as distinct from the Dionysian striving of the will, or as maintaining power over it in any way. Under the conditions of Deleuze's ontology, Schopenhauer's will would always already contain the Apollonian forms of the *principium individuationis*. When set into motion, the result is perpetual interchange between singularity and individuation, between difference and repetition, in a punctuated and contrapuntal flux of life. This forms the basis for Deleuze's metaphysics of rhythm.

More broadly, for Deleuze, Being is not a unity—as it is for Plato's *eidos*, or Schopenhauer and Nietzsche's *Ur-Eine*—but a creative multiplicity. In the long view of Western intellectual history, Deleuze returns to Plato, if only to diametrically invert his metaphysical priority from unity to multiplicity. In doing so, Deleuze would seem to have circumvented a dualism that has haunted philosophy for millennia. Mimesis, which for Plato represented the threat of a dangerous multiplicity, is no longer a corrupting force, or something consigned to a separate Kantian realm of cognition at a remove from things-in-themselves. Traditionally opposed spheres of being and becoming, the phenomenal and the noumenal, appearance and essence, are reconceived of as structurally coextensive linkages of singularities and individuations, melded together by the logic of a Spinozist monism. Thus, in their collaborative works Deleuze and Guattari will follow the lead of Nietzsche's topology, and declare with a certain metaphysical bombast that it is all part of a vast cosmic process of pluralized coextensions, a rhythm of difference and repetition, without paradoxes, contradictions, or aporias.

With regard to music, Deleuze's metaphysics would then respond to the nagging paradoxes of Schopenhauer's Platonism (for which certain aspects of music are selectively taken to be consubstantial with being) by claiming to have overcome the disjunction of the immediate copy altogether. For Deleuze, there is no contradiction between mediation and immediacy. A work of art is a mediated individuated bloc of sensations with a single purpose of consolidating the immediacy of creative, dynamic, affective powers.

Schopenhauer's paradox will not disappear entirely, of course. In his collaborative books with Félix Guattari (and with Guattari's expertise in psychoanalysis and greater familiarity with music), Deleuze and Guattari will describe music as an "a-signifying semiotics"—something like a ghosted version of Schopenhauer's immediate copy, but posed in the vocabulary of postwar French structuralism. Music is immediate insofar as it is "a-signifying" or affective, but it retains semiotic relations and mediations. But few consequences will be drawn from any residual tensions. According to what I call their contrapuntal dialectic of rhythm, sensation is always something both immediate and structured; there is thus no real aporia to its ineffability, and likewise no absolute exceptionalism to music. In this sense, Deleuze and Guattari are instructive for this study because they propose to close the gap between music and language and follow the logic of ineffability past any alleged exceptionalism for music. To thinkers where all arts are linkages of pure sensation, there can be no true hierarchy of the arts. Each has only a nominal sense of specificity.

*

In the passages above, I have deliberately moved quickly through all four philosophers for the sake of synoptic comparison. As the book proceeds through subsequent chapters, I shall slow considerably and offer full arguments about what I think each thinker is up to with respect to music's ineffability and how these differences are developed dialectically, historically, ethically, and musically. In the end, this book will argue that Schopenhauer's paradox of the ineffable is a property of music's sensory specificity, and is subject to dialectical elaboration insofar as it is taken to be philosophically productive. Once Schopenhauer's Platonic solutions have been cast away, one can recognize that the paradox of the ineffable is something both mediated and immediate—and that it serves as an invitation, even a summons, for thinking. How one chooses to develop and explain music's immersive and affective Dionysian power as something always subject to Apollonian mediation, how one triangulates various conceptions of musical form and style or situates its meaning in relationship to social life—these things are forever contested.

But the claim of this book is that the problem cannot be understood well if only one thinker is here to help us understand it. Four philosophers, united by a common set of influences and interlocutors, allow us to see a wide array of differences and similarities concerning Schopenhauer's paradox of music's ineffability. In the center of all of it is the fact that music has a specificity, one of sonic, immersive intensity. Its philosophical significance is neither exclusively semiotic or language-like nor entirely formal and abstract, but a conflicting negotiation of both, forever conditioned by the sensory impact of immediacy and the constitutive structures of mediation—that paradox of the unmediated copy. It is not musical form per se, but the general form of this problem that philosophy is so poised to explain.

CHAPTER I

Bloch's Tone

And closer still, in effective existence, regarding not perspectives but perplexities, there appear the (always overtaking) moral guiding images and ideals, and the topically still unidentified no-where whither music leads.

—ERNST BLOCH, *Philosophy of the Future*

And the creative darkness in which [music] is still shrouded is not the gloom of the Schopenhauerian will, but the incognito of the Now which drives through everything, is hidden in the world itself. Music in its unsurpassable nearness to existence is the most closely related and most public voice of this incognito, that of the welling existere which in concentric preludes seeks to be clarified here.

—ERNST BLOCH, *The Principle of Hope*

Ernst Bloch's *The Spirit of Utopia* (1918) begins with an enigmatic sentence that bristles with problems in translation: *Ich bin an mir*. It could be rendered literally as "I am at myself." But the preposition *an* indicates a multitude of linkages: it also might be translated as "I am upon, on, or to myself" or even "I am caused by myself." For many, including one of Bloch's more recent translators, it is the ambiguity in possible relations between "I" and "myself" that is instructive.[1] It encapsulates the complexity of Bloch's "self-encounter," which does not aim at a transparent sense of self-knowledge. Instead, the ambiguity echoes a nonlinear practice of self-reflection that aims to disclose latent utopian meanings from the fabric of the existing world.

The difficulty of the prose is itself a tool to facilitate the meditation; Bloch's writing demands a great deal of interpretive and meditative labor since utopian meanings cannot be put plainly in propositional terms. Of course, some sense of horizon, futurity, and hope nonetheless guides the inquiry. Adopting the vocabulary of an idealist, Bloch variously describes his horizon as "the problem of the We in itself," "the inconstruable, absolute question," and "the one, the eternal goal, the one presentiment, the one conscience, the one salvation."[2] Such an "inconstruable" vision of utopia—a collective *Geist* in the sense of a soul, spirit, or an intellectually metaphysical entity—cannot be explicitly described or explained in the pages of the book; it exceeds what can be practically represented. It can be arrived at only obliquely, dialectically, and hermeneutically through complex meditations that unfold within one's concrete experience of self-reflection, since for Bloch, utopia always retains a material, historical, and existential basis.

Many of Bloch's meditations dwell on a phenomenological paradox fundamental to the experience of time. Generally speaking, for Bloch, we are absent to ourselves; we "trickle away" and remain blind to our own potentialities. Through an exacting practice of a "self-encounter," however, we can become aware of this noncoincidence, a nonidentity, obscurity, or absence intrinsic to the experience of oneself—something he calls the "darkness of the lived moment." In contrast to vitalist philosophers and empiricists who embraced the notion of a "stream of consciousness," Bloch maintains that one can never experience the vanishing now as a present moment. Rather, he holds that the consciousness of time is a flickering, intermittent rhythm, linked transitively to absent structures of cognition.[3] And by attending to these paradoxical absences at the heart of the lived moment and opening oneself to oblique temporal displacements, one can glimpse utopian potentialities. The "darkness of the lived moment" is an important component of many of his writings. In *The Spirit of Utopia* and *The Principle of Hope* (1959), Bloch develops it into a theory of the undetermined utopian traces of *Noch-nicht-bewusste*, or the "not-yet-conscious," and in *Thomas Münzer als Theologe der Revolution* (1922) and *Heritage of Our Times* (1935), he develops a parallel concept of uncanny historical dislocations—*Ungleichzeitigkeit* or the "non-synchronous."

In this way, alongside the matrix of self-reflection, Bloch's thinking is consistently engaged with the Marxist-Hegelian question of historical development. In *The Spirit of Utopia* Bloch foregrounds a particular historical context: the aftermath of the dehumanizing Great War. In his analysis, the ultraviolent means unleashed by modern weaponry alongside the rise of alienated labor and the commoditized life of the machine age have led the world to lose grip on a primordial *techne*: as Bloch says, we have "unlearned how to play." He describes this alienated life as one of a sanitized and rationalized "lavatoriality" that has lead to the "pervasive destruction of the imagination." His subsequent writings, too, draw profoundly on the specificity of Bloch's given historical moment. In *Heritage of Our Times,* Bloch responds to Germany's emergent urbanized bourgeois culture in the 1920s and '30s, with particular attention to the ways it reshaped the conditions for modern life and was itself transformed by the rise of National Socialism.

This historical context is key to understanding the social meaning of Bloch's utopia. In his view, instrumental reasoning has led us into a reified age where technology reigns supreme. The slow obscurity of a self-encounter gives us a locus with which to disrupt the normative functions of knowledge and discern latent meanings both within us and in our surrounding worlds as traces of a utopian potentiality. Among the wide range of historical phenomena that, from the stance of a self-encounter, were ripe for critical reflection, nonsynchronous revelations, or not-yet-conscious insights, Bloch held a particular regard for works of art. At risk of criticism from those on the left who felt progressive thought should be rooted in practical and economic concerns or popular forms of culture (his early alliances and subsequent differences with György Lukács have a rich publication history), Bloch's conception of socially grounded potentiality typically privileged encounters with rare, exceptional, and often obscure expressive objects.[4]

Bloch's approach to art was in many ways inspired by Schopenhauer. For Bloch, behind the veneer of modern appearances or a "technological cold" lies the heat of a primordial material unity with nature, something akin to a noumenal thing-in-itself. For Kant, knowledge of the thing-in-itself was strictly inaccessible, since it stood by definition outside the coordinates of possible experience. Yet, as we can recall from the opening prelude, for Schopenhauer aspects of the thing-in-itself were in fact accessible to rational knowledge. Schopenhauer posited the thing-in-itself as a unified and primordial force, energy, or will that he took to undergird the existence of all individual beings. And he found that it was particularly through the interior experience of one's own body, specifically expressions of desire and unconscious motivation, that one could glimpse this primordial energy.

In consonance with Schopenhauer's view, for Bloch too there was an inner nature to all things that typically escaped ordinary thinking, perception, and representation. But for him, the true goal was to use the self-encounter to become indistinguishable from this greater materiality of nature, in order to glimpse traces of the undetermined, of the purely potential, of the utopian. In such an exceptional experience, it is as if our apparatuses of sense perception are removed from their ordinary functionality, and fleetingly taken to be indistinguishable from objects in our surrounding world: "Suddenly I see my eyes, my ears, my state: I myself am this drawer and these fish, I am these fish of a kind that lies in drawers; for the difference vanishes, the distance lifts between the artistic subject and the artistically represented object that is to be reborn to a different materiality than a mere thing's [*zu einer anderen als zu seiner bloßen Dingmaterialität*], reborn to its essence as the inmost principle of its potentiality, of all our potentiality."[5]

An extraordinary episode that dissolves the reified framework of our experience constitutes the crux of Bloch's views of art. Given a society alienated by an Apollonian structure of knowledge that has devolved historically into instrumental reasoning, Bloch holds that, from the meditative stance of the self-encounter, unusually powerful aesthetic experiences are effectively capable of joining us to a collective material potentiality latent, but concealed, in all things. So important is this gesture that it is worth considering a second description of it. In the passage below, the greater substance of nature is envisioned as somehow both corporeal and dreamlike:

> It is a substance [*Stoff*], an alien experience [*fremd gebundenes Erlebnis*]. But we walk in the forest and we feel we are or could be what the forest dreams. We walk between the tree trunks, small, incorporeal [*seelenhaft*], and imperceptible to ourselves, as their *Ton*, as what could never again become forest or external day and perceptibility. We do not have it—all that moss, these strange flowers, roots, stems and shafts of light are or signify—because we ourselves are it, and stand too near to it, this ghostly and ever so nameless quality of consciousness or of becoming-inward.[6]

Notice the central role here of a musical term: *Ton* or tone. From the matrix of the inward self-encounter, we can become the earth's musical tone, its sounding body (and note, too, that *Ton* means "clay" in German). In doing so, we will become indistinguishable from the nocturnal interiority of the forest and its "ghostly and ever so nameless quality of consciousness." Bloch's sonic and earthly *Ton* serves as a "nameless" dialectical linkage between the spheres of the material and incorporeal, the practical and metaphysical. The substance of the earth, of nature and the cosmos, might then overcome the reified coldness of the represented world in order to reveal traces of dreamlike potentiality.

This key usage of the word *Ton* is not fortuitous. While Bloch can be ecumenical about which of the arts may trigger such experience, like Schopenhauer, the amateur pianist often gave a distinct privilege to music among the arts. And this privilege is especially palpable in the pages of *The Spirit of Utopia*. In contradistinction to a "clairvoyance [*Hellsehen*]" based in sight, there Bloch argues that the true *Geist* of utopia instead comes from a "clairaudience [*Hellhören*], a new kind of seeing from within" because "the visible world has become too weak to hold the spirit. . . ."[7] With reference to a typically elaborate mélange of Wagnerism, mysticism, and theology, Bloch hears music as aspiring to disclose the ineffable, as if the immediacy of Schopenhauer's immediate copy could be obscurely disclosed through music:

> ... we want to allot to music primacy in what is otherwise unsayable, this kernel [*Kern*] and seed, this reflection of the colorful night of dying and of eternal life, this seed-corn of the inner, mystical ocean of the Servants, this Jericho and first dwelling of the Holy Land. If we could name ourselves, our Master [*Haupt*] would come, and music is the only subjective theurgy. It brings us into the interior's warm, deep Gothic sanctum which alone still shines in the uncertain darkness, indeed out of which alone the light [*Schein*] can still come that must wreck and burst apart the chaos....[8]

Here, Bloch inverts the usual hierarchy of sight over sound; music bears within itself a particular utopian *Schein,* an apparent connection to "the interior's warm, deep Gothic sanctum" that will "wreck and burst apart the chaos" of the alienated world. In this passage, Bloch also adopts a term, *Kern*, that Schopenhauer associated with the will, when he claims the force of music can be heard as a "seed" or "kernel" for unearthing the ineffable character of utopia.

A section of *The Spirit of Utopia* on the topic of musical underscoring in stage drama describes the powers of sound in more detail. Bloch recounts, in his own words, something of a cliché of musical aesthetics (one Schopenhauer states as well) when he writes that music makes stage action more vivid, more real, and more present to the spectator—that "sound makes every event more acute, penetrating, sensuous," that "it lets us sense something as real," and that it "makes things immediate, urgent, intelligible, and that all more grippingly the more the music ventures out into full extent of the action...."[9] Revealing some of the complexity behind the claim, however, Bloch adds two pages later that while music has an "amplifying, intensifying, actualizing power,... sound makes things flowery, dulls the edges, and clothes every reverie in pleasant reality."[10] Upon close examination, this might strike one as a bit of an uneasy mixture: music penetrates into the actual reality of things, overcoming the mediation of Apollonian representations in order to make an event come to life. But at the same time, so strange and absolute is music's power that intensifying may also mean decorating, dulling, even distracting; underscoring may intensify and blur the action all at once.

At the center of this ambivalence lies an ontological characteristic of music that is important to Bloch: a lack of reliable mimesis in relationship to dramatic narrative. The music is not there to merely parallel the effect of the representation, the stage action, or the moving image. Intrinsic to the force of music is an ambivalence between the heat of sensual intensity and the coolness of palliative distance; and this ambivalence is a sign of something ontologically distinct about music, a trace of a "deeper stratum of reality" that is "musically reversing the inside outward," "an unchanging, characteristic intensification" that is entirely other than the visible world of the stage or screen, but yet still remains meaningful [*sinnhafte*]: ". . . the quieter, deeper kernel, some last decisive reversal and substantiation of destiny arrested in the manifestation [*Schein*] of a musical 'reality,' in the manifestation [*Schein*] of a unchanging, characteristic intensification that brings the meaningful [*Sinnhafte*] instead of the manifestly obvious [*Sinnfälligen*], makes it mythical, that is, reveals precisely the other, deeper stratum of reality."[11]

Here we encounter a version of music's profound exceptionalism. For Schopenhauer, music, as an unmediated copy of the will, speaks the nocturnal thing-in-itself, an interior, noumenal unity behind the spatial-temporal representation of existing beings. While Bloch rejects aspects of Schopenhauer's broader philosophy, he concurs here, that music's power supersedes any particular emotional states ("It is hopeless to allocate to the music already definite emotions.").[12]

In this way, Bloch is undeniably Romantic in its rejection of specific emotions, and accordingly proximate to positions espoused by Wackenroder and E. T. A. Hoffmann. Yet Bloch's aesthetics may also strike some readers as somewhat akin to the metaphysical formalism of absolute music made famous in a debate between Richard Wagner and Eduard Hanslick during the middle of the nineteenth century. (Whereas Hoffmann and the Romantics rejected the specificity of individual emotions, Hanslick went further and argued that "tonally moving forms" autonomously expressed specifically musical ideas.) And indeed, Bloch himself frequently seems to praise the Hanslickian concept of absolute music. At the same time, in a way that was distinctly romantic, Bloch also repeatedly affirms the sensational *Intensivierung* of music's empirical force: "It is too strong, too un-abstract, too moving, too ontologically charged: it surges [*es wogt*]. . . ."[13] This fusion of absolute music and Romantic sensationalism makes for a philosophically complex mixture.

This chapter argues that Bloch's approach to music's Romantic exceptionalism is made unique by virtue of its dialectical confrontation between two contradictory halves: formalism and materiality, rationalization and singular exemplarity, speculative autonomy and embodied immanence. Schopenhauer, we can recall, ultimately sought to resolve this paradoxical admixture with Platonic solutions. By contrast, Bloch's conception of the musical tone sustains an aporetic dialectic that holds these two halves in a balance without resolution: neither side, the material nor the ideal, the sensory nor the formal, dominates. For Bloch, as for Hegel before him, certainly the tone is the central unit of musical inscription; it is what music is made out of. But for Bloch the tone is peculiar in its complexity. It is both technically precise and metaphysically efficacious; it is a "sensory riddle" that joins the lightness of areal form to the immersive nature of sonic intensity, and in this way serves as a unique vehicle for utopian speech: ". . . only the tone, this sensory riddle [*dieses Rätsel der Sinnlichkeit*], is not so laden by the world and is sufficiently phenomenal for the end, that—like the *metaphysical* word—it can return as a final material moment in the fulfillment of mystical self-perception, laid immaculately on the gold ground of receptive human latency."[14] Bloch developed this unique conception of the tone by adopting and transfiguring the concept from a range of eighteenth- and nineteenth-century thinkers, highest among them Hegel, from whom we learn the most about why and how Bloch deploys it. By this chapter's end, I will describe the ways in which Bloch's undertaking, while certainly indebted to a wide array of thinkers from Wackenroder and Hoffmann through Eduard Hanslick and Arnold Schoenberg, was specifically formative for Adorno's views on music.

If the general form of such an aesthetic experience is loosely indebted to Schopenhauer (for whom music is paradoxically an immediate copy of the thing-in-itself), this chapter argues that the method by which specific works are granted the powers to disclose a utopian meaning is, broadly speaking, Hegelian and dialectical. In particular, over the course of this chapter I will argue that Hegel's dialectical theory of the tone, his conception of *Geist* as externalized matter, and his developmentalist teleologies of the history of art are each adopted and subsequently reconfigured in Bloch's hands. And yet, notwithstanding Bloch's innovative and imaginative approach to the tone, in my view, Bloch's writings on music do not yet operate with a negative conception of the dialectic. For that, one will have to turn to Adorno. Rather, we might say, on the whole, that Bloch develops a certain version of Schopenhauer that has been significantly reframed by Hegelian dialectics. It is between these two thinkers, I contend, that one can understand most vividly and distinctly the intricate structure of Bloch's philosophy of music.

1.1 THE TONE

If music is to do detailed speculative work for Bloch (and, as explained in chapter 2 of this book, for Adorno as well), how are we understand its grammar in such a way that it can serve as the backbone for a dialectical method? How does the tone serve as the foundation for the utopian potential of complex musical works? Let us first sketch in historical terms what the tone was, in order to get a sense for the way Bloch adopts and redeploys it.

Before all the wavering and inconsistent musical *écriture* we would come to hear as music over the course of the twentieth and twenty-first centuries (from *Sprechstimme* and *musique concrète* to vocal grain and autotune), German composers, critics, theorists, philosophers, and scientists focused much of their attention on the discrete vehicle of musical literacy par excellence: *der Ton*. In their hands, the tone was not merely a symbolic or practical denotation of a note; neither was it just an empirical envelope of finite sonic consistency set aloft by ubiquitous living-room keyboards. It was, rather, a dialectical conceit that linked the practical act of sounding a pitch with a form of intellectual reflection. It functioned symptomatically as a modifier for many compound nouns that figured prominently in German music criticism, theory, and aesthetics of the eighteenth and nineteenth centuries: *Tonkunst, Tonkünstler, Tondichter, Tonsetzer, Tonnetz, Tonpsychologie, Tonempfindungen, Tonverschmelzung*, and so on.

In this context, the tone was the central unit of musical writing: discrete and continuous, articulated and moved, consistent but borne by inconsistency. In Bloch's philosophy, it was something even more. The tone was akin to a musical logos, an ontological unit of sound that was less semantic and more gymnastic, aerobic, and acrobatic as it managed to link the flux of sonic processes to the latent ideals of utopia without a linguistic system of referential coordinates. Of course, whatever its exact relationship to language actually was for Bloch will remain the most difficult and unresolved question. But that it had a unique character and a highly dialectical flexibility is central: for Bloch, music could indicate a utopian potentiality in a way that no other art or medium of expression could.

Consider the etymology: The German tone, the English "tone," the French *ton*, and the Italian *tono*, among other European descendants, can be traced to the Latin *tonus*, meaning "a sound, tone, accent." Like the Greek *harmonia*, which derived its meaning from the physical practice of carpentry, the Latin and Greek roots of tone have a practical origin. The Greek infinitive "to stretch" is *teinein*. The Greek *tónos* denoted "that by which a thing is stretched, or that which can itself be stretched, cord, brace, band."[15] *Tónos* also indicated a "firmness of body" more generally, triggering an associative range of the term that we retain in modern English. The Greek *tónos*, of course, had sonic meanings as well: "a pitch of the voice," an accent on a syllable of a word, a measure or meter, or a harmonic mode.[16] The Latin derivative, *tonus*, like the Greek root, retained its physical backbone. Lewis and Short state that *tonus* denoted "the stretching, straining of a rope."[17] As a musical term in the Middle Ages, *tonus* had a range of technical meanings as well: in addition to a sound, tone, or accent, it could denote a mode, the interval of a major second, or a short formula in the recitation of plainchant.[18] But the linkage between a finite yet flexible body and an ideal form constituted a key axis of meaning. Given a slack medium like ropes and airwaves, tone denoted consistency, strength, maintenance, end-to-end integrity, held provisionally but with breath, despite falling, ascent, unpredictability, and flux elsewhere—an effortful and virtuous gesture towards eternity.

Curiously, the German word *Ton* has frequently been mistranslated into English as "note."[19] While meanings and usages between the words "tone," "sound," and "note" have undoubtedly blurred in modern parlance, something philosophically particular is lost in this mistranslation. Consider first that "note" has a somewhat independent etymology, one that can be traced to the Latin *nota*, which designated a mark, a sign, a letter, an inscription, or a word. Within the discipline of music, the English word "note," the German *die Note*, the Italian *nota*, or the French *note* generally prescribes the execution of a single musical sound, and implies a normative medium of musical notation. As a condition for its intelligibility, then, the musical note relies upon a metaphysical structure: tones that are played—physically stretched and sustained—are taken, understood, and even ontologically reified as being identical with their discrete visual insignia. Because English translations of "tone" were written during the past half century, one might speculate that, by then, the medium of musical notation was so naturalized as a musical a priori in ordinary language that a tone could not be thought of otherwise than as a note. Whatever the case, one of the goals of this inquiry is to understand better some of these lost meanings of the tone by thinking of it as a living dialectical practice, as a term with a range of meanings, with the *range* being essential to its meaning.

In turning back to widely read sources of the late eighteenth century, one finds that the complexity of the term's meaning is palpable. The broad array of meanings we still retain in the English "tone," and which are traceable to the aforementioned Greek and Latin origins, were reflected in Johann George Sulzer's *Allgemeine Theorie der Schönen Künste* (1771).[20] There, Sulzer gives tone a multimodal range of meaning that branches out to three separate definitions, applied to the domains of music, theater, and painting respectively. The one for music alone is complex, as Sulzer writes at the outset: "where it retains in fact its proper meaning, yet is used to indicate very different things."[21]

Sulzer goes on to describe tone as indicating at once the timbre of different instruments, the register of an instrument, a whole tone of a scale, and a general pitched component of a scale. Outside music, the meanings of "tone" proliferate further. In speech and drama, "tone" denotes the characteristic sound of a vocal delivery beyond the semantics of the language, principally its moral and affective styling. In painting, tone and *Tonarten* (a word that also denotes a musical key) indicates the ineffable character or mood of a painting, often traceable to its palette of colors.

In the high era of German Romanticism around 1800, the semantic flexibility of the tone often harbored a powerful sense of metaphysical depth. Wilhelm Heinrich Wackenroder's 1797 story of the imaginary *Tonkünstler*, Joseph Berglinger, outlined the stakes of what tones could do in the hands of an exceptional talent. The first half of the story recounts young Joseph's anguished prayers in the face of authorities (both his father and God) about what it would mean to risk everything and venture out into the world and devote his life to music. His self-reflective yearnings, simultaneously alienated and ambitious, were typically romantic, and had as their focus speculations about the strange powers of musical tones, which were not merely practical or pedagogical but an ontological foundation for music that could eliminate physical boundaries between subject and object, and induce unheard forms of compassionate intoxication. The story's narrator, who had apparently spent time rifling through the young man's papers, reports that he found a poem that offered a trace of Joseph's private speculative life:

Open to me the human spirits	*Öffne mir der Menschen Geister,*
I, masters of their souls	*Daß ich ihrer Seelen Meister*
Through the power of tones	*Durch die Kraft der Töne sei;*
my spirit penetrates the world,	*Daß mein Geist die Welt durchklinge,*
Sympathetically they infuse	*Sympathetisch sie durchdringe,*
and intoxicate in fantasy!	*Sie berausch in Phantasei!*[22]

Musical tones were not simply Pythagorean abstractions; for Wackenroder they were intoxicating potencies that linked, both passively and actively, the *Geist* of the young Joseph Berglinger's private fantasies to the totality of the *Menschen Geister*. A year later, in an essay on musical aesthetics, Wackenroder offered an evolutionary trajectory to this ecstasy of metaphysical infusion.[23] Echoing the outlines of a common speculative narrative of the time, Wackenroder proposes that the *Schall* [sound, clang, echo] of nature was intellectually transfigured by a self-conscious and evolutionarily advanced *Geist* into the register of tones and *Tonkünste*.²⁴ As he states, a primordial *"Schall oder Ton"* of primitive drumming, various "undeveloped emotions," and the occult secrets of cave dwellers developed historically into a music that was "a sensual copy of and testimony to the beautiful refinement and harmonious perfection of the human mind [*Geistes*] of today." From the perspective of his typically romantic worldview, Nature teleologically determined much of this evolutionary outcome in advance. Though Wackenroder's plainly developmentalist theory of the tone was not in any way paradoxical in the way that Bloch's was, it still retained the structure of an idealist dialectic. At no point could the tone leave behind the raw material of its sensual origins. Wackenroder's definition of tone is based in a co-constitutive mixture of intoxicating bliss, spiritual immateriality, and formal perfection; but the primitive emotions of *Schall* are preserved in the harmonious tones.²⁵

Across a wide range of Romantic writers in nineteenth-century Germany, the tone was typically defined by this dialectic between sensation and ideal beauty, between materiality and form. Consider E. T. A. Hoffmann's writings.²⁶ In his famous review of Beethoven's Fifth Symphony, Hoffmann lauds Beethoven for his sovereign handling of the "*Innern Reich der Töne* [inner realm of tones]." For Hoffmann, the composer's singular control of instrumental musical forces resulted in a numinous "purple shimmer" that sounded a depth far beneath the articulation of any particular emotion, at once sensationally intense and intellectually synthetic of the work itself. Or consider a lesser-known essay that appears in the diaries kept by the young Robert Schumann, entitled "Die Tonwelt" (1828).²⁷ Like Wackenroder, Schumann bursts with aesthetic speculations about the transcendent potentialities of tones, summoning imaginary conversations with sympathetic speculators who understand music to operate at the borderlands of representation. Yet as John Daverio has emphasized, Schumann was typically dialectical in his assessment of the tone's spiritual existence. Even as the precise meaning of a *Tonwelt* remained in some sense ineffable, Schumann thought of tones as harboring noumenal depths only insofar as they were sculpted and related by intellectual reflection.²⁸

There were less dialectical approaches, of course. Eduard Hanslick popularized a formalist view of the tone. His highly influential theory of *tönend bewegte Formen*, or "tonally-moving forms," was laid out in his often-revised book, *Vom Musikalisch-Schönen* (1854). There, Hanslick argued vociferously against the idea that music was meaningful (or beautiful) insofar as it was capable of expressing feelings and emotions. For Hanslick, musical form found its fundamental coherence and value through sonic patterning and grouping that cleared the ground for a purely objective process of mediation between audience and work. In line with Wackenroder and Hoffmann, such an objectively determinable musical beauty, a teleological accomplishment of sorts, was likewise thoroughly mediated by the intellectual knowledge of *Geist*. Perhaps ironically, however, Hanslick's theory often affirmed its basis in sensuous particularity, even as it argued for the primacy of moving tones themselves as the content of musical form.

If Hanslick's theory of the tone was oriented towards form, others directed their understanding to the concept's empirical and sensational side. Exemplary in this regard are the late-nineteenth-century scientists Hermann von Helmholtz and Carl Stumpf. Helmholtz's exploration of *Tonempfindungen* investigated the sensation of tone with the first truly empirical synthesis of acoustics and physiology, allegedly shorn of any metaphysical pretenses or aesthetic premises. Stumpf's *Tonpsychologie*, and specifically his concept of *Tonverschmelzung*, for its part, examined the way in which we psychologically fuse dyadic intervals into Gestalt tones.[29] The inquiries of both scientists examined the tone with an unprecedented register of fine empirical and perceptual detail. And yet, as Benjamin Steege has argued, Helmholtz's thinking (and, I would argue, Stumpf's as well) inevitably remained dialectical; both thinkers required some form of a priori sonic organization in their quests to "emancipate sensation."[30] And for both, there was no greater a priori than that of the tone itself—the concept best equipped for handling music's dialectical basis in both the ideal and the empirical.

Notwithstanding discourses with strong orientations towards formalism or empiricism, for many practical thinkers of music a balance between the two poles of the tone's dialectic remained key. During the decades immediately preceding Bloch's *Spirit of Utopia* in the climate of fin de siècle Vienna, a wide constellation of musical thinkers placed the tone at the center of their more systematic assessments of music. To consider only the most influential—Guido Adler, Heinrich Schenker, and Arnold Schoenberg, who wrote foundational texts for modern musicology, analysis, and music theory respectively—for all three, the tone was a taken to be the central building block of music, and cast within the ambit of some kind of developmentalist teleology.

Adler (who incidentally took over Hanslick's post at the University of Vienna) defined the very scope of the academic field of musicology as bearing an intrinsic link with the identification of tones. In the opening paragraph of his seminal 1885 article "Umfang, Methode und Ziel der Musikwissenschaft," Adler echoed a version of the typical speculative teleology from primitive sound to evolved tones when he argued that "natural song" fell short of a proper *Tonkunst* insofar as it "breaks forth from the throat freely" and thus remained "unclear and unorganized."[31] Though he did express interest in comparative musicology and thought of transcription as an important scholarly tool, in the ideal frame of Adler's vision, historical musicology would be oriented around critical editions of *Tonkünste* subject to notated organization, comparison, and measurement. Ultimately echoing debates that would continue to resonate in the modern writings of Carl Dahlhaus and Karol Berger, the authoritative inscription of *Tonkunst* took its place axiomatically as the central object of *Musikwissenschaft*. The music was only subsequently and secondarily linked to literary texts, aesthetics, and social contexts.[32]

The canonical teleology that culminated in the historical growth of exemplary *Tonkünste* was likewise an important theme of the opening to Heinrich Schenker's *Harmonielehre* (1906). The seminal music theory text begins from a premise identical to Hanslick's: that the visual and linguistic arts are originarily mimetic, but music is a distinct exception—it is not clear what music imitates. From this observation, Schenker, paralleling Hanslick further, then draws the conclusion that, in order for music to develop into a similarly sophisticated form, it must be mediated by ideas.[33] With an aim of discerning the unified harmonic architecture of great works, Schenker claims that the motif is the logos of music's ideal mediation: only once tones are strung together into motifs can they repeat, grow, and develop into a vast, organically coherent totality: "The motif, the motif alone, creates the possibility of associating ideas, the only one of which music is capable."[34] Lying behind this equation of motives and ideas is Schenker's metaphysical belief that tones have their own latent potential—they contain something like an Aristotelian conception of form that seeks its own development and resolution.[35] Equally central is a point consonant with Hanslick's formalism: that evolved music becomes nonmimetic, that its form is an ideal product of an evolved *Geist*.

Arnold Schoenberg held a similarly Aristotelian view of the tone's living potentiality ("The tone lives and seeks to propagate itself"). But for Schoenberg, music in its historical development always retained imitative links with nature (specifically the natural properties of the overtone series, consonances, and so on). Mimesis was never overcome into a sublimated realm of ideal tonal freedom or organically unified works. In fact, Schoenberg saw the potentiality of the tone as a source of irresolvable problems that spurred the history of musical material toward a militantly progressive teleology: "We shall have no rest, as long as we have not solved the problems that are contained in tones."[36] In Schoenberg's view, highest among those problems was the Pythagorean comma, typically swept under the rug of equal temperament. This was a problem that was inherent to the physical nature of tones, even latent in the material itself, leading us to a kind of revolutionary teleology directed away from the systematic syntax of tonality. As Schoenberg put it: "These chords also carry within themselves that which will eventually overthrow the system."[37]

Notwithstanding such a powerful teleology, in many other ways Schoenberg's progressive view of harmony was stripped of much of Schenker's organic metaphysics of unity. For Schoenberg, though the tone was still the basic material of music, questions of consonance, dissonance, and tonal syntax were taken to be lucky accidents, contingent tricks that took advantage of certain phenomenological aspects of sound. But they did not have any necessary or natural law as their basis. In his *Harmonielehre* (1911), Schoenberg even questioned the superior excellence of equal temperament, and espoused a degree of cultural relativism and constructivism about tonal harmony, remarking that non-Western scales adhered, in their own way, to their own imitations of the tone's natural sonic properties.[38]

*

Across this range of thinkers, the tone was a musical individuation based in an empirically discrete pitch of a certain length. But the dialectical life of its ideal being—the way the sensuous materiality of a pitched sound was negated by the ideality of form and given dramatically teleological weight of "speaking" musical organization—this process was central to the life of the concept.[39] This idealist dialectic would be important for the next generation of music theorists in the early twentieth century, most notably in the metaphysical "energetics" of tonal flux developed by Ernst Kurth and August Halm.[40] A tone, if thought of ideally, must also be played, heard, and sensed—negated in remaining mediated by its sensuous particularity. True to the meanings of its Greek and Latin roots, only in maintaining the contradictory spheres of the ideal and material, the formal and the ephemeral, could the tone become and remain what it is.

Such was the intellectual heritage for both Bloch and Adorno as they wrote about the powers of music in the face of social and political catastrophe. To keep us from swimming in the nocturnal depths of Schopenhauer's ineffable noumenalism, music needed to be inscribed and understood through a sophisticated and precise dialectical system of sonic writing. For them, it was the tone, that sensory riddle, the mysteriously translucent "metaphysical word" that could function as a constitutive abstraction and enable speculative paths for music to "think" beyond philosophical impasses that seemed to press beyond, and thus unsettle, the limits of language.[41] The tone was a minimal unit of mediation; it was the single, discrete Apollonian unit of Schopenhauer's immediate copy.

1.2 THE NATURAL KLANG

From these relatively loose treatments of the tone's dialectic, let us consider the intricacies of its philosophical structure. No thinker of the nineteenth century was more elaborate and exacting than Hegel in thinking the tone dialectically. In Hegel's view, the tone's origin is still more archaic than a primitive *Schall*. Consider Hegel's account of natural sound, or *Klang*. Prior to any mediation by *Geist*, Hegel thinks of the immanent, physical origins of sound as still more material—as something inhuman, a product of matter alone. In book 2 of the *Encyclopedia*—his *Naturphilosophie* of 1830—Hegel thinks of sound in its origin and essence, as a product of the "determinations of materiality," the world of mechanics, of "heavy matter" in the physical universe.[42]

Yet even here, sound is not exclusively physical and material, a product of the "mutual externality" of bodies.[43] It is still dialectical in that it undergoes a process of becoming independent, ideal, and relatively free from materiality as an "inner vibration of the body within itself." Hegel understands this inner vibration—*Erzittern*—as an ideal elasticity. It is something like a *Schall* without human hands, one that takes shape as an elastic vibration between bodies—an ideal but ephemeral form of cohesion.

Hegel's dialectical logic of "double negation" explains how the elastic cohesion of sound rises from materiality to ideality while still preserving its materiality. It first involves a negation of the independence of each individual, external body. The second step involves the way in which this processual negation of the two individual bodies is in turn perpetually negated by the higher unitary cohesion itself. What results is a resonance between two negations—one against separate externality of the two bodies and the other from the perspective of the elastic cohesion itself. This process then resonates fast enough to become a buzzing rhythm that in effect re-coheres as its own ideality. But it remains dialectical: the cohesion of elastic vibration does not leave materiality behind in its resonance. It preserves the immanence of physical body even as sound acquires form, reflecting the fullest dialectical meanings of the Latin and Greek roots of the word "tone." Presaging the dialectical form that will be central to Bloch's conception of the tone, Hegel's theory of sound is at once unitary and divided, and hence necessitates an oscillation that is simultaneously stable and unstable:

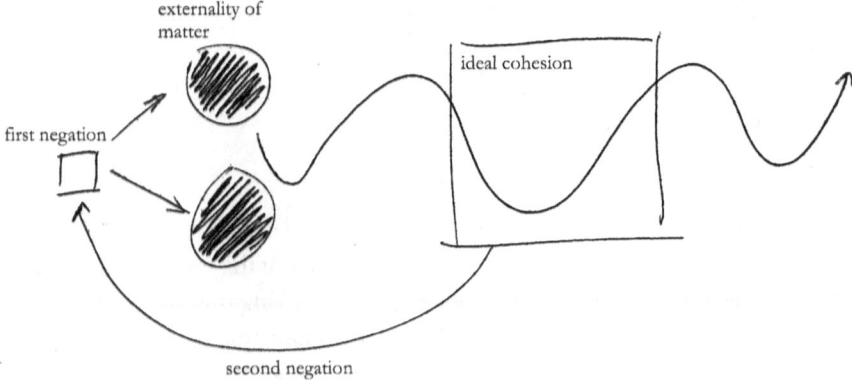

FIGURE 1.1. Hegel's *Klang*. Drawing by the author.

> The ideality posited in elasticity is an alteration which is a double negation. The negating of the persistence of the material parts in their mutual externality is itself negated as the reestablishing of their asunderness and their cohesion; there is a *single* ideality as an alternation of the two mutually sublating determinations, the inner trembling [*innere Erzittern*] of the body within itself—*Klang*.⁴⁴

Figure 1.1 illustrates the logic in play. On the far left, a small box indicates the first negation—that of the externality of material bodies, represented with two shaded circles on the left. The second arrow that stretches from the right to the left across the bottom of the diagram ("second negation") indicates the way the ideal cohesion of sound (represented by the box around a wave that extends to the right) achieves its unity by logically negating this first operation. As Hegel says, *Klang* is the *Klage* (action, claim, charge, accusation) "of the ideal in the violence of otherness [*Klage des Ideellen in dieser Gewalt des Anderes*]."⁴⁵ With the word *Klage*, Hegel suggests the steely irruption of clarity into the murky fabric of the real; in his dialectical conception, sound negates its material foundations twice over, bearing upon its buoyant, gravity-defying surface the ephemeral, weightless quality of an ideal potentiality. Sound then "becomes *free* in the *negation* of the self-subsistence of its mutual externality."⁴⁶ It preserves its material foundations, even as its ideal elasticity enacts a register of freedom, inner vibration, resonance, and reverberation that is "freely determined by the nature of its cohesion."⁴⁷ For Hegel, the ideal form of a sound is intrinsic to the material operation of nature.

1.3 THE EXPRESSIVE TONE

Hegel's account of musical tones in the *Lectures on Aesthetics* has a remarkably similar logic and structure. The logic of double negation is still central, though it appears here theorized in prose that is extraordinarily compact, and with slightly different conclusions in play. Most readily, let us first note that the addition of humans to the dialectic is what will allow the ideal elastic unity of natural sound to acquire the first traces of self-relation, of externalization, of *Geist*. Moreover, what is negated is no longer just the divided externality of indifferent matter, but the spatiality of another art form: painting. In fact, Hegel defines music in general as a negation of the "peaceful separatedness" of visual arts in the form of a sonic flux that results in an oscillating vibration of a musical tone: "The cancellation [*Aufhebung*] of space therefore consists here only in the fact that a specific sensuous material sacrifices its peaceful separatedness, turns to movement, yet so vibrates in itself that every part of the cohering body not only changes its place but also struggles to replace itself in its former position [*in den vorigen Zustand zurückzuversetzen strebt*]. The result of this oscillating vibration is the *tone*, the material of music."[48]

This echoes, in the realm of human art, how Hegel understands sonic vibration to negate the gravity of material bodies in the *Naturphilosophie*, but with a key difference. When Hegel defines the musical tone as the material of music in the context of the *Aesthetics*, he takes recourse to the deepest and most dialectical meanings of the aforementioned etymologies of *tónos* and *tonus*. Likewise, for Hegel as for Bloch after him, there is no stable eternity of repose for a tone, as there would be for a strictly Pythagorean ideality. The tone, in its vibration, is defined by the effortful striving of its own self-reproduction, of the muscular maintenance of bodies. There is no phase in which it rests on the laurels of its own autonomy.

Next, Hegel explains more explicitly how this vibrational flux of music, fraught with labor, can be thought of as overcoming, teleologically, the "peaceful and un-desiring" spatiality and separateness of painting. Here Hegel digresses quite illustratively when contemplating the resultant powers of music, and begins to describe how the sense of hearing is "more ideal than sight" because, when listening to "the result of the inner vibration of the body [*Erzittern des Körpers*]," it hears the inward depth of the subject, the "ideal breath of the soul":

> Now, with the tone, music relinquishes the element of an external form and a perceptible visibility and therefore needs for the treatment of its produc-

tions another subjective organ, namely hearing which, like sight, is one of the theoretical and not practical senses and it is still more ideal than sight. For the peaceful and un-desiring contemplation of works of art lets them remain in peace and independence as they are, and there is no wish to consume or destroy them; yet what it apprehends is not something inherently posited ideally but on the contrary something persisting in its visible existence. The ear, on the contrary, without itself turning to a practical relation to objects, listens to the result of the inner vibration of the body [*das Resultat jenes inneren Erzitterns des Körpers*] through which what comes before us is no longer the peaceful and material shape but the first and more ideal breath of the soul [*die erste ideellere Seelehaftigkeit*].[49]

Hegel then echoes a sketch of the logic of sonic double negation from the *Naturphilosophie*, and based upon this premise, gives us a vivid image of music's ephemerality. Not only is the tone's vibration built upon the virtuous labor of its imperfect musculature [*Erzitterns des Körpers*]; the artistic result is a self-annihilating point of vanishing, an ephemeral flux:

> Further, since the negativity into which the vibrating material enters here is on one side the cancelling of the spatial situation, a cancellation cancelled again by the reaction of the body, therefore the expression of this double negation, i.e. the tone, is an externality which in its coming-to-be is annihilated again by its very existence, and it vanishes of itself.[50]

In this final, quite delicate (but very famous) move, Hegel describes in slightly more detail how he understands the ephemeral tones of music to contain "inner subjectivity" and an "ideal breath of the soul" as opposed to simple Pythagorean pitch-fixity. In the context of the *Naturphilosophie*, the *Klingen* [resounding] of a tone was described as something independent and ideal by comparison with earthly matter (fighting gravity, having an inner ideality of *Klang* predicated upon double negation). In the passage below, it will sacrifice this ideal possibility by externalizing in sensuous musical form the object-free inner life of an empty and abstract subject "without any further content."

> Owing to this double negation of externality, implicit in the principle of tones, inner subjectivity corresponds to it because the resounding [*Klingen*], which in and by itself is something more ideal than independently [*für sich*] really subsistent corporeality [*real bestehende Körperlichkeit*], gives up this more ideal existence [*ideellere Existenz*] also and therefore becomes a mode

of expression adequate to the inner life.... What alone is fitted for expression in music is the object-free inner life, abstract subjectivity as such. This is our entirely empty self, the self without any further content.[51]

Notice that Hegel claims the "inner subjectivity corresponds to [tones]" because the less organized sonic resounding—*Klingen*—has an "independently existing corporeality," a "more ideal existence," that must be negated and sacrificed.[52] For Hegel, the temporal flux of music, as an *Erzittern des Körpers*, expresses the abstract and free subjectivity of one's "inner life" by negating the external spatiality of the physical world.[53]

1.4 BLOCH'S MAGIC RATTLE

Like Hegel, Wackenroder, and arguably many other thinkers of the tone mentioned above, Bloch's conception of the tone aims at transfiguring subject and object alike: that the "*inward* can *become outward* and the *outward* like the *inward*."[54] But if Hegel ultimately decides in favor of dematerialization and the eventual overcoming of the sensuous mediation of art (as in his famous "end of art" thesis), Bloch's conception of the tone dispenses with the strong teleology towards subjective independence. While remaining deeply indebted to Hegel, Bloch refocuses the dialectic on the tone's unresolved contradiction between metaphysical translucence and concrete materiality, which, in his view, is uniquely capable of utopian speech.

To understand Bloch's version of these developments, consider how the philosopher adopted and transfigured Hegel's conception of *Geist*. In the opening of *The Spirit of Utopia*, Bloch pivots from the matrix of the self-encounter to the question of the object: an old pitcher [*Krug*], a primordial tool, an archaic prosthesis. Here, Bloch explores the way a pitcher might retain vestiges of concrete labor congealed into lost meanings.[55] He writes that these pitchers "preserve the old things, like farmers: literally" and that they "are adorned with a certain, however weak sign, the seal [*Siegel*] of our self."[56] Not only is the *Krug* a seal of our collective past; it exemplifies the primordial form of the technical prosthesis that is also a necessary and constitutive aspect of all art. In Bloch's view, external artifacts and works of art alike contain congealed traces of humanity (labor, experience [*Erlebnis*], life). By focusing on technical objects rather than works of art, Bloch repurposes hermeneutics—typically a practice devoted to the linguistic interpretation of religious, legal, philosophical, literary and artistic objects—in order to show how an ordinary, material, nonlinguistic tool might reveal a possible action that is unforeseen and universal.

In the *Lectures on Aesthetics*, Hegel describes exactly this primordial externalization as a process intrinsic to the development of human history. For Hegel, nature alone was immediate to itself, single, and indifferent. But, springing up from the smallest traces of *Geist*, there emerges a teleological movement of externalization that progresses toward self-realization and "reduplication" through the work of a reflective human: "The things of nature are only *immediate and single*, but man as *Geist reduplicates* himself, inasmuch as prima facie he *is* like the things of nature, but in the second place just as really is *for* himself, perceives himself, has ideas of himself, thinks himself, and only thus is active self-realizedness."[57] Hegel separates this process into theoretical and practical components. The theoretical half is focused on the actualization of ideal self-recognition.[58] Setting the stage for the logic of Bloch's *Krug*, the practical component is based in the sensuous particularity of externalization, as the "stubborn foreignness" of matter is formed and technically externalized through complex registers of cultural evolution—from tools, clothing, and an ornamented body, all the way up to larger technological systems and complex works of art.[59] As a dialectic, the practical half constitutes a mirror of *Geist's* self-realization as a free, self-conscious subject. Notice here that both Hegel and Bloch use *Siegel* to describe this process, a word that indicates a metaphysically precise imprinting of inner spirit onto outer materiality:

> ... man is realized for himself by *practical* activity, inasmuch as he has the impulse, in the medium which is directly given to him, and externally presented before him, to produce himself, and therein at the same time to recognize himself. This purpose he achieves by the modification of external things upon which he impresses the seal of his inner being [*welchen er das Siegel seines Innern aufdrückt*], and then finds repeated in them his own characteristics. A boy throws stones into the river, and then stands admiring the circles that trace themselves on the water, as an effect in which he attains the sight of something that is his own doing. This need traverses the most manifold phenomena, up to the mode of self-production in the medium of external things as it is known to us in the work of art.[60]

How might music serve to imprint the *Siegel* of the self, in particular the collective, socially determined self? In Bloch's speculative account of the origins of music, the philosopher asks: "How do we hear ourselves at first?"[61] His answer is something akin to Hegel's boy throwing stones into the river, or Bloch's old pitcher. It is grounded in a primordial vision of the immanent, externalizing activity of our bodies: "We hear only ourselves.... An endless singing-to-oneself, and in the dance."[62] Like Wackenroder's primordial *Schall* of primitive drumming, or Adler's speculative theory of a unformed song, Bloch's musical *Siegel* begins from an archaic self-relation in sound, a musical *alter Krug*, posed from the viewpoint of an existential self-encounter.

Beyond the voice, soon musical instruments allowed humans to externalize Hegel's ideal elasticity of sound. In an essay from the 1930s, Bloch explores the evolutionary history of music through the figure of a single object—something like a musical old pitcher—the "magic rattle." For Bloch, the sound of the magic rattle was indistinguishable from its extramusical function: "... the original rattle rattled as the thing it was; the rattling sound is merely its verb, as it were."[63] Before the tone circulated as a self-conscious form of musical writing mediated by *Geist*, sound was instrumental and functional: "There was a time when the musical tone did not appear such a free agent. It was linked quite specifically with the instrument producing it."[64] With the magic rattle, the powers of music were trapped in the aura of its immediate space and time, in the *Krug* itself: "Thus here the sound [*Laut*] is an attribute of the instrument, to which it is linked in a purely material sense. Its sonorousness [*Lautsein*] is used for magical purposes, for healing the sick, driving away evil spirits and summoning good ones. But it is not primarily the sound [*Klang*] which performs the spell, but the actual magic drum being used."[65] Bloch's speculative origin of music undoubtedly echoes the aforementioned accounts from the eighteenth and nineteenth centuries. Only by way of a developmental teleology did the tones become the sign of aesthetic autonomy—"the ringing and tinkling broke loose from the ringing brass and the tinkling bell." In so doing, the tone eventually comes to assert power and authority over the technical substrate of the musical *Krug*.[66] It enacts a developmentalist liberation of the *Erzittern des Körpers* into *Geist*, through a process that effectively turns the tables on the material prosthetics of musical instruments, so that the tone could now use the instruments for its own free and artistic self-reproduction: "The tone showed so much strength in turning from the attribute of a thing into the very thing that matters [*Hauptsache*] in a developed state; from an adjective into a substantive; from a contingent and secondary quality of objects [*zufällige Nebenbei*] that were rubbed, struck or blown, to instead an 'artistic' empire ['*künstlerischen*' *Weltreich*], with melodic and above all human relations of its own."[67]

Of course, this development contained contradictions; the artistic empire of organized tones retained its material supports. If the magic rattle was a primordial musical jug, a handy primitive tool that embodied only the most basic technical sophistication, the next archetypal revolution in music came from the ancient Greek pan pipe, or syrinx. A wooden flute that consisted of a series of tubes laid out in a linear row, of increasing length (and deepening pitch) from one side to the other, the syrinx was "the first instrument which did not emit fearsome or muffled sounds [*Schreckgeräusche oder dumpfe Laute*] in isolation but gave out a well-ordered series of tones [*wohlgeordnete Tonreihe*]."[68] Though the *syrinx* did not yet have the "soul [*Seele*]" of the modern flute or horn, we here have the first degree of spiritual abstraction, "the opening up of the auditory field [*Hörraum*]."[69] The clear and distinct nature of the panpipe's sounds signaled the proper birth of the tone in all its ordered combinations, and furnished the foundations for the emergence of music history in the West.

1.5 THE TONE'S INEFFABLE UTOPIA

How, then, does Bloch uniquely understand the well-ordered tone to be a carrier of utopian potentiality? Here, finally we shall discuss explicitly how the tone encapsulates Bloch's view of music's ineffability. In "Magic Rattle, Human Harp," Bloch stages his own comparison between the sonic and the visual, one that parallels Hegel's argument in the *Aesthetics*: "The vibrating tone travels. It does not remain in its place, as color does. True, color is likewise emitted to catch the attention, but then it stays put. For a white to detach itself from a garment, or a wall, is unthinkable. In contrast, the whole of the surrounding air can be full of a sound [*Klang*]."[70]

For both Hegel and Bloch, the tone is an ephemeral vibration, a flood of movement that negates the spatiality of color, painting, and vision. And for both, musical tones are produced through a historical negation of externalized matter mediated by *Geist*, such that music reflects a *Siegel* of the self. But Hegel's historical account, for its part, begins from the physical elasticity of *Klang* and ends in a metaphysics of subjective inwardness embodied by tones. As is the case with the other arts as well, Hegel's dialectic ultimately turns towards the freedom of the subject, in this case the inner life of the soul.

In my view, Bloch's tone acquires and retains utopian meanings by refusing to resolve, teleologically, the tone's material substrate into the Hegelian realm of subjective independence. By contrast, Bloch's tone deliberately and agonistically retains the tension between these two halves—the physical and the metaphysical, the material and the ideal—and then keeps the tension alive in order to remain aporetic and open-ended in his conclusions. As a consequence, the musculature of the tone's material substrate is never fully overcome or sublated by something like an ideal soul. Bloch hears the tone as a *Siegel* of collective potentiality by virtue of its delicate and shimmering translucence, a permanently undecidable admixture of Pythagorean abstraction and material concreteness.

Consider a key passage of *The Spirit of Utopia*, a sentence Bloch found so important that he reprinted it as the epigraph to a section on music in *The Principle of Hope*. Much of it can be read as a sequel to Hegel's view of the tone:

> The tone comes with us and is We; unlike the visual arts [*bildenden Künste*], which seemed previously to point so far above us, out into the realm of the rigorous, objective, and cosmic, but which in fact stop at our graves, it [the tone] emulates good works by accompanying us even beyond the grave. This is precisely because the new, no longer pedagogical but real symbol in music, appears so very low-lying and such a mere fiery eruption in our atmosphere [*so sehr niedrig, so sehr nur bloßer feuriger Ausbruch in unserer Atmosphäre scheint*], even though it is actually a light in the farthest and absolutely innermost heaven of fixed stars [*obwohl es doch ein Licht am fernsten, allerdings innersten Fixsternhimmel ist*].[71]

Here, the tone "goes with us and is We [*Der Ton geht mit uns und ist wir.*]." It goes with us, collectively, because it is our old pitcher, our tool, our prosthesis, but it also "is we" because this sonic tool is a constitutive, even ontological, external condition—or *Geist* if you will—that makes us who we are. If, by comparison, the visual arts (what Hegel described as our "peaceful and undesiring contemplation of works of art") formerly embodied the ideal qualities of "the severe, the objective, the cosmic," Bloch now claims that visual images are finite and transient; they "stop at our graves [*bis zum Grabe mitgehen*]." The musical tone, by contrast, with its contradictory mélange of formal autonomy, inward materiality, and nebulous ephemerality, serves as the building block for a constellation of "good works" that "also go with us beyond the grave [*aber noch übers Grab hinaus mitgehen*]."[72]

Following the typical tropes of Romanticism from Wackenroder and Hoffmann, among many others, there are no rules for how this is to be done; ultimately the tone must be rendered "no longer pedagogical." Bloch envisions a tone that is a "real symbol in music"—a messianic musical logos that uniquely blends two contradictory halves of a dialectic without sublation: a latent material potentiality that appears "so very low-lying and such a mere fiery eruption in our atmosphere" while actually revealing a deeper ideal of the infinite, of hope, spirit, and utopia: "a light in the farthest and absolutely innermost heaven of fixed stars." The secular, collective resonance of the utopian tone contains a strange brew of contradictions. The material fire of the tone's inner potentiality is consistently interwoven with the light of its ideal telos.[73]

If the above epigraph exemplifies Bloch at his most poetic, elsewhere Bloch discusses the tone's dialectic a bit more plainly. Like the Schoenberg of the *Harmonielehre* (1911), who emphasizes the historical contingency of harmonic tinkering over the immutability of natural laws, Bloch's conception of the musical tone has its basis in material and historical actions. It is supported by "synthetic" human choices: "So nothing here may sound by itself then. Only in us can it blossom and awaken. The tone is intensified by us, qualitatively colored and at once dispersed. We alone are the ones who raise it up, even more: who make it define and animate itself with our life . . . to mention only the perfect fifth: all of this is only beautiful because it was chosen, because it occasions further, synthetic relationships. . . ."[74]

In the chapter on music in *The Principle of Hope*, Bloch explores this duality at length, breaking subject and object into the vocabulary of feeling and form, of sentiment and mathematics, of ephemeral *Stimmung* and cosmic eternity: "While music as *Stimmung* remains in the shaft of the soul, indeed appears the most subterranean [*chthonischste*] of all the arts, so-called *musica mathematica* becomes completely celestial [*uranisch*], lands in heaven."[75] Just a few pages later, Bloch follows Hegel (and Goethe before him) and states that music shares with architecture the integrity of "cosmic proportions," one that is, however, always integrated with the materiality of social life. In this way, music contains a "latent subject" in its tones—what he elsewhere calls the "will of the subject," the Marxist equivalent of Hegel's "ideal breath of the soul"— that speaks a peculiar nonsemantic language: "But even if architecture according to 'cosmic proportions' never let people forget that it was primarily and ultimately oriented to social needs and human proportions, then this was even more true of music which, like no other art, is related to the latent subject and to the object which entirely corresponds to it. The language sought and intended in music therefore lies much further beyond available designations and even beyond the Become-nesses [becomings, potentialities] designated therein [*darin bezeichneten Gewordenheiten*] than any other art."[76]

This "sought" utopian language of tones is Bloch's version of Schopenhauer's immediate copy. And it is tricky to unearth. Consider first that what Bloch means by the "subject" here is quite different from Hegel's conception of subjective freedom. Let us recall briefly their parallel accounts of music's relationship to subjective inwardness. In the passages of the *Aesthetics* quoted earlier, Hegel considers hearing to be a more "ideal" sense than sight, a counterintuitive claim unless one notices exactly why and how Hegel claims it is so. Hegel holds that music is an expression of inner subjective feelings (this is typically described as the central thesis of Hegel's writings on music), and spends much of his discussion of the medium in the *Aesthetics* on the topic of text setting and word-sound relationships. (He is well known as less than keen on a formalism of "music alone," which he took to be a relatively arcane and academic form of art.)[77] The inner expression of these feelings is based in the experience of feeling oneself sing, of understanding the singing voice as a *Siegel* of one's inner spirit, as an "ideal vibration of the body" and "the breath of the soul." What results is the expression of an "object-free inner life," a "free unstable soaring [*haltungsloses freies Verschweben*]" of tones that take "the soul of tone, working itself free from spatial matter, in the qualitative differences of sound and in the movement of the ever-rolling stream of time."[78]

Bloch would agree with Hegel that the musical tone bears a unique capacity of externalizing the inwardness of the subject. But Bloch recasts the ideal freedom of Hegel's enlightenment subject into the collective potentiality of a meta-subject ("To know itself, for this the mere I must go to others"); for him, the tone no longer reveals the inner flux of emotions or the soul, but instead unearths the latent utopian potentialities of the social whole.[79] It appears only from within concrete experience of the existential self-encounter, grounded by the solitary individual ("*Ich bin an mir*"). And it is Kierkegaard rather than Hegel who, in Bloch's view, refocuses the emphasis of such a self-reflection on the domain of concrete experience: "Kierkegaard posits the task for *subjective* un-Hegelian thought: to apprehend oneself as existent and to understand oneself in existence."[80]

Moreover, the goal of such an existential self-encounter is not the self-conscious actualization of subjective freedom, but something in line with Schopenhauer, a more obscure practice of sensory indistinction. To recall some of Bloch's opening words in *The Spirit of Utopia* (quoted at the opening of this chapter): "We walk in the forest and we feel we are or could be what the forest dreams." The forest could dream, we could be that dream, sharing the material potentiality of all that is. Music for Bloch, as for Schopenhauer before him, is exceptionally forceful in inducing these spells of indistinction, because in musical experience one is overcome, even overwhelmed, by music's lack of particularity, of its gapless continuity that aspires to its own system, sui generis: "Music quite simply dominates, and wants to be absolute; there is fundamentally no other music but absolute music, music which speaks *per se* in its absoluteness, music now explicable only purely speculatively. What has truly been musically designed and musically thought through to its conclusions will in the long term acknowledge no gaps between its worlds, where, like Epicurus' real gods, the gods of poetics can lead whatever hermeneutically superfluous existence."[81]

Notwithstanding the rhetoric of speculative abstraction here, Bloch's theory, of course, is quite different from Hanslick's theory of music (or Schenker's for that matter). Bloch is often critical of formalisms that subscribe to anything approaching a transcendent metaphysics, and he frequently reminds us that music comes from humans alone; its translucence is not a symptom of its transcendence.[82] He is likewise critical of the overly technical and "austere" analysis of music because it does too little "justice to the need, the exuberance of the artistic will and its objects."[83] Both halves of the tone's dialectic must be held together in a contradictory tension.

In *The Principle of Hope,* Bloch distinguishes once more (following Hegel) the tone's utopian translucence of tones from the arts of painting or poetry. What he calls here a *bewanderte Klang*—a skilled, evolved, music of tones that is both emotional [*affekthafter*] and intellectually illuminating—gets at a natural potentiality that unites all things. Music is, in this way, an "intensive root" of utopia (earlier I mentioned that Bloch used the figure of a "kernel [*Kern*]" or "seed [*Samen*]" to indicate latent potentiality) that flowers into a pastoral symphony and projects a numinous landscape of our unreified nature:

> Music reflects [*spiegelt*] reality in the aura-appearances [*Aura-Erscheinungen*] of its "naturing" which have not yet been controlled or grasped in pictorial or even often in poetic terms. What skilled music [*bewanderte Klang*] thus conveys, in a statement as emotional [*affekthafter*] as it is illuminating, is intensive root, signaled social tendency, or—in the varied pastorale—a newly de-reified world of nature overheard as a sound-figure [*Klangfigur abgehörte*].[84]

This naturing "logos" of the musical tone, and the corresponding possibility of hearing a "de-reified world of nature" and a "signaled social tendency," is a phenomenon that is at once the most embodied and the most semantically empty.

This dialectical conception of the tone is the basis of Bloch's view of music. And it serves as a response to Schopenhauer's unanswered paradox of the immediate copy: to strike listeners so deeply on the material level of sensation and still say nothing in particular is to say, quite precisely, what cannot ordinarily be said about society—an unpresentable *Geist* of collective social potentiality that nonetheless retains a grounding in human action and experience. In this way, the ineffability of music is dialectically productive for Bloch. The tone, as its fundamental unit, points towards "something vague" without referring to anything in particular. Its autonomy, in tension with its material foundation—a Marxist *Erzittern des Körpers,* if you will—is what makes the tone into a "metaphysical word" that perplexes us as it speaks with a "delicate translucent body [*zarte, durchsichtige Leib*]":[85]

Certainly, and here we can finally discuss this, it is not by chance, that it is precisely the tone properly understood, the tone which is utilized by human beings, radically wrapped-up [*umgebrochene*] that musically strikes—that it is just this delicate translucent body [*durchsichtige Leib*] which is chosen as the vehicle of musical circumstances.[86]

The tone's delicate translucence embodies music's notoriously ghostly and imprecise semantics. As an exemplum of the ineffable, it cannot tell us what utopia is; the tone allows music to bear eccentric metaphysical circuitry and speak, obliquely, a fragile or weak *Siegel* of social meaning. It must be at once unmoored from concrete nomenclatures and propositional declarations, yet be practically linked to a history of embodied practice. In a way that is redolent of the ancient meaning of *tónos* and *tonus*, which signified both a physical stretching of a rope and the virtuous and formal pose of the voice, Bloch's conception of the tone links the physical potentiality of collective life to the unbounded potential of a utopian horizon.

Just as, for Hegel, the flux of music negates the spatiality of visual arts, Bloch also claims that the secular dialectics of the musical tone replaced the cultic mythology of ancient societies. He claims that ancient cultures relied largely on "pictorial clairvoyance," a kind of "guaranteed heaven full of nothing but visibilities and objectivities." But after the disenchantment of the world, a "guaranteed heaven" based in cultic iconography no longer held sway, and philosophy "has actually been forced, been graced, to aim at practical action, at substance as process, at truth as the sublation of the world."[87] Given this immanent need for praxis and social change, Bloch understands the secular potentiality of musical tones to replace the mystical depth of ancient visual culture in the historical course of European modernity; as he puts it, "music has grown and become constitutive."[88] This development is paralleled by a secularization of much sacred music, in particular choral music of the eighteenth and nineteenth centuries, which for Bloch, was transformed from the ritual function of an "ancient congregation" into the existential plainness of a "thousand-fold cry."[89]

As described in the introduction and prelude to this book, Bloch's translucent conception of the tone—a dialectical exchange of inner and outer—could be said to embody a more rigorous handling of Schopenhauer's paradoxical theory of music as an immediate copy. A copy, of course, by definition, would seem to require mediation; and for Schopenhauer, music operates beneath the mediations of representations. The musical tone is both inward (the Dionysian thing-in-itself), and outward (an Apollonian individuation). It maintains this tension of outer and inner, of copy and original, of mediation and immedi-

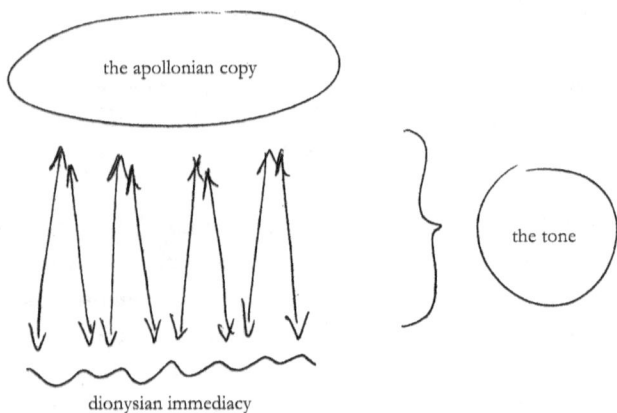

FIGURE 1.2. Bloch's tone. Drawing by the author.

acy, with the force of an intransigent and mysterious contradiction. In Bloch's hands, Schopenhauer's paradox of the ineffable is embodied in a dialectical unit of musical expression—the tone.

Figure 1.2 may give us a clearer sense of the contradictions at play. On the bottom a wavy line represents "Dionysian immediacy"—the blind forces of the will in their undisciplined state. Above, a wide oval represents the Apollonian form in which music individuates or "copies" the Dionysian forces of the will. Bloch's dialectical conception of the tone maintains the contradictory tension of these two poles without resolution, so that neither the Dionysian nor the Apollonian sides win out. They depend on each other for their coherence, but there is no ideal moment in which the contradictions are *aufgehoben* in a Hegelian manner.

As the tone might be said to address Schopenhauer's paradoxical formulation of the immediate copy, so might it address the theory of temporality Bloch develops over the course of his career concerning the "darkness of the lived moment." Though the connection is only occasionally hinted at in Bloch's writing (and the linkage between music and time is nowhere near as strong as it is for the Bergsonian intellectuals in this book), consider that, for Bloch, the tone is an entity that is both present and absent.[90] It embodies the flux of experiential time that seems immersive, real, concrete, and inescapable. Yet, as Hegel's logic of double negation reminds us, the tone's negative being is ephemeral and self-annihilating in both directions. At the center of the vanishing now of musical experience there is a certain darkness, an ephemerality that resists positive knowledge. Devoid of secure, semantic content, the ephemeral and muscular tone thus aspires to a developed form mediated by *Geist*, in order to speak a sui generis language according to a code that resists normative intelligibility and aims at unforeseen, latent, and untimely disclosures. Its dialectical character is philosophically perplexing and productive.

In the final third of this chapter I argue that Bloch develops a deeply historical conception of musical material that will be foundational for Adorno: he concretizes Hegel's scattered speculative teleology of the various arts into a teleology of music history directed at particular musical *Ereignisformen*, or event-forms. These are Bloch's ethical externalizations of the *Geist* of utopia.

1.6 THE EVENT-FORMS

How exactly does a translucent and ineffable tone, with its unstable dialectical structure, provide the grammar for utopia? In ethical terms, how does one do it well? Answers to this question are only partially developed in Bloch's work—Adorno develops fuller explanations. But some of the basic ideas are set up here. Let us recall that the ostensible autonomy of the tone is exactly what allows it to speak about social life in a hidden register. Bloch's dialectics of the ineffable exemplifies a chthonic or subterranean linguistics in which music is taken to harbor concealed, secret, and nonsemantic messages. Music's chthonic linguistics first cropped up with the Ikhwan Al-Safa, Wackenroder, and Schopenhauer, and will be further developed in Adorno's writings on music. For Bloch, this secret disclosive power is unique to the formal malleability of the musical tone as an ordered sound composed of contradictory and undecidable halves. In the late modern world of music, at the moment the tone wins a striking sense of independence from the world (via Apollonian counterpoint, rule-based composition, and so on), it can begin to speak in an obscure register about our real inner potentiality. That is, when musical composition develops independently of its psychological and social functions into the realm of pure form, it paradoxically begins to speak about society more clearly.

Consider, first, the general structure of Bloch's conception of the history of art. Bloch bases his historical vision of *Ereignisformen*, or event-forms, on a tripartite syllogism that Hegel develops in the *Lectures on Aesthetics*. For Hegel, very roughly, there are three basic schemas by which art is mediated by *Geist*. The first, symbolized by the unfree and fixed forms of *Geist*, is exemplified by Egyptian architecture that preserves the dead. The second is dubbed "classical" and is exemplified by Greek sculpture that elegantly and adequately depicts the visible freedom of *Geist*. The third is Romantic and is exemplified largely by forms of painting, music, and poetry that depict the inward freedom of *Geist*, particularly in Christian art in which the represented "Idea" is a freedom that is invisible and spiritual, rather than concrete.

In the opening of *The Spirit of Utopia*, Bloch describes a parallel version of this tripartition in the realm of visual ornament. His summary of Greek classicism in a section entitled "The Appeal of the Greek" is largely faithful to Hegel, as is his summary of Egyptian art in "The Egyptian Volition to Become Like Stone." Where he departs from the Hegelian script is in the third art form of the tripartition. There, Bloch concurs nominally with Hegel that, in the development of art, "only Christian life truly breaks through the stone." But whereas Hegel views this third schema as an emblem of inner subjective freedom, Bloch sees modern art as externalizing a "vital trace" that stems from the deeper materiality of nature: "This vital trace already bends upward towards us from that place where no one yet is. It is the same force expressed in lava, in hot lead thrown into cold water, in the veining of wood and above all in the twitching, bleeding, ragged or peculiarly compacted form of internal organs."[91]

The potentiality of this natural life force, what Bloch describes as "the free spirit of the very movement of expression," externalizes itself in what he calls the "Gothic line." In the realm of visual ornamentation, the "Gothic line" appears in excesses of baroque design. In doing so, according to Bloch, it externalized the *Siegel* not of a free subject, but an a priori utopian potentiality: "a spiritual *a priori* of construction, of architecture, to a mundanely useless construction for the sake of a great *Siegel* to another world."[92] The ornaments of the "Gothic line" are functionless and wild. They are a surplus; the pedagogy and practice of such ornamentation is excessive and poetic. Such a liberation of vital movement induces an uncanny communion with the reality of natural flux, in all its valueless materiality:

> "Gothic line ... contains all this agitation within itself; this line is restless and uncanny like its forms: the protuberances, the snakes, the animal heads, the streams, a chaotic intertwining and twitching where a warm amniotic fluid and the heat of incubation stands, and the womb of all suffering, all delight, all births and all organic images begins to speak; only the Gothic has this fire at the center, over which the deepest organic and the deeper spiritual essences bring themselves to fruition."[93]

This is how Bloch would describe the formal qualities of the art and music that induce the exceptional spells of indistinction in the self-encounter. The elemental flux of water, animals, fire, air—this greater unity of nature—in a somewhat Schopenhauerian vein, constitutes the basis for the universal potentiality of matter. We might say that the "event-form" is the musical equivalent of this "Gothic line." And, like Hegel's general tripartition outlined above, Bloch positions the modern event-form as the third term of a three-part syllogism of music. Each portion of the syllogism has parallel equivalents in music. The first schema, the Egyptian, is paralleled by the primordial "singing-to-oneself" discussed earlier that eventually, via the tone, externalizes itself into an independent history. The second schema, the classical one, is based in two giants of eighteenth-century music. The first is Mozart, who externalizes the nebulous innocence of "singing-to-oneself" into a graceful framework of tones. (Bloch had in mind three of his most famous operas: *Le Nozze di Figaro*, *Don Giovanni*, and *Die Zauberflöte*.) The other exemplar of the second schema centers on J. S. Bach's innovations in imitative counterpoint, which, for Bloch, first demonstrated the way musical tones themselves could harbor a utopian sense of depth.[94]

In the third schema of the event-forms, the tone begins to speak utopia dialectically insofar as it "wants to push towards action" as a metaphysical logos in the form of the "Gothic line." With the event-forms "the old cloister breaks; the chaotic world, the external dream before the genuine cloister, shines in."[95] In this schema, Bloch discusses a wide array of compositions from the nineteenth and early twentieth centuries (works by Beethoven, Schubert, Berlioz, Wagner, Bruckner, Reger, Mahler, Wolf, Richard Strauss, Schoenberg, and Berg). At the hands of these composers, the "cloister" (the architectural symbol of a conservative religious order) breaks out into the chaos of secular revolutions, and musical tones join us to the flux of natural materiality. It speaks a utopian message that cannot be articulated in propositional form.

The event-form of the "Gothic line" is based, partly, in a breakdown of standardized musical techniques. Music and narrative, for example, interpenetrate unpredictably, and unleash the force of music in new and unforeseen ways. In song, verses become unhinged from their standard strophic patterns (as in lieder by Schubert, Wolf, and Richard Strauss). In the case of opera, Bloch ventriloquizes the Wagnerism of his time and argues that the traditional boundaries of arias and recitatives (arias were typically non-narrative spectacles of virtuosity and feeling, whereas recitatives often functioned to move the story along) were blurred, such that "the ringing exclamations go along with the singing, and transform it into an abbreviated melodic incident variable enough to also convey the sensations and outbursts of people in action...."[96] In a complementary reading of Bizet's *Carmen* (1875), Bloch writes admiringly of musical episodes that "are not simply set in a row, but rather, without being broken, appear open and mobile, at least insofar as they are able to momentarily follow the course of the action instead of lyrically decorating and arresting it."[97]

On a philosophical level, the event-forms exemplify a more autonomous definition of music. In the above cases of opera and song, the traditional subservience of music to text, relatively fixed since the Greek *melos* doctrine and the *seconda pratica* of the seventeenth century, was dramatically inverted. Again, echoing strains of Wagnerism, Bloch claimed that, in the nineteenth century, music began to speak more clearly and dramatically on its own terms, such that the text and drama had to find their place in its flow. Bloch writes of the tone: "The digressively deployed tone, the surge of tones and the continued accretion of tension, chaos and fate, boils over into an overwhelmingly unmelodic, recitatively melismatic, motivically thematic and as a whole purely symphonically developing type of music, which—in itself already making a mockery of any well-considered text—not only follows the action, but itself generates action, a still indeterminate, nameless action, into which the theatrical application and a textual 'justification' now have to be installed."[98]

Bloch understands the "Gothic line" of these "digressively deployed" tones to be not only based in the dialectical form of counterpoint, but also equally linked to the theory of harmonic motion. Following from the work of Ernst Kurth and August Halm, who explored the processual and energetic character of tonality, Bloch describes tones as having a kind of agency, particularly insofar as voice leading implies a metaphorical sense of "gravity" towards cadences.[99] Paralleling his dialectical view of the tone, Bloch's emphasis on the energy of processual harmony reflects the way he understands the "numerical" character of harmony to stand in a dialectical relationship with the contingency of chosen combinations that were "heard" and "deliberately pursued":

> [The tone] rejuvenates itself, builds bridges, forms relationships of a fifth, and insofar as it treads the path of octave, fifth, third, in other words the path of the first melody, defines for itself certain points in the harmony to which it is drawn quite independently of our wishes, purely numerically. . . . [Yet] things would absolutely not even really continue if only the natural chord progression predominated, if there were no new leading tones, scales, suspensions, anticipations, fragments of other directions that were intermittently heard and then immediately, deliberately pursued.[100]

Note the tension between the natural potentiality of harmony, flowering through tones like a plant, and the historicity of specific choices, in particular the treatment and emphasis of dissonances. The "digressive" and energetic autonomy of an event-form's musical tones make explicit and vivid use of pungent and dynamic sonorities.

1.7 A DIALECTICAL ACCOUNT OF MUSIC HISTORY

Let us now explore more precisely the way tones develop and evolve to meet Bloch's needs of utopian speech in the course of music history. In line with the generic form of the Hegelian tripartition, as well as Max Weber's diagnosis of the link between rationality and history, the exceptional event-forms of the nineteenth century presuppose, historically, a highly systematic and rationalized conception of musical material.[101] In *The Principle of Hope,* Bloch describes this process by placing particular emphasis on the influence of the scholastic tradition: ". . . the traditional rationalization was a blessing for the polyphony which began in the eleventh century; it was not Pythagoras but rather the closeness to the scholastic mode of thinking and teaching which made possible the miracles of subtlety constructed by the Burgundian-Flemish contrapuntalists."[102] Bloch mentions two treatises that exemplify the early rationalization of the tone: Philippe de Vitry's *Ars Nova* (1322) and Jacques de Liège's treatise *Speculum musicae* (c. 1330). The former is a landmark in the emergence of modern musical notation associated with the *ars nova*. The latter is an extended account of speculative music theory associated with Greek harmonics, and also includes discussion of church modes, as well as discant and mensural music.[103] In Bloch's writings, references to medieval sources like these occur amid other references to music's role in the quadrivium of the liberal arts where music stood in the company of other branches in mathematics (specifically arithmetic, geometry, and astronomy). In the history of musical thought, Bloch understands this medieval scholastic tradition to be an antecedent of seventeenth- and eighteenth-century rationalism, as well as a prerequisite for music's emancipatory collision with expressive subjectivity in the "Gothic line" of the nineteenth-century "event-form."

It is not, however, in such formal techniques of musical composition that the "Gothic line" becomes emancipated. In Bloch's view, the event-forms only came to life by way of the numinous ingenuity of the composers as subjects, who scaled the heights of compositional techniques, and managed to channel the warm effects of music into a utopian canon of exemplars. Bloch writes of these exemplary composers in *The Principle of Hope*: "There certainly are stars in music, but they are stars which have formed only as human names."[104] Great composers, exceptional humans, ingenious subjects, who infuse pedagogical and automatic techniques with a humanistic exemplarity, are the structural pillars of Bloch's "innermost heaven of fixed stars." In fact, so singular were individual composers to Bloch's conception of music history that they could relate to one another in a way that was independent of events in actual history. When Bloch recalls the *Geist* of music history in its singular immanence, the malleability of the exceptional and ahistorical powers of composers can wield their power to scramble historical chronologies and disassemble chains of causality: "Just as the great masters freely used the different forms of song, fugue or sonata insofar as the '*Geist*' of the relevant passage required it—just in this way we can set Mozart before Bach [as in Bloch's account of the second schema], or derive from Mozart's, Bach's, Wagner's forms a sequence of composition and its objects...."[105]

As a result, Bloch's immanent *Geist* of music history contains an extraordinary amount of variability and recombination, even nonlinearity; it does not bear a steady Hegelian evolutionary progression. And this is a crucial point: Like many of his privileged objects of study, the history of musical tones embodies the logic of nonsynchronicity [*Ungleichzeitigkeit*]. Just as actual history is uneven and nonlinear, artifacts of our expressive culture reflect, often obliquely, this nonlinearity.

This nonlinear *Geist* of tones flows, metaphysically, through the bodies of individual composers, becoming in some sense immanent to music alone: "A whispering is perceptible, which [a composer's] inner self obeys, and transindividual dispatches that determine their work's design...." Under this Romantic condition, "individuals become categories, and the entire sequence of geniuses, foremost those of music, begins to pass into a system of categories having to do with our consciousness of ourselves...." This deeply idealized "system of categories" supported by the exceptional ingenuity of individual composers means that the history of music is not based primarily in its technical history (as it will be for Adorno's *Tendenz des Materials*). It is certainly dialectically linked to techniques, but again, it is really the human exemplars—the most celebrated composers and the singularity of their subjective compositional ingenuity—that provide the tone's dialectical support.[106]

Prior to the nineteenth century, the great era of event-forms, two composers stand out as harbingers of the innovations to come. With Franco-Flemish composer Orlando de Lassus, composer of the *Penitential Psalms* (1584), "complete freedom has been won" and "everything is ready for expression to the broadest extent" because of a certain harmonic sophistication. With Lassus, "the tonal edifice has been built, the range, the perspective, the transcendence of the tonal space, [are prototypically] all truly and properly 'musical' for the first time...."[107] Lassus's dialectical counterpart in polyphony is the Italian

Giovanni Pierluigi da Palestrina, who served as the Raphael to Lassus's Rembrandt and actualized an "intimate harmonic simplicity" that induced a multidimensional mode of listening "that coordinates vertically below and horizontally only above, where the total melodic effect occurs."[108] In Bloch's history of music, Lassus's and Palestrina actualized freedom because they broke the blind adoption of academic rules. With them, the tone is finally "no longer pedagogical"—they "refuted academicist construction for its own sake."[109]

Part of what makes Lassus and Palestrina so exemplary, however, is the degree to which these composers typified the following of rules even as they broke them. Indeed, Bloch held in high esteem the formal integrity of the sixteenth-century *ars perfecta* of vocal polyphony, just as he recognized that the historical path of rationality could not be undone and was an a priori for any utopian act of thought. He even drew an analogy between logic and the study of counterpoint: "Counterpoint is the variation of the theme in several voices, *ex una voce plures faciens* [from one voice make many]; by inversion, imitation, reversion and so on. Scholastic logic taught variations and combinations of formal elements of judgment, *ex uno judicio plures faciens* [from one judgment make many]; through conversion, contraposition, subalternation, modal consequence, and so on."[110]

In venturing this comparison between music and logic, Bloch seems to express a certain admiration for a bygone form of musical rationalism. And indeed, like Adorno after him, Bloch admired the structural impersonality of musical form for its generative integrity and its autonomous character, particularly in the realm of counterpoint. But he also recognized that the autonomy of music, despite all its evolutionary accomplishments mediated by *Geist*, ran the risk of becoming technologized, reified, and alienated. (Some readers may note the similarity to the pathology of formalism Thomas Mann narrates in his 1947 novel *Doctor Faustus*). Bloch's qualification, as always, is dialectical: rationalization must always be linked to the subjective embodiment of human action.[111]

When it comes to the event-forms themselves, the condition of nonsynchronicity means that some of the most revolutionary occurrences of musical "genius" are engaging in curious and uncanny dialogues with the musical past, in various forms. In fact, as I will argue in the final section of this chapter, Bloch's celebrated event-forms make use of archaic or outworn techniques that have been refashioned in modern contexts, inducing strange juxtapositions and discontinuities of historical time.

The ability of tones to speak utopian messages through musical event-forms is due to a peculiarity of the tone's aporetic dialectics. As it will for Adorno, this idealist plane of musical tones unfolds at a remove from "any economic-social pragmatics or morphological synoptics."[112] This is the crux of Bloch's Marxist dialectic: the tone's nonlinguistic abstraction, an ineffability based in a sui generis medium of sonic translucence, is paradoxically what allows it to speak utopian meanings.[113] The autonomy of the musical tone, a historical fact, is something that, as a product of the Enlightenment, can then speak back to society concretely and universally through its form alone. For Bloch, as for Adorno, music should not be directly instrumentalized for the purposes of social praxis (as in socialist realism, protest songs, committed literature, and so on). Just as the numerical and structural powers of the tones must be linked with embodied envelopes of muscles, compositional choices, and exemplary geniuses of the nineteenth century, only through the historical passage of Apollonian rationalization and abstraction does an event-form speak, reveal, or externalize the *Siegel* of the utopian metasubject.

1.8 UTOPIAN MUSICAL SPEECH

Given Bloch's dialectical orientation, it is ultimately in musical examples that one can fully appreciate how Bloch brings the ineffable abstraction of musical tones to life as utopian meanings. Consider Bloch's interpretation of the fugue in *The Principle of Hope*.[114] Seemingly abstract, ornate, and impersonal, for Bloch, fugues strangely reflect our own historical quest from centralized authority to democracy in the "Gothic line" of tones alone. Historically speaking, while they exemplify the tone's quintessentially rationalist orientation towards the intricate compositional order of imitative counterpoint, the impact of such formal sophistication in music has a social analogue: "The lower tension [of the fugue, as opposed to the dramatic structure of sonata-allegro form] and the more intense composure reflect an order of society divided into estates which as such is past...."[115] The hierarchical and ordered tones, according to their formal logic alone, dialectically crystalize a reflection of the order of society.

As it is for order, so is it for its subsequent transfiguration. From the late eighteenth century onward, as the dramatic sweep and textural clarity of sonata-allegro form rose in popularity, fugues generally fell out of fashion but persisted in a strange afterlife, turning up in odd places as fugatos—fugue-like passages in operas, symphonies, and sonatas. For Bloch, fugatos show how archaic formal procedures for musical composition (like imitative counterpoint) can, by way of a novel and nondoctrinaire citation, let a fugue "break away from its old ground." And the fugato's peculiarly understated nature speaks a kind of unconscious, nonlinguistic message; in contradistinction to the brave-hearted potentiality yielded by heroic sonata form, the fugue "ranks lower" because it "[overcomes] dynamism without having known it." This is a virtue and actually a source of productive tension, for a fugato's configuration of tones "produces or can produce *a restless rigid effect*," as illustrated "most uncannily in the fugued chorale of the armored men in *The Magic Flute*."[116]

The passage referred to in Mozart's opera is a famous chorale setting at the beginning of the finale of act 2 (example 1.1). In the scene, Tamino approaches the pyramid and encounters two armed guards who, echoing a creed of the ancient Egyptian goddess Isis, tell him that if he can overcome the fear of death, he will be rewarded with enlightenment. There are multiple archaisms in this moment of the opera. The chorale Bloch heard in the opera is in fact based on one of the first Lutheran chorales, "Ach Gott, vom Himmel sieh darein" (1524), probably attributable to Martin Luther himself, disseminated widely in the *Achtliederbuch*, and subject to a rich afterlife in the seventeenth and eighteenth centuries (Jan Pieterszoon Sweelinck, Johann Pachelbel, Heinrich Schütz, and J. S. Bach all wrote settings). Mozart's particular setting begins with a C-minor fugato of lilting and weaving strings, delicately meandering in staccato lines of eighth notes and whispering a charming canon at the unison, topped with lyrical halos of scalar descents in the violins. In the context of an opera rife with stylistic references, the contrapuntal passage reads like a "sampled" reference to aristocratic order, a simulacrum. When the guards begin singing the Lutheran hymn with a new text inspired by Isis ("Der, welcher wandelt diese Straße voll Beschwerden"), Mozart sets the melody in austere impersonal octaves, as if the singers were passive and obedient vehicles for tones that transcended them. The rigidity and intricacy that fell out of fashion in the late eighteenth century here return as a fugal simulacrum, shorn of its aura. In tortured, tense, and fragmentary form, the fugato reveals the abstract potentiality of the tone, which in its self-referentiality can act as an agent of a humanity struggling to envision itself as shorn of the shackles of Old World doctrine and authority.

The funeral march in the second movement of Beethoven's "Eroica" Symphony (1804) echoes a similar fragmentary sampling of old social orders. Bloch writes: "A new expression is formed here, it continues in the fugato of the funeral march in the Eroica, which would scarcely have been written without Mozart's example and, now absolutely a dynamic cortège [a procession], is not *quietas in fuga* [repose in flight (or literally, fugue)]."[117] After opening with the famously brooding C-minor dirge, and following it up with a very short and relatively underdeveloped trio in the parallel major, Beethoven widens the rhetorical scope of his *Marcia funebre* into an strange tapestry of contra-

EXAMPLE 1.1. Wolfgang Amadeus Mozart, *Die Zauberflöte*, K. 620, act 2, "Der, welcher wandert diese Straße voll Beschwerden," mm. 15–25. Source: Friedrich Eunicke (1764–1844), piano reduction, first edition (as a single volume), Bonn: N. Simrock, n.d. (ca. 1793), plate 4.

puntal experiments, weaving the ceremonial heaviness of the main theme into brief fugatos, laced with scalar climaxes and effecting sublime trances. Example 1.2 shows the beginning of this episode, in which each passage attempts to escape the heavy shackles of the dirge's inexorable adagio, while never acquiring quite enough energy to peel itself away. Abstract gestures of human grasping and questioning seem to radiate from the fugatos, lending a sense of struggle to each episode, while each pulsing string chord cascades, one past the

EXAMPLE 1.2. Ludwig van Beethoven, Symphony no. 3 in E-flat major, "Eroica," op. 55, mvt. 2, mm. 114–21. Source: Ludwig van Beethoven, *Symphony no. 3 in E-flat Major, "Eroica"* (New York: C. F. Peters, 1900).

next, punctuated by silences and whispered cadences. But the fugato cannot break its melancholy spell.

Beethoven's *Marcia funebre* is a sampled demonstration of intricate authority and self-referential reason, a shard of music's history littered with dead fragments. The struggling fugatos indicate a language of potentiality, not accomplishment. Their medium is the tone, assembled in constellations that are cluttered with the noise of past compositional techniques. Very far from the roller-coaster excitement of sonata-allegro form that makes the process of thematic development and juxtaposition into a series of heroic cliffhangers and codas, the fugato (example 2.2) is all tense self-reflection and struggle, a broken musical interiority that "experiences *itself only* the development."[118] Here, there is no literal mimicry of hope in music. The universality of utopia is something that cannot be simply presented, represented, or even indicated; it must be obscurely interpreted through the abstract and translucent tone of the fugato. Music's ineffability is a perplexing impetus to a utopian insight.

Later in the nineteenth century, the tense crosscurrents of the fugato's proclivity for self-reflection undergo an "after-ripening" in fugal passages of romantic works by Wagner, Richard Strauss, and Berg. What was a cipher of potentiality and inner struggle in Mozart and Beethoven is, in these composers' hands, let loose in episodes of raucous contrapuntal antagonism. Bloch writes: "It is even more curious that the fugue form proper, when used in a symphonic context, also develops a powerful element of impatience, namely feud, as in the fighting fugue in the 'Meistersinger' and the veritable bickering fugue in Strauss' 'Sinfonia domestica'; both fugues, moreover are especially learned and complicated."[119] Or, famously, in Berg's *Wozzeck* (1922), the fugue takes its place alongside the strictures of other archaic forms, which are each sampled explicitly and exhaustively: "Berg's 'Wozzeck,' this extremely atmospheric-dramatic work, has inventions and passacaglias built into it, and precisely the singing voice which is heightened to the highest dramatic expression is dynamically involved, without any stylistic incongruity at all, in the exposition of a double fugue."[120]

In no single autonomous work alone are such techniques made legible. In Bloch's view, it is only in the translucent dialectics of the tone that music remains linked both to the history of its forms (fugue, passacaglia, invention) and to a constellation of innovative acting, musical bodies. The result is dialectical: formal interpretations of a repertory or a technique are in perpetual contradiction with a practical and social meaning. The fact that this contradiction is never reconciled in language—only in an energetic fabric of musical tones—is what gives music its perplexing and ineffable specificity. In these examples, it is explicitly through the cipher of linear counterpoint that music sings a metaphysical revelation via its ineffable form.[121] An ideal trajectory of music history is reconfigured by the archaic contrapuntal technique of a few exemplary composers. My use of the passive voice is key to the structure of Bloch's dialectic; the tones remain agents. The tones obliquely speak, and they do it through a nonsynchronous musical technique, a historical disjunction, an event-form. Without language, music thus reveals a latent potential that is universal to humanity.

By comparison, sonata-allegro form, unlike the fugue, is a more straightforward and direct exemplar of utopian revelations, in which the first and second theme wrestle out a conflict in order to arrive at a higher form of self-conscious reflection. Bloch writes that "in Beethoven, the objective principle of the sonata, the double thematics and its conflict, was brought to maturity, one can also say to consciousness."[122] Reflecting the agency the tone acquires amidst Bloch's neo-Hegelianisms, the sonata is capable of "detaching itself" from the past history of musical techniques in order to serve as the medium of the heroic tone. In an echo of August Halm's *Von zwei Kulturen in der Musik* (1913), Bloch holds that the sonata takes up a dialectical opposite to the fugue and its self-imposed internal tension; by not allowing the Romantic angst of the *Sturm und Drang* to devolve into unintelligible hysteria, the sonata structures it into a dramatic conflict, one that is analogous to social conflict, and thus to the universal hope for social emancipation. "Thus the sonata *ab ovo* [from the beginning] already detached itself from its forebears, the orchestral suite and the Bachian concerto, especially from its opposite: the fugue, by virtue of its weather-like quality, by its performance in dynamic curves."[123] Finally, the two themes of the sonata, like the tone itself, are anthropomorphized in Bloch's vocabulary as two souls standing at the precipice of genuine historical self-consciousness: "On the other hand, the incipient social antagonism was sublimated to the conflict of the two souls in one breast, a conflict which was certainly contemporaneous with music, and: it became dialectical in the sonata."[124]

In still another vein, the adagio, that frequently overlooked portion of a symphony that is typically lyrical, even sentimental, and lacking the metaphysical gravity of the first movement, is given a contrary casting by Bloch, and venerated as a moment of self-reflexive intensity. Bloch writes that "even in the struggle of the sonata at least the quiet movement rests, the *andante* and *adagio* rest from conflict."[125] In an echo of his reading of the *Marcia funebre*, the adagio offers repose from struggle and signals a potential for self-reflection, the key ingredient to the revelation of a utopian potentiality. Now using Mahler as a referent, Bloch reflects on the adagio, heralding humanity from a metaphorical distance: "A self-approaching is thus there, it is Mahler's music itself, mingled with the calls of the watch, roll-calls, cortèges, signals, with a kind of melismatic dispatch from a distant headquarters."[126]

With reference to the slow, distended, and sinuous texture of the final movement of Mahler's *Das Lied von der Erde* (1912), Bloch writes: "Its last word, the 'Song of the Earth,' moves with an unresolved suspension into an immense Eternal, eternal; despite the retained and finally omitted tonic. The new music no longer contains the dynamism of the Romantic, it appears so to speak as the paradox of a highly extroverted *adagio*, but it intends [*intendiert*] just as much Unattained as the dynamic, if not more."[127] Here, Bloch uses the word *intendiert* dialectically to show how the diaphanous suspensions at the closing of *Der Abschied* have a monadic integrity that owes little to the programmatic imitation of subjective struggle; their internal serenity—a projected sense of the eternal from the embodied—reaches for the "Unattained" by way of a formalized tension. Famously, the alto soloist's D (on the word "*ewig* [eternal]") is held in a minor seventh over the cellos, who are supporting the line with an E, and it creates the feel of a not-quite-resolved tonic in first inversion before it finally descends to the root, just after the singing has stopped.

For Bloch, this exquisitely crafted suspension embodies the metaphysical potential of an ineffable tone on a pillar of muscular support, which he reads as a *Siegel* of collective potentiality. Just after this, in a poignant insight, the philosopher reiterates his view that musical techniques alone lack meaning: "If one considers a musical piece in its technical aspect, everything is correct but means nothing, like an algebraic equation."[128] Its dialectical opposite places the listener in an unresolved tension between poetry and procedure, subject and object; in the peculiar medium of tones, music as the ineffable art par excellence "says everything and defines nothing."[129] The event-forms, as in Bloch's extraordinarily unique theory of the tone, sustain the contradictory halves of the tone in a perplexing dialectical oscillation. By virtue of a chthonic linguistics of the tone Bloch derived from Schopenhauer, this oscillation can similarly be understood to disclose latent meanings from the fabric of a reified society.

*

Like a wide range of thinkers in the eighteenth and nineteenth centuries, Bloch understands the tone as powerfully constitutive of musical material; its combinations and internal logic are the determining grammar of the mediation of music by *Geist*. And yet what Bloch is asking of music is something in some ways quite new. Adorno famously credited Bloch with having rehabilitated the heretofore discredited category of utopia. He did so quite uniquely, via a mélange of Schopenhauer and Hegel, through which he accorded music a metaphysical intensity that was Romanticized and exceptional. In so doing, he took the first step towards a dialectical task Adorno would attempt to complete: specifying more precisely how to ethically and musically "speak utopia" within the confines of a teleological history.

At issue here is an effort to prescribe a musical ethics appropriate to the modern age. Bloch, however, sees little utopian value in the details of a composition's technical elements alone, which he refers to as "the lifeless melismatic or harmonic or contrapuntal components." The singularity of the composer as an exemplary subject is what carries us to the door of utopia. We would then be subject to a "Beethovenian blaze," a "mysterious place" fused with the composer's "original vision." Curiously, Bloch claims that the same is true for virtuoso performers, who engage in a "miracle of transformation," one in which "everything suddenly plays itself," and we experience the composers as "essential ciphers and objects."[130] Recapitulating a well known social construction of the conductor as the cipher for the heroic composer, Bloch views a good conductor neither as a mechanical "pedant" nor as one of the overly "subjective swindlers," but as a steady handmaiden to the actualization of the musical work.

No doubt the deeply speculative and metaphorical connectivity of Bloch's idealism has a certain quaintness nowadays. His metaphysical hypostatization of these expressive subjects—composer, performer, and conductor alike (constructions typically taken as ideologies of the subject linked to nineteenth-century Romanticism)—will be dramatically overturned in Adorno's work in favor of a far more impersonal and structural *Tendenz des Materials*, an exacting *Versprachlichung*, and a subject facing the bleak (though always incomplete) silence of an inhuman modern condition. But so careful and so exact is Adorno's thinking that he never fully succumbs to the dogmatic claims that he is so often regarded as holding. As often as he thinks of the narrow life and death of musical language in the idiom of tonality, he explores the possibility, very equally, that there are numerous other musical languages. This is especially the case when Adorno is fascinated by a musical object for which there appears to be no one methodology.

Adorno himself acknowledges how much he adopted from Bloch. For him, the tone is still the Apollonian unit of musical writing. Its ineffability is articulated dialectically and historically, rather than cosmologically or Platonically. As I have argued, Bloch certainly did not invent this historicist and dialectical theory of the ineffable musical tone; he offered a distinct vision of on it based in a wide array of precedents. From Schopenhauer he derived a paradoxical conception of music's ineffability, that of the immediate copy of the will. Eschewing any of Schopenhauer's Platonic solutions to this paradox (along with Schopenhauer's pessimism), Bloch adapted the productivity of Schopenhauer's theory to Hegel's dialectical conception of the tone. The result was a mystical, interpretation-driven philosophy based around the perplexing and unstable aspects of the musical tone as a locus of new social and political potentialities. Through untimely or nonsynchronous uses of compositional techniques, an array of ethical "event-forms" went further than any other kind of music in bringing these potentialities to life. I hope that understanding the unique nature of Bloch's intellectual synthesis sheds new light on the contours and limitations of Adorno's project. And I further hope this comparative assessment of two German intellectuals inspired by music sets Jankélévitch's, Deleuze's, and Guattari's approaches into vivid relief.

CHAPTER 2

Adorno's Musical Fracture

In 1964, Bloch and Adorno engaged in an illustrative conversation about the nature of utopia, moderated by the writer and then radio host Horst Kröger, who had found notoriety as the author of an autobiographical novel about his experiences growing up during the Third Reich. Kröger opened the discussion by suggesting that during the polarized age of the Cold War, utopia now appeared as something of an outmoded concept. Adorno responded, jumping in immediately. After a quick nod to Bloch, crediting him for having been first to rehabilitate the category, Adorno claimed that despite undeniable technological progress (the mid-century wonders of television, space travel, and supersonic flight), modern technology had addressed utopian desires by deadening them with the administered pleasures of the culture industry. In his view, we were now part of a social totality run by the capitalist law of exchange value, domination, and control.

When Bloch responded, the differing views between the two men were immediately palpable. Bloch could agree only partially, for he wanted more generously to leave open the realm of a latent potentiality. For him, the reign of what he called, in *The Spirit of Utopia,* the alienating hand of "technological cold" was not supreme; in poetry, in art, in music, in the character of tones themselves, and in everyday desires "there is a residue" of something undetermined, utopian, and hopeful. From the perspective of intellectual history, Bloch emphasized how the principle of utopia had survived and been reborn from Thomas More (an island) through the French Revolution (a popular emancipation), Marxism (a revolutionary meta-subject), and onward. Through the history of the idea, "the content changes, but an invariant of the direction is there, psychologically expressed so to speak as longing . . . a longing that is the pervading and above all only honest quality of all human beings."[1]

Notwithstanding Adorno's opening move, which was, perhaps predictably, a dark and fatalistic one, a key point of agreement between Bloch and Adorno emerged by the interview's end. Adorno was, as it turned out, unwilling to concede all potential freedom to the ideological powers of the social totality. In fact, what Bloch referred to as a "residue," a "longing," or a "direction," was for Adorno an axiomatic desire for immortality, the one thing that keeps us from a Heideggerian cult of death, an empty materialism of finitude and transience: "Without the notion of an unfettered life, freed from death, the idea of utopia, the idea of *the* utopia, *cannot* even be thought at all."[2] He cautioned, however: "One may not cast a picture of utopia in a positive manner." To think of unfettered life by way of a picture, a positive concept, or the form of the commodity was to short-circuit its strangely paradoxical form: utopia must first acknowledge the weighty existence of death, domination, and the existing world in order to conduct a "determinate negation" of it.

To some of this Bloch, in fact, nominally agreed; he would of course oppose the commodification of utopia. By contrast, he emphasized its processual tendency and its open-endedness: "There is no such thing as utopia without multiple goals. In a non-teleological world there is no such thing." But he also stated that to think utopia was to conduct "a critique of what is present." With a sense of affability, at this point the dispute appeared to be a question of emphasis rather than substance. But there was a limit to the common ground. After Bloch had gone on about his view at some length, rather than engage his interlocutor's formulations any further, Adorno simply reiterated his own in stricter form: "Yes, at any rate, utopia is essentially in the determined negation, in the determined negation of that which merely is, and by concretizing itself as something false, it always points at the same time to what should be."[3]

While deeply informed by Bloch's example, here Adorno reminded his audience a bit more plainly that utopia, for him, is resolutely negative. It is thoroughly compromised by objectivity and reason, and can have no positive image, concept, or propositional form. Utopia allows itself to be as false as everything else, but as a resistant falsehood, it can negatively and often nonconceptually point backwards to what might have been—a strange truth conveyed as a kind of "truth content" or *Wahrheitsgehalt*. This is Adorno's way of thinking of a life without domination, a life freed from death.

In his 1960 review of Bloch's essay collection, *Spuren*, Adorno expresses similar reservations over Bloch's open-ended conception of utopia and his inclinations to write about almost any kind of cultural phenomenon (not merely great works of art). Certainly, given how open Adorno was about Bloch's influence on him, the essay is still in many ways admiring of Bloch as an intellectual. But the reservations are there. One of Adorno's lines of critique is that Bloch is too undialectical. He claims that a certain musical oratory of naive and unsystematic philosophy begins to flow on the page that does not allow the reader to adequately understand the relationship between Bloch's "metaphysical intentions" and the "plane of fact." The charge is one of naive immediacy, something Adorno yokes to Bloch's expressionism, a kind of fiery protest against reification of all forms. This he calls "the pseudomorphosis of dialectics," whereby "even though the content owes a great conscious debt to dialectics, the style is essentially undialectical."[4]

In this vein, Adorno also protests at the inclusiveness of Bloch's field of objects and facts: "There is nothing which cannot be regarded as a Blochian trace, and this indiscriminate use of everything comes close to meaning nothing."[5] While always crediting Bloch with a singularity and virtuosity of thought, by the end of the review Adorno has drawn a line in the sand over the steadiness of his dialectical method. For Adorno, the universality Bloch employs—that of utopian ideals—seems to actually subsume its data into a certain greyness. Since Bloch is willing to discern utopia positively (rather than negatively, as Adorno would), his method risks becoming systematic, drowning and subsuming the cultural object, and improperly speaking for traces that ought to be read as "the involuntary, the unobtrusive and the unintended."[6]

As a consequence, Adorno felt that Bloch's dialectics had succumbed to an expressionistic din that lacked a solid negative method of immanent critique. He recognized Bloch's rhetorical powers, but critiqued his method as a sophistry that "chooses the incognito of the blusterer [*wählt das Inkognito des Schwadroneurs*]."[7] By way of a musical point of comparison, Adorno claimed that Bloch was akin to a "saloon-bar pianist who plays wrong bass notes, and who sits there poor, misunderstood, trying to make the marveling onlooker who buys him a beer believe he is Paderewski."[8] More precisely, Adorno suggested that Bloch was in fact an uncanny competitor to this boasting tavern musician, with a voice that was strangely absent and mechanical, of another time, somehow both aged and anticipatory: "[Bloch] vies with the showman from the unforgotten fairground; his voice reverberates like the automatic organ [*ein Orchestrion*] in an empty saloon which is still waiting for people to show up."[9]

In Adorno's view, the naive philosophical barrel organ was rhapsodic and indefatigable. And not without reason: Bloch's conception of *Geist*, as we saw in the last chapter, is of an extraordinary nonlinear connectivity; it is far less beholden to the weight of ideology or the integrity of the isolated and autonomous work. Thoroughly Hegelian but somehow inverted in method, and wildly contrapuntal in its treatment of cultural objects, Adorno nonetheless seemed to lose patience with Bloch's style even as he admired and respected the man's words. As he put it in his review: "Specific analyses are few and far between; it is rather as if the devotees of Hauff's fairy stories had forgathered in a circle around someone from that Oriental corner of Swabia where there is a town called Backnang and an interjection that goes 'Ah-um,' and bit by bit this and that emerges; progressively, of course, with a conceptual movement which keeps mum about Hegel, but knows him backwards."[10]

Even if Adorno did not share Bloch's abiding interest in the innocence of childhood and fairy tales, there was unquestionably an aesthetic axis that the two men shared: a conviction that music, above all the arts, had an exceptional way of allowing one to think, glimpse, or even reveal utopia. And it was music's language-like capacity—not any one musical language, but the fact that it resembled language in its outlines, in its rhythms, and phrases, in the conventions of tonal syntax, and overall in its increasingly sophisticated development—that allowed it to share a goal of philosophy: the mystery of the undetermined, the unthought.

The central argument of this chapter is that what distinguishes Adorno's philosophy of music from Bloch's (and from that of any other writer, for that matter) is the tremendous exactitude he uses to follow through on this suggestion. Like Schopenhauer and Bloch, Adorno does not claim that music is a language. Yet Adorno places an extraordinarily strong emphasis on the way music, in the course of its historical development, acquires language-*like* properties as the conventions of harmonic syntax become standardized for musicians and audiences alike. For Adorno, this Apollonian teleology culminates in the onset of atonality, when the rules of these conventions fracture and musical works become capable of questioning, critiquing, and revealing a utopian truth.

It is there—at the moment of critique and failure of music's language-like capacities—that the paradoxical questions of music's ineffability, and its associated powers to "speak" a perplexing utopian truth to philosophy, come to the fore. This point of contact between Bloch and Adorno—music's ineffability—will be subject to a detailed discussion in section 2.4. At the end of the chapter, in section 2.6, I will discuss Adorno's writings on Mahler in order to show how and why these writings press against the limits of Adorno's commitment to the exactitude of musical form, and yield what I described in the introduction as a "paradox of the vernacular." But my first aim will be to delineate, in precise and comparative terms, both the rise and fall of this "language-like" capacity in ways that are closely attentive to the philosophical commitments of Adorno's method.

2.1 ADORNO'S TONE

Let us begin with the broad outlines of Adorno's definition of music, from its prehistoric origins to its life as a modern work of composition. We might recall that Bloch's account of music's origin was fundamentally sonic. With a speculative gesture that echoed Rousseau, Wackenroder, Adler, and many others before him, Bloch described a series of ruptures and externalizations that stretched from undeveloped song to sophisticated composition—"singing-to-oneself," the magic rattle, and the syrinx, up through developed *Tonkünste* and the event-forms of the nineteenth century. Adorno, by contrast, did not conceive of music's origin as predominantly sonic. Prior to music's mediation by *Geist*, Adorno followed the Greeks in conceiving of the origins of music as woven into an extramusical web of imitative gestures and rhythms. Adorno writes in the draft of his unfinished study of musical performance that music, in its origin, was an imitation of gestures, of rhythms of life:

> Music inherently contains a mimic element. Regardless of what share the imitation of nature's sounds may have had in its origin, it has no doubt always stimulated imitation through gestures, whether those of dance or of work, of its own accord: it "demonstrated" gestures at the level of their magical use in order to elicit, or perhaps regulate, those of people.... Music is the echo of the animistic shudder, the mimicry of the invisible, feared facial expressions of the natural deity, a reflex of appeasement that still lives on in the latest delusions about the therapeutic effect of music....[11]

As discussed in the introduction, in Plato's *Republic* (one of the texts Adorno likely had in mind when writing this passage), the *ethos* doctrine relies upon the concept of mimesis to correlate musical modes with various emotional states and ethical behaviors. In Aristotle's *Politics*, music was likewise understood to be mimetic of various emotions and therapeutic in its uses, particularly for developing the moral character of youth. Moreover, the Greek concept of *mousike* did not isolate music from its social function; the word denoted a broader set of cultural practices that joined music to dance and recited poetry. In each case music was conceived of not as abstract or formal, or as exclusively sonic, but as a multisensory practice that was frequently imitative of the extramusical.[12]

Though he affirmed the multisensory character of music's origin, in the unfinished manuscript on musical performance Adorno also speculates in vivid terms what it would have sounded like for "mimetic impulse [to] ineluctably find their voice" in music prior to any self-conscious mediation by *Geist*: "The first units of musical writing are the rigidly even drumbeats of the barbarians" or "cultic dances and songs withdrawn from the unity of remembering and change."[13] Adorno's stereotyped caricatures of "primitive" music are akin to Bloch's magic rattle—drumbeats, dances, and songs "withdrawn" from all the historical development that Adorno associates with the evolved history of music in the West.

Notably, for Adorno, such "primitive" music would not have existed in an organic or natural state prior to discipline. Prior to mediation by *Geist*, music would still have been based in "units of musical writing" that were themselves disciplinary even if they were not yet rational. With the advent of musical notation, however, a decisive rupture took place. Adorno writes that musical notation was not a simple affordance to one's memory. It reorganized musical time into a dispossessed form of reproduction:

> Musical notation therefore cannot have come about as a mere aide-memoire, as the harmless preservation of an elusive substance. It rather points to precisely the *disturbance* of that organic state in which the memory is at home, and where the distinction between now and before is not firmly established. That means: to power. Musical notation is an element of discipline. It dispossesses the memory by supporting it.[14]

While for Adorno ancient mimesis was originally disciplinary, the history of music (as well as history in general) is also a developmental one where qualitative changes take hold; new technologies have a discernable impact on the kind of discipline that exists in society. In this way, notation changed both the form and the content of music; it liberated music from ritualistic practice into a spatialized image of composition proper.[15]

It is within the context of this teleological historical development that one can discuss the central role of the tone. In modern Europe, Bloch and Adorno both claim that the tone took precedence as an axiomatic unit of musical sound. They both conceive of it as a rational product of the way *Geist* mediated music; the tone was both integral to, and a product of, the systematic pedagogy of counterpoint, the emergence of a common-practice syntax of tonality, and the expanding powers of rationality. Once these systematic qualities of the tone's rationalization were in place, the tone could take up its role as a language-like unit of expression and serve as the foundation for the larger unity of a musical work. From a modern point of view, Adorno writes: "[Music's] resemblance to language [*Sprachänlichkeit*] extends from the whole, the organized linking of significant sounds, right down to the single sound, the tone as the threshold of merest existence, the pure carrier of expression [*dem Ton als der Schwelle zum bloßen Dasein, dem reinen Ausdrucksträger*]."[16]

How might one parse this rich statement? In ordinary German, *Dasein* means "existence."[17] Here, Adorno suggests that musical techniques, and the tone above all, are products of a history that is externalized in all that exists. Hegel's technical meaning of *Dasein*, however, may also be in play here. Hegel used the term to denote a "determinate being"—an elemental and dialectical "being-one [*Einssein*] of being and nothing."[18] In a way that recalls many of Bloch's dialectical interpretations of the tone, the above definition would suggest that the determinate and specific oneness of Adorno's tone might be understood as a unity of the ideal consistency of the tone and its inconsistent, vibrational non-being—a condensed contradiction in dialectical form.

In other ways, however, Adorno's view of the tone has different emphases than Bloch's. If for Bloch the tone's exceptional power came from an aporetic translucence that enabled the flux of sound to be both ordered and embodied, for Adorno the tone's dialectical character was more profoundly circumscribed by various apparatuses and writing systems, its possibilities congealed into an unconscious repository of musical instruments. Thomas Christensen has shown how four-hand piano transcriptions were a key mode of musical reproduction in the era before the phonograph, and in fact carried with them metaphysical biases in their paper, ink, wood, felt, and wires.[19] By allowing symphonies and operas to traffic in living rooms, repeatable, excerpted, slowed down, and otherwise embodied, shorn of their orchestral timbres, the notes on the page could reveal themselves dialectically as the skeletal tones of music.[20] They served as a printed foundation for the dialectical circuitry of sensuous action and cognitive playback.

Adorno recounts the following memory: "As a child, I learned through piano duets the music which we are accustomed to calling classical. There was little from the symphonic and chamber-music literature that was not pressed into service at home with the aid of those oblong volumes uniformly bound in green. They seemed to be made to have their pages turned, and I was allowed to turn them long before I could read the music, just relying on my memory and ears."[21] Far from the gestures of ancient mimesis, these reified media of the nineteenth century held sway over Adorno's recollections; pianos were mirrors of imaginary tones, musical typewriters of extraordinary potentiality. Neatly dividing octaves by twelve, passive and ready for the recollected choices of amateur pianists, this sonic furniture was the gateway to the boundless articulation of tones. The transcriptions were integral to an Apollonian discipline of dots, slurs, trained bodies, and evening soirées that enabled an intimate practice of musical possession.

As it was for pianistic playback in the domestic sphere, so was it for composing. Echoing the logic of anamnesis as established in Plato's *Meno,* in which all knowledge is a form of recollection, for Adorno musical composition was akin to a process of recollection and discovery, based in the very formatting of the piano keys:

> The child trying to pick out a melody on the piano provides the paradigm of all true composition. In the same tentative, uncertain manner, but with a precise memory, the composer looks for what may always have been there and what he must now rediscover on the undiscriminating black and white keys of the keyboard from which he must make his choice.[22]

Tones come into sensory existence from a reservoir of historical combinations at the threshold of the keyboard, a threshold that is neither in the voice nor in the mind alone. It is in the dialectical linkage between the piano as an object (a piece of musical furniture laden with sedimented *Geist*) and the cognitive act of recollection, both structured by domination and discipline. It is something like a deliberately alienated version of Bloch's self-encounter, determined far more powerfully by the structural side of the technical object and its discarded possibilities than by the existential givenness or creative ingenuity of the embodied subject: "The power of an original musical intuition traces figures in the fine dust of discarded opportunities and it is these [figures] which often have to be deciphered if the nature of the composition is to be revealed."[23] In contrast to Bloch's highly spiritualized and aporetic tones, which delicately intertwined the warmth of intoxicating force with the areal quality of pure form, Adorno's tone was an exemplary instance of historical discipline, bound tightly within the dialectical force fields [*Kraftfelder*] of technical mediations. Because Adorno's conception of composition is confronted by the impersonality of fixed choices of "what has already been there," it becomes clear that his searching nostalgia is not an affirmation—it could not be a positive one, and certainly not of Bloch's ingenious composer-subjects—but only a distant, negative, and fading memory. For Adorno, the modern rationalization of material and the mechanization of musical reproduction have taken over and foreclosed positive access to what Bloch heard as music's utopian potentiality.

If the reifying powers of *Geist* were this all-powerful, how might one ethically write music that is capable of resistance? For Adorno, the greatest risk and temptation in the modern age was naive escapism—an ahistorical mimicry of music's primitive, cultic power, one indulged variously by Stravinsky, jazz, Tin Pan Alley, and the like. Adorno describes this music as an ecstatic mimesis of the emotional power of cinema, the flux of sexual excitement, and the powers of the commodity form:

> The ecstasy takes possession of its object by its own compulsive character. It is stylized like the ecstasies savages go into in beating the war-drums. It has convulsive aspects reminiscent of St Vitus's dance or the reflexes of mutilated animals. Passion itself seems to be produced by defects. But the ecstatic ritual betrays itself as pseudo-activity by the moment of mimicry. People do not dance or listen "from sensuality" and sensuality is certainly not satisfied by listening, but the gestures of the sensual are imitated. An analogue is the representation of particular emotions in the film, where there are physiognomic patterns for anxiety, longing, the erotic look; for smiling; for the atomistic expressivo of debased music. The imitative assimilation to commodity models is intertwined with folkloristic customs of imitation. In jazz, the relation of such mimicry to the imitating individual himself is quite loose. Its medium is caricature. Dance and music copy stages of sexual excitement only to make fun of them.[24]

This paragraph is as emblematic as any when it comes to Adorno's withering critiques of pleasure in mass culture, but his reasons are more interesting than the judgment itself. His complaint is that a primitivist recuperation of ancient mimesis is ahistorical and cynically exploited by market interests. It would ignore the self-consciousness of musical form mediated by *Geist*, a direct analogue of the broader historical development of dominance, discipline and rationality. The reification of ancient mimesis into language-like tones in music is now a historical fact; resistance requires that we first recognize it and fracture it from within. A fully dialectical practice of musical resistance must fracture the reified object of disciplined tones, and match this formalist operation with a parallel discipline of structural listening. Both sides—composition and reception—must remain honest in their relationship to history.

Those critical of this kind of formalism in Adorno's thought certainly have no shortage of evidence: music, for him, was far more often described as autonomous and intellectual than as sensual. In a passage that appears two years later in an essay entitled "Music and Technique," Adorno describes notation as a carrier of nonsonorous "intellectual content." The key medium for music's conceptual character, it was based in a "mnemonic" that "[objectivizes] an imagined, spiritual reality":[25] "Musical script [notation] not only constitutes the basis of performance, but is also something independent of performance, just as reading to ourselves something that has been written enables us to objectify an intellectual content regardless of whether it is transmitted to others."[26] Not all that far from a Platonist conception of the musical work one may associate more readily with analytic philosophers such as Peter Kivy and Roger Scruton, the nonsonorous structure expressed by the visual script built on musical notes retains an immaterial element, "something independent of performance" that, like the printed word, allegedly remains fixed and durable regardless of any actualized performance. In his famous 1961 Darmstadt lecture "Vers une musique informelle," Adorno states again that musical notation allows music to belong to another "order" of time, something other than mere empirical succession, a musically immanent time: "As soon as the notation is actualized—that is to say, the piece is played—it merges with empirical time and possesses chronological duration, even while appearing simultaneously to belong to another order of time, namely that of the work which is immortalized, as it were, by being written down."[27]

Adorno's conception of the tone is mediated by notation, the visual and practical medium of elaborate musical combinations. Under the disciplinary condition of a composition lesson, the archaic rupture of spatialization gave music an identity more substantial than capricious improvisation. The powerful objectification of notation allowed music to become mediated by *Geist*, so that it could develop beyond its primitive origins in ancient mimesis. In *Aesthetic Theory,* Adorno writes: "Mimesis in art is the pre-spiritual; [mimesis] is contrary to *Geist* and yet also that on which *Geist* ignites. In artworks, *Geist* has become their principle of construction...."[28] It must be underscored, however, that even as Adorno emphasizes the visual, printed insignia as a "principle of construction" that disciplined the sounds of Western music into well-ordered sequences of tones mediated by *Geist*, his formalism was never undialectical. Adorno was explicitly wary of what he heard to be a bloodless hyperformalism that emerged midcentury with integral serialism, in which the twelve tones become reified to the point of losing any kind of critical power. In "Vers une musique informelle," Adorno criticizes modernist compositional practices for their supposed overreliance on the unit of the tone. In French he remarked, "*Ce n'est pas le ton qui fait la musique*," and insisted that modernism should still retain internally relational, flexible, and phenomenological aspects of musical form.[29] In a parallel to Bloch's dialectical insistence on the embodied usage of music's formal tricks, Adorno claimed that an experiential register was essential for an ethical and resistant form of modern music—or what he termed *musique informelle* (a term he likely borrowed from European Abstract Expressionist painting of the postwar period).[30]

In other instances Adorno similarly maintained that a resistant modernism retains vestiges of collectivist mimesis. Writing about Schoenberg in *Philosophy of New Music* (1949), he echoes Bloch's assertion that "the tone goes with us and is We" when he writes that modernist polyphony is an oblique afterimage of the social character of ancient mimesis:

> ... Music altogether, and especially polyphony—the indispensible medium of new music—arose out of the collective practices of dance and cult is not simply left behind as a mere 'point of departure' through music's development toward freedom. Rather, the historical origin remains palpably implied long after music has broken away from any collective practice. Polyphonic music says 'we' even when it lives uniquely in the imagination of the composer without ever reaching another living person.[31]

Thus, broadly speaking, for Adorno, the Dionysian collectivism of musical experience is never entirely eliminated by the Apollonian development of *Geist*, even as technically advanced compositions sublimated much of this ancient past into the exacting criteria of rules. In fact, hearing a collectivist utopia in a modern composition is only possible because something of this ancient social character remains in all music. This is not an argument made often by Adorno, but it is a significant one when it does arise.[32] And its rarity is part of the point: the *informelle* musical experience, or a suppressed collectivism, could never positively be unearthed; the risk of a false and regressive collectivism was too vivid in Adorno's mind. What remained of this social character in music could only be heard obliquely and negatively.

This leads us to a second, modern type of mimesis that is central to the possibility of utopia. In *Aesthetic Theory*, Adorno expresses the view that resistant music is capable of imitating a "natural beauty" or a "divine name" by way of rationalized, historical material. As an example, he cites Anton Webern's twelve-tone works, which he admired for their resistant form. In his view, Webern transfigured the tone—at once music's "pure vehicle of expression" and its central emblem of discipline and domination—into something that paradoxically resembled a natural *Klang*. Webern did this not by a mimetic shaking of Bloch's magic rattle, or any nostalgic imitation of Hegel's *Erzittern des Körpers*, but by way of a deliberately fragmented version of music's language-like character, one that was built upon a "subjective sensibility" mediated by *Geist* as much as it was marked by the modern fact of reification.

> The pure expression of artworks, freed from every thing-like interference, even from everything so-called natural, converges with nature just as in Webern's most authentic works the pure tone, to which they are reduced by the strength of subjective sensibility, reverses dialectically into a natural *Klang:* that of an eloquent nature, certainly, its language, not the portrayal of a part of nature.[33]

In Webern's atonality we find a "pure expression of artworks," an inescapably modern possibility predicated upon narrow and exacting criteria. Yet in order to speak a utopian truth, "authentic works" had to preserve a new form of mimesis not based in the resemblance of anything concrete (as in "the portrayal of a part of nature"). This modernist "language" or "eloquent nature" is, like Schoenberg's polyphony, an afterimage of the original, ancient mimesis of the arts. In this modern mimesis, the work of art is overdeveloped into a second-order system or "language" of imitation caught in the false circularity of its own abstracted conventions. Amidst the falsehood of its own form, the resistant work internally contains gaps, fissures, and contradictions. Utopia is a dissonant fusion of nature and *Geist*. Its fractured form resembles, negatively, a state of absent nature, a life without death, a truth without violence.

It is by way of this modern mimesis—structured by *Geist*-mediated tones but speaking obliquely against them—that Adorno will redevelop Schopenhauer's paradox of the ineffable from a simple paradox into an elaborate method of immanent critique. For in Adorno's view, it is by speaking a muted, formal, and nonintentional language of the ineffable that one can articulate a desperate failure of representation in sensuous form.[34] In order to better understand how Adorno conceives of modern mimesis as bearing utopian content in a modern composition, we should first get a more detailed understanding of how he inherits Hegelian views of history and society, and transforms them into a unique dialectical method.

2.2 ADORNO'S CONCEPTION OF HISTORY

Like Hegel and Marx before him, Adorno's conception of history is based in a logic of totality.[35] Adorno's notion of totality is (a) thoroughly social and (b) committed to a teleological principle of universality. But Adorno rejects the standard Hegelian accounts that end in an emancipated, self-conscious human subject, as well as the Marxist variant that ends in the self-aware collectivity of a proletariat. In Adorno's view, both these subjects of universal history have failed to actualize themselves: the proletariat never revolted, and Hegel's self-conscious bourgeois subject ushered in a new realm of economic exploitation, objectification, and alienation as a result of industrial capitalism. Adorno concludes that despite these failures, there still is a universal history; but it is now one of violent domination over humanity and the natural world alike.

In *The Dialectic of Enlightenment* (1944), Adorno claims (with Max Horkheimer) that "myth is already enlightenment, and enlightenment reverts to mythology"—by which the authors mean that the logic of domination is already at work in the rituals of the pre-scientific world, just as our modern selves maintain an unwavering mythological fidelity to the powers of reason.[36] Under this schema, the progress of history does little more than increase our power of domination and the means for control. Equally famous is a passage from *Minima Moralia* (1951) that flips Hegel's formula celebrating the triumph of Reason from *The Phenomenology of Spirit* (1807)—"The true is the whole"—and makes it into its catastrophic opposite: "The whole is the false."[37] In *Negative Dialectics* (1966), his philosophical crowning achievement, Adorno links Enlightenment knowledge with the powers of technology, tools with weapons, and ideas with control, and writes: "No universal history leads from savagery to humanitarianism, but there is one leading from the slingshot to the megaton bomb."[38]

As a result, out of the immanent flows of history, neither self-consciousness nor a collective meta-subject of history ever reveals itself. Subjects in the existent world are contaminated with the irreversible momentum of a rationalized reason that has dominated consciousness with unreflective mechanics (and a sense of moral guilt—a damaged "life that does not live"). We still have subjects in the existing world, but from the viewpoint of what Adorno calls "transcendent critique," it is the intellectual's task to expose the ideological character of modern life and show that the subject's capacity to act is reified and lifeless. Adorno's resultant question: If this is the situation of society and existing subjects, what do we do about it?[39]

Adorno's ethics asks us to find a way to try and overcome the systematic administration of existence in order to experience something other than lifeless domination. This task is dialectical, and Adorno calls it "immanent critique." Through an immanent critique one critically and ethically engages with a particularity—an artwork or a philosophical reflection, both of which are as much a product of history as we are—to disclose a utopian negation of all that exists. Such an operation might momentarily sunder the world's existing law of identity and exchange value ("The whole is the false") into a principled refusal that speaks the language of the nonidentical. If it is successfully resistant, it reveals something Adorno calls *Wahrheitsgehalt*, or a utopian truth-content, resistant to the falsehood of the social whole. Exemplary in this regard would be an artwork that fragments and disrupts a language of intentions and concepts, both of which Adorno takes to be complicit with the violence of domination. In the following passage from *Aesthetic Theory*, Adorno gives utopian truth-content the name "divine creation." It is akin to the aforementioned ability to think of life without the telos of death, without the dominating consciousness of intentions.

> The total subjective elaboration of art as a non-conceptual language [formalism] is the only figure, at the contemporary stage of rationality, in which something like the language of divine creation is reflected, qualified by the paradox that what is reflected is blocked. Art attempts to imitate an expression that would not be interpolated human intention.[40]

The utopian disclosure of the nonidentical is based in the aforementioned possibility of modern mimesis. Modern mimesis allows a work of art to "imitate an expression that would not be interpolated human intention." The modern Apollonian conceptualization of the materials of art is a prerequisite for discerning utopian meaning in a particular object. Once an artwork is formalized, it can attempt to "imitate," and thus fracture, the nonintentional character of reified life. Of course, "what is reflected is blocked"—the mimesis is negative. In Adorno's hands, Schopenhauer's paradox of the ineffable is thus made to speak as a contradictory dialectic: one only discloses utopia by blocking positive access.

Discerning utopia in modern art can transform the perplexity of the ineffable into a dialectical productivity, but for Adorno, getting it right requires a precise balance of operations.[41] In his 1949 essay "Cultural Criticism and Society," Adorno explores the general nature of this balance by distinguishing between "transcendent critique"—a bird's eye critique of all that exists—and "immanent critique"—a critical engagement with the terms of a particular artwork or situation. He describes their dialectical entwinement:

> The alternatives—either calling culture as a whole into question from outside under the general notion of ideology [transcendent critique], or confronting it with the norms which it itself has crystallized [immanent critique]—cannot be accepted by critical theory. To insist on the choice between immanence and transcendence is to revert to the traditional logic

criticized in Hegel's polemic against Kant. As Hegel argued, every method which sets limits and restricts itself to the limits of its object thereby goes beyond them.[42]

A transcendent critique may initially appear to be the more radical of the two: from an intellectual perch, one can critique the falsehood and injustice of all that exists. But Adorno emphasizes that the position one espouses in transcendent critique cannot be a pure one, in which the speculative work of the intellect can do away with the intransigent nature of particularities, with its complicity in the violence of reason.[43] In fact, for Adorno the very idea of an autonomous intellect is a symptom of a social condition:[44]

> The position transcending culture is in a certain sense presupposed by dialectics as the consciousness which does succumb in advance to the fetishization of the intellectual sphere.[45]

A transcendent critique partnered with immanent critique, by contrast, explicitly acknowledges the social basis of the powers of reason. Such a dialectical linkage enables one to un-circuit the reified autonomy of the mind, even if only negatively or momentarily, by mooring the transcendence of ideology critique to sociohistorically situated works of art. And in so doing, it discloses an inconsumable play of "consistency or inconsistency" that can disrupt "the structure of the existent" by showing us not simply *that* ideology exists in general, but *how*, in particular cases, ideology projects particular falsehoods:

> Against this struggles the immanent procedure as the more essentially dialectical. It takes seriously the principle that it is not ideology in itself which is untrue but rather its pretention to correspond to reality. Immanent criticism of intellectual and artistic phenomena seeks to grasp, through the analysis of their form and meaning, the contradiction between their objective idea and that pretention. It names what the consistency or inconsistency of the work itself expresses of the structure of the existent....[46]

Both immanent and transcendent critique are enabled by the normative powers of reason, but it is the particular mimetic apparition (or "pretention") of the work of art, due to its lack of objective generality, that harbors the dissonant elements that are best equipped to disrupt the closure of the whole. Both operations of the dialectic are required, however. If Adorno's method only involved immanent critique, his method would risk short-circuiting the governing power of ideas in favor of an aestheticized singularity or difference, a fetishizing of sensuous particularity, even a romantic cult of art worship. And Adorno is mindful of this risk: just as one cannot assume an intellectual position of transcendent critique outside history, neither can one analyze a particular artwork without the ideological weight of the social totality in mind: "Dialectics must guard against this [abstract intellectualism] no less than against enthrallment in the cultural object. It can subscribe neither to the cult of the mind nor to hatred of it."[47] Both poles of Adorno's method—transcendent and immanent—must be kept afloat for his dialectic to maintain its structure.[48] For, as he says: "Dialectics means intransigence towards all reification."[49]

2.3 TENDENZ DES MATERIALS

In this way, an immanent critique of what is ideologically reified in musical composition requires more than emancipatory appeals to the powers of music; it requires an equally precise conception of ideology in the domain of music. One has to acknowledge that the telos of domination is real. This is the function of what Adorno calls the *Tendenz des Materials*, or the tendency of the musical material. Like Schoenberg, Adorno insists that "music knows no natural law," and like Bloch, he claims that "only through its historical characteristics does music acquire its relation to the unattainable."[50] Yet far more narrowly than either, Adorno conceives of musical material as a precise history of compositional techniques.[51] His *Tendenz des Materials* is all-encompassing: it entails the increased rationality of pedagogy and the rules of form, the congealed repositories of living room pianos and piles of sheet music, and even the reification of our emotional responses.

And his famously narrow rules for the production of a utopian work were not merely contingent preferences of a mandarin German intellectual in exile. As I will try to show here, their narrowness is a symptom of Adorno's method. His conception of transcendent critique, like its musical variant, the *Tendenz des Materials*, is based in an idealized practice of Apollonian recollection, one that leaves itself flexible enough to make exacting choices about musical form.

Consider, from a comparative point of view, what Adorno meant by the term "historical" within the realm of music. What distinguishes a recollected version of Adorno's *Tendenz des Materials* from a typical historical account of music in the field of musicology? A recollected history of music is not narrated in great detail; it is not based in the subtleties of cultural history beyond a schematic claim that all history has a social foundation. The *Tendenz des Materials* is characteristically recalled in a singular, cognitive act so that it may be put to dialectical use. It is grounded in facts, but it is assembled and recalled at a remove from the actions of individuals, at a distinctly immaterial level of abstraction. It is fueled by the powers of speculative thinking, which, aligned with the economy of Adorno's shorthand, give the philosopher a range of flexibility in formulating dialectical links.

Adorno's "paradigm of all true composition" is dependent upon the same speculative gesture that the *Tendenz des Materials* requires: that of recollection. Here, in an echo of the child's discovery of possible melodies at the threshold of the piano's tones, composition requires a transcendent critique in the domain of musical material. Through the circuit of an idealist gesture, it relies upon a Platonism that recalls something already there in the mind. As he explains in *Aesthetic Theory*: "The object of art's longing, the reality of what is not, is metamorphosed in art as remembrance. In remembrance, what is *qua* what was combines with the non-existing because what was no longer is. Ever since Plato's doctrine of anamnesis the not-yet-existing has been dreamed of in remembrance, which alone concretizes utopia without betraying it to existence."[52] It is something like a narrower and more elaborate vision of Bloch's utopian "not-yet-conscious." For Adorno, a utopian meaning ("the reality of what is not") can be revealed in a work of art if the object—as well as one's immanent critique of it—are together routed through an exacting recollection (a transcendent critique, or *anamnesis*) of the false and ideological character of history: "what is *qua* what was."

In nineteenth-century German musical thought and the other nascent disciplines of the *Geisteswissenschaften*, there were certainly precedents for such an idealized conception of music history. Franz Brendel, the great defender of Wagner and Liszt's avant-garde New German School is typically credited with having imported the Hegelian model of an evolutionary history into the realm of musical style in his 1852 compendium *Geschichte der Musik in Italien, Deutschland und Frankreich*.[53] In a parallel vein in the field of art history, Heinrich Wölfflin and Alois Riegl codified the loose speculative conception of a history of art into one with a relative autonomy of formal development that was in some sense independent of the social and cultural networks that supported it.[54]

Unique to Adorno's idealized conception of music history, however, is an economy and flexibility that he wielded in the name of an interpretive praxis. Let us consider an example. In a 1932 essay entitled "Some Ideas on the Sociology of Music," Adorno mentions Max Weber's *The Rational and Social Foundations of Music* (1921) and then immediately proceeds to recount a few important highlights of the *Tendenz des Materials*: "There can be no doubt that the history of music exhibits a progressive process of rationalization. Its different stages are the Guidonian reforms, the introduction of mensural notation, the invention of continuo and of equal temperament, and finally the trend to integral musical construction, which has advanced irresistibly since the time of Bach and has now reached an extreme."[55] If this is intended as a summary of Weber's *Grundlagen*, readers of the 1921 essay will quickly realize that is not exactly representative of his text as a whole.[56] The narrative Adorno recounts in the quotation above echoes key elements of Weber's book, in particular passages in the second half that describe several technical innovations in the history of Western art music. But Adorno passes over much of the book's first half, which covers Weber's research in the field of comparative musicology (*Vergleichende Musikwissenschaft*) and describes the ways different world cultures deal with structural imperfections in the codification of musical scales, namely the Pythagorean comma.

Adorno's selectivity here is not merely symptomatic of his Eurocentrism—though it is that, to be sure—it is also symptomatic of the method and form of the teleology. If the *Tendenz des Materials* were detailed, comparative, and multilinear, it would risk complications that might loosen the coherence of his transcendent critique, which is perforce a brief but impactful conception. In the quotation above, Adorno links four exemplars in a single sentence, and subdivides them with the metaphorical name *Stufen*, or "stages":

1. Guido of Arezzo's eleventh-century linear staff notation, which constituted a reliable method of fixing pitch (alongside the solmization of the hexachord, and its associated pedagogy),
2. the mensural notation developed towards the end of the thirteenth century, which refined and regularized the notation of complex rhythms,
3. the harmonic shorthand of figured bass and the early uses of equal temperament in the late sixteenth century, and
4. the modern rationalization of the compositional process from J. S. Bach's early eighteenth-century music up through the systematic procedures developed by twentieth-century integral serialists.

Adorno, who studied composition extensively with Alban Berg, as we know, had considerable musical expertise. A speculative conception of these key technical inventions in the history of Western art music would have been fairly easy for him to cobble together from memory—particularly in shorthand. And that was the point: to recall it, in fairly general form, all at once. While, for Adorno, the actual workings of music history did not unfold in a way that was entirely linear or uniform, recalling this history as a dialectical gesture was nonetheless akin to what Leslie Blasius has called "the idealist historicization of music theory."⁵⁷ It linked together key moments in the history of music for the purposes of rhetorical persuasion and dialectical movement.

It is also instructive to note that, given the ubiquity of book-length music histories at the time, we need not assume that Adorno only had Weber by his side when recalling these key historical turning points. A parallel account of the *Tendenz* appears in Paul Bekker's *Musikgeschichte: Als Geschichte der musikalischen Formwandlungen* (1926). In fact, Bekker's book contains a striking passage in which the Guidonian hand and mensural notation are described together as key precedents for vocal polyphony and modern musical notation:

> The new polyphonic singing, as we have seen, required that the pitch and the duration of tones should be fixed in the notation. Guido's method offered the proper basis for fixing the pitch. But to express duration a new method was to be gradually worked out. The characters were now given a common form, to which special signs were added indicating the duration of each tone in relation to the rest. A system of comparative fractions was thus introduced into notation; tones were measured by their relative duration. Hence we now speak of a mensural or measured music. Music develops its own rhythm, independent of the language meter and divisible into mathematical relations, which are expressed in the notation. These achievements in defining pitch and duration are still apparent in the musical notation of today.⁵⁸

Bekker's *Musikgeschichte* was written with a broad audience of nonspecialists in mind, which partly accounts for what twenty-first century readers are likely to sense as an overtone of Whiggish presentism. But, in fact, presentism is key to the structure of the idealized teleology. In Adorno's *Tendenz des Materials*, the value of a recollected history lies in its relevance for what currently exists. Structured by a transcendent critique, the current state of musical material, as well as our experience of it, is taken as a product of an Apollonian telos of increasing rationality and formalization.

This developmental teleology was not merely focused on the precision of modern notation and rationality; Adorno explicitly prioritized the idea of music's autonomy by hypostasizing the influential work of figures like Hanslick and Schenker as well. If the two were not always mentioned by name, their ideas were assumed to be axiomatic for the *Tendenz des Materials* and undergirded the unity of its recollected shape. He describes the process in *The Philosophy of New Music*: "Traditional music became 'autonomous' as its tasks and techniques separated from their basis in society."[59] Methodologically, this sentence belies quite a delicate point, presaged in Bloch's conception of the tone but made clearer and more consequential by Adorno: Autonomy is not an a priori ontological characteristic of music; it is dialectically only made manifest in music because of certain practical and technical breakthroughs in its known history.

Like its twin, universal history, the speculative conception of an autonomous *Tendenz des Materials* is based in the operation of transcendent critique: outside the empirical world, a provisional intellectual perch lets us name and critique musical development and reification in different ways, with slightly different exemplars. The conception can be thought of as above or outside the realm of what exists because, remaining transcendent, the freedom to isolate and recall the content of an ideology is not entirely subsumed by the powers of the ideology itself.[60] Its claim on all that musically exists is successful if existing musical practices can be heard as congealed versions of this history. Should the conception hold, the *Tendenz des Materials* can serve as the steady ground for an immanent critique of a resistant musical object.

We will thus not be surprised to find that the fullest description of the *Tendenz des Materials* emerges in Adorno's celebrated writings on a composer who shared exactly this deep interest in the entwinement of historicism, formalism, and praxis: Arnold Schoenberg. So essential was the composer's influence on Adorno that we could venture that it is impossible to understand his thinking without Schoenberg (his music as well as his theory were clearly as significant an influence on Adorno as Wagner and Bruckner were for the young Ernst Bloch). In fact, Schoenberg felt the historical and practical weight of the musical material as intensely as Adorno had, writing in the *Harmonielehre* that his textbook was a study not in eternal or natural rules, but in practical conventions. In his commentary on the composer in *The Philosophy of New Music*, Adorno extends this idea by explaining that musical materials are neither natural in their resonant properties nor psychologically normative in their effects, but historical in their value and meaning.

By historical, Adorno means that generations of rule-based compositions have codified conventional and expressive attributes of tonality into a set of clichés (only intensified by the twentieth-century culture industry). This was the necessary cost of music's development toward autonomy. As he put it in an essay written in 1953: "Music, by dint of its disposition over the natural material, is transformed into a more or less stable system, whose individual moments have a meaning that is at once independent of and open to the subject."[61] Tonal conventions available to the expressive aims of a subject became reified, dialectically, by virtue of their independently repeatable objectivity. The syntax of tonic, predominant, dominant, tonic, for example, became wired into millions of listening bodies. As a consequence, the effects lost their luster, which in turn transformed the options available to composers. Now, one must deal with the fact that "not everything is possible in every age."[62]

Many of these intellectual gestures in Adorno are also there in Bloch's philosophy of music, in a somewhat less teleological form: (1) music as an exceptional vehicle for utopia; (2) a historical conception of musical material; and, as we shall soon see, (3) its ethical exemplification by an array of compositions that resist reification. Comparatively speaking, as I will argue in the remainder of this chapter, what distinguishes Adorno's view of music is neither the conception of utopia nor the ideological impact of rationalization that limited what was musically possible, but the rigor of his dialectical method. Adorno's narrow and exacting vision of the broken rules of form is best understood not simply as an empirical preference for fractured modernism over expressive Romanticism, but as a symptom of the method's axiomatic adoption of transcendent critique.

2.4 MUSIC'S LANGUAGE-LIKE INEFFABILITY

Having established the building blocks of Adorno's method, let us focus closely on Adorno's elaborate treatment of music's ineffability. Here, many themes in Schopenhauer's paradox and Bloch's writings on the tone will return, but in highly aporetic, formalized, and negative terms.

If the *Tendenz des Materials* denotes the cognitive gesture of Adorno's teleological conception of musical material in the modern age, the teleology's exact content is a language-like trajectory. In his important 1956 essay "Music, Language, Composition," Adorno revives the ancient concept of mimesis once again in the context of modernist aesthetics. There, he zooms up on the modern moment of the *Tendenz* and discusses the way music and language have come to formally resemble one another amid their shared status of advanced development:

> Music resembles language [*Sprachähnlich ist sie*] in the sense that it is a temporal sequence of articulated sounds [*Laute*] which are more than just sounds [*Laut*]. They [the sounds] say something, often something human. The better the music, the more forcefully they say it. The succession of sounds [*Laute*] is related to logic: there is right and wrong. But what is said—that does not allow itself to be detached from the music. It does not form a system of signs.[63]

In a relatively condensed form, here we have Adorno's dialectical account of Schopenhauer's paradox of the ineffable. In Adorno's view, music shares three properties with spoken language: (1) a basis in temporally sequenced sounds; (2) rhythms, accents, syntax, phrases, idioms, sentences, structures, and rules that develop historically; and (3) the ability to say something exceptional, humane, or critical. Note that all three aspects of music's turn towards language are integral to the developmental progression of music towards formal autonomy.

As it develops into an increasingly formalized art mediated by *Geist*, music undergoes a *Versprachlichung*—a turn towards language. In Schopenhauer's terms, one might say that the Apollonian "copy" of the immediate copy is consistently subject to language-like reification. The Dionysian gestures and ecstasies of ancient music, in all their mimetic physicality, have become compositionally expressive, conventional, normative, and concept-like.[64] Over centuries in Western Europe, chord progressions gradually turn into "generated vocables" and harmonic paradigms and cadences become "recurring symbols, insignia that bear the stamp of tonality."[65] As exemplified by the early seventeenth-century *seconda practica* in Italy, or later trends such as the eighteenth-century *Affektenlehre*, the particular impact of chords and other musical elements approximated the impact of words and concepts that might be correlated to a field of subjective emotions and intentions. In the process, individual chords acquire a syntactical sense of particularity that can link them to general contexts.

A textbook music theory example is apt in this regard. Consider one from Schoenberg's *Harmonielehre* (1911). In a section of chapter 4 that discusses short phrases of diatonic triads in the major mode, Schoenberg offers a few simple progressions in three different spacings in order to show how one can move from the tonic outward and back again while maintaining both common tones and smooth voice leading. In example 2.1, measure A is in open position (chorale spacing). Measure B is in close position—keyboard style. The final measure has the upper two voices clustered together. The fact that they are in a textbook is a perfect, in fact self-verifying demonstration that they are likely worn out as paradigms (or are referential of general types).

To our ears, these chords may sound weary and empty, but not without traces of Dionysian immediacy—color, a glimmer of elegance, even seductive shadings. Indeed, Adorno would have heard them with a certain strangeness. The chords are ancient mimetic passions congealed into modern clichés; the physicality of the gestures they disciplined appear only in ghosted outline. They now stand on the page of a textbook as emblems of the highest and most

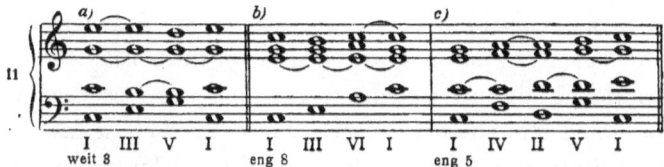

EXAMPLE 2.1. Arnold Schoenberg, "Harmonielehre," 53. Source: Arnold Schoenberg, *Harmonielehre* (Vienna: Universal Edition, 1922).

disciplined of music's literate practice; their rationalization over time led to their aesthetic and spiritual reification, as they were, in the hands of so many listeners, eventually "sedimented like a second nature."[66] For Adorno, since chords, like concepts, are emblems of domination, harmonic paradigms are akin to musical "lexical items," "universal ciphers," and "congealed formulae," without signifieds that "provided space for musical specificity just as concepts do for a particular reality" when plugged into various musical contexts. This is not mere rationalization of material, but an ideological codification of music's Dionysian power into Apollonian grammars of sense.

With these thirteen chords at Adorno's fingertips, one can finally confront the question of musical meaning and the ineffable. If asked to address utopia concretely, Schoenberg's textbook progressions, language-like as they are, curiously stammer. For music has no signs. This is true for Adorno no matter the kind of music: a magic rattle, Bach, Schoenberg, or the jitterbug. What all of it says is *abgründig*—cryptic, vague, ambiguous, an abyss. If language gives relatively precise definition to concepts and intentions for the purposes of communication, music (in line with the muscular translucence of Bloch's tone) gives definition only to physical and emotional gestures. Thus, among all the arts, Adorno hears music as a dialectical riddle, quietly redolent of Schopenhauer's paradox. Music speaks; it has a way of sounding a bit like a language, but the result is resonant and acrobatic, not semantic, and thus it cannot indicate anything precise.

Adorno does not understand this ambiguity of meaning as a weakness; rather, he claims it is a virtue. In speaking to us as a sense-laden appearance that is "at once distinct and concealed [*bestimmt zugleich und verborgen*]," music tries to name the name itself; it attempts to articulate what cannot be articulated.[67] Or it behaves subjunctively "as if it were in fact the name immediately."[68] In this way, its meaning is ephemeral and nonspecific; intentions "appear only intermittently."[69] Or, in another aqueous metaphor, "intentions stream into it" willy-nilly because of its imprecision.[70] Or it plays kaleidoscopic games as it "refracts its scattered intentions away from their own power and brings them together in the configuration of a Name [*Musik bricht ihre versprengten Intentionen aus deren eigener Kraft und läßt sie zusammentreten zur Konfiguration des Namens.*]."[71] Or it absorbs meaning "through a connectedness that preserves meaning even as it moves beyond that meaning with every motion [*durch einen Zusammenhang, der erst die Bedeutung errettet, über die er in jeder einzelnen Bewegung hinwegträgt*]."[72] It is not clear what music does with intentions, but they are there. And it seems to be saying something, we just don't know what.

Adorno's points here have an important precedent in Walter Benjamin's thinking. In his seminal 1916 essay "On Language as Such and on the Language of Man," Benjamin sketches an early version of the linguistic turn when he writes that "every expression of human mental life can be understood as a kind of language."[73] For Benjamin, every medium is language-like, as are all our mental contents and communications—everything. He says: "We cannot imagine a total absence of language in anything."[74] In the ordinary world, of course, we are stuck with a vast multiplicity of languages. Benjamin posits that beyond this multiplicity there is "one blessed paradisiacal language of names"—"proper names" that are coextensive with things-in-themselves.[75] As he says: "All higher language is a translation of lower ones."[76] The higher language is a divine language; one akin to the word of God, an indication that is coextensive with its object. That is, the word of God is the faculty of indication itself, as a real totality encompassing the eternity of creaturely communications: "the unity of this movement made up of language."[77] The proper name, which is unique to its object, exemplifies the "unity of this movement" of mental contents, and for Benjamin: "things have no proper names except in God."[78]

In Benjamin's writings, the language-like medium of music has no privileged role in furnishing access to anything outside of the epistemological constraints of language. But Adorno thinks otherwise. Like Schopenhauer, Nietzsche, and Bloch, Adorno endorses music's exceptionalism—despite his notoriously exacting criteria for resistance—and claims that music, by virtue of something not all that unlike Bloch's metaphysical logos of the tone, copies the immediate, names the unnameable. As Adorno says dialectically, therein lies a parallax: "Music distances itself from language by absorbing its peculiar strength."[79] By this he means that music leaves behind semantic indication when it becomes autonomous—as absolute music—just as it acquires, dialectically, the ability to speak the thing-in-itself or name the unnameable. Autonomous music speaks a utopian meaning ("That is how it is [*Das ist so*]") because it does not have to define the word "*das* [that]" in any particular positive way, but can define it negatively, ambiguously, through disrupted formal circuitry. Music's modern mimesis remains in the barest outlines of language—the adverb *so* indicates an unspecified similitude (*Das ist so*).[80] In Benjaminian fashion, music tends toward "the absolute unity of thing [*Sache*] and sign" only to reveal a resistant "demythologized prayer" that negatively indicates the shape of a utopian "language of divine creation."[81]

Music's ability to "name the name itself" is not based in a fullness, presence, or a coextension of sensation (as it will be for Deleuze and Guattari). For Adorno, at the moment of music's Dionysian immediacy, there is a copy—a refusal, a swindle. Apollonian mediation is always there as a refusal of representation: "[Music's] relation to the thing that it cannot represent but would like to invoke is therefore endlessly mediated."[82] When sound hits us, we are confronted by codes, patterns, ideologies, and histories. There is no fullness of sensation; there is always something dead and empty that leaves us gesturing towards the ceiling like a fool: "The name appears in music only as pure sound [*reiner Laut*], divorced from its bearer, and hence the opposite of every act of meaning [*Bedeutungs*], every intention toward sense [*Sinn*]."[83] To this extent, "music provides the prototype of untranslatability."[84]

This is Adorno's theory of the ineffable. He recognizes more powerfully than Schopenhauer, Nietzsche, or Bloch did that we cannot stare the meaning of utopia in the face. The form of ideology says otherwise; access to the ineffable is barred by the ideological weight of transcendent critique, which ensures we can never commune with the realness of the Dionysian void: "Music gazes at its listener with empty eyes, and the more deeply one immerses oneself in it, the more incomprehensible its ultimate purpose becomes. . . ."[85] Thus, notwithstanding any deep immersion in its sensory impact, as a blank formalism, a language in outline alone, music is perplexing and incomprehensible. It is instructive to note that Bloch, like Adorno, recognized music's developmental tendency towards the abstraction of a language-like form. For Bloch, however, this language-like development remained a latent horizon for the future, not a concrete actuality. As Bloch put it: "Now still a fervent stammering, music, with an increasingly expressive determinacy, will one day possess its own language: it aims at the word which alone can save us, which in every lived moment trembles obscurely as the *Omnia ubique* [everything everywhere]: music and philosophy in their final instance intend purely toward the articulation of this fundamental mystery, of this first and last question in everything."[86]

For Bloch, music would eventually—given enough time—become language-like. In his view, music's *Versprachlichung* is a horizon of possible expression, still deferred. For Adorno, by contrast, the congealed physicality of music has already been reified in the language-like conventions of tonality. And by claiming that music had already passed through the formal development of linguistic convention, Adorno can thus make a parallel claim that resistant music would break with it—negatively.[87]

An illuminating explanation of Adorno's understanding of the language-like character of tonal harmony appears in a short essay called "On Punctuation." There, Adorno discusses the way music and language, in a state of advanced development mediated by *Geist*, began to resemble one another. The embodied flux of linguistic sentences and phrases had musical parallels: the punctuation marks of sentences were analogues to tonal cadences:

> There is no element in which language resembles music more than in the punctuation marks. The comma and the period correspond to the half-cadence and the authentic cadence. Exclamation points are punctuation marks like silent cymbal clashes, question marks like musical upbeats, colons dominant seventh chords; and only a person who can perceive the different weights of strong and weak phrasings in musical form can really feel the distinction between the comma and the semicolon.[88]

Harmony and percussion punctuate the flow of musical information into language-like phrases which can be combined according to conventions. In this passage, which echoes the question at the opening of this section, we might discern another instance of modern mimesis in Adorno's writings. This one seems to be an internal product of *Geist*, based in a comparative set of resemblances drawn among the various formalisms of the modern arts. That is, since each of the arts has become increasingly formalized and autonomous in the modern age, they are all increasingly capable of imitating one another *as forms* (as opposed to imitating events, gestures, and emotions drawn from outside the realm of art). Thus, in the twentieth century, comparative linkages abound across the arts: Kandinsky's abstraction imitates Wagner's *Lohengrin*, Schoenberg's music imitates the workings of language with its themes and sentences, the poems of Mallarmé and T. S. Eliot aspire to musical form, and so on.

In this instance of modern mimesis, forms of music and forms of language cross-pollinate, spawning utopian mimeses in both. On the one hand, modern music becomes fractured and syncopated by the linguistic punctuation that, ironically, helped it circumvent its own norms. On the other hand, poetic language becomes resistant by eliminating conventional punctuation and becoming more musical:

> . . . it can hardly be considered an accident that music's contact with the punctuation marks in language was bound up with the schema of tonality,

which has since disintegrated, and that the efforts of modern music could easily be described as an attempt to create musical punctuation marks without tonality. But if music is forced to preserve the image of its resemblance to language in conventional punctuation marks, then language may give in to its resemblance to music by distrusting punctuation marks."[89]

For Adorno, modern music that fights the reification of normativity is not mere *Klang*—which Hegel had explained was a subjectless property of colliding objects. Circuited through disciplined tones, harmonic exercises, and Apollonian recollections of compositional methods, resistant compositions are, rather, *Klangfiguren*, an articulated temporal sequence of sounds based in the teleology of the *Tendenz* but fragmented into a negative object. Resistant composition requires the punctuation of tonality speaking back in a way that breaks it apart. Amidst this breakage, the many surface resemblances between music and language enable a utopian practice of modern mimesis that reestablishes an artwork's relationship to society only by negating it. After all, music is now formalized, modern, and purportedly asocial; modern mimesis returns it to social life, but in fractured form.

As Adorno put it in 1957: "If in fact music, in Schoenberg's remark, says something that can only be said through music, then it assumes, as a result, a quality that is at once unfathomable [*abgründiges*] and emphatically contingent."[90] For Adorno, Schoenberg's commitment to autonomy was "emphatically contingent" because, like Hanslick, Adler, and Schenker before him, he supported the timeless banner of musical autonomy in one form or another, while remaining situated as actors in contingent moments of the nineteenth and twentieth centuries. And it was the contingency of their situation that gave social meaning to their claim to autonomy. That is, music was still relevant to society even if it claimed only to be a language-like abstraction; and in fact, its very abstraction is what made it so apt for a society that had become profoundly alienated from itself.

Getting it right was never easy. In *The Philosophy of New Music*, when Adorno is in the midst of outlining criteria for Schoenberg's fragmentation of the formalized language of tonality, he singles out a dissonant cliché for failing to meet the criteria of genuine fragmentation: the diminished seventh chord, which he heard as saturated with the sound of ideology: "Even the more insensitive ear detects the shabbiness and exhaustion of the diminished seventh chord and certain chromatic modulatory tones in the salon music of the nineteenth century."[91] This is likely a shorthand description of Schoenberg's description of the same chord in the *Harmonielehre* (1911):

Wherever one wanted to express pain, excitement, anger, or some other strong feeling—there we find, almost exclusively, the diminished seventh chord. So it is in the music of Bach, Haydn, Mozart, Beethoven, Weber, etc. Even in Wagner's early works it plays the same role. But soon the role was played out. This uncommon, restless, undependable guest, here today, gone tomorrow, settled down, became a citizen, was retired a philistine. The chord had lost the appeal of novelty, hence, it had lost its sharpness, but also its luster. It had nothing more to say to a new era.[92]

At the coda of Beethoven's Sonata op. 27, no. 2, certainly his most famous, an emotional and passionate subject is gasping at the limits of his own expressive domain. These measures (example 2.2) occur in a culminating moment of movement three. The structure of the sonata as a whole is highly idiosyncratic, ramping up tension from the famous adagio sostenuto, to the spritely scherzo and trio, and finally to a ravishing and furious presto agitato in sonata form with four different themes and a very compact development. In what initially would appear to be a final statement of the first theme following the recapitulation, the bass line descends beneath rising arpeggios on a iv^6 harmony followed by a i $^6_4$ which then falls with incredible dramatic force on $\#\hat{4}$ F_x. From here, the keyboard crashes upward in six diminished seventh chord rolls, which are notated out. Beethoven then repeats the six pulses of fully diminished seventh chords a half step lower, ratcheting up the tension further and setting the stage for an overwhelming (and even schizophrenic) coda that conveys an ambiguous fury stuck between crisis and defeat.

The implication is that in 1803 this gesture would have brought down the house at public concerts in Vienna. Diminished seventh chords divide the octave symmetrically and contain nested tritones that can pivot between distant key areas; in the nineteenth century they only became more popular as ways of destabilizing the security of a tonal center. It is akin to a nineteenth-century tone cluster, a Dionysian drumbeat grimacing at the weight of the *Tendenz des Materials*, that punctuates a climax within the dramatic Apollonian orders of a sonata-allegro form. But Adorno might challenge us to hear these chords as empty shadows of their former selves, clouded by stacks of audiocassettes, piano recitals with drifting attention from audiences, and habituated terror in horror film soundtracks.

In 2002, Charles Rosen, by way of a citation of Proust, described the Beethoven sonatas as the "steak and potatoes" of art music.[93] For him, they brought the loftiest accomplishments of humanity into the miniaturization of the domestic sphere. One could easily surmise the ambivalence Adorno would

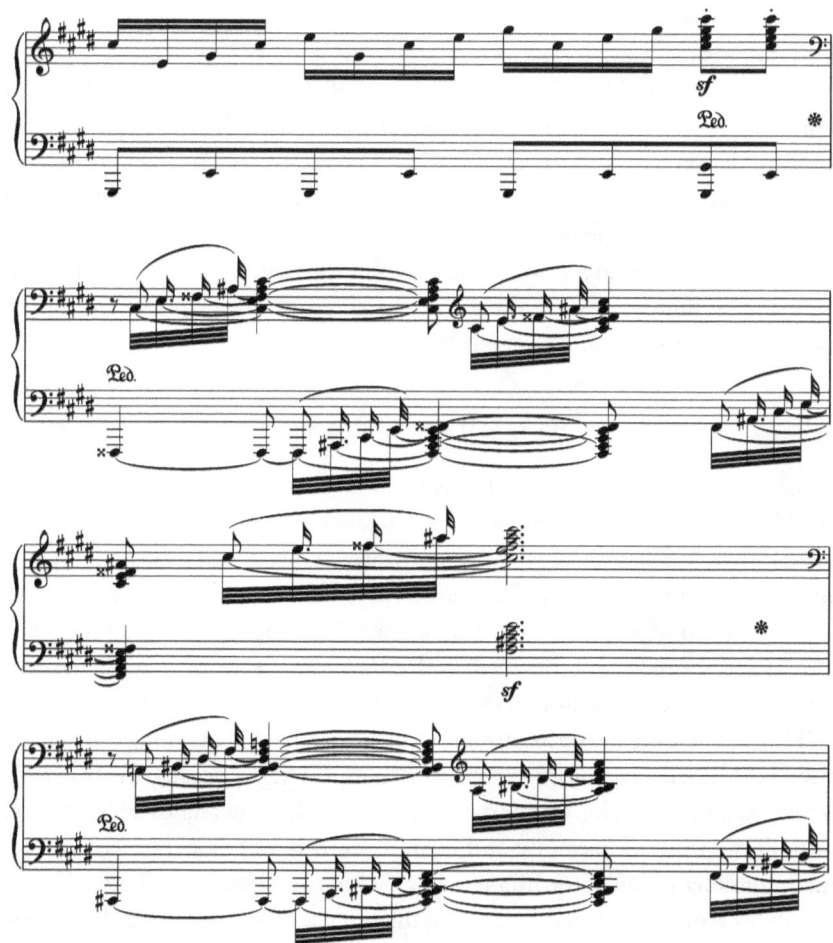

EXAMPLE 2.2. Beethoven, Sonata no. 14 in C-sharp minor, "Quasi una fantasia," op. 27, no. 2, mm. 162–66. Source: Beethoven, *Sonata no. 14 in C-Sharp Minor, "Quasi Una Fantasia"* (Munich: G. Henle Verlag, 1952).

have felt in considering Rosen's culinary metaphor. In his writings on Beethoven, Adorno describes compositions in Beethoven's late style—the *Missa Solemnis*, the late quartets, the Ninth Symphony, the last piano sonatas, the *Bagatelles* op. 126, the *Diabelli Variations*—as uncannily resistant, nearly 140 years after their composition. But Adorno at the same time complained that the heroic gesturing of the middle-period symphonies was systematically and chronically neutralized by the mass media. Likewise, here, in one of the most popular (and overplayed) passages of Beethoven's expressive rage and fury, the replicability of these sounds may have foreshadowed the seeds of music's reification.

To make a point like this, the *Tendenz des Materials* must be simplified so that it can be rendered quickly, enabling Adorno to fluidly develop a dialectical formulation. In summoning this Apollonian circuitry, one acknowledges the reified kitsch of the diminished-seventh chord with a transcendent critique about the ideological character of tonal harmony. Doing so, one can see why it is necessary in Adorno's view to fragment tonal syntax from within and create a music that mimics an absent nature, or a "life that does not live," with fractured and inconsumable punctuation.[94]

2.5 THE IMMANENT CRITIQUE

No account of Adorno's view of music would be complete without an analysis of his most exacting vision. Mere dissonance, a clashing refusal of a key, is not enough, for dissonances, too, can become conventional and reified. For music to resist reification in late modernity, what Adorno requires is an explicit return to objectivity from expressive subjectivity, in which all the learnedness and formalism in the *Tendenz des Materials* develops opaque barriers to the sensory consumption of musical flux.

Thus, in hearing music as utopian with Adorno, we are no longer in a metaphysics of Bloch's ingenious event-forms, supported by the singularity of composers as subjects. The Wagnerian visionary of the nineteenth century, who bent all the rules of harmony and form to the will of his magisterial and all-encompassing vision of the human unconscious, has been reconfigured into a late style centered on the resistance of the object, of ordinary chamber music, of mechanisms, gasping subjects, and fractured compositional alienations.

Such a genuinely resistant musical work understands the problems it inherits from the *Tendenz des Materials*. Akin to a hermetic, gnostic, and dialectically twisted Platonism grounded in embodied practice, this anthropomorphism must be sustained, since musical objects, for Adorno, are themselves knowledge: "... the *character of cognition* is to be demanded of any music which today wishes to preserve its right to existence. Through its material, music must give clear form to the problems assigned to it by this material which is itself never purely natural material, but rather a social and historical product; solutions offered by music in this process stand equal to theories."[95] The properly resistant musical work can only arise out of a triangulated dialectic between the immanent and objective problems of musical form inherited from the *Tendenz des Materials*, the material itself, and the labor of the composer. It is the resistant musical work's job to be something technically organized, autonomous, and monadic, but also something that is linked to society insofar as it is inconsumable, and refuses to comply with dominant social norms. It is an object of congealed cognition that contains a multitude of subjective remnants.

Famously, Schoenberg's music is a key exemplar that meets Adorno's narrow criterion, but not because the composer himself shared Adorno's condemnation of society's administered misery, dominated by the principle of exchange value. For Adorno, Schoenberg was actually quite politically naive, as he was single-mindedly focused on his "'supposedly specialized' [area] of problems without respect for a presupposed social reality."[96] He virtuously composed resistance with techniques alone. Specifically, Adorno discusses two components of Schoenberg's compositions that reflect a critical relationship to the *Tendenz des Materials*: (1) the renunciation of the inherited language of tonality and (2) the recuperation of linear counterpoint.

Consider a composition of Schoenberg's that would meet many of Adorno's demanding criteria for an ethical work. In 1911, the composer wrote a song based on a German translation of a poem by the Belgian symbolist Maurice Maeterlinck. Bearing the title *Herzgewächse* (The Foliage of the Heart, or "Feuillage du cœur" in Maeterlinck's 1889 original), the short song is often seen as a minor precursor or preliminary study to Schoenberg's much more widely known song cycle *Pierrot Lunaire*, op. 21 (1912). Like *Pierrot* and the other works of Schoenberg's Expressionist or "free" atonal period, the song is short and economical and is heavily circumscribed by the form of the poem. Through-composed, and packed with arabesques and asymmetrical changes in direction, it bears an unusual if not surreal and ancient instrumentation: soprano, celesta, harmonium, and harp. Below is the poem in the original French, followed by Schoenberg's setting in German and an English translation that follows Schoenberg's German:

Feuillage du cœur	*Herzgewächse*	*Foliage of the Heart*
Sous la cloche de crystal bleu	Meiner müden Sehnsucht blaues Glas	My tired melancholy blue glass
De mes lasses mélancolies,	deckt den alten unbestimmten Kummer	covers old indefinite sorrows
Mes vagues douleurs abolies	dessen ich genas	From which I recovered

S'immobilisent peu à peu:	und der nun erstarrt in seinem Schlummer	and which is now paralyzed in its sleep.
Végétation de symbols	Sinnbildhaft ist seiner Blumen Zier:	Its lush flowers are symbolic:
Nénuphars mornes des plaisirs	Manche Freuden düstre Wasserrose,	some gloomy water lilies' joys,
Palmes lentes de mes désirs,	Palmen der Begier,	palms' yearning,
Mousses froides, lianes molles.	weiche Schlinggewächse, Kühle Moose,	supple vines, cool mosses,
Seul, un lys érige d'entre eux,	eine Lilie nur in all dem Flor,	A lily among all these flowers
Pâle et rigidement débile,	bleich und starr in ihrer Kränklichkeit,	pale and rigid in its sickliness,
Son ascension immobile	richtet sich empor	arranges itself up
Sur les feuillages douloureux,	über all dem Blattgeword'nen Leid,	over all the foliage of grief.
Et dans les lueurs qu'il épanche	licht sind ihre Blätter anzuschauen,	Light is seen from its leaves,
Comme une lune, peu à peu,	weißen Mondesglanz sie um sich sät,	white moonlight sows around itself,
Elève vers le cristal bleu	zum Krystall dem blauen	to the blue crystal
Sa mystique prière blanche.	sendet sie ihr mystisches Gebet.	it sends its mystic prayer.

In Maeterlinck's poem a deep isolation, through the prism of a rare and alienated psyche, reveals the underside of historical reality. For Adorno, we might say this unnamed singer—not even a subject—experiences a profoundly melancholic solitude. On the face of things, there are no other people here; not a single word links this singer to a friend, to a lover, to exchange, to society, to anything. If the first stanza speaks in the first person and openly testifies to solitary despair under the cloak of blue glass, the last three stanzas are impersonal or in the passive voice, as if the speaker of the poem has shifted into a trance, watching a bizarre animation without worldly consequence. We have only a small clue to the social world, giving us a backwards glace to something past: "De mes lasses mélancolies [of my weary sorrows] / deckt den alten unbestimmten Kummer [covers old indefinite sorrows]." In this line, the speaker articulates a "weary" or "indefinite" memory of an intractable sorrow, leaving her abandoned to symbolic hallucination. The melancholy speaks after the fact of abandonment, animating the singer's testimony, setting free a strange play of unmoored and delusional signifiers.

In late modernity, society is deeply structured by symbols, exchanges, traditions, and conventions. But in this experience of melancholy, we touch a zone where nature carries symbols that embody a sorrow that has lost its means of reference. It is a form that has been abandoned by its own language. If nature in the Romantic tradition can serve as a transcendent or sublime escape from the fallen world, for this despairing modernist, symbolist escape is exorbitant. *Herzgewächse* sings without relation to the world now. The speaker in the poem is singular, hallucinating, praying with a self-arranging lily through a broken musical language, doomed to miscommunication.

The gestalt and the sonic details of *Herzgewächse* are openly fractured. The cosmic trio of instruments that accompanies the soprano is subdued, otherworldly, and disorderly. In example 2.3, consider the harmonium's opening melody. It soars upward, hinting at the melodic drama to come in the next two minutes, but with characteristic disjunction, as if its commas, semicolons, and periods were misplaced, keeping it from landing on tonal cadences and achieving punctuated, consumable forms of closure.

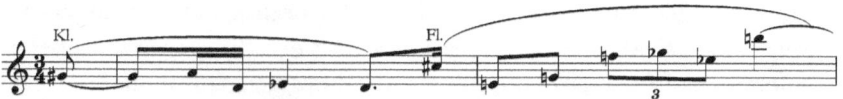

EXAMPLE 2.3. Arnold Schoenberg, *Herzgewächse*, op. 20, mm. 1–2, harmonium part (right hand)

Then consider the opening vocal line, shown here in example 2.4. The first two stanzas combine speechlike declamation in a long opening phrase that meanders jaggedly upward to a C♯5. Surrounding the singer, the band's accompaniment lacks much in the way of textural regularity. The vocal melody sounds as if it were surrounded by a collection of strewn ornaments and metallic objects; the celeste and harp decorate the line with pointillist gestures.

EXAMPLE 2.4. Schoenberg, *Herzgewächse*, op. 20, mm. 1–4, soprano part

By the second half of the piece, as the composition soars into a dramatic series of vocal poses with the soprano at the top of her range, much of this opening material has fallen by the wayside. The setting of "richtet sich empor über all dem Blattgeword'nen Leid" (example 2.5) is far more sustained and expressive than the recitative-like opening, and it indulges in obvious text painting, in which a lily—the central object and agent of this poem—blooms and takes shape over the foliage.

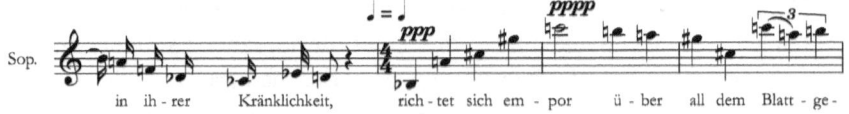

EXAMPLE 2.5. Schoenberg, *Herzgewächse*, op. 20, mm. 15–18, soprano part

Given an overall lack of regularity and repetition at the musical surface, one might assume that language and convention have been abandoned entirely. Yet, during the so-called "free" atonal period, nearly a decade before Schoenberg's development of the twelve-tone system, dead fragments of Apollonian musical languages remain everywhere. A quick glance at the harmonium part in measure five shows a consistency of Schoenberg's part writing that stretches throughout *Herzgewächse*. Many of the chords in the harmonium part are major and minor triads, though without the normative punctuation of tonal cadences, they collide with one another as if they were blissfully unaware of their overlapping dissonances.

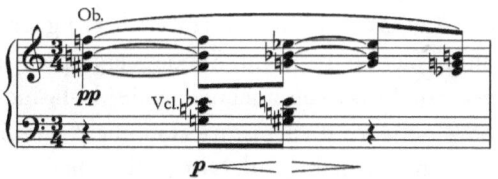

EXAMPLE 2.6. Schoenberg, *Herzgewächse*, op. 20, m. 5, harmonium part

In example 2.6, five harmonium chords are isolated from the texture. A paragraph of formal details that points to this measure requires a series of leaps of the eye, the mind, and an imaginary ear.[97] But any loss of flow on the printed page is symptomatic historical evidence of the *Tendenz des Materials* in a late modern state of overdevelopment. In the right hand line of this measure, the two stacked intervals (P4, d5) collapse inward in a manner not dissimilar to a tonal cadence. The d5 (B–F) resolves downward to a P4 (B♭–E♭), the P4 (F♯–B) resolves inward to a m3 (G–B♭). The new chord is a major triad in first inversion, a stacked m3 and P4. Yet its harmonic functionality is absent because of what is happening in the left hand: a C-minor triad in second inversion (a P4 beneath a m3) that resolves to a first-inversion E major chord (a m3 below a P4) just as the right hand lands on E♭ major. The harmonic verticals that result, both before and at the moment of this simultaneity, are chromatic and dissonant collections, not functional harmonies. The end of this short phrase jumps downward as the right hand moves to an augmented triad, (two stacked M3s). And at the same time, a harp figure joins in on this last beat, with two trichords that move up a half step in parallel motion: a M3 (D♭, F) stacked with a tritone (F, B):

EXAMPLE 2.7. Schoenberg, *Herzgewächse*, op. 20, m. 5, harp part

The smooth voice leading certainly helps the fingers move more easily between chords at the harp, and allows these instrumental parts to unfold with some sense of organization. Yet an important dimension of smooth voice leading—dissonance treatment—is essentially absent: Schoenberg's voices resolve intervals in ways that no longer verge towards consonance.[98] And this has a crucial consequence for the aural effect: without the predictable tonal punctuation, one is unlikely to hear Schoenberg's voice leading as rhetorically effective in the same way as one would if one were hearing tonal cadences. For Adorno, this would in fact be the point: Schoenberg openly allows the ear's warmest teleological comforts to be sidelined while old-fashioned Apollonian formalisms that have outworn their historical moment puzzlingly remain behind, as symptoms of the "wrong world." Normative musical expectations are thus disrupted and yet preserved in outline as mere shadows of their prior functionality; this is why the "new art is so hard to understand."[99]

Schoenberg, one might predict, saw it slightly differently—naively, almost of necessity. In 1911 the composer sent a copy of the autograph manuscript of *Herzgewächse* off to Wassily Kandinsky for publication in the *Der Blaue Reiter* almanac, a collection of Expressionist prints, children's art, primitive art, and folk art. Along with the manuscript, Schoenberg sent in a famous text entitled "Das Verhältnis zum Text [The Relationship to the Text]." The short essay discusses the composer's ideas about how the relationship between a poetic text and musical setting should be understood. Here, he asserts that there should be no strong correlations between the meaning of the words and the movement of the music. Music should be be purified of programmatic, denotative, narrative parallelism in order that the essential idea embodied in the musical work may be spoken purely: "Thence it became clear to me that the work of art is like every other complete organism. It is so homogeneous in its composition that in every little detail it reveals its truest, inmost essence. When one cuts into any part of the human body, the same thing always comes out—blood. When one hears a verse of a poem, a measure of a composition, one is in a position to comprehend the whole."[100]

If we followed Schoenberg's Romantic organicism too closely, there would be no immanent critique of *Herzgewächse* at all, for if the work actually carried such self-sufficiency and transparency, it would speak the musical idea immediately, in the manner of an autonomous monad.[101] By contrast, of course, Adorno focuses on how the unity of the monadic work is structured by all that it is not. What makes it resistant is neither the singularity of the subject's ingenuity, nor the organic autonomy of its "inmost essence." Music's resistance comes through a tangled knot of relational *Kraftfelder*—technological force fields—that link the historicity of the *Tendenz des Materials* to the particularity of the music's technical puzzles. And, practically speaking, Schoenberg was indeed delightfully mistaken about the organic unity of his music; as many have noted, *Herzgewächse* is rife with text painting. In the second half of the song, a lily that arranges itself into the sky is set to a soaring vocal melody and clothed in pixie dust of harps and celeste plunks that gently descend beneath.

In example 2.8, the celeste, harmonium, and harp play 44 attacks in one

EXAMPLE 2.8. Schoenberg, *Herzgewächse*, op. 20, m. 18. Source: Arnold Schoenberg, *Herzgewächse* (Vienna: Universal Edition, 1920).

measure alone, structured by 3:4 polyrhythms at the level of the thirty-second note. The effect is something of an ornamented carpet of sound, of nocturnal dust settling beneath the stars. While the text painting is somewhat loose and nonsynchronous, Schoenberg's text setting nonetheless entails echoes of a kitschy referentiality, as native to Tchaikovsky's *Nutcracker* (1892) as it would be to a mid-century film score. Schoenberg's resistance is never simply that of the cloistered formalist. Broadly speaking, a latent history of surface-level mimesis in music was as central to the *Tendenz des Materials* as were harmony and counterpoint. One might even say that the colorful pictorial qualities of these passages lend credibility to the inconsumablity of its surface, by keeping Schoenberg moored to a legible form of historical fidelity.

To be sure, such mimetic traces were typically fragmentary, and often outnumbered by the historicity of learned techniques.[102] In a matter analogous to Karl Kraus's view of language, which attempted to eliminate the unnecessary and superfluous in order to arrive at a language that showed itself to be the proper medium of thought, and not unlike Adolf Loos's reduction of decoration in architecture in favor of function, Schoenberg's atonality undeniably prioritized motivic and formalist development over decorative mimesis. Yet for Adorno, ultimately, the virtue of Schoenberg's compositional method was his singular sense of dialectical balance. In his view, the composer "never behaved 'expressionistically,' superimposing subjective intentions upon heterogeneous material in an authoritarian and inconsiderate manner. Instead, every gesture with which he intervenes in the material configuration is at the same time an answer to questions directed to him by the material in the form of its own immanent problems."[103]

It is the immanent problem of musical organization. How can one, increasingly, after the collapse of a normative *Versprachlichung*, write resistant music but ensure organization? Schoenberg's refuge was the old-fashioned and historically systematic domain of counterpoint. According to Adorno, the composer "is *emancipated* and produces that form of polyphony known as 'linearity'" by using contrapuntal techniques that allow the music to retain order, even after the "vertical" language of tonal sonorities has been exhausted. This ensured Schoenberg's link with the *Tendenz des Materials*:

> ... an alert polyphonic thinking is required at every moment, as is also that capacity for transparency, for classifying the individual parts into main event, secondary event, and mere background, that shows Schoenberg the contrapuntalist to have been a polyphonic composer in the narrower sense. All counterpoint also has an analytical function, the dissection of the complex into distinct parts, the articulation of simultaneous events in accordance with the relative weight of its components and according to similarity and contrast.[104]

What Adorno describes here as an "alert polyphonic thinking" would be dramatically codified in the twelve-tone technique after 1923. But in the early atonality of *Herzgewächse*, Schoenberg's polyphony is strikingly dialectical; his formalism is crosscut with mimetic kitsch, fused with pixie dust and dramatic gestures, and set to mind-altering, even woozy poetry. A recent generation of music theorists has ventured more systematic analyses of Schoenberg's free atonal period.[105] But on the whole, the polyphony of this period was typically less systematic than the twelve-tone method (which, incidentally for Adorno, flirted with the danger of pedagogical reification). And, from Adorno's point of view, precisely by virtue of its intuitive simplicity, Schoenberg's early atonality exemplifies resistance all the more powerfully. For key to Adorno's immanent critique of the musical work is the degree to which historical musical language is not completely shattered; *Herzgewächse*'s resistance was based in its twofold link to the past—one of both rejection and continuity. Its historically aware formalism was always a contradictory one.[106]

Looking back to Bloch at this moment of heightened technical specificity, one notices a striking parallel with the *Ereignisformen*. For Bloch, we can recall, the archaic fugato became an anticipatory citation of historical material in Mozart and Beethoven's hands, a formal technique stuck in a nonsynchronous context, where it was repurposed as a carrier of latent potentiality as opposed to hierarchical order. By comparison, we might say that Adorno's immanent critique enacts a more specified form of Bloch's nonsynchronicity. From an Adornian point of view, *Herzgewächse*'s mellifluous voice leading devoid of tonal cadences is evidence of consistent Apollonian procedures from a past that is no longer present, outwardly bent on expressing an alienated sense of freedom. In this way, Schoenberg's music harnesses a utopian resistance against modern reification by simultaneously disrupting and maintaining remnants of the conventional circuits of musical consumption, circuits that have been denuded of their ideological functionality. The narrowness of the immanent critique prescribes how music "speaks" utopian truth without speaking; it is an elaborately dialectical version of Schopenhauer's paradox of the ineffable, attuned to the failures of a reified world.

2.6 THE PARADOX OF MAHLER'S VERNACULAR

It is not easy to compose music as strikingly and as dialectically resistant as Schoenberg's. Unquestionably, by way of what Shierry Weber Nicholsen has called an "exact imagination," Adorno often maintained an exceptionally narrow range of what would constitute resistant art.[107] The many kinds of music that failed to meet this high standard of resistance are well accounted for in the secondary literature on Adorno—jazz, Tin Pan Alley, primitivism, neoclassicism, the hyperformal atonality of total serialism, and the like.

Stranger, however, are murkier cases where Adorno's criteria for resistance seem to shift around with a sense of ambiguity and indecision. A key example is Adorno's 1960 monograph on Gustav Mahler. Mahler represents a very different case study than that of Schoenberg. Mahler's music is late Romantic, not modernist. It is full of tonality and of references to vernacular song. To our modern ears, his music can sound somewhat redolent of film music. It is often imitative, though for Adorno it imitates strange totalities like universal history.[108] It contains narrative and characters, even epic sweep. It seems more unabashedly Wagnerian, trafficking in clichés that are products of nineteenth-century ideologies of the *Volk*, of nationalism, of the subject, of all that is withered and regressive in the space age of 1960. Yet, for Adorno, it is striking that Mahler's music remains utopian in its meanings; that it "timidly, with obsolete means, anticipates what is to come."[109]

Between Schoenberg and Mahler the common cause of resistance is not without some empirical justification; there are surface commonalities between the two composers. In an echo of Schoenberg's "dialectics of loneliness," Adorno is attracted to the rancor, controversy, and discontent that Mahler's music famously attracted from critics, notwithstanding its pervasive use of familiar musical materials.[110] In the sphere of religion, both composers experienced discrimination that stemmed from their Judaism, and assimilated to different degrees—Mahler to Catholicism, and Schoenberg to Lutheranism. In a summation of his view of Mahler, Adorno writes: "Suffering [is] the tacit precondition of everything he says."[111] And yet, despite these commonalities, in order to account for the pervasive presence of tonality and vernacular musical materials in Mahler's music, Adorno must alter the dialectical balance of his immanent critique. He shifts the weight of resistance off of the Apollonian, formal procedures of polyphony and counterpoint over to the murkier terrain of subjective alienation.

The exact manner in which Mahler's resistance manages this tilt towards the subject is a delicate and complex matter. For Mahler's music is not simply an externalization of subjective alienation unmediated by the *Tendenz des Materials*; Adorno still hears it as having formal integrity. The telling question turns on what kind of formal integrity is required; for when it comes time to isolate the resistant elements themselves with a degree of technical precision, Adorno's answers are often tentative and exceptionally paradoxical (even for a dialectician).

Mahler's use of harmony is exemplary in this regard. For Adorno we know the language-like character of tonal harmony bears a strong ideological imprint. Yet Mahler's symphonies unfold as if they are oblivious towards their own harmonic exhaustion: "[Mahler] charges tonality with an expression that it is no longer constituted to bear. Overstretched, its voice cracks."[112] Adorno adds that there is an electrical, even fiery, intensity to Mahler's use of tonal harmony: "Mahler heats [tonality] up from within, from an expressive need, to the point that it again becomes incandescent, speaks as if it were immediate."[113] Then, if tonality, in all its fiery immediacy, can still be resistant despite a sense of ideological exhaustion, how should it be used? Are there still narrow and exacting criteria, as there are for Adorno's immanent critique of Schoenberg?

Rather than break apart tonality from within, one might say that Mahler takes an exhausted means from the *Tendenz des Materials* and drains it of its power even further, to such a point where it sounds overextended. Suddenly, at the other end, with the most ordinary, kitschy, and childlike of means, an experience of subjective alienation begins to seep through the inadequate simplicity of ordinary harmonies. "[The First Symphony] draws its power, paradoxically, from the lack of a ready-made musical language for such experience. Through its troubled contrast to the innocent means it uses, that experience is more compelling than if the complaining dissonance were set completely free and so became the norm."[114]

Mahler's Symphony no. 1 (1888) reflects a resistant potential quite different from that of Schoenberg's shrieking atonality. The composition's use of tonality espouses something like a latent uprising of the vernacular, a revolution without criteria: Mahler's use of major and minor "sabotages the established language of music with dialect."[115] This applies to other conventional means as well: pentatonicism, whole tone scales, caricatured imitations of Asian scales, exotica—musical orientalism that projects verisimilitude.[116] In other contexts, Adorno would reject these materials as ideological and ahistorical. But in the Mahler study, reified materials are framed as citational, made distant from their usual emotional effects, and adopted in a fashion that is self-aware. In this way, they de-circuit the Romantic projection of interior emotions, and speak more abstractly and impersonally of alienation in history and society. Along these lines, as an alternative to an expressive atonal dissent that fragments music's tonal *Versprachlichung*, Mahler's music is based in a style at once clichéd and uncannily detached, a "specific atmosphere" in which familiar idioms sound alien: "Mahler was both a part of musical culture as a master saturated with its language, as yet separate from it, produces the specific atmosphere of his language. It is at once colloquial and that of a stranger. Its strangeness is heightened by the overfamiliar element, absent from compositions so deeply at one with their language that it changes dialectically with them."[117]

When Adorno speaks of a "specific atmosphere," "hazy designations," or an "incommensurable presence" in Mahler—is it still possible to be technically precise about resistance? Adorno's description of Mahler's resistance is rife with striking paradoxes and equivocations. In his view, the music is neither programmatic nor formal, and yet is somehow precise in the Hegelian sense of being a "sensuous appearance of the Idea." The whole world is in there, and it is a wrong one. But beyond that it gets tricky. Perhaps there are no solid criteria for why this music works or does not. Just generally, that it does. The point is that we may never know, or that every composition sets its own rules (as in "compositions so deeply at one with their language that it changes dialectically with them").

This is what I called, in the introduction to this book, the paradox of the vernacular: it occurs when the objective universality of formal Apollonian means (the *Tendenz des Materials*, Western notation, tonal syntax, the orchestral tradition, and the like) is made to speak through an array of dialects formed by the experience of an alienated historical subject. In the modern paradox of the vernacular, resistance emerges from a local idiom that perturbs the centralized formalism of an established mode of knowing and sensing the world. Such a vernacular resistance raises complex questions for musical analysis.[118] For the resistance seems to disguise itself, and somehow elude the precision tools that could help one decide exactly what constitutes a legitimate fracture of the *Tendenz des Materials* (in the manner, say, of conservative polyphony and voice leading in Schoenberg's early atonality).

The criteria for Mahler's disruption remain formal in outline, but because the resistance is vernacular, the exact techniques remain opaque in terms of their precise historicity. The closer one gets to pinning down a detail or a source of resistance, the further one seems to be drawn laterally to the perplexing oddity of the whole or to the physiognomy of the subject as the locus of resistance. The effect is somewhat hallucinatory, hypermodern, and difficult in spite of its familiarity: "His tonal, predominantly consonant music sometimes has the climate of absolute dissonance, the blackness of the New Music."[119] The unconscious voice of a damaged life speaks through ordinary sonic coordinates, and the result is a stunning and strange apparition.[120]

Amidst all the ambiguity, Mahler's music retains a formalist precision and design that is based in the syntactical integrity of its own internal language. In Adorno's view, this formal architecture prevents listeners from simply being lost in "rapt immersion," Wagnerian phantasmagoria, and the like.[121] In particular, Adorno discerns a formal integrity in Mahler's manipulation of motives that saves it from Wagnerian leitmotif semantics (though many would claim this formal integrity for Wagner as well). Musical themes are abstract characters, bearing intentions in their own language, sui generis:

> The composition has swallowed the program; the characters are its monuments.... Mahler's medium is that of objective characterization. Each theme, over and above its mere arrangement of notes, has its distinct being, almost beyond invention. If the motives of program music await the labels of the textbooks and commentaries, Mahler's themes each bear their own names in themselves, without nomenclature.... [His method] works with a musical-linguistic material in which intentions are already objectively present.[122]

With its sophisticated internal design, Mahler's music thus retains the status of high art. The composer's métier remained steeped in the know-how of the *Tendenz des Materials,* which kept his music from triviality and the vulgar mimesis of ideology. As a consequence, the vernacular sources, the dialects, in the gestalt of the epic work, appear in another register, as citational and framed:

> The borrowings from the forms of folk song and popular music are endowed by the artistic language into which they have been transported with invisible quotation marks. . . . The conflict between the high and the lower music . . . is renewed in Mahler's music. His integrity decided in favor of high art. But the breach between the two spheres had become his special tone, that of brokenness.[123]

Adorno then compares Mahler's accomplishment—a fractured fusion of high and low—to those of others who have failed to execute such a collision properly. He mentions Stravinsky's primitivism, and credits Mahler by comparison for demonstrating a subjectivist strength that "complains of the futility of its own exertions" as it "[descends] from the superstructure, tears up and changes what it encounters."[124] In Adorno's view, Mahler unties, liberates, unfetters, and demythologizes the infantile, the vernacular, and the kitsch "from the fragments and scraps of memory"—everything left behind in history. Mahler lets the "trace of past suffering" speak in its own musical language. That is, if commerce and ideology merely exploit the dialects of vernacular longing, Mahler sets it free in order to reveal its falsehood. While his music may sound collectivist on the surface, it bars uncritical forms of identification by making its falsehood explicit.[125] The composer does not cathect to suffering, assimilating it as a cheap social psychology or a primitivist fetish—that would amount to something "malicious" or archaic. Rather, Mahler excavates it in musical form from the psychic depths of the alienated and melancholic subject.[126]

Over the course of his study, Adorno develops customized strategies for describing these mind-bending paradoxes of Mahler's *Versprachlichung.* One involves hallucinations of the extramusical. In a way that beautifully parallels Schopenhauer's linguistic indecision over exactly how music copied the will (paints, narrates, objectivizes, expresses, mirrors, and so on—as discussed in section 0.1), Adorno often describes Mahler's music as reaching into literary, visual, and olfactory registers. Take literary narrative. From the local level of thematic development to the scope of the gestalt, the music defies autonomy and unfolds with narrative sweep, even epic proportions: "In historical-philosophical terms, Mahler's form approaches that of the novel. Pedestrian the musical material, sublime the execution.... Mahler's gesture is epic, and naïve. Listen: I am going to play something such as you have never heard."[127] But curiously, in this symphonic narrative, no real story is ever told. There is no programmatic realism that depicts stories or characters encoded in the symphonic tapestry. Instead his music imitates, at an abstract remove, the *way* the stories are told—it adopts narrative structure in outline.

In Adorno's writings on literature, Peter Uwe Hohendahl has discerned a similar adherence to a modernist practice of comparatively abstract "representation" against György Lukács's "realism."[128] For Hohendahl, Adorno's conception of resistant literature in works by Proust and Kafka is built not around a realistic depiction of social facts, but around an abstracted "representation of a theoretical model" that more obliquely reveals social discontent.[129] Likewise, in his treatment of Mahler, Adorno seems attracted to the deliberate emptiness of the musical narrative—a lack of reality—that gives us no particular characters or program with which to identify or perceive. Such an abstracted narrative rearticulates the stuttering inability of music to refer to anything concrete—its highly developed ineffability. In Adorno's words: "While [Mahler], chained to the unconceptual and unobjective material of all music, can never say what the music upholds and what it opposes, he seems to say it nevertheless."[130] We can recall that, for Adorno, music "seems" to say something—*Das ist so*. But music does not define the pronoun *das;* it is mimesis of something without a real referent.

Mahler's epic symphonies are also somewhat visual in their impressions. Adorno writes: "Not through its individual intentions, but only through the tissue in which they light up and fade, is this medium accessible to thought, in its totality."[131] There is something image-like, almost cinematic, about the processual unfolding of Mahler's epic sense of scale. It harnesses resistance through an optical sequencing of narrative elements, not a specific expressive modality or harmonic technique. Adorno writes: "He does not organize his work through harmony in detail, but uses harmony to create light and shadow in the whole, effects of foreground and depth, perspective."[132] If the luminous feel of a symphony's epic size is a criterion for resistance, it is a strange one. It would mean that music's resistance is, again, no longer specifically musical, but instead appears as an extramusical medium—a hallucinated optics of lighting techniques, shading, and foregrounding. Thus, in yet another echo of music's ineffability, Mahler's extrasensory potential draws together a scene devoid of any particular content.

The music even gives the impression of a distinct aroma. At one point,

Adorno refers to a comment of Schoenberg's on Mahler's use of musical form. Schoenberg claimed that Mahler's critics often referred to his forms as a "potpourri"—a montage of successive musical scenes without much in the way of formal architecture.[133] But in Adorno's view, the loose assemblage of olfactory forms can trigger a kind of noumenal, subterranean commentary—a latent and vernacular formalism without syntax. Adorno expands upon this thought powerfully:

> The potpourri satisfies more than one of Mahler's desiderata. It does not dictate to the composer what is to follow what; it demands no repeats, does not de-temporize time by a prescribed order of contents. It assists the decayed themes it accumulates to an afterlife in the second language of music. This Mahler prepares artificially. In his works the potpourri form, through the subterranean communication of its scattered elements, takes on a kind of instinctive, independent logic. Jacobinically the lower music irrupts into the higher.[134]

The emptiness of the narrative, the naive harmony, the formal integrity of its characters, the epic sweep and scale, the sensory associations of visual imagery and olfactory assemblage—Mahler heard and composed emancipatory utopian truth in all of it without lapsing into a regressive form of identification. The innocence of the musical details infuse the ephemeral appearance of the totality, while maintaining a certain monadic necessity:

> [Mahler's] movements, as wholes, would like to endow their musical content with the for-the-first-time quality that evaporates from each individual element, the endowing having the force of command, just as in Austrian dialect the word *anschaffen* (to get) also has the meaning "to command." All willfulness in the mastery of material he puts at the service of the involuntary.[135]

On a level of musical material, this is an astonishing claim for Adorno's methodology. For it is no longer clear what the criteria are for musical ideology, for what is worn out and false. It is certainly clear that falsehood is still in play; Adorno consistently maintains that vernacular materials are ideological. But there is some kind of involuntary repetition of the vernacular here that contains the seed of disruption. The German verb *anschaffen*, which can mean to get, acquire, buy, or purchase, here has a vernacular Austrian meaning ("to command") that is only dialectically attributable to the word by virtue of is sociolinguistic moorings. The meaning of *anschaffen* is, formally speaking, not in the denoting operation of the word alone. And in Adorno's elegantly twisted dialectical play, exactly that vernacular meaning that requires social context—to command—is ironically one that itself denotes formal imposition, not subjective freedom. One is commanded to express by the necessity of the vernacular.

This ironic twist of meaning exemplifies the paradox of a vernacular formalism. By definition, the *Tendenz des Materials* is predicated upon the structure of an ideal and universal recollection of musical form, in particular the conventionality of a tonal *Versprachlichung*. It depends upon the historical inheritance of normative harmonic techniques, the musical analog of a grammar book and a dictionary. But a profoundly alienated subject like Mahler, who, by virtue of his use of dialect, is commanded to disrupt the norms of the whole—this insistence of the vernacular challenges Adorno's method by espousing critical resistance and reified conventions at the same time. The result is elusive and inconsumable, despite the ideological familiarity of its means: "The dignity of Mahler's musical language lies in the fact that it can be entirely understood and understands itself, but eludes the hand that would grasp what has been understood."[136]

In some ways, Adorno's reading of Mahler is as historicist as his reading of Schoenberg—both maintain an exacting and faithful relationship to the *Tendenz des Materials*. The difference would concern what constitutes a practice of fidelity to the musical material. In Schoenberg the criteria are clearer, in part because Adorno spends many of his writings on modern music elaborating why Schoenberg felt it was historically necessary to move beyond a tonal *Versprachlichung*. But with Mahler there are no firm criteria, other than the astonishing particularity of the works themselves, that harness the innocence of musical material and wield vernacular dialects in a way that taps into unforeseen negative possibilities. To Adorno's ears, aspects of Mahler's music may sound programmatic, schmaltzy, and regressive. But the assembly is so large and ungainly, so naive in its grand scope, so multisensory in its effects, that it seems to resist consumption. Perhaps Adorno knew that Mahler's music could never be the epic and heroic collectivism of the future; rather, it was always a dying Romanticism, a late style that could never fully espouse an effective ideological function.

In a manner redolent of the intermedial verbs that surround the paradox of Schopenhauer's immediate copy, Mahler's criteria for resistance evaporate into extramusical hallucinations and metaphors. For Adorno is asking us to hear something with precision whose resistance is essentially ineffable. Its Dionysian immediacy systematically vanishes into literature, optics, and olfaction. And so, one can easily feel unsure of what music is made of. Certainly, Mahler's symphonies are notated. Scores, at face value, are based in notes and tones, a literate musical practice mediated by *Geist*. But beyond that general observation, can one be sure what forms and techniques truly resist? An immanent critique worthy of the name presses forward with the business of isolating formal particulars. Adorno describes a precise detail of harmonic motion:

> Relevant in this way is the almost vanishingly insignificant feature at the very beginning of the Ninth Symphony. There, in the serene D major, an accompanying voice of cellos and horns brings a B-flat into the cadence. The minor pole of the old polarity is represented by a single note. As if by the application of acid, grief has drawn together in [the B-flat], as if it were no longer expressed at all, but precipitated in the [musical] language.

Here, Adorno mentions a dissonant B♭, a flattened sixth, in the pastoral opening of Mahler's Symphony no. 9 (1909). As a formal trick alone, it is relatively empty. In the context of the symphony, however, Adorno hears the flattened sixth as a fusion of an "almost material concretion of the moment" and a "generality of a life":

> In itself, in isolation, the flattened sixth would be banal, too naive for what is meant. But it is healed, like the conventional element in general that is also tolerated by the late Mahler, by the density of the experience of fragility: the alienated musical means submit without resistance to what they proclaim.[137]

The flattened sixth is a textbook technique of Apollonian harmony, but the fragile and alienated life that has seeped into its impersonal formality animates it with utopian power, an imprecise meaning that cannot be put into words. Exactly why this particular harmony and not another is left unelaborated in the Mahler study; Adorno often sticks to the brief labeling of sonic details, alongside the occasional passagework of blow-by-blow musical descriptions. If, in Adorno's *Mahler*, any musical naiveté can have significance given an epic context of fragmentation, old age, and fragility, an immanent critique is no longer primarily about the objective reification and fracture of musical form—as in the death of harmony. Instead, Mahler, the alienated composer, summons resistance with vague criteria: the ephemeral sequencing of narrative movement, the multiplicity of vernacular languages required for its externalization, and an array of uncanny illusions. The weight of Adorno's historicity remains in force as a kind of moral necessity because Mahler's music still seems aware of tonality's affective, mimetic exhaustion. It is just that Mahler somehow manages to compose without exhaustion, even as he does not know why, or formally, how.

In an anticipation of what Jankélévitch was to theorize just a year later in *Musique et la ineffable* (1961), I would suggest we have something akin to Adorno's formalism of the ineffable. It is an elaborate dialectical articulation of Schopenhauer's paradox maintaining that music acquires its exceptionalism in appearing as a perplexing object. But unlike Jankélévitch, a more openly Dionysian thinker of the ineffable who rejects talk of alienated subjects and will consistently pin his search for an ethical musical practice on music's evasive temporality, Adorno insists that the ephemerality of music is inextricable from reification.[138] For Adorno, there is still the question of negativity—of a fractured language—even as he acknowledges in the Mahler book that the terms for recognizing that language have become blurred. Jankélévitch will similarly emphasize the perplexity and productivity of music's ineffability, and also underscore the multiplicities of its significance. But he will propose to break with music's language-like character altogether.

In an unusual passage that appears the end of his study of Mahler, Adorno meditates on the sublime fade-outs of the final song in *Das Lied von der Erde* (1909), and explains that, now that we have the planetary consciousness of the mid-century space age (thanks to satellite photography), the night stars are no longer distant anthropomorphic images, but logical possibilities of alternative worlds. The quaint ritualistic hope of the night sky no longer speaks the meanings it once did; we now know how huge and cold the universe is. Ours is a "disenchanted nature" devoid of metaphysics. But it carries a tiny silver lining: one can harbor, with Mahler, decades after his death, a "melancholy hope for other stars, inhabited by happier beings than humans."[139]

Adorno here indulges in a stellar speculation, seemingly free of ideology. Is he truly capable of positively imagining life on other planets outside of the structure of domination? Shouldn't his meditation be recast as a moment of negative impossibility, in which a star is a false image within one's horoscope, rather than a material vehicle for positively imagining another world? Notwithstanding his notoriously exacting commitment to form, in moments like these of subtle and responsive dialectical thinking, the contours of Adorno's conception of ideology remain remarkably contested and flexible.

Similarly, Adorno is in an improvisational mode as he responds to the many ways in which Mahler's music might be heard as inconsumable or resistant. There is never just one argument in his book on Mahler, and the plain appearance of what he is confronting—the obvious importance of tonality, kitsch, and vernacular sounds—is one he has no way of completely answering. It is here that he espouses an immanent critique that is far more Benjamininan—far more weighted on the rich side of the particular artwork than on the transcendent critique of ideology. One could even argue that it is somewhat Blochian in its emphasis upon the category of the exceptional subject, and upon the somewhat sidelined role of negation and what Nicholsen has called "exact imagination." There is still a conception of ideology at work, but Adorno is much less firm about what the criteria are to resist it.

2.7 THE CURVE OF INCONSISTENCY: MUSIC'S SCHRIFTCHARAKTER

In a 1934 essay that has received a substantial amount of attention in the Anglophone secondary literature entitled "Die Form der Schallplatte [The Form of the Phonograph Record]," Adorno argued that in the age of the phonograph, music now "approaches decisively its true character as writing [*Schriftcharakter*]."[140] Adorno's word, *Schriftcharakter*, can be taken in a very special sense. The thrust of the passage steers us away from reading it with connotations of pencils, pens, and staff paper, and closer to something expansive, akin to a musical version of Jacques Derrida's concept of *archi-écriture* that he proposed in *Of Grammatology*—the general inscription of life on matter.[141] *Archi-écriture* accounts for all processes of lived formation: genetic code, instincts and habits, tools and techniques of the body, social systems, and oral languages.[142] In this all-encompassing sense, Adorno understood a needle without a consciousness to be capable of "writing" without the mediation of symbols, inscribing a real musical singularity in material space, in "this and no other acoustic groove."[143] Surpassing centuries of manuscript paper, the *Tendenz des Materials,* its *Versprachlichung,* and so on, music's *Schriftcharakter* designated an inscription that was mechanically faithful to the real inconsistency of musical time.

But there was something specific to Adorno's usage of *Schriftcharakter* that would make it inassimilable to Derrida's broadened concept of writing. Contra Derrida's adherence to the linguistic turn, for Adorno, music still presented a special case to philosophy. Phonograph records offered a qualifying remainder to any sense that linguistic signs constituted a governing form of life itself. This was because the *Schriftcharakter* of recorded music surpassed the bounded form of the sign so that music could write itself as a form of resistant truth. In the process, it became, quite dramatically, something that remained at once utterly lifeless and infinitely real. In one of his characteristic dialectical reversals, for Adorno it was by overcoming the strictures of symbolic notation that sound recordings would reveal music to be at once materially written and also capable of disclosing a revelation of the nonidentical.

At the end of the essay, Adorno's speculative thought flowers into a brief spell of eschatological theology. He suggests that listening to a phonograph record might "transform the most recent sound [*Klang*] of old feelings into an archaic text of knowledge to come."[144] It is a trace of a speculative practice that saw mechanical reproduction as emancipatory—more at home in Walter Benjamin's writings than it would be under the conservative historicism Adorno would subsequently develop from 1940 to 1948 in *Philosophy of New Music*.[145] Adorno ends "Die Form der Schallplatte" by venturing an evocatively messianic speculation, an obscure premonition of the apocalypse that offers a vague hope for divine futures: "Ultimately the phonograph records are not artworks but the black seal [*Siegel*] on the letters that, in circulation with technology, are rushing towards us from all sides; letters whose formulas trap [*verschließen*] the sounds [*Laute*] of creation, the first and the last sounds, judgment upon life and message about that which may come after."[146]

It was not for nothing that the media theorist Friedrich Kittler claimed that the phonograph surpassed the ordered sphere of scales and symbols to write something real.[147] The form of the phonograph record is a wave. It is an externalization of music—a *Schall* or *Klang* without a secure grammar of historicity, an electrical writing oblivious to the world's historical languages. It may happen to record historical tones and *Tonkünste*, but the dialectical half of inconsistent muscles, ropes, and voices that supported Bloch's hermeneutic link between musical tones and society suddenly did not need human breath and air; the *Schall* was newly expedient, free of the ancient dialectic, transmitted in a continuous medium of inscription. It is remarkable then that Adorno heard "*Laute* of creation" on the phonograph, a choice of words that presages Adorno's usage of the same term in his later essay, "Music, Langauge, Composition" to denote a quasi-linguistic stammering. In this instance, Adorno's *Laute* are something like encoded, humanly produced sounds that contain the element of a liminal potentiality, inscribed to speak out, off the mechanical *Schall* on a *Schallplatte*. These *Laute* would, of course, not be stuck in a "primitive" immemorial past of Bloch's magic rattle, but would instead be right there, very modern, in front of us, stuck on vinyl, in our ears, quite close to our sentiments and commutable for all eternity. Would their grooved inscription be a victory of Dionysian immediacy?

For Adorno, alas, it was not. Several years later, as he worked in exile in the United States on the Princeton Radio Project in an abandoned Newark brewery, the fragmentary glimmer of hope induced by the phonograph had vanished; now he would complain that sound recording was a tool of unreflective commercialism that extinguished music's lived temporality: "The phonograph record destroys the 'now' of the live performance and, in a way, its 'here' as well."[148] And its sister technology, radio transmission, due to its exceptional powers of dissemination, threatened the originality of musical works: "In radio the authentic original has ceased to exist and, as a category, [the original] has fallen behind the actual state of technical development."[149] The background hiss and hum of these sound media constituted what Adorno called a "hear-stripe" (*Hörstreife*)—a vulgarized copy of music's immediacy. If at first, in the long drafts of the unfinished study entitled "Radio Physiognomics," Adorno's argument meanders as he searches for the best way to condemn the technology, he eventually turns to the Judaic image ban, explaining that the *Hörstreife* violate a well-known idea in nineteenth-century musical aesthetics: that music cannot be a picture of anything. It was an echo of Adorno's response to Bloch in the 1964 radio conversation: that no positive image of utopia can be given. Only through an immanent critique's "determinate negation" can one break open the reification of all that exists.

Between the musical tone and the phonographic wave, why does Adorno's method of immanent critique seem to require the mediation of musical notation? And what consequences does this have for any "Adornian" analysis of music? Notation is a well-defined unit which makes for a similarly well-defined Apollonian history, a simultaneous ground of autonomy and reification. As Adorno's Mahler study demonstrates, vernacular means do not make for well-defined unities of formal resistance. They can entail empathy, sentimentality, biographical criticism, murkiness, ineffability, multiplicity, and vague criteria. It is difficult to discern their exact relation to ideology.

In the course of an immanent critique, the *Tendenz des Materials* is typically neither relational, plural, nor empirical, but—following from Bloch's conception of the tone and the Hegelian structure of a universal teleology—immanent, singular, and speculative. If an empirical history of music is diffuse, complex, subject to contestation, and consistently bound to extramusical affairs, the *Tendenz des Materials* is formal, based in purely musical matters, and only secondarily and dialectically linked to history and society. It is through the idealism of its circular reasoning, then, that this speculative history of music passes through the nineteenth-century development of absolute music to acquire its most essential attribute—autonomy, conventionality, and a language-like character—in order to give Apollonian structure to Schoenberg's defiant gestures. As a consequence, negativity may be impossible for Adorno unless we can agree on the reification of a transparently accessible and formalized *Versprachlichung*—the *Tendenz des Materials*.

Thus, for methodological and not merely empirical reasons, Adorno typically limits the applicability of immanent critique by concluding that music's historicity bears an ontological link with the attributes of musical notation: abstraction and standardization. Insofar as such a conception of the *Tendenz des Materials* based in a universal conception of form is necessary for Adorno, contingent or wave-based forms of musical reproduction are likely to remain suspect, liminal forms in his conception of musical material, the murky criteria that cannot reliably harbor the ethical powers necessary to negate the horrors of modern society and produce a utopian truth.

We can read this difficulty—this methodological befuddlement for Adorno and his reader—as an instructive one for how the ineffable singularity of an ethical practice of modernism can be specified. For as our Francophone thinkers broaden the criteria for resistance, in particular by focusing attention on the Bergsonian axis of temporality rather than that Apollonian resistance of form (and its attendant ideologies in Adorno's thought), I would argue that they do not dispense with the question of a dialectic—of how musical particularity is linked to an ethical and resistant compositional practice.

If asked why the literate tradition has been studied more than any other, music scholars might respond by claiming "it is the easiest to study." A philosophical reason is not necessary when merely practical ones can be taken as self-evident. Indeed, the original aim and continued affordance of the literate medium has been to standardize transmission, to make music written, repeatable, and ultimately amenable for what Adler had taken to be the foundation for the publication of critical editions. The narrow formalist criteria of Adorno's *Tendenz des Materials* are extensions of this process. For those interested in an expanded vernacular conception of musical modernism, of material imperfections, of sonic impact, "musicking" and oral force, it remains incumbent to search for and track down the ephemerality of musical form itself, to negotiate the murkiness of its mediations.

This is what, in my view, Adorno heard and saw in the wave: a manifestation of the closure of the dialectic between inconsistent flux and consistent material without the normative security of the tone's dialectic. In the 1930s, as the phonograph took hold, the tone collapsed into the wave, as it is now inscribed at every moment of its becoming. The inconsistent violence of Hegel's *Erzittern des Körpers* is now continuously the carrier of its own nonmuscular support, without unity or dialectical boundaries. In the age of the phonograph, it is as if one did not know what kind of *Geist* mediated it, what kind of historicity, what kind of form. Though, as is the case with Mahler, it seems something is up; and interpretive acrobatics will still open the music. But the criteria are not neat. The complexity of this question is as apt an illustration as any of how and why the ineffability of music can be so perplexing an impetus for the philosophically unthought.

It is exactly the mind-bending multiplicity of music's curvatures that will be the locus of music's ontology in the next chapter, which turns to the musical thought of Vladimir Jankélévitch.

INTERLUDE

Wittgenstein's Silence

Perhaps the most cryptic and haunting of Ludwig Wittgenstein's many propositions proposes to utterly silence the din of speculative dialectics. We read it at the end of his only completed book, the *Tractatus Logico-Philosophicus* (1921):

Wovon man nicht sprechen kann, darüber maß man schweigen.
Whereof one cannot speak, thereof one must be silent.

Like Vladimir Jankélévitch, the chief speculator of the next chapter's story, Wittgenstein was a philosopher surrounded by pianos and pianists. His mother, Poldi, one of his sisters, and his two older brothers all played. In fact, Paul, the younger of Ludwig's two older brothers, following an injury in World War I that required a limb amputation, would go on to a celebrated international career as a one-armed virtuoso. Ludwig himself did not excel at piano, but developed an ear for matching pitch by whistling, managed to teach himself the clarinet, and attended countless concerts and private rehearsals that featured works by well-known Viennese composers—Haydn, Mozart, Beethoven, Brahms (who was apparently an occasional guest at the family home), and the like.

But the whistling philosopher was also something of an aesthetic conservative. He tended to avoid the elaborately demanding media of modern music, reportedly even walking out on concerts featuring large-scale Romantic works by Mahler and Richard Strauss, to say nothing of music by Schoenberg or Berg. Something about the consonant legibility of simple, rounded musical phrases drew him in. In 1915, in a short-lived cognitive fit, he scribbled that there must have been some underlying grammar or logic to it all: "Musical themes are in a certain sense propositions. Knowledge of the essence of logic will lead to the knowledge of music's essence."[1]

Whatever the case, his youthful confidence in the link between the logic of prepositions and musical themes could only purport to explain short sequences of tones—seconds, not minutes, of music. It perhaps would not surprise us to find that, confronted with the gramophone in Cambridge, his listening practice, like his philosophy, collapsed wholesale into obsessive close reading and analysis.[2] He used the machine to fashion himself a temporal magnifying glass on short segments of music by repeatedly picking up the tone arm and dropping it ahead of the same passage again and again, cutting musical totalities down to jerry-rigged musical loops.[3]

Another anecdote comes to us from a diary kept by David Pinsent, an amateur pianist and a classmate of Wittgenstein's at Cambridge. It gives us traces of a still more intimate scene of listening:

Monday, December 9, 1912
Went to tea *chez* Wittgenstein at 4.30. Later we went on together to the CUMC [Cambridge University Music Club] – where we performed several songs of Schumann in our usual manner, I at the piano, he whistling.

Thursday, April 17, 1913
During the morning I did 2 hours work. Lunch in rooms at 12.30. Later I visited Wittgenstein and went with him to the CUMC where we performed several Schubert songs in our usual manner. I returned *chez moi* about 4.0.

Sunday, April 27, 1913
About 2.0. I visited Wittgenstein. Later he came to my rooms and we performed some Schubert songs in our customary manner.[4]

Wittgenstein and his classmate, nurturing what is commonly taken by Wittgenstein scholars to have been a homosexual relationship, got in the habit of taking breaks from fierce and temperamental debates about logic, and took afternoon retreats to a queer scene, together retracing the *Sehnsucht* of nineteenth-century *Lieder*, Wittgenstein whistling *ohne Worte*. It was a ritual of pleasure for two men that was also a relief from the territory of semantics; Wittgenstein may have been too shy to sing out, measure by measure, one-on-one, the extroversion hanging in the ether beyond, say, Heinrich Heine's poetry in Schumann's "Dichterliebe: Da ist in meinem Herzen die Liebe auf

EXAMPLE 1.1. Robert Schumann, *Dichterliebe* (1840), op. 48, mm. 4–12. Source: Robert Schumann, *Robert Schumanns Werke, Serie XIII*, ed. Clara Schumann (Leipzig: Breitkopf & Härtel; Farnsborough, UK: Gregg Press, 1967).

gegangen." But in the safety of a socially acceptable ritual at the Cambridge University Music Club, some kind of love (or sublimation, to borrow from the vocabulary of psychoanalysis) sprang up in the philosopher's heart, as Pinsent used his hands at the piano to support a soaring melody curiously devoid of content. The two men made a habit of recreating yearning suspensions, the philosopher's wordless air buoyed by Pinsent's delicate lacing of arpeggios.

We can only guess exactly which lieder. But it is worth recalling a likely candidate, one of the more studied openings in all of musical Romanticism. In the opening of the first song of Schumann's "Dichterliebe" (example 1.1), a sour dissonance begins with a major seventh in the absence of any real tonal context and grows, amidst a thicket of chromatic tones, into a very skeletal first-inversion B minor triad that twice resolves down a half step to the dominant seventh of F♯ minor. Schumann then swiftly changes course while we are hearing "Im wunder schönen Monat Mai," and cadences us twice into A major, only to immediately lift us up through an ascending phrase that tonicizes B minor and D major in sequence. Quite famously, the fragmentary twists and turns keep the tonal framework ambiguous enough to evoke the jagged emotional territory of an impossible romance.[5] Such complex affective traffic, structured by several media (Pinsent's piano, Wittgenstein's whistling lips, a score, the sound of Schumann's experiments in tonal ambiguity and fragmentary form, and of course Heine's unsung poetry), never constituted the substance of Wittgenstein's propositions on music, nor did they have a place in his ordinary language philosophy. A scattering of notes seems only addressed to the most basic choreography of classical form, leaving the murkier speculations on music's affective complexity arrested in silence.

Notwithstanding the weight of the verb *schweigen*, architect Paul Engelmann, a friend of Wittgenstein's, could recall exceptions that leave traces of the philosopher's unpublished astonishment. Singling out a particular line from Eduard Mörike's 1856 *Künstlernovelle* on Mozart, he recalled: "Wittgenstein was enraptured by Mörike's immortal story *Mozart's Journey to Prague,* and in it especially by the passages describing musical effects in words: 'coming as from remotest starry worlds, the sounds fall from the mouth of silver trombones, icy cold, cutting through marrow and soul; fall through the blueness of the night,' he would recite with a shudder of awe."[6]

But shuddering amidst a torrent of musical inconsistency, this once enthusiastic reader of Schopenhauer now yearned for logic. In 1947, with the ponderous modesty of old age, the philosopher qualified his reflections but remained fixated on the local particularity of a musical language; a certain kind of *Versprachlichung*. With regard to performances by Josef Labor (his brother Paul's famous piano teacher), Wittgenstein wrote:

> Think about how it was said of Labor's playing 'He is speaking.' How curious! What was it about his playing that was so reminiscent of speaking? And how remarkable that this similarity with speaking is not something we find incidental, but an important and big matter!—We should like to call music, and certainly some music, a language; and no doubt this does apply to some music—and to some no doubt not.[7]

But the philosopher left Labor's pianistic proximity to speaking at that, leaving blank—and we have to assume unthought—the precise criteria for inclusion and exclusion in music's *Versprachlichung*. By the 1960s, this hiatus had left openings for musically minded disciples of Wittgenstein, like Stanley Cavell, to meditate two decades later, in the heyday of institutional serialism, on what a truly intelligible "language" of music might have been. Wittgenstein had no name or real grammar for it; Cavell, who himself had tried his hand at being a composer in an institutional setting but had found a few weeks of lessons at Juilliard uninspiring and the advent of total serialism objectionable, opted for the nondoctrinaire and humanist name "improvisation."[8]

Though a few analytic philosophers have gone on to deepen this insight and argue that, say, certain musical practices exemplify a kind of *Versprachlichung*, here I would forgo the task of reconstruction.[9] To draw this story into the broader narrative of my analysis, let us instead take Wittgenstein's hiatus as a symptom. To his mind, a musical theme may have loosely resembled the metaphysical "picturing" that accompanied the logical assemblage of thought propositions and images. But in the absence of any further thesis, perhaps the famous chill of the *Tractatus*'s seventh proposition remains in effect, sealing music's fate with that verb that has no real English equivalent, *schweigen*—something like "to be silent" or "keep quiet." *Wovon man nicht sprechen kann, darüber maß man schweigen*. Despite Ludwig's professed love for chamber music, household pianos, public concerts, and gramophones, a befuddlement or a chiasm fell to the young author of the *Tractatus*, who seems to have sensed the multiplicities of meaning behind his whistled yearning and just left it at that, making sure he would not get it wrong.

CHAPTER 3

Jankélévitch's Inconsistency

It was exactly the confounding multiplicity excluded by Wittgenstein's silence—an unspoken philosophical hiatus—that was for several Francophone thinkers the source of intense speculative attention. In his 1976 essay "Listening," Roland Barthes wrote of a marginal philosophy of listening unique to the twentieth century:

> ... whereas for centuries listening could be defined as an intentional act of audition (to listen is to *want* to hear, in all conscience), today it is granted the power (and virtually the function) of playing over unknown spaces: listening includes in its field not only the unconscious in the topical sense of the term, but also, so to speak, its lay forms: the implicit, the indirect, the supplementary, the delayed: listening grants access to all forms of polysemy, of overdetermination, of superimposition, there is a disintegration of the Law which prescribes direct, unique listening; by definition, listening was *applied*; today we ask listening to *release*; we thereby return, but at another loop of the historical spiral, to the conception of a *panic* listening, as the Greeks, or at least the Dionysians, had conceived it.[1]

Barthes took the hiatus as an invitation to rethink the substance of what might be heard as emanating from a differential unconscious, a sense of uncertainty that induced a Dionysian panic. Like Wittgenstein, Barthes had a special passion for amateur sight-reading sessions (of Schumann in particular, who he claimed could only really be understood through the praxis of performance) but he preferred instead to speculate at the moment of befuddlement and ineffability, "playing over unknown spaces" while—always the structuralist—remaining quietly categorical in his conclusions. He denoted nonsymbolic, nonindexical listening with special names—*signifiance*, *jouissance*, release, an "individual thrill," a *geno-song*, a "shimmering" of signifiers, vocal grain, *musica practica*—all names for a body enraptured by music's inconsistency.[2]

Barthes's speculations had a Hegelian perch, sitting atop the twentieth century, "at another loop of the historical spiral," where he heard the guitars of the 1960s folk revival overtake the expressive literacy of nineteenth-century domestic lieder, and suggested that Adorno's Apollonian law—a musical *Versprachlichung*—would wither at the hands of recorded bodies that registered musical desire in peripheral, nonsemantic traces.[3] Perhaps surprisingly, though, all this led the semiotician to pessimistic conclusions about what might be meaningfully said about twentieth-century listening. Aside from acknowledging the sea of adjectives penned by music critics, he declared, quite famously: "How, then, does language manage when it has to interpret music? Alas, it seems, very badly."[4]

If Wittgenstein and Barthes stopped philosophizing with prohibitive injunctions or categorical affirmations at the threshold of music's inconsistency—what Adorno called music's *Schriftcharakter*—the work of Vladimir Jankélévitch might be best understood as an effort to keep philosophizing incessantly about exactly what might be understood about musical experience that lies beyond the orders of propositional and factual control. From similar amateur scenes of pianistic practice, Jankélévitch refused to break music down into the most empirically manageable system, or hear it as structured by the Apollonian ideology of music's *Versprachlichung*. Instead, he cultivated a set of novel speculative practices that demonstrated how our language might ethically practice just the right kind of dialectical fidelity to music's ontological inconsistency—its resistance to language altogether. In Jankélévitch's hands, the immediacy of Schopenhauer's immediate copy comes to life once again.

But let us be cautious about polarizing Jankélévitch too strongly against his German compatriots. Consider a few broad strokes of comparison. Bloch and Adorno, native to the tradition of Western Marxism, are both, generally speaking, Hegelian thinkers. Both write about music through a dialectical method that conceives of subject and object as mutually constitutive; historically, both write about the failure of a revolution of the proletariat, and turn to music to recover the potentiality of a fragile utopian meaning. Jankélévitch, Deleuze, and Guattari, on the other hand, are all roughly Bergsonian in orientation. All are suspicious of intellectual forms of mediation having too much power over real experience; they are empiricists who place a greater emphasis on temporality, sensation, and the positive forces of creativity.

Though Jankélévitch's philosophy is undeniably vitalist in orientation, it is significant that his fidelity to inconsistency continues to accept the necessity of mediation. By comparison with Bloch and Adorno, however, for Jankélévitch the necessary and constitutive forms of mediation rest in the paradoxes of one's habits of conscious reflection, rather than the vast historical universality of *Geist*, the concept of ideology, and the deterministic weight of the social totality. In holding fast to the necessity of mediation but refocusing it to the axes of temporality and experience, I contend that Jankélévitch's musical thought retains continuities with that of his German compatriots: in particular, an ethical specification of certain compositions, an insistence that mediation is constitutive of all experience of music, and a central focus on ineffability and the ephemerality of music's exceptional significance.

This chapter argues that Jankélévitch develops the form of music's ineffability to an unprecedented degree, and that he does so dialectically. He does this by loosening the ethical precision of the dialectic in order to shift its priorities away from the power of forms, techniques, and ideas towards the temporal impact of sensation. From chapters 1 and 2, one may recall that Bloch's and Adorno's dialectical methods foregrounded contradiction. For them, music's sensuous particularity develops historically as something it is not: an Apollonian abstraction of tones, or of language-like syntax. Jankélévitch's dialectic, by contrast, presumes that music is at its core a temporal inconsistency that can only be asymptotically approximated by words and concepts. In so doing, Jankélévitch stages a dialectical encounter between structure and inconsistent sensation that is incommensurable rather than contradictory.

As explained in the introduction to this book, I have purposefully retained the term "dialectic" in order to highlight intellectual continuities across national boundaries. But the term is apt for other reasons. Not only did Jankélévitch use the term in his writings (in both the Platonic and Hegelian senses), but Hegel was in fact an important influence on his thinking. Though Jankélévitch certainly did not consider himself a Hegelian, nor did he attend the famous lecture courses given by Alexandre Kojève (1933–39), it is worth noting that Hegel's works were always very close at hand. Vladimir's father, Samuel Jankélévitch, was the translator of early French editions of Hegel's *Lectures on Aesthetics* and *Science of Logic*. As a student, Vladimir studied with and was influenced by Jean Wahl, who wrote an important study of Hegel in 1929. And prior to Jankélévitch's postwar effort to purge his published writings of all things Germanic, the philosopher's doctoral dissertation on Schelling, along with his first book of moral philosophy, *The Bad Conscience* (1933), made substantial references to Hegel's writings. Moreover, as mentioned in the book's introduction, Gaston Bachelard's *Dialectic of Duration* (1936), a book Jankélévitch knew well, critiqued Bergson's concept of *durée* by claiming that dialectical operations of negation and discontinuity were essential to the processes of life.[5]

The flip side is no less true. Adorno is not always the dogmatic formalist his harshest critics claim him to be. As mentioned at several moments in chapter 2, there are many aspects of Adorno's project which can be read as Jankélévitchian. That is, for Adorno, if a Dionysian fusion with the void is impossible, a pure formalism is itself equally insufficient. One can recall, for example, that Adorno insisted that all music preserved a shadow of the sensuous rhythms of ancient ritual. Dionysian physicality, passion, and movement are there, stuck inside the chord progressions: "To the extent that music is a language, it is, like notation in music history, a language sedimented from gestures. . . . Music has as its theme the question, How can gestures be made eternal?"[6] Thus, notwithstanding Adorno's perennial emphasis on form, his dialectic still entails a mimetic mode of listening and performing that brings the music to life. In another instance, Adorno appeals to the circuitous physicality of music as a way to "innervate the intentions that flash forth."[7] The exacting dialectician is even occasionally a celebrant of what Carolyn Abbate has called, following Jankélévitch, the "drastic," though not at the cost of the integrity of the musical work (a central object of Abbate's critique): "[Music's] enigma apes the listener by seducing him into hypostatizing, as being, what is in itself an act, a becoming, and as human becoming, a behavior."[8] In all these cases, the temporal inconsistency of gesture, mimesis, and performance are taken to be structurally necessary for any kind of ethical resistance.

Moreover, as discussed at length in chapter 2, Adorno's study of Mahler and his writings on the phonograph reveal a philosopher who was in many ways uneasy with the narrow prescriptions of his own method. As discussed in section 2.6, Adorno's writings on Mahler demonstrate an uneasiness or an indecision regarding the exact formal constitution of the music's resistance; the composer's vernacular means seems to resist the precision tools of formalism. Similarly, Adorno wrote that the inconsistent wave inscribed on the surface of the phonograph record might "transform the most recent sound of old feelings into an archaic text of knowledge to come."[9] In these writings of Adorno's, the critical theorist seems to anticipate (or echo) key aspects of Jankélévitch's project—particularly the speculative multiplicity of what musical form might be, and the repeated affirmations that one may remain permanently uncertain as to how to answer that question. Though Jankélévitch himself does not focus on musical vernaculars or forms of phonographic inscription, his cool reticence against precision dialectics, his central affirmation of music's inconsistency, and his playful attempts at loquacious fidelity provide us with a parallel philosophical voice similarly perplexed by the significance of music's ineffability.

Certainly, however, a committed Bergsonian is of a different breed than we have seen so far. Before drawing together any further comparisons, let us orient ourselves within Jankélévitch's intellectual orbit, and first explore how Jankélévitch followed Bergson in overturning the strictures of Kantian epistemology.[10]

3.1 BERGSON AND THE INCONSISTENCY OF TIME

The Copernican revolution of Kant's *Critique of Pure Reason* (1781, revised 1787) attempted to secure the transcendental conditions for all possible experience in the properties of the subject, and did so by privileging the essential role of cognitive understanding (*das Verstehen*) for the experience of phenomena. For Kant, the faculty of understanding is a transcendental mediator of experience, and it filters all phenomena through representations (*Vorstellungen*). This is how the world becomes presentable at all to a conscious subject. In itself, the transcendental faculty is empty; by definition, its transcendental nature exceeds and conditions all particular experiences. It serves only as a cognitive stage for the coming of empirical phenomena. If this faculty of understanding is the a priori agent of cognition, by comparison intuition (*Anschauung*) is a passive and receptive faculty, drawn off our experience of sensibility. The passive character of intuition appears to us as a sensible experience of space and time without determination. In Deleuze's words, Kantian intuition is a "sensible empirical diversity, *a posteriori*, appearing in space and time."[11] And it appears as something separate from the active powers of understanding. For if passive intuition and active understanding were united, we would have a form of intelligence that knew reality immediately, and logically speaking, this can only be attributed to an all-knowing divine substance—what Schopenhauer, Nietzsche, and Bloch described with the Kantian vocabulary of the thing-in-itself.

Thus separated, we receive a passive sense of reality through the intuition. But only through the active faculty of understanding do we come to use concepts to make reality genuinely intelligible. It is for this reason that Kant can assert in the *Critique of Pure Reason* that, in order to produce knowledge, the faculty of the understanding must remain superior in function to that of sensibility and intuition. He writes: "Sensibility [the source of intuition], when subordinated to understanding, as the object upon which the latter exercises its function, is the source of real modes of knowledge."[12] In fact, sensibility has the potential to mislead us: "But the same sensibility, insofar as it influences the operation of understanding, and determines it to make judgments, is the ground of error."[13]

To this, Bergson suggests a reversal. He asks that we do away with the a priori faculty of understanding and its mediation by representation. Instead, he proposes to think experience immediately—real everyday experience—in order to transform intuition from its passive and receptive philosophical role into the basis for a new philosophical method. In order to do this, Bergson asks us to strip away our conventional processes of cognition and representation. This requires undoing or suspending the intellect, since intuition and intellection stand at cross-purposes: intuition is associated with vitality and creativity, whereas the intellect is associated with language, logic, and technics. If Schopenhauer separated this opposition into dual spheres of representation and will, and if Wittgenstein's philosophy attempted to map the intellectual fabric of language from within, thus inaugurating a key gesture for the linguistic turn (and rendering all that is inconsistent in musical experience *geschwiegen*), by dramatic contrast Bergson hopes to suspend it, despite all apparent difficulties: "To give up certain habits of thinking, and even of perceiving, is far from easy: yet this is but the negative part of the work to be done...."[14] If we can negate the mediations of our intellectual filters, we may then glimpse a "curve" of true experience stretching into the darkness. As he puts it: "...when it is done, when we have placed ourselves at what we have called the *turn* of experience, when we have profited by the faint light which...marks the dawn of our human experience, there still remains to be reconstituted, with the infinitely small elements which we thus perceive of the real curve, the curve itself stretching out into the darkness behind them.[15] Speculative fidelity to the "real curve" of experience has an important philosophical goal: to rescue the possibility of thinking something absolute.

One could imagine this result as following through on Deleuze's famous protest in his book *Bergsonism* (1966) against the schoolteacher who always sets the terms of a proper philosophical problem in advance.[16] By looking to intuition rather than intelligence, Bergson wants a license to overturn any kind of Kantian "transcendental" problem—transcendental problems that condition all possible experiences and that, as a priori principles, remain external to (but conditioning of) empirical reality. That is, if under the Kantian schema philosophy is resigned to merely relative thinking, such that the essence of objects or the reality of phenomena is conditioned by the faculties of a transcendental subject, Bergsonian philosophy claims to revive the intuition in the name of a new metaphysics.

In his magnum opus, *Matter and Memory* (1896), Bergson develops a metaphysical conception of spirit by way of an investigation into the indeterminate nature of one's memory. And in *Creative Evolution* (1907) he states: "Intuition and intellect represent two opposite directions of the work of consciousness: intuition goes in the direction of life, intellect goes in the inverse direction, and thus finds itself naturally in accordance with the movement of matter."[17] In claiming that the intellect is "in accordance with the movement of matter," Bergson suggests that intellect is complicit with the domination of matter's lifeless inertia, and structurally coextensive with technics. The intellect does, however, produce necessary illusions crucial for survival and communication, akin to Kantian concepts that make phenomena accessible to a transcendental subject.

Curiously, Bergson's position parallels elements of Adorno's ideology critique. As we can recall from the previous chapter, Adorno argues that the Enlightenment continues the project already at work in prehistoric myth—that is, the domination of nature for the advancement of human civilization. This is a key component of his "transcendent critique." For Adorno, however, there is no intuitive method through which to regain access to a nondominating conception and practice of life. In his view, the ideological process of domination (which reifies all that exists by rendering thought identical with technics) is irreversible; it can only be negated via an immanent critique. For Bergson, by contrast, domination can more easily be reversed; through intuitive sympathy one can fight it upstream to regain a mystical sense of the true nature of reality.

As a heuristic, let us consider how Bergsonian intuition might approach a very brief example of tonal analysis. Consider David Lewin's famous discussion of a functionally ambiguous sonority in a lied from Schubert's song cycle *Die schöne Müllerin* (1824), an analysis that has recently reemerged as a topic in music theory on account of its complex relationship with phenomenology.[18] Lewin attempted to hear the following passage of "Morgengruß" in two different ways by linking the sonority in measure 14 to two different perceptual schemas: sequentially as a first-inversion F-minor chord (iv^6 in C major) and as a deceptive substitute for a cadence in D minor (example 3.1).

Lewin spins out an extended discussion of this ambiguity because it allows him to link the analysis of musical structure to the inherent multiplicities of its actual perception. While Bergson—theorist of the "qualitative multiplicity"— would sympathize with Lewin's overall aim, the philosopher's method would

EXAMPLE 3.1. Franz Schubert, *Die schöne Müllerin*, "Morgengruß," op. 25, mm. 12–15. Source: *Franz Peter Schuberts Werke, Serie XX: Sämtliche einstimmige Lieder und Gesänge*, no. 433–52 (Leipzig: Breitkopf & Härtel, 1894–95), plate F. S. 790–809.

take exception. We certainly can hear it "as" having two different tonal functions. According to a Bergsonian intuition, however, one would not be able to apprehend the sonority in measure 14 from a discrete series of adumbrated analytical perspectives, as in a series of photographs of an object taken from different angles. Instead we would need to find the temporal "curve" that reflects the real experience of the "Morgengruß" and makes no mediating recourse to "possessing" it through a conventional tonal *Versprachlichung*. This requires overcoming the fixed dichotomy of subject-object relations and instead practicing an ethical fidelity to the vitality of musical experience itself. In so doing, we would find what Bergson famously called *durée*, a lived musical time that is not quantitative or clock-based, but rather that true qualitative multiplicity, a force of creative vitality and becoming, of doing and undoing, that surpasses any effort to divide, intellectualize, or territorialize it.

Like Heraclitus's flowing river whose water is never the same at two different points, intuition brings us into *durée*'s endless novelty; it gives us access to the incessant, immeasurable change of life. For Bergsonian intuition is essentially the intuition of time—time as an absolute. If for Kant, time is an empty transcendental form for the coming of all possible empirical syntheses, for Bergson time is genuinely productive and in no way conditional of what is possible. Quite the opposite, in fact: time is creative enough to force something impossible into the field of possibility.

Of course, this does not mean that we are to simply turn off our intellects and let Schubert's haunting sequence pass over us in dumfounded silence.[19] Jankélévitch will press for an alternative. As a student of Bergson and the author of a definitive monograph on him, the philosopher shared his teacher's fascination with the powers of intuition: philosophy, for him as for Bergson, is typically blocked by concepts and intellectual reflection. To practice philosophy well, one must become oriented towards the lived temporality of actual experience. Like Bergson, Jankélévitch held that in making use of our intuition, we would not find transcendental guard rails at the core of our reasoning minds. In fact, by being faithful to our intuition, we would put our intelligence in reverse, to focus on what might be pre-intellectual, or presupposed for intellection. In Jankélévitch's words: "Becoming does not permit the object to be divided into sectors, according to its corporeal limits; it is much more the dimension according to which the object undoes itself without end, forms, deforms, transforms, and then re-forms itself. A succession of states of the body, that is, change itself, dissolves the limits fossilized by our mental habit of splitting and dividing."[20] But Jankélévitch dwelled far longer on a problem Bergson left unsolved, namely a paradox that echoes in Schopenhauer's paradox of the ineffable and inhabits any experience of *durée*'s real curvature: How can one speak of it (or reflect on it) if it cannot be named or measured without being boxed in by concepts? Does not our very effort to stabilize *durée* in language (by, say, writing a book about it in order to understand it better) keep us from accessing its true being?

Like Schopenhauer's tension between the will and its musical copy, it is a paradox that inheres to a ubiquitous dualism in modern European philosophy, one that Alain Badiou has characterized as a divide between life and concept, or between body and idea.[21] For Jankélévitch, the dualism initially appears to be one of mutual exclusion between the quantitative and qualitative, the discrete and the continuous: ". . . the one clear and precise, but impersonal; the other confused, ever changing, and inexpressible, because language cannot get hold of it without arresting its mobility or fit it into its common-place forms without making it into [reflective] public property."[22] But a closer analysis reveals that Jankélévitch puzzled deeply over how the two realms might relate in the terrain of his philosophy.

3.2 THE APORETIC SOURCE OF FIDELITY

In his *Philosophie première* (1954), Jankélévitch develops this dualism as one between quiddity (a conceptual and intellectual order) and what he calls "quoddity." Quoddity is the "thatness" of something, its indescribable and contingent existence as a specific fact. As it is for Bergson, separating the two orders is a crucial first step, allowing us to experience "the first manifestation of metaphysical *seriousness*" that involves preserving the contingent facticity of quoddity from any and all quidditive reduction. Jankélévitch asks us to insist on "the acceptance of the entirely-other-order and the refusal to reduce the absolute difference of kind to differences of degree—diminutions

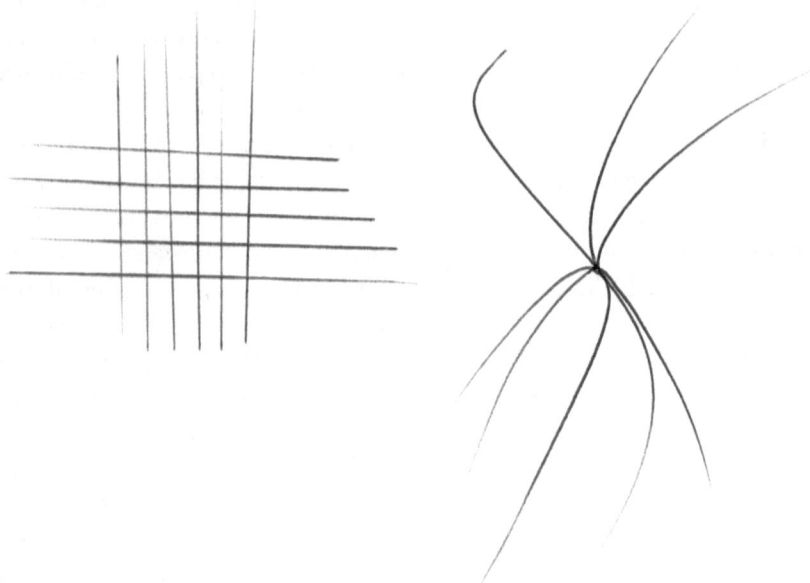

FIGURE 3.1. Quiddity versus quoddity. Drawing by the author.

or augmentations—the fundamental heterogeneity of this [quidditive] order and 'the other.'"[23] Figure 3.1 provides a sketch of Jankélévitch's dualism. On the left, quiddity organizes this force of absolute creativity into an Apollonian grid of symbols, definitions, and concepts mediated by the intellect. On the right, I have represented quoddity with a star of irregularly radiating lines that reflect the qualitative multiplicity of *durée* at work in the concrete facticity of every instant.

From here, Jankélévitch's account of the dualism differs markedly from Bergson's. If towards the end of his career Bergson forwarded mystical assertions claiming that the orderly work of intelligence should simply be overcome, in books like *Philosophie première* Jankélévitch shows us that quoddity or *durée* cannot be presented to experience without interventions from quidditive, symbolic filters.[24] These orders are permanently and paradoxically enmeshed within one another. In fact, Jankélévitch's solution to the problem of presenting quoddity was highly conscious of this paradoxical structure, and uniquely performative in its practical solution.

In 1927, when the philosopher taught his first large lecture class as a doctoral student in the Institut Français in Prague, his public crowds numbered over a hundred. The twenty-four-year old philosophy instructor who was still experimenting with teaching techniques found the piano to be an exceptional pedagogical tool. As he put it to Louis Beauduc, his college roommate at the École Normale Superieur: "I have to tell you that I had to rent a piano at the Institute [*Français* in Prague] to play a few musical quotations during class. This resonating instrument, installed in the lecture hall, helped energize the crowd even more than my eloquence did; these things never fail to elicit their effect . . . to paraphrase Saint-Simon in another context, it must excite the masses to organize themselves."[25]

Punctuating his lectures with pianistic flourishes was a practice that would prove fruitful, both pedagogically and ontologically. As chair of moral philosophy at the Sorbonne, Jankélévitch gave public lectures that were, by some accounts, speculative rhapsodies at blistering speed that were ornamented with a flurry of musical examples he rattled off at the piano. This practice left a striking impression on his colleague Emmanuel Lévinas, who suggested that Jankélévitch's style of delivery was attempting to show his audiences in real time how language and music might try to keep up with the astonishing evanescence of *durée*. It was an improvisation struggling for serenity, a virtuous calibration of attention and inattention that mistrusted the "facile" analysis of quidditive habits. As Lévinas recalled:

> Jankélévtich had a certain way of speaking; a bit haltingly, in such a way that, in the perfect clarity of the statement, each word sprang up new, as if unforeseeable in the word that preceded it. As if, here, thought never left the flowing waters of its spontaneity, mistrusting the facile aspects of language, its verbal habits and its rhetoric. An original thought—from the depths—but a poetic thought as well: inspired words, which is to say a thought that, by some marvel, only keeps or recreates the secrets of its source in the act of expression. That is how I heard Jankélévitch even in his everyday utterances—how his public lectures on philosophy rang out, or his musical commentaries with piano accompaniment, or his indefatigable interventions on behalf of the 'humiliated and offended,' and the rights of man.[26]

His spontaneous loquacity was above all faithful to the poetic originality of thought itself. When copied down on the printed page for a book manuscript, Jankélévitch's rhapsodies could saturate individual sheets of paper. One might imagine the philosopher's arm and hand locked into the tempo and cadence of thought. In a reproduction of an autograph manuscript from his 1966 book *La mort* (figure 3.2), Jankélévitch penned marginal notes in ecstatic tessella-

FIGURE 3.2. A page from the autograph manuscript of *La mort* (1966). Photograph of Jankélévitch's manuscript published in Guy Suarès, Vladimir Jankélévitch, *Qui suis-je?* (Lyon: La Manufacture, 1986), 49.

tions that leave us with the trace of a visual utopia and an inaudible music that hoped to approximate the real quoddity of cognitive speed. Drawing together linguistic performance with musical sound, Lévinas went on: "The rhythm and breath of his spoken words still orchestrate, for my ears, the printed pages of his work."[27]

Of course, Jankélévitch's actual lectures, given with notes in hand, weren't really wholly improvised, nor in a rigorous ontological sense could they be. Just as Lévinas suggested that he could hear the real-time music of ecstatic speech when caught under the spell of Jankélévitch's printed words, the philosopher's live performances in the lecture hall required a whole range of quidditive supports—detailed preparations, skills, structures, and idioms. In a radio interview that Jankélévitch did for France Culture, the writer and poet Vera Feyder asked him directly: "Do you ever improvise [your lectures]?" To which the philosopher responded, wryly: "Not at all. I do not improvise. I pretend [*Je fais semblant*]. What cunning [*Quelle rouerie*]! I prepare my course very carefully."[28]

This apparent paradox is key to his speculative practice; Jankélévitch harbored no naive supposition that one could simply enter into some kind of sympathy or presence with the quoddity of musical time. Rather, a philosophy based in real experience required a highly learned form of fidelity. In this interview, Jankélévitch was modest about his own performative prowess as he acknowledged that he adopted a "trickery [*rouerie*]" or "cunning" through which he appeared to be improvising even as his lectures were highly structured. Such a practice would seem to emulate the praxis of musical performance with score in hand. That is, despite the intense speed and the clanging piano at the ready, there were always vast vocabularies of quidditive structures, scores, and lecture notes by his side, setting in motion an oddly paradoxical charade.

In his book on Liszt, *Liszt: Rhapsodie et Improvisation*, Jankélévitch describes improvisation through a metaphysical vision of an "initial moment of invention" or a "chromos of the real."[29] In music, for Jankélévitch, such an improvisation is exemplified by Liszt's eschewal of a Germanic logic of thematic development, and a virtuosic adoption of dramatic verve, impersonal grace, playful arabesques and arpeggios, and nonlinear and wandering transitions that emulate the improvised dynamics of embodied thought. But the improvisation is scored; scripted mediation is always necessary. Similarly, in the lecture hall, at the piano, making music or philosophical thought purely and immediately present was strictly speaking impossible; his audiences were instead left witnessing the sonorous traces of his calculated fidelity towards the un-presentable inconsistency of time.

In Figure 3.3 I have represented this fidelity to (and courageous acceptance of) music's inconsistency. The curve of quoddity is the facticity of an irreversible musical experience. It stretches from left to right. A receding grid in the center of the figure that points upward to the right represents one's quiddi-

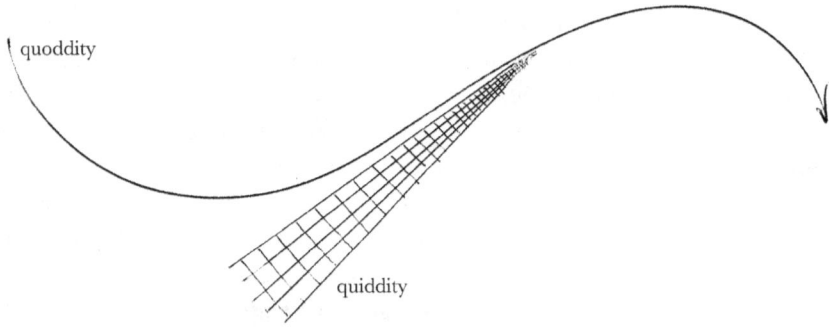

FIGURE 3.3. Quiddity's fidelity to quoddity. Drawing by the author.

tive and linguistic fidelity to the quoddity of music's temporal inconsistency. It approaches in the manner of an asymptote. This speculative practice of a "fidelity to inconsistency" had a deep structural mooring in Jankélévitch's philosophy. In the *Philosophie prèmiere*, Jankélévitch had already spoken of a wholly-other order of an eternal improvisation, an immanent force of creation coursing through the life of all creatures. He went on to show that this original creativity is never presentable to any one of us through conscious experience. Creatures created by the eternal improvisation are never consubstantial with the drastic powers of the creator—there is a structural disjunction between creative life itself and its creaturely actualization. He wrote: "There is an *eternal improvisation* that reduces itself neither to [a] parousian 'primacy' of eternalism nor to a historical 'precedence' of creationist anthropomorphism. — The creature itself is entirely posited positivity; posited within the continuous, the creature is never contemporary with primordial position. . . ."[30] In Latin, Jankélévitch then made this division clear when he wrote, "*Creatura fit* [the creatures are made] *Creator facit* [The creator makes]"; the creator does the creating; the creature is made.[31] Thus a gap presents itself between the sheer inconsistency of creativity and the quiddity of particular creatures.

Since, following Bergson, Jankélévitch's creativity is coextensive with *durée*, this gap has an important consequence for Jankélévitch's experience of time: "No person is ever witness to the creative instant in its interval; its knowledge is prospective or retrospective, always anticipatory or occurring in delay in that it is of a certain thickness—before or after the fact, but never right on it, never in sync with it."[32] The instant of creativity—the quodditive coming of a factical event—cannot be witnessed in the ordinary flow of time; put otherwise, the pure creativity of the instant never appears in a simple empirical present. Instead we are resigned to a dialectical oscillation between quodditive freedom and a quidditive "reifying inclination" that keeps us in an infinite game of "hide and seek" between the infinity of time and the reifying order of symbolic grids.

Such a philosophical position on time has points of resonance with aspects of Bloch's aporetic dialectic of the tone, which relied on an unstable and contradictory fusion of form and sensation that never arrived at an ideal Hegelian reconciliation. Still more directly, it echoes the temporality of what Bloch described as "the darkness of the lived moment."[33] For Jankélévitch, likewise the sensational flux of time appears in its disappearance, through an evanescent temporal play of difference that refuses self-sufficiency. Time is marked by its fragile ephemerality. We may recall from chapter 1 that Hegel described the flux of time as a "double negation" in his *Lectures on Aesthetics*—a phenomenon that destroyed itself in its becoming. With this in mind, we might think of Jankélévitch's conception of ephemerality as a version of Hegel's thesis without *Klang's* sublation ("the *Klage* of the ideal in the midst of violence").[34] Largely eschewing the structuration of Apollonian support, Jankélévitch's inconsistent time remains in a perpetual state of incommensurability: language and concepts cannot exhaust music's inconsistency. Though it is not a contradiction in the strict Hegelian sense, it is still based in incessant mediation: Jankélévitch's quidditive supports (his voluminous rhapsodies of prose) must remain talkative and hyperactive, ever faithful to the inconsistent flux of time.

This produces a distinctive "Jankélévitchian" oscillation that is not only musical, but creatural—immanent to life itself: "That is why the creature is a combination of a supernatural operation and a formed reality: in itself, it experiences at once the infinite recurrence of conscience and of freedom, which is perpetual relation with the beyond, and the reifying inclination which makes it consume its own initiatives."[35] Note that there is still reification here, which Jankélévitch associates with the powers of consciousness, "formed reality," and the intellect which consumes the freedom native to quodditive becoming. This consumption is one that describes a creature in an insoluble and aporetic dialectic between consciousness and a "supernatural operation," oscillating as an "infinite recurrence."

Here we come up to the Jankélévitchian leitmotif: endless things may be said about quoddity, *durée*, or music's inconsistency because the language of concepts has explanatory and poetic power to give us some sense of the unpresentable. It is just that this dialectic cannot fully and adequately present the unnamable vitality of quoddity. As a consequence, philosophy is in the double business of the *je-ne-sais-quoi* (which names a modesty regarding our inability to present quoddity) and a *presque-rien* (the remainder following an infinitesimal but inexhaustible effort to approach it).³⁶ It is in this way that Jankélévitch's philosophy is a kind of ethics; if we cannot speak directly of quoddity, than we have an obligation to speak incessantly past Wittgenstein's use of *schweigen,* and maintain a form of fidelity towards its nonpresence. This is the only "positive science" for philosophy—one of modesty and continual effort that results in perpetual paradox and impossibility.

As it is for life itself, so it is for the moral decisions that humans inevitably confront. In *Forgiveness* (1967), Jankélévitch explains that a true act of forgiveness does not simply acknowledge the transgression one has incurred. In order to truly forgive someone, the forgiver must overcome the quodditive specters of self-interest, calculation, and retribution in order to harness a fidelity towards the quoddity of the "pure event" by wagering a "gratuitous gift" to a real personalized other in excess of all intellectual understanding.³⁷ This faithful act of discontinuity, this "sudden decision," this "instantaneous event" leads to an aporetic "disappearing appearance"—for the total generosity intentionally required by the forgiver is strictly unpresentable: "Absolute selflessness ... is rather an ideal limit and an inaccessible horizon that one approaches asymptotically without ever attaining it in fact."³⁸ Consequently, forgiveness is not presentable in propositional form, nor is it even properly thinkable in intellectual form. Instead, philosophy expounds upon what true forgiveness is *not* in order to remain faithful to the unpresentable instant of a true moral action; for "only an apophatic or negative philosophy of forgiveness is truly possible."³⁹

With respect to temporality, this paradox of negativity structures our very experience of time, any "continuation of an interval." For this reason, the instant (as opposed to the interval) acquires special significance in Jankélévitch's philosophy. Contracting Wittgenstein's grammar of musical phrases much further to the infinitesimal *punctum* of the gramophone needle, Jankélévitch's musical instant is in itself quoddity or infinite creativity, a point of time that cannot be presented, analyzed, or sustained; it serves as a horizon (sensible but ungraspable) for quodditive knowledge. We can only attempt to harness the essence of the quodditive instant with positive, spatial, intervallic, quodditive apprehensions of time; we can at no point find a way to escape a negative relation with quoddity. He writes: "We can take, in the smallest being of the instant, only a consciousness itself *almost* inexistent, which is to say trans-discursive and intuitive: not so much a kind of Gnostic clarity, it is the only positive science of sur-truth to which might be given to us to claim."⁴⁰ In other words, we cannot fully claim knowledge of an infinite, quodditive, inexistent, transdiscursive, and fully intuitive *sur-truth* (something like an unmediated quoddity, or the Kantian thing-in-itself). We can only know something that is almost this.

Which is why the loquacious piano-playing lecturer kept such detailed notes. His so-called improvisation was marked both by real-time attention to the passing moment and a performative fidelity to the quodditive nature of the real. Real quoddity cannot be experienced without the intervallic mediations of quidditive, discursive preparations structured by concepts, language, and the intellect. Contra Bloch and Adorno, who adopted a Hegelian conception of history, cognition is no longer wedded to the telos of a universal history; it is more easily undone by appeals to intuition and lived temporality. Though of course never entirely: Jankélévitch's philosophy is still apophatic, and it requires a negative mode of argumentation, in which the thing in itself—quoddity, musical inconsistency, and so on—cannot be made present to consciousness.

In this way, Schopenhauer's paradox and its troubled efforts to copy the will without distortion still hold sway over the structure of musical experience. One might recall Adorno's version of Schopenhauer's unmediated copy, his dictum of the ineffable: "Music reaches the absolute immediately, but in the same instant it darkens, as when a strong light blinds the eye, which can no longer see things that are quite visible."[41] Bloch, Adorno, and Jankélévitch would argue together that reification and cognition are perpetual, even inescapable. These Apollonian supports structure the dialectical form of the ineffable; they condition every element of music's sensory impact, disallowing any present, purely sensational, or Dionysian communion with music. And yet, for all three philosophers, the refusal of music to disclose its exact meaning is a source of philosophical perplexity and inexhaustible fascination.

3.3 CHARME

"Music is the daughter of time. It has to defend itself, having neither the stability nor the durability of the written work."
—VLADIMIR JANKÉLÉVITCH[42]

For Jankélévitch, music's quoddity, containing at once an exceptional fragility and an unsurpassable power, unleashed multitudes from its noumenal interiors. Listening remained, for him, a notoriously delicate practice as it was never fully present, flooded with aesthetic surpluses and thus incessantly unstable and forever attempting, however impossibly, to run free of quidditive inscription. If Bloch and Adorno assigned speculative origins of music in discretizing instruments like "rigid drumbeats," the Greek syrinx, the tone, and early forms of notation—if they, in short, committed themselves to hearing music in the context of some necessary and constitutive Apollonian form of mediation—

Jankélévitch heard music as exemplary of an inexhaustible improvisation fueled by the inconsistent vitality of life itself.

It is not a total refusal of form. Rather, Jankélévitch's question becomes: How does one remain dialectically attentive to the inconsistency of musical time without reifying any one form of mediation or inscription? Without recourse to the historical coordinates of an ideological *Versprachlichung* that we find in Adorno's thinking, what is philosophy to say about music? If the only solution were an affirmation of a performative presence or *praxis*, there would be no philosophical reflection, only musical doings. But for Jankélévitch, no less than Bloch and Adorno, the precise way in which one comprehends music's perplexing formal character is at stake (as well as an attendant ethics of musical composition).

To recall Lewin's analytical remarks about Schubert's "Morgengruß," Jankélévitch would reject the proposal that we multiply possible points of view analytically about an object in order to circumvent a normative tonal *Versprachlichung*. When Jankélévitch writes about actual music (and he has written an enormous amount on specific repertories—his printed musical examples easily outnumber Adorno's), he does not enjoin us to silence, but instead engages in an entirely different ethics of imprecision, coolness, and distance that avoids the use of any one system of interpretation or analysis.

In my view, Jankélévitch looks for new ways to approximate musical reality through a multiplicity of circulating and swarming miniature philosophies of music that, while remaining at a certain distance from semantics, logic, and analytical specificity, hope to touch on the *mystère* of a musical instant, and heighten our attention to its inconsistency. Far from eschewing attention to musical detail, Jankélévitch hews closely to the details of musical surfaces by adopting what Steven Rings has called a "deictic" approach to sonic detail.[43] It is a practice I propose to think of as an unwoven dialectic: a rigorously attentive—but nonsystematic—fidelity to music's inconsistency.

In Jankélévitch's unwoven dialectic, the particular and the general are no longer linked by the tone, the Apollonian weight of the *Tendenz des Materials* or a particular hermeneutic method. Standing above the multiplicity of his reflections, Jankélévitch posits a generic principle that replaces the normative syntax of an Adornian *Versprachlichung*: *charme*. *Charme* stresses the contingency (as opposed to the syntactical integrity) of musical experience. The origins of the French *charme* can be traced back to two Latin words—the verb *canere*, which can mean to sing, recite, or sound, and the associated noun *carmen*, which indicates a song, poem, play, charm, prayer, incantation, ritual, or magic. In his philosophy, Jankélévitch makes productive use of these Dionysian associations, which are at once sensory, metaphysical, and ethical; the term *charme* signals how an indicated feature of a musical score might exemplify the impact of its real, underlying inconsistency. Metaphysically, in line with his highly aporetic ontology, Jankélévitch hesitates to define such impact positively, instead stating it negatively. In *Fauré et l'inexprimable* (1974) he writes: "Any nature that one assigns to *charme* (for example, grace, nature, or simplicity), it is always *something other*, for the good reason that it is not a 'thing,' a *Res* [in Latin: occurrence, deed, condition, case, thing, object, being, matter, affair, event, fact, or circumstance]. In itself it is nothing, and itself it *is* not: made of nothing, which is to say, it is itself one for Nothing."[44]

Put otherwise: *charme* itself is not. In a manner structurally linked to Jankélévitch's approach to the instant, *charme* cannot be fully presented. Under the condition of Schopenhauer's paradox, any exemplification of creativity or inconsistency—the thing-in-itself, the will, Dionysian forces, *durée*, *charme*, and so on—is only insofar as it is not. From the standpoint of an unwoven dialectic, positivity and negativity, presence and absence, gestures of revealing and concealing stand in permanent conflict, keeping our interpretations and our experiences from resolving into explanatory formulas. The absolute can be glimpsed and thought as a quoddity for an instant, but it must be kept strictly at a transfixing distance, enjoining us to an ethics of fidelity right at the point of musical experience which, in Wittgenstein's intellectual practice, remains cloaked in silence.

Like Adorno's view of music's ineffability, Jankélévitch's method has an equally negative structure. But by comparison with Adorno, the exact criteria for an ethical form of resistance have been eased substantially; Jankélévitch's mode of attentive fidelity is not one of historically aware dissent, but is instead one of innocent, seemingly naive, and paradoxical distancing. His musical ethics will motion toward atmosphere, toward coolness, toward neoclassicism, toward multiplicity, toward mechanism and magic. In aesthetic and stylistic terms, the divide mirrors a nationalist convention. As opposed to the emotionally invested Germanic resistance against the exhaustion of tonal harmony, Jankélévitch celebrates a cool, Gallic, neoclassical distance, a calculated naiveté of history.

Eschewing self-conscious dissent against the forms of the past, Jankélévitch's *charme* is closer to time than to space, having "something nostalgic and precarious about it . . . [it is] some unknowable something having to do with insufficiency and incompleteness, which heightens itself through the effect of time."[45] Such perpetual insufficiency and incompleteness remind us that *charme*'s temporality is not goal-directed. Like Bergsonian intuition, *charme* provides a creative ground for the production of new problems by sustaining itself with an aporetic logic: "*Charme* does not provide us with the solution to a problem but is much more a state of infinite aporia that produces a fruitful perplexity; and in this, is more ineffable than untellable."[46] This is due to *charme*'s evanescence, as irreversible and alive as Bergson's *durée*. It reveals the new just as it must conceal our memory of the past: "*Charme* is always coming into being: because succession does not grant us a present moment except by concealing an anterior moment, and this alternation creates all that is melancholy in temporality."[47] It is thus infinitely fruitful, a source of inexhaustible fidelity: "With this *Charme* (the musical act), there is nothing to 'think' about, or—*and this amounts to the same*—there is food for thought, in some form, for all infinity; this charm engenders speculation inexhaustibly, is inexhaustible as the fertile ground for perplexity, and the same charm is born of love. Infinite speculation, as soon as it becomes exhilaration pure and simple, is analogous to the poetic state."[48]

Infinite speculation, Jankélévitch held, would have no allegiance to a single universal hermeneutic. Out of an original negativity—"There is nothing to think about"—our fidelity to music's *charme* would engender infinite productivity, a courageous and virtuous exposure to music's inconsistency. And it spawns speculative multiplicities. The criteria for an ethical practice are deliberately, even rigorously loosened, through the operation of an unwoven dialectics. How do we know *charme* when we experience it through music? Can we isolate it in musical techniques that we usually consider to be finite and quidditive? Yes: despite its structural alliances with quoddity, *charme* undoubtedly congeals in quidditive musical topoi that Jankélévitch could isolate by looking at scores. Though the philosopher's ensuing landscape of speculations on music is vast, here I offer descriptions of six.

Inexpressive Expression. Music with *charme* embodies what he calls an "inexpressive espressivo," a term that stands in stark contrast to any claims of organic wholeness, developmental integrity, and formal self-referentiality so closely associated with German musical aesthetics. Leveling an implicit dismissal of "meta-musical" monuments by Beethoven, Wagner, and Brahms that, as he sees it, all hope to "speak" to listeners through some form of *Versprachlichung*, Jankélévitch writes almost exclusively about music coming out of Russian, Slavic, French, and Spanish traditions since the mid-nineteenth century. Jankélévitch's bias towards an alternative (non-Germanic) repertory supports his argument that fidelity to the inconsistency of music is best understood by exploring the nonlinguistic and oblique musical realms of the inexpressive, the mechanical, the odd, the naturalistic, and the uncanny.

Aimless Juxtaposition. If one listens with Jankélévitch to the orbit of the inexpressive, one finds that "the musical universe, not signifying any particular meaning, is first of all the antipode to any coherent system."[49] Consequently,

EXAMPLE 3.2. Antonín Dvořák, Trio, "Dumky," op. 90, B. 166, mvt. 6, mm. 1–26. Source: Antonín Dvořák, *Trio, "Dumky," op. 90, B. 166* (New York: Dover, 1988).

a Slavic *dumka*—an instrumental balladic elegy, usually melancholy and set in a minor mode, and based loosely in the imitation of popular Polish and Ukranian folk ballads—is here rendered as music in which specific meanings have been effaced. Modern instrumental *dumka* are just a "little thought, a nascent and groping thought, the opposite of rigorous sequence."[50] Stripped of the lyrical content held by their nineteenth-century Ukranian *dumka* ancestors, the later instrumental settings by Czech composers like Dvořák and Janáček open music to its inner multiplicity—to an infinity of possible meanings.[51]

One might recall Dvořák's "Dumky" trio in E minor (1891; example 3.2), which sought to capture the spirit of Slavic folk song through transcribed melodies among the violin, cello, and piano, and to depict, recalling Liszt's *lassu/friss* structure, stark juxtapositions of affect. In this, the final movement of the trio, the themes take on a freewheeling and rhapsdic life of dialogue and play may have had a personal resonance for Jankélévitch, who was of Ukrainian heritage. The main theme is declarative and rambunctious, but gives way to strikingly lyrical and romantic passages led by the violin and cello. Dvořák sees little need to integrate the two halves into a coherent compositional whole.

In 1890 Dvořák wrote of his own work: "[The trio] will be cheerful and sad. In some places it will be like a serious song, in others like a happy dance but in a lighter style, more popular, so-to-speak, and short: this will result in it being suitable for both demanding and less demanding minds."[52] Jankélévitch's demanding mind listened not simply for the realism, but also for the abstraction and impersonality of the composed result. For him, the work resembled "meditation" in its many moods, but this music bore no content, and thus actualized no consequences. Jankélévitch articulates a refusal of music's *Versprachlichung*—not the tonal syntax altogether, but the metaphysical conceit that there is anything akin to reflection, semantics, or a fracture of musical logic. He instead values a neoclassical discipline of the impersonal that exemplifies music's specificity as a nonlinguistic medium. Shorn of its intrinsic linkages to systems and a language-like mediation by reason, Jankélévitch levels an implicit rebuke to Schenker, Schoenberg, and the Hegelian slogan that art is a "sensuous appearance of the Idea" when he writes: "The meditative musical reverie is not 'meditative' except in a manner of speaking, because it has no object on which it mediates and never untangles the consequences implicit in an idea."[53]

Creative Repetition. In an anticipation of Deleuze and Guattari's theory of rhythm (explored in chapter 4), Jankélévitch holds that there is no strict repetition in musical form because time is irreversible—all music is subject to *durée*. Thus, musical repetition is re-colored by incessantly new affective resonances: "The second time around, the inchoate musical phrase becomes or-

EXAMPLE 3.3. Erik Satie, *Vexations*, m. 1. Source: Erik Satie, *Vexations* (Paris: Max Eschig, 1969).

ganic; the second time around, that which was arbitrary and unusual assumes a more profound sense."[54] Or, between any two empirical moments, musical repetition induces trance-like sequences of incessant alteration: "Between first and second occurrences, an interval of time has passed that renews the iterated sound and makes an incantation out of insistence, magic out of monotony, progress out of stationary repetition."[55] With this in mind, one might recall Erik Satie's legendary *Vexations*, a highly chromatic composition for solo piano that repeats a single theme 840 times (example 3.3). Amidst such mind-bendingly slow, delicate, and aimless iterations, the coming of each repetition of the theme triggers, for listeners and performers alike, a changing constellation of perceptual impressions. Repetition always produces a difference. It is an atonal music box; and our attention is called to the involunatary imperfections of odd spellings, disjunct dyads, and the absence of telos.

Uncommunicative. Inexpression or inexpressive music is a particular musical work that has no interlocutors; it does not outwardly seek to express any content through the means of musical form. "Allocution—the communication of meaning and the transmission of intentions—is out of a job where music is concerned."[56] This is not something only relevant to performances. Quite the contrary, musical works suffice to actualize it; a sonata is a "soliloquy without interlocutors." Consequently, "[the listener] is no longer an interlocutor, but an outsider, a witness."[57] An inexpressive expression sustains this paradox: while music might "express" itself, it expresses nothing *to* listeners. Musical works retain a perplexing sense of indifference, if only to nourish an inexhaustible series of speculative efforts.

Unemotional. Inexpressive melody is too ambivalent and nebulous to approach the specificity of speech: "Music does not 'explain' word by word, nor does it signify point by point; rather it suggests in rough terms, not being made for line-by-line translation or for the reception of indiscreet intimacies, but rather for atmospheres, spiritual evocations."[58] These vague evocations can set the stage for strange inversions, jokes, masques, mysteries, and rhetorical puzzles. Take Ravel's *Le tombeau de Couperin* (1917; example 3.4) for solo

EXAMPLE 3.4. Maurice Ravel, *Le tombeau de Couperin*, "Prélude," mm. 1–3. Source: Maurice Ravel, *Le tombeau de Couperin* (New York: Dover, 2001).

piano. Jankélévitch writes: "Expressing himself *a contrario*, Ravel composes five serene, smiling dances for five friends killed in the war. A musician who expresses himself this way, in reverse, is also confiding in us, but in an indirect or oblique way, which one must interpret counter-intuitively."[59] In music written as a memorial for friends killed at war, one might expect to hear dirges and lamentations—music that is slow, heavy, contemplative, quiet, and uses minor harmonies—all topoi readily signifying mourning. Instead, with the exception of the ruminative menuet, the *Tombeau* puts us in an inexplicable dreamland of wistful, dancelike, even exuberant fantasy. Its opening measures are emblematic of the thematic material of the piece: flowing triplet arpeggios in circular (constant up and down) motion, spinning out into more threaded passagework that ascends or descends in sequences. In the first four bars, no strong tonic is established. The right hand circulates in a pentatonic collection, but the left hand is too close in register to anchor the leading hand in any fundamental. The result is a light and airy sway between something that mixes D major and E minor (mm. 1, 3), and G major and A minor (mm. 2, 4). But the effect is a palette of impersonal arpeggios and diatonic colors; its exact relation to a lost friend is oblique, ironic, mechanical, elegant, even puzzling.

Other music might surprise us with a profound sense of irony, setting in motion semantic reversals and uncanny revelations: "This is the function of humor and the puzzling ruse in Satie. Humor is always good as an excuse: it is the alibi and the pretext that allows one to say serious things in play, in short, a way of being serious without seeming to, rather as irony serves to convey great truths under the guise of smoke and jesting."[60] Or a dim coolness of emotion might transfix us with its low-key mode of address: "To look for the half-light, paint in half-tones, half-say, with a lowered voice: in all these forms of allusion and of continence, a quasi-ascetic will shows through, the will to arrest oneself in mid-flight on the way to exaggeration. *En sourdine:* muted."[61] Or, potentially, music could flood one's experience beyond the borders of individual control: "In *Adieux à la geunnesse* [a popular melody in lower Brittany harmonized by

Bourgault-Ducoudray], music exhales the sweet melancholia of irreversibility and regret about the years that have fled into the past."[62] Unspecifiable atmospheres might cloud one's listening practice with a swirl of involuntary, even Proustian, recollections.[63]

Mimetic. Inexpressive musical topoi imitate oceans, sunsets, creatures, perceptions, and technologies, not human voices and their personalities. That raw mimetic quality of music that for Adorno had been sublimated into the normative syntax of tonality is, in Jankélévitch's view, still alive—not as an *Affektenlehre*, a primitivism, or an erotic means, but as imitations of natural, impersonal, and mechanical objects and processes. In these examples music imitates noises and, in doing so, marks its distance from expressive, language-like mediation.

Impressionism in particular remained reticent in the face of any declarations of *appassionata*, and left room for synesthetic simulations and aimless processions of mechanical objects. In *La mer* (1905), for example, "Debussy put a stethoscope to the ocean's chest, to the tide's lungs, to the heart of the sea and the earth; thus his symphonic poems never behave like narrative, with proper closure. In *La mer*, the human persons' face has utterly disappeared."[64] In another vein, Prokofiev's *Visions fugitives* (1915–17) meanders through a series of colorful worlds and alien perceptions; Bartók's cycle for solo piano entitled *Out of Doors* (1926) incorporates the sounds of birds, cicadas, and frogs; and Messiaen's *Catalogue des oiseaux* (1958) builds a string of pianistic episodes based in the imitation of bird calls. And a multitude of larger works mimic the futurism of the machine age: factory machines in Prokofiev's ballet *Le Pas d'acier* (1926), industrial clamor in Alexander Mosolov's song *Iron Foundry* (1926), car horns in George Gershwin's *An American in Paris* (1928) and cannons in Shostakovich's Symphony no. 11 (1957).

Organic Totality. A philosopher who wrote his doctoral dissertation on Schelling, one of the great German Idealists, did not purge his thinking entirely of this nineteenth-century tradition, even if German names were expunged from his postwar publications. His concept of *charme* names a singular musical totality that cannot be understood as an assemblage of component parts; thus, its organic singularity is such that it could be disfigured with the removal of just one element: ". . . *Charme*—it is always total; that is, it exists, or does not; it is not a total equal to the sum of its parts but an indivisible and impalpable totality such that displacing one syllable is enough to cause something qualitative to fade away."[65] No specified technical feature is a guarantor of musicality; every bit of music is conditioned upon a multitude of relationships that are symptomatic of its indivisible singularity: "One can make the more general point that nothing is musical per se, neither a ninth, nor a dominant chord nor a plagal cadence, not a modal scale—but anything can become musical, given the correct circumstances. Everything depends on the moment, the context, the occasion, and a thousand conditions that can transform an acoustic novelty into spiritual insincerity or pedantry, or make a brilliant discovery out of a banal little chord."[66] It is a striking echo of the way Adorno shuttled impatiently from narrative to optics to olfaction in an effort to capture the resistant potential of Mahler's symphonic epics. Jankélévitch's theory of *charme* evokes vague atmospheres, vibes, and strange feelings from banal materials and a lack of syntactic specificity. For him, the "thousand conditions" of a work's totality are what make ordinary harmonic materials potentially ethical. Notice too that in this passage, Jankélévitch seems to be implicitly aware of the risk of ideological reification; chord changes can wear out. The solution, however, is not negative atonal dissent, but compositional atmospherics infused with a singular totality of grace.

Music that is inexpressive, unemotional, uncommunicative, repetitive, mimetic, full of odd and improbable juxtapositions and singular in its construction—if the sheer variety of ideas in this speculative multiplicity is a bit disorienting, this is precisely an effect that makes sense within the purview of Jankélévitch's ontology. In order to avoid listening to an inconsistent multiplicity of music through the lens of a consistently systematic metaphysical or hermeneutic frame, Jankélévitch's unwoven dialectics of the ineffable took the opportunity, empirically, upon unique experiences of each work, to maintain an ethical mode of philosophical "exhilaration" by incessantly speculating anew about what the music might be doing. He floods his reader with a scattering of ideas that have no strict coherence other than their affirmed opposition to any kind of *Versprachlichung*. Rather than claim to resolve or decode Schopenhauer's paradox of the immediate copy, Jankélévitch multiplies this impossibility into a detached practice of loquacious fidelity.

This is Bergsonian to the core: speculative multiplicities are unleashed by virtue of an unwoven dialectics between musical details and music's quoddity, leaving significant room for page-by-page reformulations. And it leaves little residual guilt over social totalities, ideologies, or neglected transcendentals—necessary mediators for the comparatively exacting dialectics we find in thinkers among the Hegelian tradition of Western Marxism. We also might note how thoroughly Jankélévitch has sought to purge the existential centricity of feeling-oneself-sing, of Hegelian teleologies of tones, and of other Germanic metaphysical conceits of sonic self-presence. Certainly Jankélévitch discusses scores—it is not as though he has dispensed with literacy tout court, or the dialectical mediation of musical time by form—but his privileged objects are now unfocused and distant: vibes, styles, mechanisms, attitudes, landscapes, and atmo-

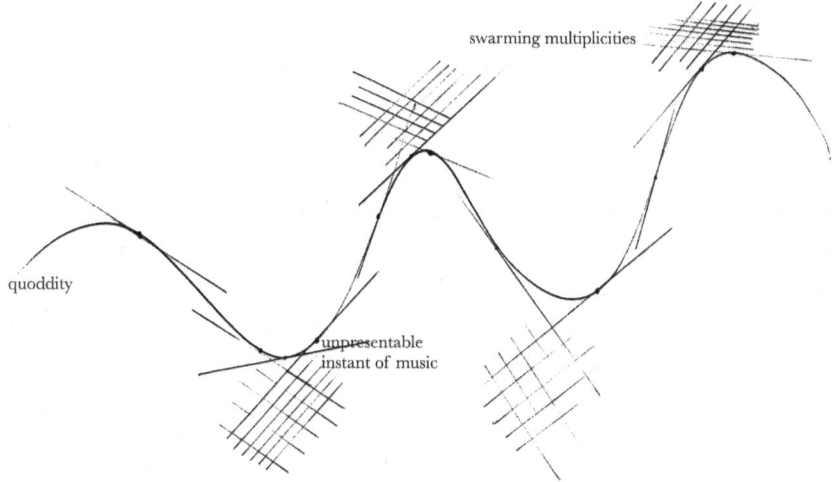

FIGURE 3.4. Music's speculative multiplicities. Drawing by the author.

spheres. The exacting rules are gone, but the dialectic remains; Jankélévitch's philosophy feeds off the inexhaustible vitality of sonic inconsistency, such that every new section on a new musical detail becomes a clean slate.

In figure 3.4 I offer an illustration of Jankélévitch's method. The quoddity of musical inconsistency is represented by the curved sine wave stretching from left to right. At various tangents, grids of quidditive discourses swarm in multiplicities, in their effort to remain faithful to the inconsistency of musical time. But this dialectic is one of asymptotes and asides rather than particulars and totalities—its loquacity traffics in oblique descriptions and quixotic changes in direction, rather than in focused interpretations of details, fragments, or hidden depths. It is incommensurable rather than contradictory; for Jankélévitch music and language are subject to a strict gap or hiatus. His unwoven dialectics are based in a hyperactive fidelity actualized through an ethics of impersonality and inexpression. And the kinds of forms Jankélévitch prized at its center were based principally neither in tones, harmonies, nor syntax, but in a flood of inconsistency. When Adorno heard the phonograph's inconsistency as a trace of music's *Schriftcharakter*, he balked at the lack of clear dialectic. By comparison, Jankélévitch inventively pursued music's ineffability with a sense of philosophical and ethical approximation, and found, as did Bloch and Adorno, that it enforced distance and impossibility as much as fascination and perplexity.

3.4 COSMIC SILENCE

Finally, let us return to the philosophical nature of Jankélévitch's conception of the ineffable to assess some of his deeper metaphysical claims. Jankélévitch insisted repeatedly that the musical basis of *charme* was not itself transcendent. Nonetheless, as Jankélévitch heard music's inconsistency, he contended that a very specific kind of transcendence could take shape that had its immanent basis in the embodied experience of real space and time. It was a uniquely ephemeral transcendence, a quoddity somewhat akin to Adorno's *Wahrheitsgehalt*, which would be impossible to apprehend with a sense of communion or presence; it was restless and transitory.

Though he occasionally adopts the terminology of Neoplatonism, Jankélévitch's ephemeral conception of musical transcendence is quite unlike a journey from Plato's cave. It is not oriented around an ideal of eternity or of neo-Pythagorean correspondences, as it was for Schopenhauer. To the contrary, it is a fragile escape from immanence with a paradoxical structure that echoes the negativity of Adorno's "divine creation." In an obscure instant, one may glimpse what an escape from our finite world might be like, but only by way of a ephemeral opening or "vanishing apparition" of what is absolute. In an echo of Jankélévitch's instant of pure forgiveness, an ethical musical experience can trigger moments of exemplary virtue (*caritas* or charity, grace, enchantment, etc.). As he writes: "For us, the Absolute itself is a vanishing apparition. Musical rapture is an escape from immanence—but it also does not breach that wall; it merely makes an opening, similar to the opening cleared within our human condition by an innocent, highly fragile emotion, caritas. By virtue of that sharp point, a soul enchanted by music, the almost-nothing, escapes its finitude."[67] In this "vanishing apparition," we never fully escape our immanent, finite condition. This is the paradox of a maximally ephemeral transcendence embodied by an ethical musical experience—it can only be glimpsed before being, in that very instant, concealed once again: "Expecting to become immortal listeners at an eternal concert, human beings end, after the celebration, as finite beings once again, just as a composer, who is never an unflagging genius, will sink and become an imitation of himself, a mere continuation of his beginning."[68]

The final two chapters of *Music and the Ineffable*, entitled "The Charm and the Alibi" and "Music and Silence," offer a condensed version of Jankélévitch's fragile philosophy of transcendence. Like the aforementioned theses on musical aesthetics that the philosopher describes in the "inexpressive espressivo," in these chapters Jankélévitch interprets *charme* widely, with an open multiplicity at his disposal. He describes it as a form of musical innocence that is uniquely humanizing; he suggests that music is analogous to the voice of God, not offering concrete answers to one's prayer, in a way that is redolent of Bloch's "inconstruable question" or Adorno's "demythologized prayer." Finally, Jankélévitch insists that listening properly requires a sense of grace achieved only through a distinct openness to the unexpected, and he ends with a metaphysical gesture that has more than a tinge of existentialism to it: that music itself is perpetually in a liminal, temporal state between existence and inexistence, between articulation and silence, between being and nothingness.

Jankélévitch gives this deeply metaphysical multiplicity a name: divine inconsistency. It is divine in a metaphorical sense insofar as these speculations have an impossible transcendence as their aim. And it is inconsistent because no single link between music and transcendence can be prescribed by philosophy without developing a paradox that obliges us to a pragmatic amnesia in service of the multiple. The ground of any transcendence must remain inconsistent, drawn from a void that is intrinsically unstable, demanding more fidelity than adherence, more courage than understanding. I group Jankélévitch's metaphysical speculations about music under three headings:

1. Musical transcendence comes through innocence and spiritual attunement. Against a Germanic aesthetics of historical and philosophical self-consciousness, Jankélévitch calls on composers and listeners to approach music with an innocence that reflects Bergson's philosophical orientation away from intellect towards quoddity's action and intuition. Quoddity means go, practice, play, compose, improvise, tinker, and don't think about it: "In general, the creative imaginations are completely absorbed in a naïve state of being, taken up by the deep, blind toil of Doing. Don't read what they profess, but listen to what they do."[69] The intentionality, passion, desperation, and narcissism of an autonomous subject would be blockades to true action. Only with the heavy burdens of ideology and self-consciousness laid aside, could one be properly attuned to the arrival of the unexpected, a genuine event: "The over-informed conscience transforms despair into theater of the *Disperato*. But grace has a surprise in mind, and it sweeps us off our feet: the grace that is refused to those who overact, whose repentance is interested or mercenary, will fulfill us when we stop posing for the gallery or eyeing our own merits, when the agent no longer usurps the position of witness."[70]

Jankélévitch's orientation towards the "drastic" action of musical time urges us to listen with a sense of innocent spirituality, with an ethical comportment that is analogous to prayer. Jankélévitch pursues this analogy with religion by referencing the distinction between monotheism and "paganism." He contends that pagan gods speak concretely, always too little or too much, whereas the monotheistic God of the Abrahamic religions remains silent, speaking only through a form of immanent, universal grace: "Music, as if it were a canticle sung by God, does not answer our questions directly. No, it is the pagan oracles that give answers when one goes to consult them, and they invariably say too much, these little, loquacious gods. And if they speak that way, it is doubtless because they know nothing. God, he himself, remains silent, preferring the answer in arpeggios or nightingales, the high cries of his swallows or the murmur of the prophetic leaves."[71] As archaic as the language of theology is here, note the striking proximity to the ineffability of Bloch's "inconstruable question" and Adorno's "demythologized prayer." For Jankélévitch, as for Bloch and Adorno, the specificity of music's ineffability is akin to paradoxes that inhere when one attempts to address the infinite, the thing-in-itself, or the Benjamininian "divine name." In fact, gestures that are analogous to theology serve all three philosophers studied so far—Bloch, Adorno, and Jankélévitch—not because their view of music is religious, but because a negative theology is based in an analogous structure of the ineffable, one that, as discussed in the introduction to this book, finds its precedents in Plotinus's dialectic (whose *Enneads* was the subject of Jankélévitch's master's thesis). The thing-in-itself (or the one beyond Being, for Plotinus) is inexhaustible, unpresentable, and even unknowable, yet, in the case of music, somehow endlessly copied. Fidelity to inconsistency goes hand in hand with philosophical perplexity.

2. Following Bergson, organisms are bodies, and as bodies, they are organic totalities infused with a sense of unity that undergoes incessant change (by way of *durée*): "All spiritual reality possesses thus by its nature a certain total virtue that makes it engulf all imported modifications and reconstitute at every step the its total organism. This is an organism continually transformed."[72] Spirituality is immanent to *durée*, and accessible through intuition. One's virtue is based in the absolute unity between the matter of the organism and its creative and spiritual life as a totality: "And as this totalization carries, in all moments, on all the elements of the spiritual organism, we will have to say that not only the contents of life *survive* in themselves in time, but that they *relive* themselves—partially in each of the contemporary contents, and totally in the spiritual person that they express."[73]

With respect to the spiritual totality of the organism, music has the specific and exceptional power to enact this qualitative multiplicity of *durée*: it imitates concrete emotional states in constant flux and counterpoint. In an echo of Bloch and Adorno's veneration of music's polyphonic character, for Jankélévitch, musical polyphony uniquely imitates a certain kind of affective interpenetration:

This mutual immanence, so difficult for the faculty of understanding to grasp, is something that our arts, by contrast, seek to imitate; but none succeed better than music, doubtlessly because music, by the grace of its polyphony, possesses more means than any other art for expressing this intimate interpenetration of states of the soul. Does polyphony not allow motion in parallel among several superimposed voices that express themselves simultaneously and harmoniously, while remaining distinct and at the same time opposed?[74]

Readers of Bergson's *Time and Free Will* (1889) may recognize this as an elaboration of one of Bergson's statements about music.[75] Jankélévitch develops it in his *Bergson* monograph by way of two musical examples: Liszt's *Faust Symphony* (1857), and Debussy's *Pelleas et Melisande* (1893; example 3.5). Both demonstrate how polyphony has the unique capacity to imitate the complex texture of contrapuntal and overlapping emotions:

> One remembers the mysterious prelude to *Pelleas* where in the 18th measure Debussy is struggling to set Golaud's and Mélisande's themes, expressing there the tragic union that will establish itself between two destinies. Does one not admire also the wonderful subtlety with which Liszt, in the *Faust Symphony*, shuffles around the most opposed emotions: Faust's love and speculative anxiety in the first movement, Faust's love and Marguerite's love in the second? The themes confront one another, they mix, contain one another, and each in the other carries the signature of all the rest.[76]

After a hushed theme unfolding as the mere murmurs of strings, we hear Golaud's motif: an oscillating but transfiguring whole-tone sound mass played by the winds (mm. 5–6). This motif returns in broader strokes just six measures later, followed by the more animated and descending solo motif associated with his lover, Mélisande. The moment that interests Jankélévitch occurs in measure 18, when the two motifs (Golaud's and Mélisande's) are presented at the same time over an A pedal point.[77] Since music can conjoin two motifs that are associated with two distinct characters (and their attendant emotional states in the narrative), we might say that the music makes this paradoxical mélange between Golaud and Mélisande into something metaphysical that uniquely imitates the emotional complexity of life: "Thus it makes interior life at all moments: it associates in paradoxical counterpoint the experiences that appeared unrelated, so that each of them carries testimony of the entire per-

EXAMPLE 3.5. Claude Debussy, *Pelléas et Mélisande*, act 1, scene I, rehearsal no. 2, mm. 1–12. Source: Claude Debussy, *Pelléas et Mélisande*, first edition (Paris: E. Fromont, 1902).

son. The 'total mixture' that the Stoics proposed like a paradox—is it not a continually lived reality?"[78]

If Bloch and Adorno shifted the emphasis of the ineffable to Apollonian mediations, Jankélévitch shifts attention back to the emotionally saturated potential of lived reality. But he does so in a way distinct from Schopenhauer, as well as from Schopenhauer's Wagnerism (as it would eventually come to be received and understood), which held that music disclosed a secret interior history of the will, or extracted Platonic essences of individual emotions in musical form. Jankélévitch, by contrast, proposed that music embodies, with a great deal of transparency, unique mixtures of otherwise unrelated emotional states. In their non-semantic impersonality and mystery, these embodiments exemplify metaphysically the holistic texture of an individual's life.

3. Finally, at the conclusion of *Music and the Ineffable*, Jankélévitch defines music in relationship to the lack of life—silence—the stark emptiness of the cosmos. He does this by proposing that music, silence, and existence are related in two somewhat opposed ways. First, music can be thought of as akin to a concrete existence—a sonic life that passes ephemerally in the silence of the cosmos. Or it can be thought of as a solace—a silent respite or shelter amidst the noise of the cosmos.

Jankélévitch first proposes that music is equal to existence. This means music is akin to a living life, an existing thing, a warm being standing firm against the void of the cosmos; this music would be equal to existence; music would coincide with all existent beings. Silence for its part, would be nothingness.

MUSIC = EXISTENCE
SILENCE = NOTHINGNESS

Under this schema, music is like a finite creature, but the silence surrounding it is infinite. One can understand this most pointedly by imagining a mutual heat death of music and the existence of life, a twin decay into the cold and silent emptiness of the universe: "If existence—which we suppose to be fragile, superficial, and provisional—tends asymptotically towards nothingness, then music, gradually exhausting all possible combinations of sounds, tends inexorably toward silence."[79] Thus, Jankélévitch reminds us that all music ends in silence. Unlike in Schopenhauer's Neoplatonism, here there is no eternal being of Pythagorean harmony linked to the mathematical properties of consonant intervals. Instead, music is equal to a fragile assertion of a life, an existence that is spiritual in its bare possibility, destined however to return to the cold emptiness of the universe. It has a birth and a death. It is a parenthesis of living existence, a life: "In this case, it is the world of noises and sounds that would constitute a parenthesis in the backdrop of silence, and that would emerge from an ocean of silence, like a ray of light that illuminates homogeneous space, the black void of the *chora*, for a few instants."[80]

Music and existing life share attributes, like duration, structure, rhythm, movement, mutability, making, and creating, that imply succession and continuation—properties of existing beings. By contrast, silence and nothingness are empty. In sharing these formal attributes, music and silence are uniquely reflective of one another. We might say that Jankélévitch hears music as an ephemeral Pythagoreanism of the cosmos. Its life and bare existence—not its structure, its tonal form, or its narrative content, but just its ephemeral facticity—is itself the carrier of its infinity, its potentiality for transcendence: "As something similar to a work of art, life is an animated, limited construction that stands out against lethal infinity; and music, as something similar to life—as a melodious construction, magic duration, an ephemeral adventure, and brief encounter—is isolated, between beginning and end, in the immensity of nonbeing."[81]

The second schema contends that music *is* actually silence, or that silence is actualized in musical works, providing a sense of silence as a relief from the noise of existence. This is the solace argument; the nothingness of the void is pure noise, and we have erected a sanctuary of spiritual transcendence with music. We might say that it is Jankélévitch's ethics in its sparest outlines: music is a solace, a meditation of law against the chilling hyperchaos of the universe, a transcendence of grace and virtue structured by a Bergsonian definition of creation.

MUSIC = SILENCE
EXISTENCE = NOISE

Under this schema, music lifts us above mere existence into a silent meditation. "... Now this [proposition] has been inverted: the person assailed by cacophony, covering his ears, wants to protect his slip of a silent garden, shelter his little islet of silence, because henceforth it is silence that insulates, and not noise."[82] In this instance, when music is equated with silence, it is linked to the existence of particular musical objects. Thus, unlike in the above proposition, where silence is infinite, here silence is finite, actual, real; but it safeguards the infinite as a silent potentiality in a cold universe of noise. And silence as music is never full—as long as human beings are around, we end up with the dust of a *presque-rien* instead of an absolute silence: "It is not just that silence is the nothingness of a single category of sensations within the plentitude of all other: silence itself is never complete."[83]

Silence also enables transcendence in a manner similar to that of innocence or prayer. Here, though, Jankélévitch quietly reverses his statement about music requiring a kind of innocence; he uses the concept of silence to refuse the possibility that any meaning could be given over in the plentitude of a present experience without a nagging aporetic disappearance. Being conscious of a musical object would not do the trick: the truth appears in music's vanishing into silence. Thus silence serves as a perpetually incomplete negation in which the quiet of the silence's *presque-rien* prepares us to receive truth; as it "smooths the way for the transmission of a message," it "allows us to hear another voice, a voice speaking another language, a voice that comes from elsewhere. This unknown tongue spoken by an unknown voice, this *vox ignota* [unknown voice], hides behind silence just as silence itself lurks behind the superficial noise of daily existence."[84]

In the manner of the Ikhwan Al-Safa, Bloch's "inconstruable question," or Adorno's "demythologized prayer," Jankélévitch's "unknown voice" is not a universal language, not an unspeakable language, but a nonlanguage that is in an intransigent foreign dialect, with tremendous sensory impact. It is already there, as a silence that is both omnipresent and ephemeral. Capturing it entails an excess of paradoxes: *charme* as unexperienceable and, strictly speaking, unactualizable. It keeps music's truth at a permanent distance, opening us to the realm of the multiple. It reflects a true ethics of a modern music that creatively restates the Bergsonian "problem" of a philosophy of music in an unfolding series, a multiplicity, that answers to no transcendental law save that of *charme*'s immanent potentiality.

3.5 UNWOVEN DIALECTICS

To return to the broader philosophical frame with which we began, when Jankélévitch adopts Bergson's anti-Kantian injunction to use one's intuition to creatively restate philosophical problems over and over again, he quite practically does so from paragraph to paragraph. So many things can be said of music in different contexts, and from different points of view, that a philosophy of music need not be totalizing or systematic in its revelations. We saw in chapter 2 that Adorno is flexible in his approach to Mahler—to some extent despite himself and his exacting practice of immanent critique. Jankélévitch, by comparison with Adorno, takes this flexibility as axiomatic. In his view, intuition is far too inconsistent, and fidelity to quoddity obliges us to practice inconsistency. *Charme* does not reduce music to an unreflective metaphysics of presence, to an immanent *durée*, or to an exemplary practice of musical embodiment—it instead multiplies potentials, and endlessly differentiates the experience of music into new fields of interpretation.

It was Jankélévitch's virtuoso performances that struck an assistant of his at the Sorbonne, Catherine Clément, as exemplifying an extraordinarily unique form of fidelity to music's unpresentable ephemerality.[85] But Clément, in her own philosophy, proceeded to elaborate a different facet of music's inconsistency, one that would curiously be quite important for Deleuze and Guattari. She focused on what she called the *syncope*, an inconsistency of embodied time, an interruption or rhythmic stuttering marked by the incessant punctuality of articulation, an irreducible symptom of difference within all musical form. As she put it: "The queen of rhythm, syncope is also the mother of dissonance; it is the source, in short, of a harmonious and productive discord. . . . Attack and haven, collision; a fragment of the beat disappears, and of this disappearance, rhythm is born."[86] While Clément did not practice her fidelity to music's syncopated inconsistency as a loquacious approximation to specific musical passages or by way of swarming multiplicities, she developed her own style of intervention, recounting the quodditive irruptions of syncopation into all that was quidditive in the history of philosophy.

But what was unnegotiable for Barthes, Jankélévitch, and Clément alike was a distinct sense that music could do something for philosophical practice that language could not quite accomplish on its own. All three listened to music precisely because they could hear it as engendering a speculative practice of fidelity to an inconsistency inherent to musical time that language could only specify inadequately. Of course, Jankélévitch did not think of music's being as exclusively temporal—a whole range of musical techniques and linguistic commentaries were necessary mediations for one's apprehensions of music. For him, musical material is neither a passive medium for our personal expressions nor something utterly impersonal, objective, and disinterested; it subsists in the inconsistency of dialectical crosscurrents. He wrote: "Far from being amenable to the winds of our desire, this servant of intention will make use of its own master. The material is neither a docile instrument nor a pure obstacle."[87] Doing and learning are intertwined. Even if the dialectic is dramatically slackened from Adorno's strong negations of ideology, a loose version of it is nonetheless still at work for Jankélévitch: all composition and performance is a conversation with the material. In an echo of Adorno at the piano, techniques are necessary mediators insofar as they are recalcitrant in the face of one's passionate desires to make them into vehicles for the communication of interior states.

We can recall that, while Bloch and Adorno emphasized the ephemeral and temporal qualities of music, their Hegelian dialectics took recourse to the tone as expressively handled by a genius composer (in the case of Bloch) and the fractured form of a specific work (for Adorno) as essential mediators for any kind of utopian meaning. By comparison, Jankélévitch's unwoven dialectics recover transcendence by remaining faithful to the blankness of music's overarching inconsistency, nonexpression, and silence. With regards to Adorno's most vividly dialectical account of musical material—"gestures made eternal"—we might say that Jankélévitch practices an austere fidelity to the Dionysian flux of gesture rather than its historical development and fracture of its life as an Apollonian form. In the process, Jankélévitch reimagines musical autonomy in a newly paradoxical form—as the eternal vitality of its ephemeral inconsistency.

If one were willing to read Jankélévitch's dialectical method against the grain, it would be possible to draw out further the ways in which his privileged attachment to inconsistent temporality may not be without its own limitations and contradictions. While he unleashes the usual multiplicity in his use of the Ancient Greek verb *poiein* (to make, do, or produce), in which "the composer, the performer as active re-creator, and the listener as fictive re-creator all participate together in a sort of magical transaction," it is worth remembering that his musicological writings focus on a highly selective repertory.[88] As James Currie has remarked critically with respect to Jankélévitch's philosophy of music, behind all the freewheeling multiplicities, the philosopher's empirical preferences for an aesthetics of French impersonality over Germanic expressionism might also be read as smuggling in some form of un-thought or repressed disciplinary totality, one that has no acknowledged role in Jankélévitch's system.[89] Were the philosopher around to shield himself from this critique, his primary line of defense would likely be ontological; he would argue that the intrinsically complex nature of music's immanent, technical, and material substrate keeps his philosophy in the realm of the multiple, and within the logic of the paradox, so that "the essence of music in fact never consists in this or that."[90] Only with a presupposed openness to music's technical substrate, an orientation to the multiple, could we legitimately remain clear of any kind of *Versprachlichung*.

The question of whether or not dialectical closure is necessary and irreducible among these philosophies must remain an open one for now; this chapter has only attempted to analyze what is uniquely characteristic of Jankélévitch's thought. Bloch and Adorno brought to the fore elaborate dialectical contradictions that hoped to show us how music could indicate an unnameable utopia,

Roland Barthes and Catherine Clément found ways to categorically affirm the notoriously difficult to describe parameters of praxis and voice, and in the final chapter I will argue that Deleuze and Guattari affirmed music's rhythmic coextension with sensation and the cosmos. All these thinkers confront the paradox of Schopenhauer's immediate copy, but in twentieth-century European intellectual history, none of them went on to conclude that the operation of describing and analyzing music induces an inexhaustible fidelity (and a concomitant perplexity) to its temporal inconsistency. Such a practice not only offers aesthetic insights about the music Jankélévitch prized, but also gives us a distinct vision of how a philosopher might preserve the incommensurable operations of an unwoven dialectics that enjoins us to reflect productively on musical experience as an exemplification of the quodditive real.

In contrast to the neo-Hegelian historicism variously developed by Bloch and Adorno, Jankélévitch's affirmative philosophy of music opens the floodgates so that the divine inconsistency of *charme* is coextensive with the full multitude of its immanent actualizations in music. It rejects a historicism that attaches metaphysical significance and a spatial logic to compositional development and tonality, and opposes the universality of an Apollonian metalanguage like an Adornian *Versprachlichung*. Positively, this means that Jankélévitch can create a new field of concepts that are responsive to a wider multiplicity of musical forms. In this way, *charme* is not cause for mere skepticism or silence. Rather, because mediation is still constitutive of our experience of time, music provides an exceptional occasion for one to practice an unwoven dialectics embroidered around the inexpressive flux of music's inconsistent and ephemeral temporality. Subject to such an ethics, it becomes a nexus of one's loquacious fidelity.

If the philosophers discussed so far (Schopenhauer, Nietzsche, Bloch, Adorno, and Jankélévitch) each adopt and develop the form of music's ineffability, the final thinkers in this book, Deleuze and Guattari, will be the first to try to close the gap between music and language, and claim that there is no fundamental paradox or aporia at the center of musical experience. In their view, music is exemplary of a coextensive rhythm of sensation based directly in the creativity of virtual forces. Deleuze and Guattari go further than Jankélévitch to replace and overturn the Hegelian proposal of an aesthetics based in the "sensible appearance of the Idea" through their theory of a "sensation in itself." With respect to music, the dialectics of the tone, of a *Versprachlichung*, of an attentive fidelity towards the inconsistency of musical time, turns into an intermedial affirmation of a syncopated, contrapuntal dialectic. As a result, Deleuze and Guattari collapse the aporetic mediations of the ineffable that Bloch, Adorno, and Jankélévitch link to a metaphysical aporia of an "inconstruable question," a "demythologized prayer," or a "divine inconsistency." They collapse these perplexing summons to thought and, in so doing, intriguingly revive an ancient Pythagoreanism modernized for the era of mid-century structuralism.

For many readers, closing the gap of ineffability may further loosen the criteria of what constitutes an ethical practice of modernism, and expand the "distribution of the sensible" (to refer to Rancière's phrase).[91] Yet curiously, we will find that questions about paradoxical formulations, about dialectical methods, about the nagging difficulties of using language to account for music, and about the specification of criteria for an ethics of musical composition remain strangely in effect as afterimages of methodological tensions over the boundaries of form and the power of ideas.

CHAPTER 4

Deleuze and Guattari's Rhythm

The philosopher Gilles Deleuze did not leave any indications that he had read the work of Vladimir Jankélévitch, but a comparison between their two views of music in fact reveals a great deal about both of them. Jankélévitch and Deleuze were avowed Bergsonians, if not the two most important ones of their respective generations. Just as Jankélévitch wrote the definitive interwar monograph on the philosopher in 1931, Deleuze wrote the definitive postwar account. This 1966 study, *Bergsonism*, was written when he was forty-one, and it followed in the model of his first four books, which were all studies of individual writers: Hume (1953), Nietzsche (1962), Kant (1963), and Proust (1965). In the three years after *Bergsonism*, Deleuze would publish a study of Sacher-Masoch (1967), followed closely by his most formative books: the two monumental dissertations *Spinoza: Expressionism in Philosophy* and *Difference and Repetition*, in 1968, and the famed study of language *The Logic of Sense* in 1969.

There are some basic differences between Jankélévitch's and Deleuze's views on music that can be enumerated in short order. While Deleuze's philosophy is, like Jankélévitch's, oriented in many ways toward the Bergsonian flux of lived time, Deleuze, unlike Jankélévitch, did not think of music as harboring an exclusive or privileged link to the lived movements of time. In fact, if there was an art that did have a privileged relationship to the machinery of lived time, it was decidedly not music, but film.[1] Thus, it should be emphasized at the outset that music stands in crowded aesthetic territory in Deleuze's thought. Second, we might recall that Jankélévitch based much of the thinking in *Music and the Ineffable* in an a priori negation of any kind of *Versprachlichung* in music, a theory so central to Adorno's account of music. Deleuze would agree with Jankélévitch that music should not be heard as language-like. He would not, however, hypostasize it as exceptional among the arts, or as being above or beyond language. Commonly, Deleuze positioned music as integrated with visual and textual media, since for him the senses and arts are more often combined than hierarchized. Thus, for the first time in our narrative, gone are any quasi-theological views of music—inconstruable questions, demythologized prayers, approximations of the voice of God. Such residues of Romanticism are largely absent. To be sure, under the influence of his famous collaborator Félix Guattari, music will acquire a unique specificity, but at no point will music accomplish anything words and images cannot get at in their own way.

My goal in this chapter will be no different from those that preceded it; I hope to make clear the specificity that music does have in Deleuze and Guattari's thinking. The first half of the chapter will develop the concept of rhythm as it is found in Deleuze's foundational writings of the 1960s. In the second half I will show how Deleuze, together with Guattari in the 1970s and '80s, developed this theory of rhythm into a new concept—*la ritournelle* or "the refrain" (as it is customarily translated into English)—that purported to explain the unity of music and nature through overarching, cosmic structures of rhythm and repetition.

Deleuze and Guattari's *ritournelle* is consonant with Jankélévitch's inconsistency insofar as, for both thinkers, music and sound contain an important link with the flow of lived time. But Jankélévitch's thinking suggests that language has an inadequate grasp of lived time; this is why he practices a loquacious fidelity to the inconsistency of musical flows. Deleuze and Guattari, by contrast, do not consider musical time as an exemplary instance of aporias and paradoxes immanent to the experience of the vanishing now. If Jankélévitch's fidelity to the inconsistency of musical time led him to construct sustained tributes to unpresentable musical geographies, odes to the mechanical, and speculative injunctions about the coolness of distance, Deleuze and Guattari's *ritournelle* suggests that the *Tendenz des Materials* might be largely dismantled, or "scared away." From a bird's-eye perspective, they declare with a certain metaphysical bombast that the sonic rhythms of the *ritournelle* can be thought of as a speculative extension of the cosmos.

At the center of Deleuze and Guattari's theory is an assertion that concerns sound's affective force, something they take to operate with a degree of sensational immediacy. Inspired in equal parts by Spinoza and Nietzsche, Deleuze and Guattari's *ritournelle* couples sonic material with nervous systems into a single affective substance, an "interminable presence" of virtual rhythms and forces. For such a presence to occur, the barriers between finite sounds and infinite forces become indistinct in order to make way for a new form of affective autonomy, a sensation "in itself" that is actualized from and re-sutured to the connective openness of the void: "The work of art is a being of sensation and nothing else: it exists in itself.... All sensation is composed with the void in composing itself with itself.... It is the percept or affect that is preserved in itself."[2] Such a coextensive coupling of material and sensation always crosses a boundary—"something passing from one to the other. This something can be specified only as sensation. It is a zone of indetermination, of indiscernibility as if things, beasts, and persons ... endlessly reach that [virtual] point that immediately precedes their natural differentiation."[3] And in doing so, music, like all the arts, operates at an impersonal remove from any particular musical experience: "We attain to the percept and the affect only as to autonomous and sufficient beings that no longer owe anything to those who experience or have experienced them."[4]

To be sure, in its simplest form, this theory of an affective, impersonal, and coextensional *ritournelle* can appear to be a fanciful and uncritical theory of music, as if history, humanity, mediation, and all Apollonian aspects of form have been cast into the wilderness for the sake of a single-substance vitalism. This is, however, not the full story. As argued in the prelude to this book, and as further elaborated in this chapter, Deleuze and Guattari understand Apollonian individuation to always already structure the vitality of Dionysian forces. As a consequence, the ethical and dialectical question about how one should practice music remains a complex matter of debate, even as the criteria are further loosened. As is the case for Bloch, Adorno, and Jankélévitch, particular forms and techniques are still at issue.

Moreover, just as resonances of dialectics lurk in the background when it comes to debating the contours of what music counts as ethical (or not), it is similarly fascinating to see that Schopenhauer's paradox of the ineffable turns up in ghosted forms at moments when the discussion of music's sensuous particularity is at issue. One instance occurs when Deleuze and Guattari describe the affective force of music as an "a-signifying semiotics"—an echo of the unmediated copy (discussed in section 4.3). Another occurs when Deleuze and Guattari flesh out the logic of the *ritournelle* in a way that harks back to Schopenhauer's contention that music can give one a sense of the blind, interior forces of life (discussed in section 4.4). And a final one occurs when Deleuze and Guattari claim that any gap between music and language that gives one an impression of music's ineffability is merely a practical challenge—that it is "hard to say" exactly what the potentially representational content of music is (discussed in section 4.5).

Of course, these are only moments. Most of Deleuze and Guattari's writings on music are dominated by an all-encompassing metaphysics that renders music and language inseparable from a common intermedial rhythm of sense. I read this as a peculiar twentieth-century revival of an ancient Pythagorean lineage of speculative cosmology. Its sources stretch through the Latin doctrine of *musica universalis*, medieval Arabic musical thought, and the higher liberal arts of the quadrivium, up through the English Renaissance and beyond. What joins Deleuze and Guattari to this Pythagorean tradition is their conviction that music shares, via the link of an inhuman metaphysics, a grand coextensive relationship with the cosmos. Of course Deleuze and Guattari have significantly retooled this metaphysical conviction with the aim of joining it to a modern universe for which there is no overarching harmony, no ideal cause, and no heavenly telos. Instead, their metaphysics is based in the vital structure of a cosmos composed of interlocking rhythms and counterpoints. But the parallels are striking.[5] To explain and defend this interpretation requires careful explication. With this in mind, let us turn to Deleuze's discussions of rhythm in his formative publications of the 1960s.

4.1 DELEUZE'S RHYTHM

Across the range of Deleuze's output, rhythm is theorized as a pluralized, punctuated, social, and dialectical flow of lived time. This is his most important source of distance from Bergson. If Jankélévitch distanced himself from Bergson by arguing that our experience of *durée* was not simply intuitive but instead highly aporetic and paradoxical, Deleuze distanced himself from Bergson by arguing that the vitalist philosopher too often considered *durée* to be singular and unified, even a source of intuitive freedom from matter. By contrast, Deleuze emphasized that *durée* cannot be exclusively temporal, intensive, spiritual, free, or creative. For him, "there is always extensity in our *durée*, and always *durée* in matter."[6] The rhythm of life (along with repetition, the eternal return, the *ritournelle,* and so on) makes explicit that lived time stands in an incessantly dialectical relationship with matter. Life is not only creativity and temporal flux; it is significantly punctuated, stopped, and started by the material constraint of bodies.

The same dialectical rhythm applies to the relationship between space and time. The dynamism of rhythm, as a virtual realm of differential structures and potentialities, actualizes itself equally in space and in time. Here, I quote Deleuze at slightly more length: "... Dynamisms are no less temporal than spatial. [Dynamisms] constitute a time of actualization or *differenciation* no less than they outline spaces of actualization. Not only do these spaces begin to incarnate differential relations between elements of the reciprocally and completely determined structure, but the times of *differenciation* incarnate the time of the structure, the time of progressive determination. Such times may be called differential rhythms...."[7]

Deleuze's rhythm is a punctuated time of differentiation and a dynamic time of structure. It is neither pure flux nor metrical regularity, but instead a dialectical interaction of temporal consistency and inconsistency, enmeshed in irregular cycles of reciprocal determinism. Unlike the Hegelian dialectics in Bloch and Adorno's thinking, which are based in the surfacing of contradictions, and unlike the unwoven dialectics of Jankélévitch's thought, which are based in an asymptotic approximation of temporal inconsistency, for Deleuze what I am calling a contrapuntal dialectic is a material process of rhythmic punctuation, unregulated by the power of ideas. It retains two generative operations that are co-constitutive—but they are based in an incommensurable codependence at the level of matter rather than in a contradiction at the Hegelian level of self-consciousness, history, or society. In *Difference and Repetition*, Deleuze describes these operations as a counterpoint between regular and irregular rhythms that together yield a nonsymmetrical, polyphonic multiplicity:

> The study of rhythm allows us immediately to distinguish two kinds of repetition. Cadence-repetition is a regular division of time, an isochronic recurrence of identical elements. However, a period exists only insofar as it is determined by a tonic accent, commanded by intensities. *Yet we would be mistaken about the function of accents if we said that they were reproduced at equal intervals. On the contrary, tonic and intensive values act by creating inequalities or incommensurabilities between metrically equivalent periods or spaces.* They create distinctive points, privileged instants which always indicate *a polyrhythm*.[8]

Regular cadences are a mere homogeneous relation of the identical, a mere "abstract effect." Beneath lies a productive rhythm that bears difference and multiplicity. In Nietzsche's vocabulary, one might say that Dionysian forces are immanently structured and articulated by Apollonian individuations, though without the regulative mediation of concepts and ideas. It results in a rhythm based in "evolutionary cycles or spirals whose principle is a variable curve, and the trajectory of which has two dissymmetrical aspects, as though it had a right and a left. It is always in this gap ... that creatures weave their repetition ..."[9] We might visualize this contrapuntal dialectic as follows.

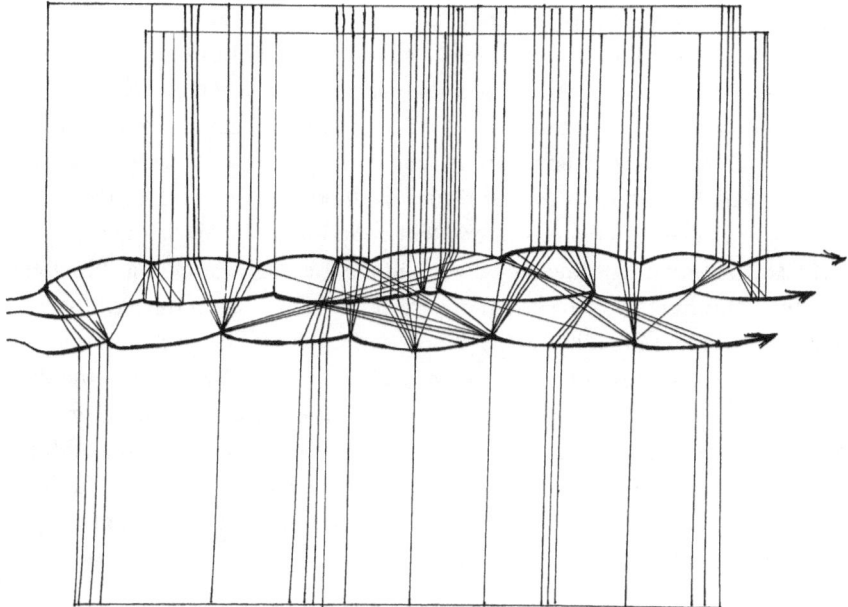

FIGURE 4.1. Deleuze's rhythm. Drawing by the author.

In figure 4.1 I have drawn two lines of temporal progression stretching from left to right. (There are only three for the sake of simplicity, though obviously various durations in Deleuze's metaphysics are nearly innumerable.) The durations crest at irregular and nonsynchronized points because they do not flow continuously. They are rhythmically articulated by stops and starts, changes in speed, variations in intensity, direction, and so on. Secondly, the three lines are socially interactive; their individual rhythms engage in a variety of relatively unpredictable dialogues with other durations. These are represented by lines fanning out from individual points; the lines could indicate a series of words that link two interlocutors, a sequence of actions or physiochemical processes transpiring between two bodies. Finally, each of the three durations has a perpendicular rhythmic stem; one stretches below, two reach upward. These rhythmic "notations" make explicit the structural asymmetry of vital, cosmic rhythms.

As a companion to his theory of rhythm, in *Difference and Repetition* Deleuze develops a novel theory of repetition in dialogue with Hume, Kierkegaard, Nietzsche, Mallarmé, Bergson, Freud, and Proust. I have written about some of its intricacies elsewhere, but for the sake of economy, here I will recount only the basic outlines.[10] Given the complexity of the above rhythms, repetition is never strict or mechanical for Deleuze; it is always dynamic and creative. Likewise, the temporal life of a creature is multiform: it involves practical syntheses of habits, skills, and anticipations, a basis in an infinitely "pure past" of potential recollections, and the possibility of engaging in singular, unforeseen creativity. Its basic logic is reflected in Deleuze's distinctive interpretation of Nietzsche's "eternal return of the same," which Deleuze reads in light of Mallarmé's famous poem "Un coup de dés" (1897), a deeply symbolic affirmation of contingency that explores the fragile aura of a shipwreck in which "nothing will have taken place but the place [*rien n'aura eu lieu que le lieu*]."[11] As he puts it in *Nietzsche and Philosophy*: "The game has two moments which are those of a dice throw—the dice that is thrown and the dice that falls back."[12] The throwing of the dice is the affirmation of unforeseen chance and risk; it is the opening of a life onto the virtual reservoir of differences. And it is a philosophical affirmation of a singular creativity. But it entails no simple operation of affirmation; every event has a relational mooring. For Nietzsche, the falling dice make of this opening an actual concrete result or "combination."

For Deleuze, in order to grasp the essence of repetition, we cannot begin hoping for patterns in what the dice actually show. This would push us back into the jurisdiction of representation. Instead, we must affirm the whole of chance and roll the dice again, throwing them to the sky. For Deleuze, Nietzsche's "eternal return of the same" is the whole of this movement. Throw: affirmation of chance. Fall: affirmation of necessity. Repeat. Throw. Deleuze does not hesitate to feel the full Nietzschean force of this affirmation: "That the universe has no purpose, that it has no end to hope for any more than it has causes to be known—this is the certainty necessary to play well...."[13] By affirming both the risk and the creativity possible in every moment, we become attuned to asynchronous rhythms that flow through the entire cosmos.

How do Deleuze's early theories of rhythm and repetition develop into Deleuze and Guattari's *ritournelle*, which is explicitly sonic? In Deleuze's *Logic of Sense*, he describes sound as a medium that links linguistic rhythm with lived rhythm in general. This gives it a vivid specificity that will be expanded in his collaboration with Guattari. But even so, it must be emphasized that, in Deleuze's later work, sound will earn no real privilege over and above language; in its effects, rhythm traverses all the senses—not just sound. As Deleuze wrote in his 1981 study of the paintings of Francis Bacon, cosmic rhythm "is more profound than vision, hearing, etc."; it is "a vital power that exceeds every domain and traverses them all" and constitutes the true "unity of the senses." This delicate tension—a proximity and specificity between sound and rhythm, and the ultimately univocal character of rhythm and sense—should be dealt with carefully. Let us proceed with a discussion of the role of sound and rhythm in Deleuze's *The Logic of Sense* (1969), one of the most important books of his early career.

4.2 THE RHYTHM OF SENSE

At a physical level, life for Deleuze is based in the aforementioned structure of rhythm. In *The Logic of Sense* he characterizes the rhythm of life as a theater of "sudden condensations, fusions, changes in the states of extended layers and for distributions and reshufflings of singularities."[14] These topologies of dynamic matter are punctuated through cycles of changes, stoppages, and a multitude of forces and intensities.[15] Here Deleuze describes rhythm as a "measureless pulsation" that physically organizes and transforms surfaces:

> [Let us consider] bodies in their undifferentiated depth and in their measureless pulsation. This depth acts in an original way, by means of its power to organize surfaces and to envelop itself within surfaces. This pulsation sometimes acts through the formation of a minimum amount of surface for a maximum amount of matter (thus the spherical form), and sometimes through the growth of surfaces and their multiplication in accordance with diverse processes (stretching, fragmenting, crushing, drying and moistening, absorbing, foaming, emulsifying, etc.).... There is therefore an entire physics of surfaces as the effect of deep mixtures—a physics which endlessly assembles the variations and the pulsations of the entire universe, enveloping them inside these mobile limits.[16]

In motion with this deep physical pulsation and its array of physical processes there then corresponds a surface layer granted a certain privilege—the metaphysical theater of symbols. Deleuze calls it a "transcendental field."[17] It marks the presence of a Mobius-strip-like "frontier" (not a dualist separation) between the depth of the corporeal body and the incorporeal surface of language. Deleuze describes this symbolic frontier as the threshold of "articulation." It appears once physical rhythms are doubled into a metaphysical register of ideational irruption and incorporeal signification; it is where language is developed and distorted, and where imaginary worlds are made palpable to sensory experience. One could think, provisionally, of this incorporeal doubling as an organizing grid. But it would not be one that parallels our bodies in any dualist or rational Cartesian sense. Following from Deleuze's univocal metaphysics, the incorporeal surface must be irrevocably tethered to the substance of physical life.

Thus language, for Deleuze, is not a projection of a second order, of falsehoods or semblances. It is the fully real and constitutive structuring of life. By way of example, Deleuze repeatedly mentions the way Lewis Carroll elides Alice's processes of eating and speaking in *Alice in Wonderland* (1865)—as if material ingestion and immaterial production were two intertwined sides of a single Mobius strip. Similarly, for Deleuze, Antonin Artaud challenges one to confront the physical reality of action and passion beneath language that points to an association of sound with the real, a "language without articulation." As Deleuze says, in something of a Lacanian proposition: "Every word is physical, and immediately affects the body."[18]

Language is further broken out into three aspects: (1) the denotations necessary for propositions to work; (2) the manifestations, desires, and beliefs of those who speak; and (3) logical or conceptual relations in language (called "signification"). Supporting this interlocking tripartition there is a fourth realm called sense. Sense is not what is denoted; it is the way something means.[19] It operates within the dynamic and embodied articulation of language; it is "what happens to bodies"; it "insists," "inheres," or "subsists" in our propositions as the "unconditioned" basis for the operation of language. In Jankélévitch's vocabulary, we might say that sense is the quoddity of language's propositional quiddity, the lived genesis of all language use. We find it in our beliefs and desires, in our intentional stances. But we can not directly say sense, because, like Jankélévitch's "irritating game of hide and seek" or Heidegger's *Ereignis*, it is the presupposed, impassive, neutral ground for the intendment of any meaning, not a propositional thing that can be said.

How, then, does sense interface with rhythm? And how does the medium of sound exhibit this linkage? In his account of psychoanalysis, Deleuze describes the emergence of sense as a "dynamic" or "historical" process, as opposed to something that is given as "unconditioned," static, or a priori. In this account, Deleuze explains that an infant's prelinguistic sounds begin as forms of socially disorganized, unacceptable, or undisciplined sounds: crying, babbling, whining, whimpering, and so on. When children acquire language, they evolve through a "history which liberates sounds and makes them independent of bodies."[20] It liberates sound, that is, into the logic of sense, into the separable expressivity of language. Eventually, children arrive at the frontier of Deleuze's ideality when the event of a "good object which holds itself aloft" takes this oceanic real of creaturely life and hones it into a voice capable of incorporeal expressions.[21]

In Deleuze's "dynamic genesis" of sense, which discusses the above process of language acquisition in psychoanalytic terms, the medium of sound and the temporality of rhythm serve as the common axis of the physical and metaphysical registers of life. Sonic rhythms are key to the advent of sense because Deleuze does not want to think of language acquisition as transcending or dominating the vital and infantile fluxes of the real. Conjoined in the form of a Mobius strip, language and the real are co-implicated in a polyphonic, contrapuntal dialectic that remains open to the deep movement of physical rhythms. For, in exemplary moments, such rhythms reemerge in art, in nonsense, in stuttering, and even in ordinary language when "schizoid fragments" unpredictably bubble up from our creaturely depths.[22]

Just as the aforementioned logic of repetition always entails the production of difference, such a contrapuntal dialectic between the physical and the metaphysical is never regular. The basis for such a rhythm is "difference in itself," not identity. Difference, the chance of the dice throw, inhabits every articulation of time. To make this clear, Deleuze uses the concept of the crack—a self-generating and unpredictable split—to indicate that the orders of the physical and the metaphysical will never be properly harmonized or synchronized with one another as correlative registers of language and bodies, of signs and referents. The crack marks the beginning of a syncopation, an irregularity, a play, a pattern of difference and differentiation, right at the frontier of sense: "The crack is neither internal nor external, but is rather *at the frontier*. It is imperceptible, incorporeal, and ideational."[23]

It is a rhythmic irruption of structure that forks out unpredictably through the sky, splits porcelain, and erupts from the volcano along the lines of least resistance, like a flow of lava. The crack is ideational, but not in the mode of a Platonic model or a Hegelian Idea. Unlike an Adornian fracture positioned within the forms of a *Geist*-mediated being, Deleuze's crack is produced concretely—by the immanent fracturing of matter. It comes to life as an unharmonious relationship between sound and silence that triggers "complex relations of interference and interfacing, of syncopated junctions—a pattern of corresponding beats over two different rhythms."[24] In Deleuze's ontology, the rhythm of sense, sparked by the unpredictability of the crack, unfolds as a polyphonic set of beats and syncopations that link together the physical and the ideational.

Finally, for Deleuze there are exemplary, even ethical, ways of opening oneself to the powers of these rhythms, and making them explicit and intense. And the role of art is crucial in this regard, not because it imitates or represents the asynchronous rhythms of life, but rather because, in line with the aforementioned theory of affective force, it can become substantially coextensive with them: "Perhaps the highest object of art is to bring into play simultaneously all these repetitions, with their differences in kind and rhythm, their respective displacements and disguises, their divergences and decentrings; to embed them in one another and to envelop one or the other in illusions the 'effect' of which varies in each case. Art does not imitate, above all because it repeats; it repeats all the repetitions, by virtue of an internal power."[25]

In Deleuze and Guattari's fully developed theory of the *ritournelle*, the sonic rhythms of music will vividly show us how one might "bring into play"—not imitate or duplicate, but continue and extend—the rhythms of the cosmos. This particularized role for music is hinted at in the closing of *The Logic of Sense*, which ends with a bit of a surprise *telos*—the "problem of the work of art yet to come." For Deleuze, such a work of art would be a goal, a "final ordering" that would repeat the genesis of incorporeal and divine sense from the depths of embodied nonsense. It would "[recover] the voice of the heights of the primary [physical] process" while "the secondary [linguistic] organization at the surface recovers something of the most profound noises, blocks, and elements for the Univocity of sense...."[26] The resultant artwork would be a formal extension of this process, not a representation of it: "a poem without figures." And the processual "verb" of modern music would present us with a particularly vivid form of expression: "What can the work of art do but follow again the path which goes from noise to the voice, from voice to speech, and from speech to the verb, constructing this *Musik für ein Haus*, in order always to recover the independence of sounds and to fix the thunderbolt of the univocal."[27]

Here we have an early outline of what Guattari will call the *ritournelle*, something like the ghost form of a speculative teleology in the medium of sound that extends from matter to life, up to art, and finally to a form of independence. It begins in the depths of cosmic noise, proceeds through the human voice up through the incorporeal sense of speech, and arrives at the flux of expressive action in a modernist form: here, the example is Karlheinz Stockhausen's *Musik für ein Haus* (1968), a four-hour multiroom performance environment. Its teleological apex is a musical "poem without figures" that will ultimately "recover the independence of sounds" as it captures the genetic forces of "difference in itself"—"the thunderbolt of the univocal."[28]

A hint of Hegelian teleology here may strike readers as something of an oddity for a philosopher who thought of himself as adamantly "anti-dialectical" in his early book on Nietzsche. Instructively, however, much like Adorno—a deeply Hegelian thinker—Deleuze and Guattari are willing to go beyond a metaphysical affirmation of the teleology towards artistic independence; by the 1980s they are increasingly tinkering with the ethical question of how to do it well. Tellingly, they even acknowledge in the midst of a section on music in *A Thousand Plateaus*: "All this seems extremely general, and somewhat Hegelian, testifying to an absolute spirit."[29] In fact, as I will argue in this book's conclusion, some kind of ethical specificity may be a common touchstone when these intellectuals turn to a prescriptive account of musical composition. Before this thread can be developed any further, however, the status of sound and music in Deleuze and Guattari's collaborative books must be brought to the surface.

4.3 A STRUCTURALIST QUADRIVIUM

With Guattari on board, sound and music are given a vivid specificity. Deleuze and Guattari's collaborative theory extends Deleuze's concepts of rhythm and sense into an elaborate musicalized vision of a cosmic *ritournelle* that accounts not only for the temporality of life and sense, but for all forms of creaturely life on a wide range of scales from the biological microrhythms of creatures to forms of human music both ordinary and extraordinary, all the way up to vast cosmic *ritournelles*. This multitiered structure, first proposed by Guattari alone and then developed in partnership with Deleuze, accounts not only for the manifestation of sense but also for the expressivity of life in general. The *ritournelle* is both sonic and material—it is a chorus of nonsynchronous but nonetheless repetitive cosmic movements. One can hear it in music, but it is based in the material habits of singing-to-oneself, of creaturely survival and sexual expression, of delineating territory and shelter, and of occasionally leaving one's milieu behind to improvise or "deterritorialize."

We might recall from chapter 1 that Bloch espoused a similar teleology of music that was developmental and marked by stages such as singing-to-oneself, classical song, and the resistant potential of modern event forms. What distinguishes Deleuze and Guattari's evolutionary narrative from the Hegelian teleologies is its structural imbrication in an underlying contrapuntal dialectics of rhythm and repetition, as opposed to a historical *Geist* of well-ordered and self-conscious forms of musical organization. Correspondingly, rhythm, rather than the tone, becomes the key sonic parameter. Such a commitment to a highly dynamic parameter rather than an orderly one reflects, as it did with Jankélévitch, Deleuze and Guattari's interest in avoiding the mediation of any kind of regulative ideality or mental representation, as was central to Hegel's understanding of the distinction between a natural *Klang* and a *Ton* mediated by *Geist*.

And dynamic it is. Deleuze and Guattari's definition of sound might even be said to recall Adorno's ahistorical and mimetic "rigid drumbeats of the barbarians." For them, sound coextensively repeats the action of material impulses;

it is a Dionysian flux of affective force, and it proposes to cast away any Apollonian *Versprachlichung* in music. Such Dionysian affirmations set them apart from the cool and impersonal distance of Jankélévitch's *charme* as well. Deleuze and Guattari think of sound as hot, intoxicating, and powerful; it summons an intensity that is ambiguous in its powers:

> Sound invades us, impels us, drags us, transpierces us. It takes leave of the earth, as much in order to drop us into a black hole as to open us up to a cosmos. It makes us want to die. Since its force of deterritorialization is the strongest, it also effects the most massive of reterritorializations, the most numbing, the most redundant. Ecstasy and hypnosis. Colors do not move a people. Flags do nothing without trumpets. Lasers are modulated on sound. The *ritournelle* is sonorous par excellence....[30]

It is a thought that returns us full-circle to Schopenhauer's Dionysian affirmations of music's "stronger, faster, effective, and infallible" sonic force. Sound is the most powerful deterritorializer; its powers can be exceptionally creative. At the same time it presents us with the threat of the greatest ideology—numbing and redundant "re-territorializations" that, in extreme cases, might even echo the masochistic instincts of Freud's death drive. Language and vision simply do not pierce, invade, impel, and drag us with quite the same intensity. It is a point that is made elsewhere in late books like *What Is Philosophy?* (1994), as well as in Deleuze's solo book on the paintings of Francis Bacon.[31] Sound invades us with a certain force; it does not necessarily require the mediation of language, representation, or interpretation; it can set us free (or delude us) with an undeniable intensity.

But does sound alone do this? Is the *ritournelle* distinctively sonic? Deleuze and Guattari put the question to themselves quite explicitly:

> But precisely why is the *ritournelle* eminently sonorous? Why this privileging of the ear, when even animals and birds present us with so many visual, chromatic, postural, and gestural *ritournelles*? ... It seems that when sound deterritorializes, it becomes more and more refined; it becomes specialized and autonomous. Color clings more, not necessarily to the object, but to territoriality.... Sound owes this power not to signifying or "communicational" values (which would privilege light over sound) but to a phylogenetic line, a machine phylum that operates in sound and makes it a cutting edge of deterritorialization.[32]

A "phylogenetic line" and a "machine phylum" are perhaps the strangest terms to be associated with their ontology of sound. Phylogenesis denotes the evolutionary individuation of a species. Extending this term to music, the advent of "specialized and autonomous" sound would not be due to an ideal or regulative principle (such as tonality, the musical work, or the concept of absolute music). Rather, according to the logic of phylogenesis, it is only through the aimless material process of trial and error—via an immanent evolutionary process akin to natural selection—that musical sound develops into an autopoietic "machine" with its own logic. In this way, Deleuze and Guattari's history of music is akin to a natural history. Well-known composers have no teleological, necessary, or unified place for Deleuze and Guattari, as early Schoenberg does for Adorno's *Tendenz des Materials*. In their vocabulary, the composer or artist is merely an empirical occasion for the instance of a "minor literature."[33] She is a contingent and "phylogenetic" individuation, free of any ideal guidance.

A materially grounded "phylogenesis" of sound proposes an immanent flip side to the transcendent views of music espoused by Hoffmann, Hegel, and Bloch and to the various forms of *Stilkritik* influenced by German Idealism (as discussed in chapters 1 and 2). Historicist traditions have recourse to idealized teleological trajectories mediated by a form of self-conscious *Geist*, the most common being the Germanic lineage from the eighteenth to the nineteenth century that stretches from Bach through Haydn, Mozart, Beethoven, and the New German School. Deleuze and Guattari, by contrast, suggest that there is something specific to the medium of sound that has a material tendency towards abstraction, a-signifying intensities, rhythmic patterning, and machinic transduction. There are still Apollonian individuations at work, but they are not regulated by the power of concepts, ideas, or historical self-consciousness. This material autonomy dispenses with a Hegelian *Tendenz des Materials* funneled through the logiclike character of a *Versprachlichung*. The autonomy of sound is based in the "ecstasy and hypnosis" of its material force.

Guattari is already tinkering with this theory in his early manuscripts on the concept of the *ritournelle*, and he does so with an explicit consideration of how music might upend the coordinates of what a Lacanian would call the symbolic order. Consider Guattari's diary entry of August 29, 1971. There, we see three themes that are central to the theory of music articulated in *A Thousand Plateaus* (1980): an ethical vision of modernism; its supersession of language, the subject, and the symbolic order in the name of a formal "transversal" or "diagonal" abolition of hierarchy; and a link of transduction between music and cybernetic machines that model the structural movements of life. He writes:

In the very first notes of really machinic music—not show [virtuoso] music—the universe is deployed, in the axiomatic sense of deterritorialized musical signs. A plane of consistency prototype. Abolition of the subject of enunciation. Generalized suture of everything and nothing. Radical elimination of the signifier. Music is the machinic art form par excellence: musician and listener both fall into musical machine, instrumental or textual. Jouissance seeks refuge in infinitely small residual differences. . . . musical enunciation grants the right of way to pure group fantasy, to what Hjelmslev describes as a collective level of apperception.[34]

Guattari's diary entry ends by proposing that music serves as a medium for "pure group fantasy"—something highly prized in Guattari's experimental psychotherapy at *La Borde*, the psychiatric clinic where he developed the practice of schizoanalysis in the 1960s. Music, he speculates here, might subvert the regulative authority of the symbolic order through an "abolition of the subject of enunciation" and the "radical elimination of the signifier."[35] Just over a decade later, in his *Glossary of Schizoanalysis*, Guattari echoes this thought in a more dialectical fashion. He proposes that music operates through an "a-signifying semiotics," by way of terms largely based in the mid-century vocabulary of cybernetics and systems theory, a discourse that was pervasive among French Marxists of the 1960s and '70s: "We have to distinguish between signifying semiologies—that articulate signifying chains and signified contents—and a-signifying semiotics that work from syntagmatic chains without engendering any signification effect. . . . An example of an a-signifying semiotics: musical writing, a mathematical corpus, computer syntax, robotics, etc."[36]

As mentioned earlier, Guattari's "a-signifying semiotics" uncannily revisits Schopenhauer's immediate copy. For Guattari, Music's immediacy would work without any referent or "signifying effect"—it has tremendous affective force. And yet it is still semiotic—still structural, still mediated in a way that is analogous to Schopenhauer's copy. An "a-signifying semiotics" is also aligned, however, with the comparatively direct, real, and "transductive" vehicles of mathematics, structure, cybernetics, and machinery—all key components of Deleuze and Guattari's metaphysics. And this direct relationship to structure is how an "a-signifying semiotics" avoids being paradoxical or aporetic. Music, like many other material processes, operates differently than do "mental representation" or "signification effects" because it works directly with material fluxes, in a process that is both structural and nonlinguistic.[37]

It is instructive to think of Guattari's structuralist vision of music's "a-signifying semiotics" in dialogue with a very old-fashioned gesture in the history of musical thought. I would suggest, in fact, that far from a mere gesture towards cybernetic futurism, Guattari's proposal might be read as a revival of ancient Pythagoreanism. For both Guattari and the Pythagoreans, there is a link of coextension between music and the cosmos via the common attribute of structure. The key difference from the Pythagorean metaphysics will be that for Guattari, as for Deleuze, the structure of the cosmos is no longer based in the eternity of whole-number ratios, and is no longer harmonic, static, or universal. In Deleuze and Guattari's metaphysics, the cosmos is upended into a teeming multiplicity of interlocking counterpoints, which find their basis in Deleuze's own metaphysics of difference, disjunction, and syncopated rhythm.

For Deleuze and Guattari, as for the Pythagoreans, the link between music and the cosmos remains structural, even mathematical. In consonance with a theory of the real that emerges mid-century in Lacanian structuralism and is further developed by Alain Badiou and Quentin Meillassoux, mathematics affords us access to the real, the thing in itself, the true being of what is.[38] Since the privileged sonic element is now mobile and combinatory rhythm rather than static Pythagorean harmonics, instead of a transcendent doctrine of eternal number, Deleuze and Guattari's "a-signifying semiotics" of music will be integrated with uncountable sensations, affects, and differential fluxes, structured as a ceaseless process of punctuated articulations. Overturning a Neoplatonic metaphysics of cosmic resemblance, Deleuze and Guattari will hold that rhythm has a "geomorphic" or "transductive" relationship to the real.

This is a speculative practice that is quite different from the Hegelian views espoused by Bloch or Adorno, both of whom maintain that music acquires its power predominantly through an idealized, and technically exteriorized, history of music. It is also unlike the Bergsonian ethics of temporal inconsistency one finds in Jankélévitch's writings, which moves beyond Hegelian historicism but retains an incommensurability—a qualitative separation—between music and language. All three—Bloch, Adorno, and Jankélévitch—place great emphasis on the paradoxical structure of Schopenahauer's immediate copy. In contrast, by tightly integrating the spheres of the Dionysian and the Apollonian into a metaphysics of rhythm, Deleuze and Guattari displace the paradox of the ineffable to a more generalized question of cosmic structure.

In fact, in my view, Deleuze and Guattari's claim that music's metaphysical significance lies in its coextension with the cosmos recalls not only Pythaogreans, but a long lineage of speculative music theory that was unfashionable in the eyes of Bloch, Adorno, and Jankélévitch: the Latin concept of *musica universalis*, or *musica mundana*, as it would be referred to by Boethius and many others after him.[39] Its first instance comes to us from a Greek source briefly alluded to in this book's introduction: Plato's *Timaeus*, a book that exerted a significant influence on Western musical thought up through the seventeenth century, thanks to centuries of summaries, paraphrases, and commentaries. So important is the text that it is worth a brief excursus.

In a key passage of the dialogue, Socrates's interlocutor Timaeus tells us that he will now explain the relationship between the soul and body. He begins, predictably, by remarking that the soul is older and "more venerable in birth" than the body, which is the "mistress" inflected by "too much that is casual and random which shows itself in our speech."[40] If this hierarchy seems self-evidently Platonic, what follows is famously convoluted. Timaeus explains that there are two different intermediate categories besides the soul and the body—a "third form of Existence" that hybridizes identity and difference into an intermediate "compound" that blends the divisible (potentially different) with the indivisible (the same). According to the myth, a demiurge took these two hybrid terms and mingled them all together in a unity, and then back into differentiations. This tripartite structure reflects a highly elaborate formal explanation of how identity and difference, the indivisible and the divisible, the eternity of being and the movement of becoming, can feed into one another outside of the deliberate mediation of any human *techne*. If in the *Republic*, Socrates's explanations of how the truth of being is mediated by human actors are largely practical and ethical (educating philosophers, training guardians, banning poets, practicing the dialectic, etc.), in the *Timeaus* the relation between being and becoming is formalized as a speculative metaphysics of number.

In line with the Platonic ontology that presumes that forms are ideal and eternal, and best articulated through the immaterial science of mathematics, Timaeus goes on to explain the differential compounds through a series of Pythagorean whole-number ratios. These are famous in the history of musical thought, and were often illustrated on a simple instrument called the monochord by stopping the string or moving a bridge at different points to change the sounding pitch of the plucked string. The practice enabled people to hear what we now measure as octaves (2:1), fifths (3:2), fourths (4:3), and so on, and to think speculatively of intervallic pitch relations as a real manifestation of cosmic universality. Timaeus glosses all this as resulting in a cosmic "fabric" of divisions and subdivisions, down to the very smallest and most complicated and dissonant subdivision—256:243—something like a minor second that's a bit flat.

This Pythagorean formalization was both obscure and numerically precise enough to inspire centuries of commentary.[41] In medieval Europe, practical musical application of the harmonics took on increasing importance. We have very influential treatises, for example, by Aristides Quintilianus and Boethius, which try to develop and explain this text in a more compositionally instructive way.[42] The Ikhwan al-Safa, too, described elaborate Pythagorean correspondences between the sounds of the four-stringed oud and a vast universe of natural substances.[43] In early modern Europe, music theorists like Gioseffo Zarlino undertook sophisticated efforts to prescribe structural complexity around the resonant possibilities of Pythagorean harmony. Broadly speaking, however, it is important to note that, for the Pythagoreans, music was not primarily heard or thought of as expressive or aesthetic, but instead, given music's privileged relationship to number, it was viewed as a structurally impersonal extension of a divine harmony. Among the liberal arts in medieval Europe, after Boethius, music comprised a portion of the medieval *quadrivium* (next to mathematics, astronomy, and geometry), which was taught after the *trivium* (rhetoric, grammar, dialectic) because it was understood to be an exact and more advanced discipline closer to the study of philosophy.[44]

Under the condition of Pythagorean metaphysics, music was not exceptionally privileged because it said obscure things that language could not get at. That would risk ascribing a romanticized lens of the ineffable to a distant moment in the intellectual history of music. Music's ancient exceptionalism stemmed from the view that music wasn't saying anything at all; it was just taken to be one with the metaphysical belief in the truth of number as the real foundation of the universe. I would venture this as the key point of contact between Deleuze and Guattari's theory of music and ancient musical thought. At a historical and geographic remove from the substantial impact of humanism, the Enlightenment discipline of aesthetics, and the epistemology of the modern subject, what carried the greatest ontological weight for music was a link of coextension posited between music and the universe via the link of structure: the whole-number ratio.

One of the most striking visual manifestations of this link comes to us from Robert Fludd, an English mathematician and occult cosmologist who developed an elaborate theory of cosmic harmony. Fludd argued for the metaphysical unity between the structure of sonic intervals and the universe. The famous image of such correspondences can be seen vividly in his 1618 drawing seen in figure 4.2. From top to bottom, the drawing bisects the monochord into two octaves, with the sun at the center point of the bisection. On the left, Fludd extends arcs that represent the numerical proportions of the intervals from a low G (customarily represented with the Greek capital gamma) up to middle G, and on up again to "gg," an octave higher. In the corresponding arcs on the right side, Fludd indicates the upper octave intervals as formal [*formalis*], and

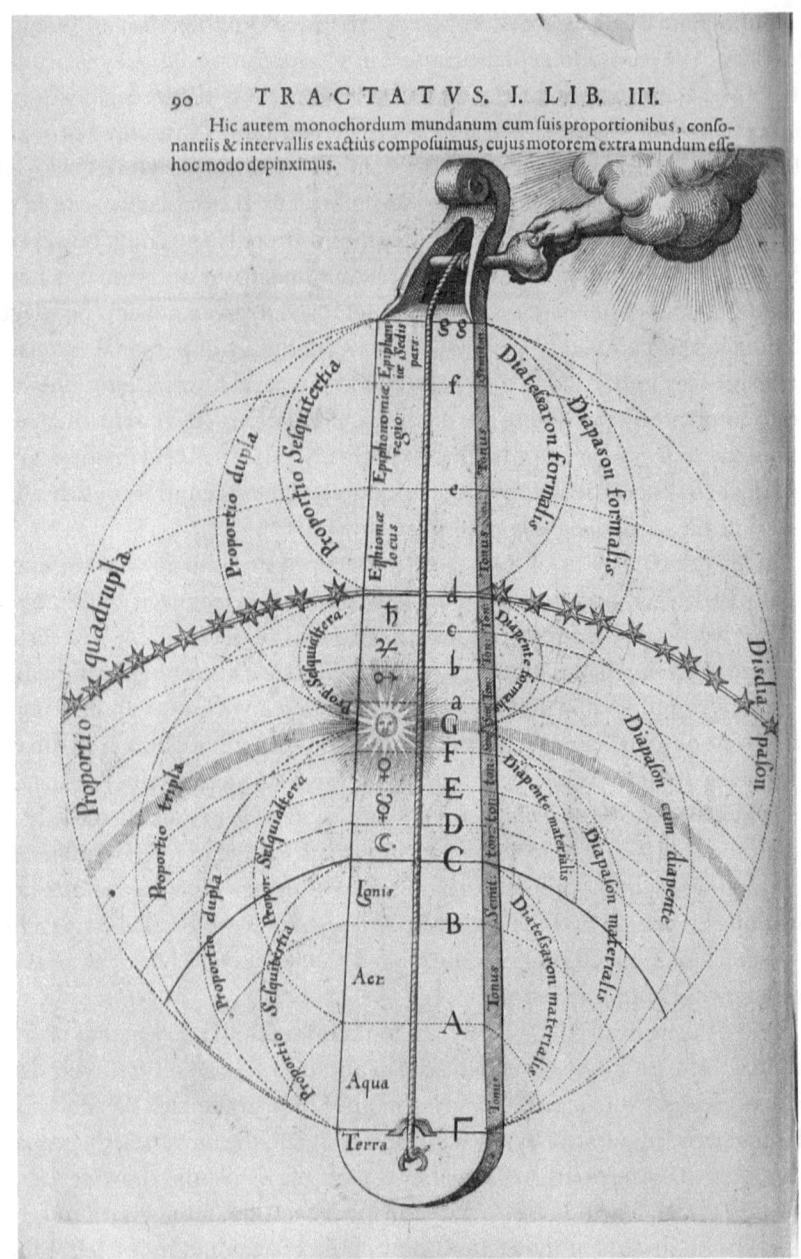

FIGURE 4.2. The "Divine Monochord" from Robert Fludd, *Turiusque cosmi . . . historia* (1617), 1:90. Source: Robert Fludd, *Utriusque cosmi maioris scilicet et minoris metaphysica, physica atque technica historia*, 2 vols. (Oppenheim: De Bry, 1617–19), 1:90. Getty Research Institute Research Library Catalog. Digitized version, internet archive (public domain).

the lower octave as material [*materialis*]. Running up the spine of the monochord is a chain of being that extends from the lower earth up through the material elements to the formal "seat of the epiphany [*epiphaniae sedis pars*]."

Joining Deleuze and Guattari to this speculative tradition is a common theory that considers music and the cosmos as structurally coextensive, linked via a common form. If, for the Pythagoreans, plucked strings were heard as extensions of the eternal form of the universe thanks to the whole-number ratios of the harmonics, for Deleuze and Guattari the same link of metaphysical coextension between music and the cosmos holds, only with the key difference that the cosmos is shorn of its ideal, static, and eternal form. Correspondingly, the structures undergirding the coextension have been inverted from the grand vertical unities of eternal harmonics and Neoplatonic hierarchies to the modular differentials and "diagonals" of twentieth-century structuralism and a contrapuntal dialectics of syncopated rhythms. But the cosmology, the metaphysics, and even the metaphor of resonance remain. And the parallels (despite the obvious contrasts) are striking.

Inspired by Nietzsche, we are told, Deleuze's ontology endeavored to overturn Platonism.[45] From a synoptic view, he could be said to retain many aspects of Platonic thought, if only to diametrically invert them. His ontology maintains the dichotomy of the virtual realm of incorporeal Being and the actual, concrete realm of ontic beings. But Deleuze transforms Plato's virtual *eidos* (which is based in the principles of identity and resemblance) into a dynamic structural event of differentiation. In contrast to the Platonic virtuality of an eternal model, the Deleuzian virtual does not resemble its actual counterparts and there is no harmony or identity among its actualizations; like the crack of difference in itself, it produces the world in rays of syncopated differences as it "resonates across all of its disjunctions."[46] Such actualizations are compatible with the cosmos only through a revival of medieval univocity where all beings are taken to be of a single substance even as they produce boundless differentiations. But nothing in the world resembles the differential crack of the event itself, an irruptive presupposition for the appearance and ramification of sense:

> The univocity of Being signifies that Being is Voice; that it is said, and that it is said in one and the same "sense" of everything about which it is said. That of which it is said is not at all the same, but Being is the same for everything about which it is said. It occurs, therefore, as a unique event for everything that happens to the most diverse things, *Eventum tantum* [the event alone] for all events, the ultimate form for all of the forms which re-

main disjointed in it, but which bring about the resonance and the ramification of their disjunction.[47]

Deleuze and Guattari's structuralist revival of the medieval quadrivium can be thought of as an extension of Deleuze's ontology, one of resonance of disjunction and difference, of a pluralized univocity. The revival is based equally in Deleuze's foundational theory of disjunctive rhythm and in the aforementioned Pythagorean themes in the *longue durée* of musical thought. It rearticulates Deleuze's claim to overturn Platonism in the medium of sound, by turning away from eternal whole-number ratios to the variable structuralism of rhythm, from static harmonics to syncopated temporalities.

To hark back to the book's prelude, Deleuze and Guattari's structuralist quadrivium also echoes quite uniquely Schopenhauer's metaphysics of music. For one, Schopenhauer, Deleuze, and Guattari all attempt to overcome a conventional conception of mimesis by positioning music as an art form that exemplifies structure rather than representation. They also share with Schopenhauer the claim to overcome the paradox of the "immediate copy" and solve the paradox of the ineffable through the link of metaphysical structure held in common between music and the cosmos. After all, like Schopenhauer, Deleuze and Guattari associate music directly—immediately—with cosmic forces, which are forces of the real—blind, and valueless.

Of course, significant differences divide Schopenhauer from Deleuze and Guattari. Deleuze and Guattari insist that these cosmic forces are plural rather than unitary. More seriously, for them the multiplicity of such virtual forces does not exist as a separate facet of life, as the will does for Schopenhauer. Rather, their conception of the virtual always already contains the processes of individuation. Dynamic and pluralized punctuations of rhythm, structured by a contrapuntal dialectic of individuation, of space and time, would replace the unified eternity of a will that Schopenhauer understood to operate outside of space, time, and causality. Finally, Deleuze and Guattari do not view music as having any exceptional proximity to the will; rather, the metaphysical pulses and rhythms of the cosmos pluralize all the arts with one another.

4.4 THE RHYTHM OF LIFE

Syncopated, variable rhythms that are coextensive with the differential structures of life are central to the concept of the *ritournelle* in its fully developed form. In *A Thousand Plateaus*, Deleuze and Guattari define the *ritournelle* as an *agencement* (an "assemblage," "layout," or "arrangement") that lies somewhere on a vast chain of being from the primordial forces of chaos to the rhythms of creaturely milieus, motifs, and counterpoints, up through expressive territories, assemblages, inter-assemblages, and landscapes. Across the range of this metaphysically stratified chain of being, sound and life are taken to constitute the same single substance. And the musical elements of motifs and counterpoints exemplify the way the rhythms of music develop outward to coextensively repeat the temporal structure of a vast, expressive, nonhierarchical cosmos.

In a manner redolent of a German *Naturphilosophie* from the early nineteenth century, in *A Thousand Plateaus*, Deleuze and Guattari argue for the coextension between music and nature in dialogue with a range of scientific thinking drawn from outside the field of philosophy. In the footnotes to the famous "De la ritournelle" chapter of *A Thousand Plateaus*, one finds a library of texts from evolutionary biology, ethology, and sociobiology, among many others from anthropology, comparative religion, aesthetics, literature, and musicology. Let us consider one of the most important sources: German biologist Jakob von Uexküll's *Streifzüge durch die Umwelten von Tieren und Menschen*, first published in 1934 but translated into French in 1956. From Uexküll, Deleuze and Guattari seem to have derived the idea that creaturely life has a protohumanistic horizon of meaning. For Uexküll, who sought to join speculations about Kantian epistemology to nonhuman perception, each creature has an autonomous, even quasi-subjective interior semiotic environment (or *Umwelt*) that engages in incessantly contrapuntal interaction with the *Umwelten* of other creatures and objects. On one level, Uexküll's concept of the *Umwelt* helped Deleuze and Guattari blur the line between the human and animal, which they were keen to do. But more substantially, it allowed them to connect human art with prehuman structures of creaturely expression.

Deleuze and Guattari extended Uexküll's theory of the *Umwelt* with the key concept of territorialization, which they developed in dialogue with Konrad Lorenz's theory of "mutual repulsion acting on the animals of the same species."[48] The authors disagreed with Lorenz that aggression was the central causal factor in territorialization, and instead posited a more peaceful and creative notion of expression (bird song, ornamentation, dwellings, etc.). Deleuze and Guattari cite the example of the male tooth-billed bowerbird, who expresses himself by arranging leaves upside-down (bright-side-up) in a "display court" in order to form a striking visual contrast with the dark soil (figure 4.3).[49]

Deleuze and Guattari take this "display court" to exemplify a structure of creaturely expression that does not require the mediation of reflection, imitation, or interpretation. For them, the visual contrast (bright green upturned

FIGURE 4.3. Bowerbird. Photograph by Timothy G. Laman. Licensed by Tim Laman Photography.

leaves versus dark soil) articulates a structural relationship between two birds through a transductive, coextensional, machinic counterpoint between creatures and objects in their environment.

In my view, Uexküll's biosemiotics furnished Deleuze and Guattari with a novel theory concerning the relationship between the structure of life and the structure of music. For it is Uexküll's theory of the *Umwelt* that asks: What is it like for the Bowerbird? Thomas Nagel develops this question in 1974 in his article, "What is it like to be a bat?" In the article, Nagel critiques materialism (what he calls "physicalism") as having no convincing account of consciousness or experiential qualia for animal life. In his view, the interiors of creaturely life would appear inaccessible to objective knowledge. And yet Nagel insists that the compulsion to recognize the fact of an interior life in nonhuman creatures remains.[50]

Uexküll answers this question through a theory of a functional cycle (or *Funktionskreis*) that describes the interiors of creaturely experience in structural terms. The *Funktionskreis* is represented here in an early diagram from 1920 (figure 4.4), which is now viewed as a progenitor to the systems theory central to cybernetics as well as a foundation of what is now called biosemiotics. On the right half of this diagram, Uexküll represents the *Innenwelt* of

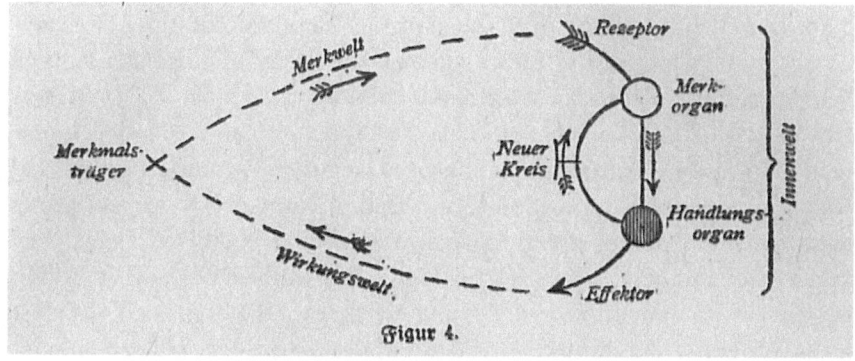

FIGURE 4.4. "Originaler Wirkkreis von Uexküll" (public domain). Source: Jakob Johann von Uexküll, *Theoretische Biologie* (Berlin: Verlag der Gebrüder Baetel, 1920), 117.

the creature as a cycle between a *Merkorgan* (above), which could discriminate particular features of the *Umwelt*, and a *Handlungsorgan* (below), which would orchestrate some kind of behavioral response. Completing the cycle is an arrow stretching out to the left with a dotted line that effects something in response to a *Merkmalsträger* (a carrier of a perceptual cue or sign in the environment), which in turn engenders a feedback loop and sends a new signal back to the *Merkorgan*. This triggers a new cycle (*Neuer Kreis*) of creaturely action and signification.[51]

If the structure of Uexküll's *Funktionskreis* is designed to represent the interior structure of creaturely life as it relates to its *Umwelt*, how does one express that philosophically, presuming that the language of philosophy is forever contaminated by anthropomorphic concepts? For Uekxüll, it is music that compellingly indicates how we might know what it is like to be a nonhuman creature.[52] Uexküll's text relies upon a range of musical metaphors: the "living carillon" (the structural unity of a healthy living cell), a musical score (a scripted model for biology's natural "plan") and a "formative melody" which appears to be a progenitor of DNA. This functional cycle he models with something he calls an *Ich-ton* or "self-tone"—in part because a musical tone seems to be able to accept the chaos of passing time while still holding itself together. Uexküll calls upon music to do the work of explaining the unexplainable interiority of creaturely life. In a strangely precise afterimage of Schopenhauer's conviction that music narrates the most interior secrets of the will, music serves as a metaphorical indicator of a creature's material homeostasis.

Deleuze and Guattari adopt Uexküll's general strategy of appealing to music, but they very carefully shear away most of Uexküll's chosen musical elements.

They leave behind two of them: the motif and counterpoint. Why these two components, which are relatively minor components of Uexküll's theory? Why not a tone, a scale, or a score—the all-important musical elements in Uexküll's text? Because most of Uexküll's elements retain vestiges of Apollonian unity and a Germanic commitment to language-like musical syntax. Deleuze and Guattari's opposition to any kind of normative *Versprachlichung* leads them to reject any governing logic of totality and unity. Of course, they retain a commitment to musical technique. But, in their view, the intertwining of motivic counterpoint—of polyphonic "lines and movements"—is most amenable to the mobile linkages and multiplicative qualities of deep ontological rhythms. Motifs and counterpoints exemplify the ontological process of disjunctive synthesis central to Deleuze and Guattari's metaphysics (and . . . and . . . and; sometimes . . . sometimes . . . sometimes, etc.) as well as the concept of the *agencement* or "assemblage," a form of fitting-together without *harmonia* (a telling contrast with an ancient Greek term originally used to denote the proper joining of wooden planks). According to Uexküll, motifs give us a sense of minimal creaturely behaviors, bits of vital movement. Counterpoints model the interaction of motifs, basic interspecies relations within the socially expressive structures of biosemiotics. As a whole, they result in a sonorous tapestry of creaturely nature—a vast *ritournelle* of flexible, diagonal, contrapuntal, interior worlds—*Umwelten*.[53]

In this reworking of Uexküll, Schopenhauer's paradox of the immediate copy seems to linger in ghosted form. As with Bloch's and Adorno's utopias or Jankélévitch's instant, in Deleuze and Guattari's discussion of Uexküll, sound and music serve as an alternative mode of knowing, an epistemological remedy for speculating about something—the will, the thing-in-itself, or the interior rhythms of creaturely life—that cannot be easily articulated through language. In this regard, once again one finds an afterimage of music's ineffability. To be sure, as the role of biosemiotics makes clear, Deleuze and Guattari do not aim to think of music as doing anything exceptional that language cannot touch, as do Bloch, Adorno, and Jankélévitch, who maintain that music is both ineffable and exceptional. Rather, Deleuze and Guattari hear music as bearing a narrow specificity, or at best a quiet exceptionalism. In reviving the outlines of an ancient Pythagorean metaphysics that is shorn of unitary order and harmonic doctrine, music, of a common structure and substance with life itself, is metaphysically thought of as extending the syncopated counterpoint of the cosmos.[54] That is, if the structuring of life cannot be easily articulated in language, music intensifies it in the medium of sound along the privileged axis of rhythm and counterpoint.

4.5 SONOROUS COEXTENSIONS

Finally, if music and lived rhythms are already structurally intertwined with one another in such a specific way, why does it matter to us? Is there a way to be ethically attentive to this coextension, to make it vivid and explicit to ourselves with music that "stands up on its own" as an "artwork yet to come?" It is with this question that Deleuze and Guattari articulate an equivalent of Bloch's *Ereignisformen* or Adorno's *Wahrheitsgehalt*. And like Adorno, they ask: How might one create music that ethically addresses the conditions of modern life?

In this context, it is instructive to note that Deleuze and Guattari's ethics is linked to a Marxist view of political economy that parallels that of Bloch and Adorno. We can recall that Bloch and Adorno proposed to recover utopia as a critique of a life that has been reified by the all-encompassing impact of technology, capitalism, exchange value, and domination. For Deleuze and Guattari, by contrast, the *ritournelle* is a productive capacity of life that precedes capitalism. That is, if Marx understood the means of production to be a historical and technological process set in motion by human societies, for Deleuze and Guattari the *ritournelles* of life are originally productive from the genetic and cellular level up through the development of modern capitalism. This is the foundation for their materialist ontology of life.

For Deleuze and Guattari, an unethical capitalism in the modern world would not just be exploitative of this labor power; it territorializes it, and in the process erases the ontological productivity of labor.[55] With Deleuze and Guattari's readings of Marx in mind, it is possible to see how the techniques and *ritournelles* of music and art are not simply asocial affirmations of affect and sense; their resistant view of art is also a way of "forewarning" the present-day fact of capitalism's reterritorializing of production.[56] Yet, for this "forewarning" to occur, there is a shift in register that needs to be discussed between a general productivity of life that precedes and undergirds capitalism (what they call "the labor of creation"), and one that is ethically produced in a work of art and is thus capable of resistance (what they call "a whole learned labor").[57] It is the tension between what life already is and what it ought to be. The following passage, which comes towards the end of the famous chapter on the *ritournelle* in *A Thousand Plateaus*, formulates these two registers explicitly:

> What needs to be shown is that a musician requires a *first type* of *ritournelle*, a territorial or assemblage *ritournelle*, in order to transform it from within, deterritorialize it, producing a refrain of the *second type* as the final end of music: the cosmic *ritournelle* of a sound machine. . . . We go from

assembled *ritournelles* (territorial, popular, amorous, etc.) to the great cosmic machined *ritournelle*. But the labor of creation is already under way in the first type; it is there in its entirety.... It is the extremely profound labor dedicated to the first type of refrain that creates the second type, or the little phrase of the Cosmos.

For Deleuze and Guattari, any "second type" of *ritournelle* that might ethically "deterritorialize" itself and articulate "a little phrase of the Cosmos" is actually already at work in the "profound labor" of all *ritournelles*. Then what makes it a deterritorialized *ritournelle* unique and distinct? How precisely can we make one with music? They continue:

> ... We do not need to suppress tonality, we need to turn it loose [*faire fuir*].... Produce a deterritorialized *ritournelle* as the final end of music, release it in the Cosmos—that is more important than building a new system. Opening the assemblage onto a cosmic force. In the passage from one to the other ... many dangers arise: black holes, closures, paralysis of the fingers and hallucinations of the ear, the madness of Schumann, cosmic force becoming *bad*, a note that pursues you, a sound that penetrates you.... We can never be sure we will be strong enough, for we have no system, only lines and movements. Schumann.[58]

Like Adorno before them, here Deleuze and Guattari are attempting to discern criteria—genuine limits—for an ethical and resistant practice of modern music. Earlier in the chapter, they offered words of caution regarding music that makes the inconsistency of noise into its core material, and leaves us with a meaningless "scribble [*gribouillage*]" or "interference/garble [*brouillage*]." As an example of this, they mention John Cage's prepared piano, an invention of the 1930s that converted the equal-tempered piano into a self-contained percussion ensemble.[59] In their view, music that has noise as its core material is "too rich" and risks becoming a destructive "resonance chamber well on the way to forming a black hole."[60] By contrast, the skilled molding of consistent sound is required a priori for any genuinely creative or "deterritorializing" work. As they say: You have to start somewhere with a solid technical foundation, and make a sonic "block of sensations" that can "stand up on its own."[61] It must be music based in a measure of "consistency" and "sobriety," yet still unregulated by the Apollonian ideality of Hegel's musical tone, in fact without any systematic guarantees whatsoever—"We can never be sure we'll be strong enough."

Then why Schumann? Was it simply that the composer's works were empirically available to them? Or is there a philosophical reason why he appears here, as a dramatic form of teleological punctuation? It first should be noted that for Deleuze and Guattari, the criteria for a deterritorialized *ritournelle* are generally not narrowly teleological; the examples they mention range quite widely, and many are cited for what appear to be openly incommensurable reasons.[62] Some composers write music that refers to birds or imitates bird song (madrigals by Janequin, Mozart's *Die Zauberflöte,* Mahler's *Das Lied von der Erde,* and many compositions by Messiaen); others write music that indexes childhood, relations between nature and territory, nursery rhymes, and folk songs (Mozart, Schumann, Berg, and Bartók). Still others are credited with advancing formal innovations: novel methods of orchestration (Berlioz), a colorful embrace of neotonality (Bizet, Chabrier), sophisticated forms of motivic transformation and development (Wagner, Debussy, Stravinsky) or cutting-edge sonic experiments (Varèse, Stockhausen, Berio, Boulez, and La Monte Young).

On the whole, by comparison to Adorno, one might note that we have a palpable loosening of criteria. In their vocabulary of a generic, rhythmically mobile structuralism of "lines and movements" borrowed partly from the writings of artist Paul Klee, all that is required is a technical aptitude to work with musical materials in a way that does not fall into the trap of excessively systematic or hierarchical methods of composition. A few vivid words regarding the *Tendenz des Materials* set this difference into relief. Deleuze and Guattari suggest that one ought to maintain a certain distance from the twelve-tone method and other kinds of musical formalism—any "new system." More particularly, when they write, "We do not need to suppress tonality, we need to turn it loose [*faire fuir*]," they use a French phrase that can also mean "scare away" or "make flee." It is a phrase that echoes Deleuze's more famous locution: "*lignes de fuite.*" What would it mean to scare off the grammar of tonality, as opposed to making explicit how exhausted it was (as Adorno understood Schoenberg's early turn to atonality)?

It is at this moment in the text that we find a reference to a chapter of Alexis Roland-Manuel's encyclopedic and multi-authored *Histoire de la musique* (1963). The reference points to a chapter written by Roland-Manuel himself, entitled "The Evolution of Harmony," which describes in nationalist terms the outlines of the death of tonality at the hands of German culture. Specifically, it counterposes this Germanic death of tonality (via the diminished-seventh chord discussed in chapter 2, Wagner's *Tristan* chord, and the loss of functional foundations to tonality) with an alternative French historicism that avoids the logic of tonal death or exhaustion. In Roland-Manuel's vision, modern French music is infused with the spirit of vernacular song, plainchant, and a renewed fidelity to Rameau and the foundations of tonality.[63] The implication, for Roland-Manuel as for Deleuze and Guattari, is that there is no teleological *Tendenz des Materials*, no *Versprachlichung*, no necessary or irreversible decline and death. This is because the "very profound labor" of the second *ritournelle* is not based in Bloch's or Adorno's historicisms, but instead in what Roland-Manuel describes as an open empiricism toward the affective appeal of musical sounds. Of course, Roland-Manuel's openness is somewhat ironically cast in the terms of a neoclassical revival. Ghosts of historical teleologies are hard to dispense with entirely. Deleuze and Guattari's ethics is still, in many ways, haunted by the dialectical problem of criteria.

Nonetheless, Roland-Manuel's alternative "evolution" of harmony would not lead most of us to Schumann, composing in 1837. Why, then, does Schumann appear at the apex of their "cosmic" theory of the *ritournelle*—indeed, at the absolute conclusion of both chapters of *A Thousand Plateaus* that discuss music? Was it simply an empirical matter of taste? Like Roland Barthes, are Deleuze and Guattari idealizing the intimacy of domestic music making because they oppose the authority of hierarchical disciplines? (Guattari's critical views of hierarchy and authority extended far beyond psychiatry and politics. In his correspondence with Deleuze, he occasionally mentions his distaste for conservatories, dogmatic schools of composition, and showy virtuosos.)[64] How might Schumann fit into their peculiar mix of empirical openness, celebrations of the minor and vernacular, critiques of formal systems, and their interest in sonic experiments?

Adding to the conundrum of Schumann's appeal for Deleuze and Guattari are the passages where the authors distance themselves from romanticism. They write, again with reference to Paul Klee: "What romanticism lacks most is a people. The territory is haunted by a solitary voice."[65] Deleuze and Guattari are not the first French intellectuals to make this point. Barthes had written just a year earlier: "Schumann is truly the musician of solitary intimacy, of the amorous and imprisoned soul that *speaks to itself* . . . of the child who has no other link than to his mother."[66] To this Deleuze and Guattari will readily respond: What we now need is a sonorous "nature or people."[67] Not a private cult of the aesthetic, but an inclusive public vehicle of sensation. To hear Schumann properly in this context would require finding a way to move beyond the introverted fantasies of domestic pianism, and to hear it as an expansive and impersonal coextension of the cosmos. A nineteenth-century discourse of impossibility and romantic limit would have to be rendered into a sonic structure of transversal connectivity.

In order to hear Schumann's music as affectively connective rather than impossible and private, one should remember that it cannot be taken as autonomous in any ideal sense; in its most intense form it will always be taken as affectively coextensive with some kind of nonsonorous being. In fact, Deleuze and Guattari hear in Schumann connections to a wide variety of nonsonic others, a diverse set of figures who are taken to be resistant to those of a normative, patriarchal society: an animal, a child, a woman, a minor literature, a madness. In "Becoming-Intense, Becoming-Animal, Becoming-Imperceptible," this aesthetic connectivity is presented as a question of musical content:

> What does music deal with, what is the content in-dissociable from sound expression? It is hard to say, but it is something: a child dies, a child plays, a woman is born, a woman dies, a bird arrives, a bird files off. . . . Musical expression is inseparable from a becoming-woman, a becoming-child, a becoming-animal that constitute its content. . . . Music is pervaded by every minority, and yet composes an immense power.[68]

As in their discussion of the bowerbird, here Deleuze and Guattari again quietly recapitulate Schopenhauer's paradox of the ineffable. They state that it is "hard to say" what the content of music is, because the specificity of sonic force—taken as a sensational immediacy—does not lend itself to ready translation into the mediated theater of sense. In their view, music does indeed translate into words. It is just that practically speaking—and their philosophy is thoroughly practical—it is something that happens with difficulty. This difficulty would need to be rigorously distinguished from the impossibility of a romantic or ontologically strict conception of the ineffable separation of word and sound; gone are Hegel's dialectical negations of one medium to another (as in music's negation of painting, or poetry's negation of music in the *Lectures on Aesthetics*). For Deleuze and Guattari, all artistic media are intertwined. Thus, with respect to the relationship between music and language, they openly report with a certain minimalism that the content of music "is something." It can be said—its force is accessible to language—but it is a challenge to say it. It is quite precisely just a practical challenge, not a metaphysical impossibility. In Schopenhauer's terms, Deleuze and Guattari would maintain that it is a challenge, not a paradox, to try use music to "copy" the immediacy of the will.

Without the structure of a paradox of the ineffable in place, for Deleuze and Guattari there is no longer any quasi-theological metaphysics of sound. And there is no aporetic or paradoxical exceptionalism of music as one finds in Bloch, Adorno, and Jankélévitch. By contrast, Deleuze and Guattari endorse music's material specificity based in the affective plainness of sound's "immense power" and some non-normative minority. There are no impossibilities, hierarchies, or metaphysical limits between media. Life and sense are structured by rhythms, sonic rhythms are part of the same substance as lived rhythm, and exemplary works of music deterritorialize these rhythms, provided that they are drawn into transversal links among media.

Then, notwithstanding the cosmic "lines and movements" Pythagoreanism of the *ritournelle*, or the creaturely phylogenesis of musical sound into an autonomous form, in the ethical form of a "work of art to come," musical sound does not stand alone as an abstraction. Deleuze and Guattari's favorite works of art pass from one medium to another. Kafka's stories tap into a sonic force that remains latent in the texts, Francis Bacon's terrifying paintings leave behind the abstraction of the medium and capture an "analogical language" of movements and expressions, Schumann's childhood fantasy pieces reach out to nonpianistic literary desires. Art tends to produce sensations that cross boundaries between media; similarly, music extends vital and cosmic rhythms in a way that is often linked with words and images.

In an ethical composition, one creates a structural coupling that enacts a substantial transformation, something that is difficult to explain dispassionately, in part because it seems naive: melded with Schumann's music, one must become caught up in its machinery like a bowerbird and his leaves, or like Uexküll's *Funktionskreis*, becoming indistinct from its workings, and turning into structural extensions, even "children," of its operations. With a certain sort of practical self-evidence, Deleuze and Guattari claim that an ethical music involves the production of minor content. It is a vernacular without specific or exacting criteria, without paradox—an affirmative, intermedial extension and intensification of what life already is. These transformations form the basis for a view of art that, as I have stated earlier in this chapter, are both affective and relational, and quite opposed to the autonomy of the object. What ultimately matters for Deleuze and Guattari is that art connect two beings with an impersonal affect or a discrete percept that, through the work of art, stands up on its own as an "interminable presence." This presence makes indistinct not the ideal coordinates of subject and object, but the material entities of thing, animal, and human.[69] Such is the basis of their definition of an affect: ". . . something passing from one to the other. This something can be specified only as sensation. It is a zone of indetermination, of indiscernibility, as if things, beasts, and persons . . . endlessly reach that point that immediately precedes their natural differentiation. This is what is called an affect."[70]

Deleuze vividly articulates this affective and sensory connectivity in intermedial terms when he considers the role of sound in what is probably the philosopher's favorite medium: film. In the "movement-image" that he associates with early cinema, a new form of visual continuity is articulated through which images function not as a series of stills, but through a dialectical link with the film as a totality. Particular images are "internalized in a changing whole," while at the same time this whole "is externalized" in the images. Sound, productively, even harmoniously, enriches the silent film by grounding its unity with a "different figure." In the sound film, for example, indirect exterior images fit the direct interior of the "direct enunciations" of music and sound, in an intermedial counterpoint that perfects the whole of the film: "With sound, speech and music, the circuit of the movement-image achieves a different figure, different dimensions or components; however, it maintains the communication between the image and a whole which has become increasingly rich and complex. It is in this sense that the talkie perfects the silent film."

In the "time-image" that develops in modern cinema, however, sound and image engage in mobile couplings as "two dissymmetric, non-totalizable" sides which are heteronomous and occlude one another through a direct presentation of lived time.[71] Here, there appears to be no strong preference for music or sound, other than for them to join the image as an equal partner in the disjunction of linear time. In fact, for the time-image, film music "no longer ensures a direct presentation of an assumed whole." Word, image, and sound become unmoored from one another. They engage in a disjunctive set of innovative counterpoints and heteronomies where the "speech act" is not necessarily communicative, where musical organization is not necessarily or exclusively musical: "[The sound] continuum now takes on the value of innovation claimed by Michel Fano in Robbe-Grillet's films (notably in *The Man Who Lies*): it ensures the heteronomy of the sound images, and must achieve both the speech-act as limit which does not necessarily consist of a speech in the strict sense and the musical organization of the series, which does not necessarily consist of musical elements."[72]

No one medium of sensation (image, word, or sound) has priority in the "time-image"; each is incessantly interwoven with the other. Deleuze even puts it plainly: "It would be wrong to conclude that there is a prevalence of sound in modern cinema."[73] The interweaving is, in Deleuze's late work, part of a generalized logic of sensation: "Whether through words, colors, sounds, or stone, art is the language of sensations."[74] According to the dictates of rhythm, at the center of this intermedial counterpoint of dissonance one can find a cinematic parallel to Stockhausen's *Musik für ein Haus*, a film that is capable of repeating with all the repetitions of the *ritournelle*. Here Deleuze describes it as a presentation of the machinery of time itself in a purified or "direct" state: "In modern cinema, by contrast, the time-image is no longer empirical, nor metaphysical; it is 'transcendental' in the sense that Kant gives this word: time is out of joint and presents itself in the pure state."[75] In order to make explicit an "out of joint" rhythm of sense, an ethical exemplar—musical, cinematic, or otherwise—has to be intertwined, even imbricated, with texts, images, fantasies, and bodies.

Consider then, Schumann's "Warum?," a famous piece from the *Fantasiestücke*, a set of character pieces written in 1837, the year of *la ritournelle* according to the chapter's title, and easy enough for Guattari the amateur pianist to have actually played. It is a delicate piece that has obvious links to the connective themes of becoming-other, becoming-animal, becoming-fantasy, and so on. This one comes third in the cycle of eight, as a moment of bracing repose, reflection, even innocence, under the mysteriously gnomic title "Why?"—following immediately after the riotous "Aufschwung [Revival, Boom, Upswing]," inspired by the character of Florestan from Beethoven's *Fidelio*. In "Warum?" suddenly we are afloat, directionless:

EXAMPLE 4.1. Robert Schumann, *Fantasiestücke*, "Warum?" op. 12, no. 3, mm. 1–16. Source: Robert Schumann, *Piano Music of Robert Schumann*, Vol. 1 (New York: Dover, 1972).

The left-hand accompaniment here is hushed, and it swings with a murmuring syncopation that harbors a slight trace of anxiety. One's attention inevitably falls on the right hand's melody, language-like in its upturned contour and speechlike declamation. If one places one's hands on these notes, however, one is immediately struck by the fact that this opening melody overlaps with the second in a way that could not be sung by a single human voice; the intertwining motifs, separated by a minor sixth, are singularly pianistic and contrapuntal. Specifically, notice the origin of the second melody: there is an evanescent pause immediately after the opening melody when the right hand's thumb momentarily joins the left hand's chiming chords on four quietly syncopated Fs. It is an entrancing oscillation just seconds into the piece. Out of these Fs, almost surreptitiously, the bottom two fingers of the right hand spawn the second melody that eventually reaches up to a C♭ atop a diminished sonority. In a delicate harmonic motion, this second melody pivots the harmony of the song with a cool change of color to E♭ minor in measure seven, which forms the foundation for a third woven countermelody an octave higher that will crown the opening with a stepwise descent at the end of the first staff.

In close listening, it is the tactile shape of this woven exchange of motifs and counterpoints that is vividly relational, connective. The second melody that emerges from the oscillations of the right hand thumb could not have come from the same opening voice; they sprout ex nihilo as structural extensions, as an unconscious tendril of melody, something akin to a sonic *Merkmalsträger*. Once this second melody has taken flight, the fifth finger of the right hand takes up those Fs, with the fifth finger chiming an octave higher. With the right hand outstretched, doing two things at once, it is as if its physical form frames the motivic dialogue. In the second half, the rhythm of the phrasing increases, and the yearning sequence of intertwining melodies ends in a cosmic left-hand arpeggio. It ultimately arrives at an otherworldly sonority: a V7 chord whose functional color has been neutered by a static A♭ in the bass, recasting all the important dissonances into ornamental intervals—seventh, ninth, and eleventh tones that waver overhead. The sonority ends with an enjambment, where our speculative reverie is sent unexpectedly back to the opening phrase.

Transparency and interlocking motivic conjunctions dominate.[76] The piece is easy to play, its structural operations open and relatively accessible. In Schumann's melodic, overlapping counterpoint, Uexküll's functional cycles are sounded as fragmentary melodies set into motion by hands; they seem to extend the interior forms of creaturely life without developmental goals. The piece is also intermedial. With its programmatic title and upturned interrogative contours, some kind of language is a central issue for these intertinwed melodies. But it is not an expressive, syntactical language. Schumann's title encapsulates every one of the piece's sounds with an open philosophical question—Why?—that, in its blankness, invites meaning while offering no exact answer beyond sensory extension. We might say that the musical sounds of Schumann's "lines and movements" are perched atop the paradox of Schopenhauer's immediate copy, but in a way that is devoid of any aporetic worries. For the sounds acquire intensity at a threshold that is affirmed to be at once potentially creatural and potentially linguistic. In staging challenging—but not impossible—connections across intermedial boundaries, "Warum?" connects one to the syncopated, out of joint, or nonpulsed time of deeper ontological rhythms. Its ethics derive from no large-scale compositional plan, no secret disclosure of a unified will, no naming of a divine name, or of any strong sense of formal integrity—not from any system or idea. It is a contingent occasion, an intermedial assemblage, a minor literature in sonic form.

Adorno might protest: Is all this coextensive affirmation not still based upon an ideological *Versprachlichung?* Certainly, under Adorno's lens, one could hear "Warum?" as an exhausted or nostalgic language of tonality with all its associated emotional triggers, worn down by generations of culture industry clichés. But in this context, the spare counterpoint of interlocking melodies is not to be heard through the historicity of its harmonic syntax. Again, Deleuze and Guattari would draw attention to the way the abstraction of piano sounds, as a vivid assemblage of sensation, might be *potentially* representational. Across the word-sound divide, in their theory, "Warum?" brings to life a "zone of indistinction" between the pulsations of physical rhythm (the sound of the piano) and the event of the incorporeal sense (a question positioned at the threshold of the symbolic order: Warum?). It is a hearing that is experientially grounded, incessantly in motion, and loosened from a narrowly teleological history into the connectivity of mobile affective couplings.[77] In this way, it might join coextensively the irregular rhythms of time and space.

Such is likewise the case for two of Deleuze and Guattari's musical favorites who have been written about extensively in the Deleuze and music secondary literature: Wagner and Boulez. Deleuze and Guattari endorse Boulez's writings on the Wagnerian leitmotif and, as Alain Badiou has done in his *Five Lessons on Wagner* (2010), they subscribe to a formalist reading of the leitmotif based the malleability of its melodic transformations staged against a wide variety of harmonic backdrops. One of their aims is to rescue Wagner's leitmotif technique from a vulgarized vocabulary of narrative semantic indication. Though it is instructive to note that, notwithstanding the formalist views of music espoused by Pierre Boulez, Deleuze and Guattari's musical preferences are not

FIGURE 4.5. Paul Klee, *Die Zwitscher-Machine* (1922). Oil transfer drawing, watercolor and ink on paper with gouache and ink borders on board, 15¼ × 19 in. Museum of Modern Art, New York. Copyright 2016 Artists Rights Society, New York. Digital Image Copyright Museum of Modern Art / Licensed by SCALA/Art Resource.

typically oriented around the high formalist monuments of mid-century abstraction (say, Boulez's *Structures* [1952, 61], a composition they likely would have known about). In line with their intermedial orientation, their interest in Wagnerian music drama focuses on the way sound can be formally transformed while remaining moored to the larger counterpoint of senses at work in the *Gesamtkunstwerk*.

This ethical practice of composition is done without strong criteria, and sits on intermedial borderlands. On a metaphysical plane, one could argue that sound is exemplary of the rhythms of the *ritournelle*. But when it comes to the ethical and aesthetic criteria for the production of artworks, Deleuze and Guattari express only marginal interest in the phylogenetic autonomy of sound such as one would find in high modernism. Their favorite works are positioned as hinges across boundaries. As Deleuze says: "... From the moment that the material passes into sensation, as in a Rodin sculpture, art itself lives on these zones of indetermination."[78] A famous example comes to us from Paul Klee, son of a composer and an artist deeply influenced by music, whose *Die Zwitscher-Machine* of 1922 (figure 4.5) elicits the skeletal wonder of Uexküll's *Funktionskreis*. It is an awkward machine, creaky, even useless, on the verge of collapse. Its form, as Klee engineered it, is undoubtedly cyclical, inviting us to play and interact by turning a crank, curved and shaded with a bit of detail and care. What happens when we turn it? A variously slowing and speeding chorus of creaturely noises, something repetitive and rhythmic but also inharmonious, giving us a dissonant and unconscious counterpoint, united by structure but not intention. These four creatures, disfigured and half-formed, provide the image of a life lived in mechanical distress, dependent on somebody else's play. But for Deleuze and Guattari, the mechanical structure of life—here rendered as a line drawing, in outline alone—is a paradoxical vehicle for its liberation, for revealing what life truly is beneath the veneer of our mental representations. Against Uexküll, one can read Klee's image, which appears as the frontispiece for the chapter of *A Thousand Plateaus* on the *ritournelle*, as a playfully imprecise drawing of the biosemiotic *Funktionskreis*, one that is explicitly attentive to rhythm and sound as delineating the structural form of cosmic life, unmediated by the regulatory frameworks of consciousness, history, and teleology.

Deleuze and Guattari drew on Klee for several borrowed concepts: the formalism of dynamic "lines and movements" and the notion that all art needs a people. (Klee famously lamented, "*Uns trägt kein Volk*." The modern artist doesn't have a people, a community. It is an early plea of the alienated modern artist, something that would still haunt Adorno in his 1931 lecture "Why Is the

New Art so Hard to Understand?") To this it is clear that Deleuze and Guattari seek a turn to a *Wahrheitsgehalt* grounded in an intermedial vernacular, something that is surreal and creative, strange and wild—modern, no doubt—but that is grounded in the alterity of the already there, of childhood, madness, oddities, creaturely forms, and expressive idioms of improvisation. By privileging the content of the vernacular as music's form, they affirm it pure and simple, and wave away the paradoxical structure that so transfixed and perplexed Adorno as resistant to formalism in his book on Mahler.

It all makes for a dizzying multiplicity, one that perhaps recalls the teeming minature philosophies of music forwarded by Jankélévitch. But differences abound: we have Deleuze's contrapuntal dialectic of rhythm, a modified Bergsonism. Equally unique is Deleuze and Guattari's structuralist quadrivium, an "a-signifying semiotics" of sonic force, a peculiar revival of Pythagorean metaphysics that gives us a vivid sense of the interior rhythms of life. Together, these two theories comprise the concept of the *ritournelle*. Finally, in ethical and aesthetic practices, one can see how it is possible to join, coextensively, these rhythms: by creating permanent and enduring affects and percepts that are multimodal and multisensory, tapping into the broadest and deepest rhythms of sense to "fix the thunderbolt of the univocal." The coextensive affective metaphysics that this ethical act triggers is a strange form of content, something that creates an affect as an "ideal coincidence": a disembodiment, a permanence, "man's nonhuman becomings," a pure presence, a "compound of sensation," "the compound of nonhuman forces of the cosmos" that is independent of any subject or object:

> The being of sensation, the bloc of percept and affect, will appear as the unity or reversibility of feeling and felt, their intimate intermingling like hands clasped together: it is the *flesh* that, at the same time, is freed from the [finite] lived body, the perceived world, and the intentionality of one toward the other that is still too tied to experience; whereas flesh gives us the being of sensation and bears the original opinion distinct from the judgment of experience-flesh of the world and flesh of the body that are exchanged as correlates, ideal coincidence.[79]

Deleuze and Guattari share with Jankélévitch the eschewal of normative Apollonian categories for musical grammar that depend upon orthodox Hegelian traditions of speculative idealism, so central to Bloch's and Adorno's thinking. Indeed, their theory of "sensation in itself" and of the rhythm of sense might be read as an inversion of Hegel's view of the work of art as a sensuous embodiment of the Idea. The Bergsonians also share an attentiveness to temporality, multiplicity, inconsistency, and openness. But whereas Jankélévitch develops a privilege for music in order to erect a neoclassical *hommage* to musical time through a loose neoclassical ethics of chastity, benign indifference, and playful multiplicity, Deleuze and Guattari connect music to the chaotic heat of lived rhythms, to the cosmic pulse of syncopation that links together all forms of life with a vast affirmative metaphysical gesture. Their contrapuntal dialectic is open-ended, nonsystematic, and attuned to the affirmation of vernacular content without strong criteria. They privilege Schumann, but only obliquely, for their reading ultimately aims at a transversal, intermedial aesthetics that is based in a neo-structural affirmation of affect. It gives us an innovative revival of Pythagoreanism fused to the intellectual aims of mid-century structuralism.

This Pythagorean revival is redolent of Schopenhauer's Platonic solutions to the paradox of music's ineffability. Indeed, both Schopenhauer and Deleuze focus their metaphysics on exposing us to the reality of the void. If Schopenhauer and the lineage in his wake (Nietzsche, Bloch, Adorno, and Jankélévitch) developed music's exceptionalism into a productive dialectics of the ineffable, Deleuze and Guattari return full-circle to Schopenhauer's Platonism, if only to upend any appeals to static and eternal harmonics. In doing so, they retain a dialectical method whereby individuation and mediation are structurally intrinsic to the virtual (or the will). Meanwhile, what once appeared to Schopenhauer an unsurpassable limit between language and the music of the will (as when he claimed that music paints, narrates, or discloses the will) is now for Deleuze and Guattari the basis of ontological and ethical transformations (becoming-fantasy, becoming-other, becoming-child). In this way, Deleuze and Guattari remix the ineffability of music's high exceptionalism into an aesthetics of porous, intermedial boundaries.

All the while, to be sure, Schopenhauer's paradox lurks in ghosted forms when the specificity of music is at issue. For musical sound still gives voice to a contrapuntal dialectic of deep ontological rhythms and makes vivid Deleuze and Guattari's distinctive metaphysical vision: an ancient and eternal Pythagoreanism inverted into an everchanging, relational, and connective theory of affective coextension. For them, the force of sound, ethically harnessed, is capable of repeating with exceptional intensity the productive rhythms of life.

CONCLUSION

A Paradox of the Vernacular

If music allows one to think something distinctly philosophical, how can a philosopher in turn be confident that a specific kind of music presents us with a successful exemplar? This ethical question is a fraught one, particularly given that the medium—the ineffable, nonsemantic, immersive strangeness of music—can be understood in ways that are quite systematic even as its effects and idioms can flow over us in ways that are often irrational and lawless. It is a question that haunted all the philosophers discussed in this book. In this conclusion, I shall first revisit this question by drawing some final synoptic comparisons among the four chapters. I will then return to the paradox of the vernacular and offer some suggestions as to how it might be applied to recent developments in modernist musical practices. Finally, I shall close by discussing how these philosophers' writings on music might be related to recent challenges to the linguistic turn in the theoretical humanities.

From the open connectivity of Deleuze and Guattari's intermedial metaphysics, consider once more the stringent formalism of Adorno's immanent critique. Deleuze and Guattari have linked their conception of "sensation in itself" to a deeper ontology of rhythm that stretches throughout the cosmos. But Adorno would remain suspicious of the idea that rhythm could bear utopian potential. In fact, in many of his writings on popular music, he singles out rhythm as a dangerously false and ahistorical parameter. For Adorno, repetition is typically the sign of a numb ideology; he raises the issue in a rich passage of a 1932 article entitled "Some Ideas on the Sociology of Music," just as he is also recapitulating Schopenhauer's paradox of the ineffable:

By virtue of its pure material, music is the art in which the pre-rational, mimetic impulses inevitably assert themselves, and at the same time enter into constellation with the processes leading to the progressive domination of matter and nature. This is [the material] to which music owes its transcendence over the operation of mere self-preservation, an ability that led Schopenhauer to define it as the immediate objectification of the will and to place it at the apex of the hierarchy of the arts. If anywhere, then music in fact reaches beyond the mere repetition of what happens anyway. At the same time, however, it will be smooth [*wird sie eben*], and as a consequence, also suitable for the constant reproduction of stupidity. The very element that raises it above ideology is also what brings it closest to it.[1]

This passage is a striking synopsis of Adorno's early views of music. It can also be read as a note from the future—a hypothetical response from Adorno to Deleuze and Guattari on the topic of rhythm and repetition. For in this passage, Adorno, in line with Schopenhauer and Nietzsche, acknowledges that music is exceptional because of its strong linkages with the irrational impacts of rhythm and mimesis. But if Schopenhauer heard in music's Dionysian forces an exceptional voice of the unconscious, for Adorno, music's rhythmic intensity led inevitably, via a historical teleology, to a petrified world of ideology, domination, and violence. And yet, as if the paradoxical qualities of Bloch's mystical and translucent tones were still finding a way to speak through him in this passage, Adorno continues to assert that music has a resistant buoyancy. By stating that music "reaches beyond the mere repetition of what happens anyway," Adorno points to music's ineffability in a way that is even somewhat redolent of Jankélévitch. Still, little utopian potential remains. Always the negative dialectician, in the final two sentences of this quotation, Adorno narrows the compass. He reminds us that, notwithstanding this "reach beyond," the appearance of mimetic immediacy in music simultaneously harbors the greatest threat of ideology.

Deleuze and Guattari are not entirely open-ended by comparison. They would likely agree with Adorno about the ideological threat that music presents. In *A Thousand Plateaus* (1980), they even claim that sound, as a medium, presents the threat of a regressive "re-territorialization." Of course they would agree with Adorno that a resistant music entails going beyond the brute fact of repetition. The crux of their disagreement is that Deleuze and Guattari do not think a formal, cognitive, historicist acknowledgment of this ideological threat is a necessary condition for resistance. For they would understand the concept of ideology to slide into a self-defeating gesture that reifies the very "re-territorialization" it aims to challenge. Deleuze and Guattari's ethics is by comparison loose and affirmative, and is based in a practical and intermedial method of doing away with the systematic power of ideas, of positively harnessing the powers of sensation in an "work of art yet to come."[2] But has it successfully cast away the regulative bearings of ideas?

The ensuing debate turns on the question of whether or not this ethical resistance requires well-defined criteria for a negativity that explicitly disrupts the ideological repetition of aesthetic consumption (as for Adorno), or whether it can happen positively because mediation is always already part of musical expression (as it does for Deleuze and Guattari). From a perch high up in a metanarrative of modern intellectual history, one might say that Adorno's negative position assumes that the power of ideas and ideologies is irreversible and pervasive. Contrariwise, while the positive position espoused by Deleuze and Guattari claims equally that modernity has cast a pall of reification over the forms of life, their practical ethics keeps open broader routes to resistance. It is between these two ethical poles—Adorno's exacting negativity and Deleuze and Guattari's deliberately inexact practical philosophy—that instructive differences among the philosophers comes into relief.

Let us quickly recall the scope of their positions. Bloch's tone emphasizes the ineffable substance of music in general; for Bloch, its nonsemantic but still concrete and material blankness harbors exceptional potential to disrupt the orders of reified life. Among an array of examples, his ethics engages historically nonsynchronous musical techniques in nineteenth-century compositions (section 1.8 discussed his interest in eighteenth-century fugal counterpoint). Adorno extends the utopian ineffability of Bloch's tone, but takes much more seriously how music is historically structured by a reified, rationalized, language-like syntax. Via the negative method of immanent critique, Adorno's ethics correspondingly specifies narrower, more counterideological techniques of musical resistance. Jankélévitch, like Bloch and Adorno, focuses a substantial amount of his attention on music's ineffability. Unlike the German philosophers, however, Jankélévitch rejects the idea that music is language-like, and turns instead to the axis of music's temporal inconsistency in order to draw our ears to a wider multiplicity of its nonsignifying dimensions. Finally, Deleuze and Guattari, in conceiving of music's sensory immediacy and formal exactitude as structurally coextensive, overturn the question of the ineffable altogether. They downplay any strong exceptionalism for music, and give sound a quiet but vivid specificity that takes its place in an intermedial play among the various arts.

Each of the philosophers, despite diverging criteria, have in common some adoption of Schopenhauer's paradox of the ineffable: that if music is a sensory immediacy, it cannot be immediate to our experience of it without taking recourse to some form of mediation. And all find this dialectical tension to be philosophically productive. Bloch and Adorno think of it primarily as an irresolvable contradiction. Jankélévitch takes it to exemplify an incommensurable divide between music and language. And Deleuze and Guattari take this divide to be an extension of a more fundamental incommensurability, an ontological polyphony that structures the differential productivity of life itself.

One might group these philosophers according to the amount of emphasis given to a modernist ethics. If Adorno and Deleuze typify a polarized contrast on the use or misuse of criteria in the ethics of modern music, Bloch and Jankélévitch might be seen as thinkers who are more concerned with general problems of music's ineffability, and less preoccupied with questions of compositional ethics. Whether through Bloch's dialectic of the tone, or through the fidelity to the inconsistency of time in Jankélévitch's unwoven dialectics, Bloch and Jankélévitch tend to focus on the ways that music allows us to grasp broader conundrums about the limits of representation and the inescapability of mediation. Certainly, their writings yield insights about the metaphysical backstory that underlies the sharper opinions held by Adorno and Deleuze. But for Bloch and Jankélévitch, the ethics of musical composition plays only an ancillary role.

Another axis of comparison concerns how specific they are in their discussion of musical details. In the framing of this book's thesis, I have deliberately selected what I took to be iconic parameters (tone, fracture, inconsistency, rhythm) that I thought captured the scope of each philosopher's writings, and helped facilitate instructive comparisons among them. But, as I mentioned in the introduction, the underlying terrain of which musical forms are specified is undeniably rugged. Schopenhauer, Nietzsche, Bloch, and Deleuze tend to keep their discussion of music in a register of vague generality. They speculate about music in general by frequently mentioning only the most basic parameters (tones, rhythm, melody, and harmony). On occasion, they name composers and works, and explore more involved issues in musical aesthetics. Bloch intermittently delves into more detailed stylistic topics. But only Adorno and Jankélévitch write about musical works in real detail. They are the musicologist-philosophers willing to discuss technical specifics; each has written multiple books about individual composers, and many scholars and musicians who are not all that inclined towards philosophy have learned a great deal from their writings.

As I mentioned in the introduction, the level of specificity these philosophers engage has consequences for the kind of philosophical work music does. For the first group—those whom we might call the loose generalists—music can more easily be made to handle fanciful and complex metaphysical content (as in the secret history of the will, a birth of tragedy, a utopian potentiality, or the interiors of creaturely life). After all, music's ineffability can be vaguely metaphysical, grand, and even bombastic in its explanatory power when only the tone as a single item of sound or an overarching cosmic rhythm is at issue. For Adorno and Jankélévitch, by contrast, the weight of the discourse falls on the side of the musical objects themselves. Late style, expressive fractures, atonal polyphony, inexpressive distance, and naturalistic mimesis are often fleshed out in elaborate and technical terms. These philosophers engage in more detailed justifications of exactly how the ineffable works—in relation to a language-like quality of music (Adorno) or a fidelity to music's temporal inconsistency (Jankélévitch). The grand metaphysical questions are still there, and in many ways their approaches are more highly developed. Yet it is curious that Adorno and Jankélévitch are often careful to approach musical notes and technical details with a delicate touch. When reading their texts, one can easily get the sense that music's ineffability pushes back against language's powers of explanation, inducing perplexity and necessitating patient dialectics—whether contradictory, fractured, unwoven, or contrapuntal.

For many, Adorno's commitment to the historicity of form remains the most productive tool for conceptualizing the ineffability of music as bearing ethical potential. It makes constructive use of Bloch's ineffable tone, while also allowing one to set and contest more precise boundaries for what counts as resistance. Even if the narrowness of Adorno's choices seem occasionally off-putting, the fact that musical form in the end—in its nonsemantic blankness—remains the proper grounds for resistance, and not sloganeering or protest lyrics, is an instructive injunction. For Adorno, one must use art's own abstracted autonomous ground, and accept the modern ideological cast of the artwork "without purpose" (in the Kantian sense) in order for art to find a mode of resistance. It also makes sense that these rules are historical. All art needs some kind of historical context, some kind of idiom, and some kind of form.

On the other end of the spectrum we have Deleuze and Guattari. If Adorno sidelined content in favor of fractured historical forms, for Deleuze and Guattari the content of music exposes a vernacular production without specific criteria—a productive rhythm of sense. Mediation is maintained, but at a level that is general and ontological, not historical or *Geist*-mediated. And because history has only diverged and multiplied criteria for resistance, there seems to be a constant imperative to loosen the rules. After all, we live on a planet teeming with a multitude of different musical forms, practices, idioms, and traditions. Shouldn't an ethics of modern music entail recognizing that we cannot limit ourselves to just one conception of form or idiom as the grounds for negation, or even to privileging the ineffability of music as exceptional among the arts? If one agrees, this would seem to make Deleuze and Guattari a more promising, open-ended alternative to Adorno. As suggested by their *lignes de fuite*, there may be naive and intuitive ways, practical ways, of doing your own thing, of making virtual forces sonorous and sensible, of creating intermedial blocks of sensation. One might even adopt Deleuze's idea of using one's "intuition as method," as the philosopher once put it in his book *Bergsonism* (1966).

Adorno might respond: Can one truly be precise about the operations of the intuition? Does intuition not confound all efforts at establishing methods and Apollonian territories? For Deleuze and Guattari, it does not. To recall Deleuze's response to Schopenhauer, individuation always already structures the will. One might be able to scare off tonality as a particularly narrow and ideological system of harmonic syntax, but one would be hard-pressed to scare off Apollonian coordinates altogether. Indeed, Deleuze and Guattari state in *What Is Philosophy?* that the foundation of all art is ultimately technique. To adopt Adorno's language, we might say that for Deleuze and Guattari there would always already be a multitude of *Versprachlichungen* at work in a musical expression.

Insofar as one agrees with Adorno that negativity requires one to be explicit about the Apollonian coordinates of form and abstraction, one can be led easily to a narrow ethics. It is one that takes what many presume now to be a minor story in the history of the world's musical cultures—the supposed breakdown of tonality—and makes it into a privileged locus of resistance. But even Adorno knew there were limits to his reasoning. He himself touched on this territory in his Mahler book and in his writings on the phonograph. In these writings he confronted objects and compositions that did not fit his narrowest criteria as did, say, the early atonality of the Second Viennese School. In so doing, he sensed that the negative fragmentation of a universally enforced Apollonian material might not be the only way to scramble the code. Adorno acknowledges, then, that one can take Dionysian vernacular routes to resistance, or adopt threads of miniature Apollonian traditions—routes that seem to change the rules unpredictably, and resist normative criteria.

For self-declared creative artists, the vernacular form of expression may be ethically axiomatic, but it is strangely an always receding terrain. No matter how much one searches for a grain of the voice, for a blue note, for a certain feel, a studied indifference or lack of know-how, a theatrical musicality that is both heartfelt and distant—no matter how twisted and wild this creative resistance gets towards the vernacular life of Mahler, the curves of the needle, or the *lignes de fuite*—no matter how weird, how schizoid, or how minor one's expression—Deleuze would argue that individuated units seem to course through these musical sounds like DNA. This is true even if the units are as bare and non-normative as Deleuze and Guattari's repetitions. As Ornette Coleman, a musician who did not just scramble forms but scrambled the rules for finding them, once said, "Repetition is as natural as the fact that the earth rotates."[3] Unbridled creativity in the vernacular is impossible; this is its paradox. It cannot do away with form or with the risk of reification, even if it marks only the minimal necessity to start, stop, and repeat.

Deleuze and Guattari hold as equally as Adorno that to sidestep the constitutive role of discipline in rhythm is as grave an error as assuming that one has immediate access to Dionysian forces. It is to risk venerating the body as axiomatically resistant beyond all norms. And it is not axiomatically resistant; rather, as Michel Foucault always strenuously argued, the body is the locus of form's organizations. Schopenhauer's copy cannot be immediate to itself. Correspondingly, ontologies of sound do not ask to be addressed with naive immediacy; rather, they can be met with asymptotic, paradoxical, or wildly metaphysical conceptions of how mediation is everywhere the condition for access.

But can one have an ethics without criteria? Though they argue powerfully for a practical and pluralized ethics, Deleuze and Guattari's open-ended intermedial aesthetics may risk a certain blandness, in which distinct sensory media threaten to lose their specificity in favor of a generalized ontological rhythm. For a philosopher transfixed by the medium of music, it may be that some level of this specificity should be retained. After all, for Bloch, Adorno, and Jankélévitch, in the real-time practice of music every moment of one's experience seems to threaten to erase mediation itself, by dumping one back in the pool of sensuous immediacy. It is the acoustic vividness of this dialectical refusal—and the impossibility of its resolution—that makes music so befuddling to many intellectuals. For Bloch, Adorno, and Jankélévitch, in particular, this strange tension becomes an exceptionally productive impetus for philosophical thought.

*

Paradoxes of the ineffable and the vernacular are not merely based in questions of aesthetics. As all of these intellectuals (and perhaps Adorno above all) emphasized, any account of form entails parallel forms of institutional discipline that are out there in the social world, ensuring intelligibility, value, and coherence for a given idiom: schools, foundations, grants, awards, cultural expectations, and commercial formats. A *Tendenz des Materials* has a sociological foundation. In this regard, it seems inescapable that music requires some kind of reified means. Apollonian forms are embedded in social and historical life, even if we are not sure of the rules and idioms one is inheriting, repeating, fracturing, and distorting. The question is: What reification is necessarily at stake? How exactly are aesthetic determinants intertwined with material ones?

If one wants to be truly dialectical in Adorno's sense, one would have to address the question of formal criteria in specific historical and social terms. In our contemporary world, how is a trust-fund artist, a debt-free artist, an artist who is a citizen of a wealthy nation, or an artist who graduated from an elite private institution positioned to resist reification in ways that the poor and marginalized are not? What kinds of ideological baggage do various supporting institutions entail, whether they are commercial, academic, grant-based, patron-based, governmental, or crowd-sourced? A frequent debate among the Frankfurt School critics was that, depending on the material basis of one's aesthetic practice, there is no guaranteed causation of artistic compromises. There are reified practices of new music that function independently from the support of the commercial market, as often as there are artistic innovators who trigger meaningful resistance to the status quo while making it big in show business.

No matter the musical idiom or means of economic support, there is always some potentially reified system one must be born into and adopt. Again, one never does away with form; there is always mediation. But this does not have to entail a conservative aesthetic perspective on creativity and resistance. One problem is that it is tricky to isolate and argue about specific musical forms without risking a conservatism, or a set of a priori judgments about any one system of economic or cultural support, depending on what forms and traditions are supported by said system. A group of musicians who studied harmony and counterpoint might find themselves turning to the institutional study of parameter-bending electroacoustic music. Those who play a form of traditional music might seek to modernize or hybridize it for a broader audience, or to transfigure it into forms of jazz and electronic dance music. In cosmopolitan locales, those with latent musical talent may go to art school, find the art market reified in its own way, and develop DIY practices that present vernacular fractures of both institutional and commercial musical expectations. Still others carve out a niche within the mainstream music business in order to develop a platform that functions meaningfully (and profitably) within the norms of the culture industry. Others may find ways to question conventions of musical form within religious institutions and practices. Endless hybrids abound.

The paradox of music's ineffability, a play of formalism and immediacy—to say nothing of the incredibly complex social forces at play in any of these scenarios—seems to permanently frustrate ethical attempts to legislate this question in any strong sense. Impassioned public discussion about the death of tonality or the ethics of the twelve-tone method, with its presuppositions of "universal" relevance, is now a quaint memory; it even seemed to be receding in 1961, the year of Adorno's famous "Vers une musique informelle" lecture at Darmstadt. But its dialectical shadows live on in the form of a teeming multiplicity; rage against the norms does not end, as artists today relentlessly probe for new directions beyond the reified and established. And gestures towards the new still call out for explanation, critique, and debate.

In this regard, a dialectical method provides one with a certain precision when discussing the parameters of an object. One can empirically describe the political economy underlying a given reification of music by explaining how patron A or record label B enabled a creative work to come into existence within a given set of expectations and constraints. One may further judge in what way the resistance of a given musical form and style is loosely reflective of whatever system is supporting the music. One can even flood the interpretive page with sonic details and critical reflections. But Jankélévitch's cool philosophy of the ineffable subverts fantasies of precision hermeneutics. It reminds us that the most rigorous response must measure its distance from the object, even it if it means turning down the volume and listening to a recording quietly. That can remind one that the musical object is more than a saturated plentitude that invites an intellectual's explanation and analysis; it is also profoundly indifferent to us, like atmospheric wallpaper, murmuring far in the background.

Made sober, one's dialectics would have to chill out. One may not be able to strictly correlate the political economy with the aesthetic decisions, in particular because—on the aesthetic level—we may not know exactly which form is in play, and, more seriously, because we may not know what the rules are for deciding which forms are even on the table. What it means to be skilled, the very grounds for expertise and legitimacy, can end up for grabs as well. For Jankélévitch, that is what is entailed in facing the medium head-on. Music is a slippery art form; the medium wears its mediations in unpredictable ways. It is not made up of words, or of representational pictures, which can make it clearer that artworks are copies of other things. Music is made up of Hegel's *Klang*—a vibrating materiality—that has an underlying, nondiscrete inconsistency to it. Music has the appearance of immediacy, and this appearance can be confusing. Indecision and ambiguity are endemic to the immersive experience of its sensuous particularity.

Not knowing both the rules and the rules for deciding them can easily leave one perplexed, or can leave one stuck assuming that an absent authority must know them inside and out, as Plato and Aristotle once were. Consequently, music's paradox of the vernacular—the search for a non-normative resistance open to a multiplicity of idioms—is closely paralleled, even exacerbated, by the paradox of music's ineffability. For if the medium itself is slippery when it comes to formal specifications, particularly in an age of multitrack recording, editing, and new media, it may be that a modern ethics of the vernacular foregrounds and even intensifies these ontological ambiguities.

Pressing ahead to address it nonetheless remains an imperative in a twenty-first century world where the modes of musical literacy have multiplied, transforming and expanding the ethics and politics of what is both sensible and intelligible. In fact, such an approach to the vernacular can serve as a basis for an act of critical and ethical listening. When music's ontology is understood to be evasive and non-normative, it becomes a puzzle that we seek to grasp, and befuddles the search for normative aesthetic judgments. If music is not readily translatable into a collection of sonic signs, it can instead be taken as a magnet for this paradox—one that transfixes in its refusal of all easy answers, and draws our thinking towards the significance of the unthought.

*

In closing, let us consider the broader intellectual context for these philosophers' writings on music. Amid the paradox of the ineffable, under the lens of these intellectuals, might music embody a challenge to the linguistic turn? The fruits of the linguistic turn's greatest humanistic export—semiotics—have had the effect of making all the world a web of intermedial discourse. It is something that the European founder of semiotics, Ferdinand de Saussure, foresaw: that semiology would extend far beyond language to account for a wide variety of structures of meaning.[4] Indeed, from literary criticism, film studies, and art history to anthropology and psychoanalysis, it would be hard to overestimate the influence of the structural theory of the sign, the importance of textuality, and the concept of discourse.

Increasingly, however, many have questioned the long-standing privilege of semiosis and representation in the humanities and social sciences, claiming that nondiscursive aspects of our experience may have gotten short shrift. Affect theory is all the rage. Realism is in. The material turn in philosophy, historiography, and anthropology draws our attention to forgotten objects, the secret life of things, hidden engineering, and inhuman forms of connectivity. Cinema is understood to be itself a mode of thought and of being; graphic novels point to ontological borderlands in different media, and literature is praised for its *Stimmung*, beauty, presence, and emotional resonance. In the wake of deconstruction, scholars have taken up the work of realist metaphysicians like Alfred North Whitehead, Deleuze, and Alain Badiou. Others have proposed revivals of and connections to scientific materialism. Interdisciplinary cognitivists have sprung up. Evolutionary theory as a materialist history has arisen. At the hands of the speculative realists, in particular, calls have been made to jump out to the great outdoors of the thing-in-itself. With Bruno Latour, actor-network theory can account for microhistory and the rhizomatic fabric of social movements. New ontologies based in the "beyond" of representation have emerged, finding fascination in the hyperchaos of the cosmos, or the dark untranslatable core of materiality.

How might music, as an instantiation of a perplexing and productive paradox of the ineffable, share common cause with such challenges to the linguistic turn? Historical answers to this question quickly encounter rugged terrain; indeed, the very terms of the question betray a strong presentist bias. The term "linguistic turn" has an arcane origin. It sprouted up in the 1960s in the pages of quite intricate debates within the analytic philosophy of language.[5] One of the central discussions focused on to what extent philosophical questions were best understood as problems of language—specifically, whether or not it was desirable to construct a correct or "ideal" language for philosophy, or conversely to take ordinary meanings of language as illustrative of philosophical truth. Their areas of concern included the verifiability of philosophical knowledge, the grounds for public agreement and consensus, and the progress of philosophy. This movement quickly fell by the wayside in analytic philosophy. What we now remember as the more influential linguistic turn in the humanities and social sciences was a parallel movement in structural linguistics that flowered into mid-century structuralism, cybernetics, and systems theory. This is what eventually sprouted the discipline of semiotics, particularly via the writings of Barthes, Julia Kristeva, and many others in the 1970s.

On a philosophical plane, the grand metaphysical gestures of the mid-century linguistic turn associated with French structuralism—that everything is structured like a language, that there is nothing outside the text and its system of relations, that everything is a sign in a grand political economy—are equally indebted to the mid-century reception of Hegel at the hands of Jean Hyppolite. Language, in Hyppolite's widely read study of Hegel, *Logic and Existence* (1952), was inseparable from a universal teleology toward self-consciousness and the absolute.[6] That is, if there were a historical progression of *Geist* that externalized human self-consciousness in a developmental history, then language was part of the substance of that progress; it structured it, and in so doing, it structured everything otherwise taken to be ineffable as immediate sensory experience. An early and influential exemplar of this tendency is Lacan's 1953 lecture "The Function and Field of Speech and Language in Psychoanalysis," which quite strongly echoed Hyppolite's position on the governing structures of language.[7]

As Gary Gutting has remarked in his recent survey of post-structuralism, Hyppolite's Saussurian emphasis on the governing mediations of language also set the stage for the most influential post-structuralist readings of Hegel that took shape in the 1960s, and sought to recover ineffability, difference, and sensation against the dominating powers of structuralism, logocentrism, and institutional authorities.[8] In this way, Gutting argues that Derrida, Deleuze, and Foucault, among others, all understood Hegel as a necessary foundation whose thesis of reconciliation (that consumed inconsistency and ineffability of experience) was unacceptable. For the post-structuralists, the structures of discourse could not exhaust what life could be, even as their elements and relations were all-encompassing.

In this context, if one were to argue that music's ineffability perturbs the linguistic turn, then, historically speaking, one would have to argue that these intellectuals were each singling out music in a way that critically responded to structuralism (with formulations like Bloch's "inconstruable questions," Adorno's "demythogized prayer," Jankélévitch's "divine inconsistencies," and Deleuze and Guattari's "forces made sonorous"). Given the post-structuralist critique of Hegelian thought—recovering the ineffable, the inconsistent, and so on, often to the point of dissolving the subject altogether—each intellectual in this book could then be understood to conform to the suggestion that music is an exemplary way of pointing beyond language, beyond the means of self-recognition, and beyond the symbolic order to the numinous and murky terrain of affects and materialities.

What is curious in this sense is that none, perhaps with the exception of Barthes, makes a move beyond Apollonian structure. These philosophers confront the sense that music is ineffable but not unspeakable, and maintain that it should be thought of as a philosophically precise form of imprecision: a copy of the thing-in-itself, the unconscious, the noumenon, the will, the forces of the virtual in a way that sustains and develops Schopenhauer's paradox of the immediate copy. It must copy what, in principle, must always remain immediate to itself. The paradox, and the move that places it somewhere beyond the linguistic turn, is that this cannot, as Adorno says, result in a system of signs. Adorno puts it aptly when he says that music remains gestural and mimetic even as it becomes increasingly formalized by modern disciplines. As it develops historically, it may become language-like, even protosemiotic in broadest outlines, though it always remains semantically blank. From a transhistorical point of view, one might argue that music is the source of a medium-specific post-structuralism. Or perhaps to say that music is ineffable is even to make an implicit rebuke to semiotics as an explanatory method.

Such a speculative connection would necessarily be mine, not theirs. Bloch, Adorno, and Jankélévitch had no strong historical relationship to the linguistic turn. For methodological reasons, they each ignored or rejected the intellectual forerunners of the linguistic turn on the analytic side: Gottlob Frege, Bertrand Russell, and Wittgenstein. With the exception of Deleuze and Guattari, their philosophies matured in time and places that had developed outside the central impact of structuralism in mid-century France. Thus, when they contemplate the specificity of music as an ineffable form, it is not done in the context of any axiomatic proposal that language structures the problems of philosophy. Deleuze, the one thinker who responded intently to the linguistic turn in his book *The Logic of Sense*, did not grant music a particularly strong privilege above any of the other arts. Consequently, according to the direct lines of intellectual influence, there is no manifest reason why these philosophers would consider music "beyond the linguistic turn."

Most important of all, these intellectuals did not intend music to critique the powers of language. At best, they chose to give music a quiet exceptionalism that focused our attention on its specificity as an art form. In so doing, they argued that it was not linguistic—that there was something specific going on with music that needed to be thought through at a certain level of philosophical precision. It exposed us to a paradoxical and befuddled borderland to representation, one that could be put to a multitude of ends, particularly at a point when the normative grammar of music is experiencing its own demise.

Jacques Attali wrote, in striking consonance with the four philosophers in this book: "My intention here is thus not only to theorize *about* music, but to theorize *through* music."[9] What Attali meant here, no doubt provocatively in the youthful age of twenty-eight, was that music allowed us to think something (in his case, a Marxist thesis about world history and social reality) that we could not think in any other way. We might add that, whether or not the reader grants music any sort of strong exceptionalism, three of these intellectuals (Bloch, Adorno, and Jankélévitch) quietly granted it some exceptional powers, and all four thought it had a vivid specificity. None concluded that music alone was the only way to convey its own intensity and formal complexity (in the manner of absolute music); all certainly went back to the printed page to express their thoughts. They only maintained that there was a specifically musical experience that was not reducible to linguistic forms of expression.

*

Ineffability need not be taken as a limit of pious refusal or austere silence; it can be an intelligent response to the specificity of musical intensity. One can take it as a peculiar injunction to be perplexed by establishing an open but undefined and resolutely candid channel between musical experience and thought, a productive puzzlement. As a music scholar, one can skirt the problem of the ineffable by adhering to a strict formalism when discussing musical details, or by pinning down music with signs. But this may come at the cost of shearing away some kind of significance. By the word "significance," I mean to indicate not a referential property but a certain weight of import, one that has a diffuse meaning with a distinct philosophical resonance. Such metaphors (import, resonance, significance) aim at something full, complex, and real in all its befuddling instability that is neither formalist nor semiotic, but which nonetheless matters a great deal.

Two paradoxes have intertwined and framed the arguments of this book. One is of the ineffable itself, a metaphysical paradox developed by all four philosophers in which music is accorded a significance that might appear to speak, but without any sense of semantic meaning. When it sounds it is strangely blank. The second is a linked paradox of the vernacular. In the modern world, musicians disjoin music from norms, even as they necessarily adopt them. They create exceptional accomplishments, work outside of centralized paths, and piece together their own discontent and thought in sound. On an intellectual level, their music suggests that the abstraction of sound in its ineffable emptiness, in its fragility and ephemerality, might allow us to imagine a different world, to negate the world with discontent, and to model the ephemerality of lived time or of an ethical rhythm of life. In so doing, the musicians encounter a parallel paradox: that of the vernacular. No matter how self-taught one is when one plays and writes music, one cannot write without a historicity, without a form, without an adoption of the past.

For Adorno, a fractured version of this adoption—however unconscious, intuitive, or naive on the part of the artist—was the mode for resistance, and it aimed at strict criteria. By contrast, Jankélévitch, Deleuze, and Guattari all loosened the rules and attempted to make something more pragmatic and affirmative in its criteria. Thus, greater multiplicities of style have fallen under the banner of novelty. But at no point do expressive bodies resist without thought, without form. Musical creativity always entails a play on given cultural norms, a shared movement in sound, formed on an inconsistent backbone. It can then lead us to a non-normative ethics that makes up its rules as it goes along. Metaphysically, one cannot make music without doing it differently; and yet ethically creativity cannot be taught, nor can it be mastered. If the creativity behind a musical object appears mysterious, it is not for reason of a divine metaphysical substance. It is because it is an index of nearly innumerable mediations.

This book could not have discerned the exact effect of musical impact on philosophy. It is very hard to discern the impact of music on anything, let alone philosophy. It is clear, though, that music has had some kind of loose effect on philosophy, in the way that music was, for Schopenhauer generally, roughly mimetic of the will. It is probably better, as it was for Aristotle, to not discern the exact effect of music, for fear of missing the point, of overthinking it, of trying too hard in the wrong way, of not doing something meaningful with it. The book did, however, assert that music is of exceptional intellectual value to these philosophers. Each of them was struck by music's nonconceptual character. None of the four Platonize music's ineffability the way that Schopenhauer did, by claiming for music the status of an eternal hierarchy of beings. They all found its perplexing specificity to be productive in a strange, dialectical way because music spoke to them in a way that was not in itself intelligible as philosophy. Though music was never language, it was still a powerful sensation with its own sense of form and structure. And it was always potentially linguistic; it always inspired thought.

Among a scattered group of musically sensitive modern European philosophers, this book has also been an attempt to show—more abstractly—how philosophy in general might listen to music. After all, to discern how philosophers as people listened to or played music is to try to answer a question with only very weak and indirect evidence. What is palpable in their writings—and what I did try to imagine in the introduction to this book—is an empirical befuddlement in the face of music that turns up as a symptom in their philosophy. These befuddlements are multiform. Some philosophers engage in silence, skating around and avoiding, boxing in, or banning. Other intellectuals idealize, loosen, underspecify, and even free-associate when accounting for music. These philosophers in particular responded to the experience of music by creating elaborate theories with exactitude, intricacy, sophistication, and detailed claims. Beyond a biography of philosophers' oddities, musical tastes, and various asides, beyond the polemics over various repertories, this book has drawn together a conversation about an irresolvable puzzle that transfixes my mind when listening to music, and is stuck somewhere up in the clouds, as much as it is apparently here and now.

ACKNOWLEDGMENTS

This book took eight years of reading, writing, and rewriting, and lots of help. What mistakes and oversights do remain are entirely my own. A huge thank-you to Elizabeth Branch Dyson for being so generous with her time, suggestions, and support from an early moment when many crucial decisions still hung in the balance. Her encouragement has been unflagging and invaluable. I owe an enormous debt to Jairo Moreno, advisor extraordinaire, who, along with the faculty at New York University in the Department of Music, let the cohorts of those years be as weird as we wanted to be. Along the way, Mike Beckerman, Cesare Casarino, Suzanne Cusick, Eric Drott, Walter Frisch, Keya Ganguly, Roger Grant, John Hamilton, Natilee Harren, Berthold Hoeckner, Brian Kane, Rob Lehman, Thomas Y. Levin, Richard Leppert, Martin Scherzinger, and Audrey Wasser each offered generous critical feedback. Carolyn Abbate read the entire manuscript and offered brilliant commentary and insight. Joey Crane was incredibly helpful in preparing musical examples, and Mark Mahoney helped with last-minute image scans. Josh Rutner compiled a brilliant index. John Hicks and Richard Leppert gave helpful advice regarding permissions. I received valuable comments from the participants of Sumanth Gopinath's sociology of music graduate seminar. Many thanks to Stephen Lett and the many wonderful folks at the Interdisciplinary Music Forum and the Department of Comparative Literature at the University of Michigan for inviting me to speak on my research on Deleuze and Guattari. And a warm thank-you to Erica Weitzman of the Department of German at Northwestern University for inviting me to present my introduction at a crucial juncture.

This book would have been impossible without innumerable conversations with so many music and philosophy scholars, both in the United States and in the United Kingdom: Amy Cimini, James Currie, John Deathridge, Benjamin Korstvedt, Clara Latham, Sherry Lee, Tamara Levitz, Judith Lochhead, Tomas McAuley, Stephen Decatur Smith, Beth Snyder, Gary Tomlinson, Naomi Waltham-Smith, and Holly Watkins. Thanks to my colleagues at the University of Chicago for their mentorship and guidance over many lunches, dinners, and colloquia: Philip Bohlman, Seth Brodsky, Thomas Christensen, Martha Feldman, Travis Jackson, Robert Kendrick, Kaley Mason, Steven Rings, Anne Walters Robertson, and Lawrence Zbikowski. Beyond Cesare, Keya, and Richard, who scrutinized the pages of this manuscript, my colleagues in the Department of Cultural Studies and Comparative Literature at Minnesota have been an ideal home of committed intellectuals: John Archer, Timothy Brennan, Robin Brown, Tony Brown, Maggie Hennefeld, Alice Lovejoy, Laurie Ouellette, Tom Pepper, Gary Thomas, and Shaden Tageldin. Thanks as well to the faculty and graduate students in the language and literature departments at NYU, who were inspiring colleagues—particularly Emily Apter, Martin Harries, Daniel Hoffman-Schwartz, Jacques Lezra, Barbara Nagel, Lauren Stone, and Magalí Armillas Tiseyra. My first mentees, Laurie Lee and Etha Williams, were tremendous forces of inspiration. I owe a different kind of thanks to Janka Nabay, Boshra Al Saadi, and Matthew Mehlan, who taught me to write music without talking so much. And above all, I could not have written this book without Emily Ruth Capper, whose love and brilliantly skeptical spirit pushed me to rewrite, rethink, and refine over and over again.

This book is dedicated to my dad. He was tireless, generous, and very patient. Like my mom and my sister, he moved through life with a philosophical spirit.

NOTES

INTRODUCTION

1. On the use of music by US soldiers in wartime Iraq, see J. Martin Daughtry, *Listening to War: Sound, Music, Trauma, and Survival in Wartime Iraq*, 219–53.

2. Plato, *The Republic*, book 3, Andrew Barker, ed. *Greek Musical Writings I: The Musician and his Art*, 131. Barker's translation of this opening phrase is "I'm no expert on the *harmoniai*." His footnote, however, offers the more literal "I do not know the *harmoniai*," which I have adopted for this quotation. While otherwise following Barker's translations, for clarity's sake I have inserted the names of the speakers.

3. Barker, 134.

4. Barker, 134.

5. For a detailed reconstruction of Damon's views of music, see Robert W. Wallace, *Reconstructing Damon: Music, Wisdom Teaching, and Politics in Perikles' Athens*.

6. Aristotle, *The Politics*, book 8, in Barker, ed., 179.

7. Ikhwan Al-Safa, *Epistles of the Bretheren of Purity*, epistle 5: On Music, chapter 16: "On the Wise Sayings of the Philosophers Concerning Music," in Owen Wright, ed. *On Music: An Arabic Critical Edition and English Translation of Epistle 5*, 162.

8. Ikhwan Al-Safa, in Wright, ed., 164.

9. These verses are attributed by scholars to the Persian poet Rudaki, though Rudaki's published "Diwan" differs somewhat from this version, which appears in the Ikhwan Al-Safa's epistle, as pointed out by Abbas Hamdani. Ikhwan Al-Safa, in Wright, ed., 165, n. 324. Translation of the Persian is Wright's.

10. On Kant's view of music, see Herman Parret, "Kant on Music and the Heirarchy of the Arts," *The Journal of Aesthetics and Art Criticism*, vol. 56, no. 3 (Summer 1998), 251–64.

11. See Peter Kivy, *Music Alone: Philosophical Reflections on the Purely Musical Experience*; Roger Scruton, *Aesthetics of Music*; Julian Dodd, *Works of Music: An Essay in Ontology*; Nick Zangwill, *Music and Aesthetic Reality: Formalism and the Limits of Description*.

12. For Jankélévitch's writings on politics, see Vladimir Jankélévitch, *L'esprit de résistance: Textes politiques 1943–1983*.

13. As Félix Guattari memorably put it: "I like that kind of inwardness I see in Descartes, seeking to find strength from within himself, and the ultra-inward writing of people like Proust and Gide; I like Jarry, Kafka, Joyce, Beckett, Blanchot and Artaud just as in music I like Fauré, Debussy, and Ravel. Clearly, then, I am a divided man: a petty bourgeois who has flirted with certain elements of the workers's movement, but has kept alive his subscription to the ideology of the ruling class." Félix Guattari, *Molecular Revolution: Psychiatry and Politics*.

14. Guy Suarès, *Vladimir Jankélévitch: Qui suis-je?*

15. Charles J. Stivale, "Pragmatic/Machinic: A Discussion with Fèlix Guattari (March 19, 1985), http://topologicalmedialab.net/xinwei/classes/readings/Guattari/Pragmatic-Machinic_chat.html, accessed June 12, 2015.

16. Deleuze had associations with the composer and conductor Pierre Boulez during the 1970s and '80s. At a 2010 panel discussion at Columbia University, Boulez mentioned his encounters with various European intellectuals (Levi-Strauss, Foucault, Lyotard, Deleuze, Umberto Eco, and Roland Barthes). There, Boulez stated that he was an amateur at philosophy but was nonetheless inspired by Deleuze's philosophical development of Boulez's concepts of the "smooth and the striated" in *A Thousand Plateaus*. He mentioned that in addition to their encounters and shared presentations in the late 1970s, he and Deleuze had engaged in personal correspondence. Cf. https://www.youtube.com/watch?v=8qtSiRpihLw, accessed February 26, 2015. Other, less well known musicians had notable interactions with Deleuze during the same period. The intellectual historian François Dosse describes a 1975 encounter with musicologist and composer Pascale Citron in *Gilles Deleuze and Félix Guattari: Intersecting Lives*, 445. In the following years, Deleuze held two seminars with the French composer Richard Pinhas on the topic of nonpulsed time and metallic instruments. See "Vincennes Seminar Session, May 3, 1977: On Music," trans. Timothy S. Murphy, *Discourse* 30, no. 1 (Fall 1998): 205–18; and "Metal, Metallurgy, Music, Husserl, Simondon" [Seminar Session: February 27, 1979], trans. Timothy S. Murphy, http://www.webdeleuze.com/textes/186, accessed December 20, 2016.

"Gilles Deleuze, Seminar Session and Vincennes" (February 27, 1979), trans. Timothy S. Murphy. On Deleuze and Boulez, see Gilles Deleuze, "Boulez, Proust, and Time: Occupying without Counting" *Angelaki* 3, vol. 2 (1998): 69–74.

17. Deleuze and Guattari, *A Thousand Plateaus*, 311.

18. Jankélévitch, *Music and the Ineffable*, 91.

19. Michael Denning, *Noise Uprising: The Audiopoetics of a Musical Revolution*.

20. Friedrich Kittler, "Gramophone," in *Gramophone, Film, Typewriter*.

21. Jacques Rancière's phrase "distribution of the sensible" refers to the a priori conditions of sensibility and intelligibility of art and the aesthetic. For Rancière, what is taken as self-evident or sensible (audible, visible, legible, and so on) in any given locale or epoch is structured by conditions that variously include and exclude. See Jacques Rancière, *The Politics of Aesthetics*.

22. Richard Taruskin, *Oxford History of Western Art Music*, introduction. He writes: ". . . the concluding chapters are dominated by the interplay of literate and postliterate modes, which have been discernable at least since the middle of the twentieth century, and which sent the literate tradition (in the form of a backlash) into its culminating phase." Later: "For the defining feature of that history [of the fine art of music in the West] . . . has been its reliance on written transmission; and what the digital revolution of the 1980s presaged above all was liberation from the literate tradition to which Boulez remained so unbendingly attached, and its probable eventual demise." Taruskin, *Oxford History*, vol. 5, 480.

23. Rose Rosengard Subotnik, "Adorno's Diagnosis of Beethoven's Late Style: Early Symptom of a Fatal Condition, *Journal of the American Musicological Society* 29 (1976): 242–75;, and "Why is Adorno's Music Criticism the Way It Is? Some Reflections on Twentieth-Century Criticism of Nineteenth-Century Music," *Musical Newsletter* 7, no. 4 (Fall 1977): 3–12. Also see Max Paddison, *Adorno's Aesthetics of Music*; Richard Leppert, ed., *Adorno: Essays on Music* (Berkeley: University of California Press, 2003); Berthold Hoeckner, ed., *Apparitions: New Perspectives on Adorno and Twentieth-Century Music*); Michael Spitzer, *Music as Philosophy: Adorno and Late Beethoven*; Lydia Goehr, *Elective Affinities: Musical Essays on the History of Aesthetic Theory*.

24. See Buchanan and Swiboda, *Deleuze and Music*; essays by Boretz, Gallope, Rahn, and Scherzinger in *Perspectives of New Music* 46, vol. 2; Brian Clarence Hulse and Nick Nesbitt, *Sounding the Virtual: Gilles Deleuze and the Theory and Philosophy of Music*; Edward Campbell, *Music after Deleuze*; Joe Panzner, *The Process That Is the World: Cage/Deleuze/Events/Performances*; Brian Hulse, "Becoming-Composer," *Perspectives of New Music* 53, no. 1 (Winter 2015): 219–37, and Judith Lochhead, Sally Macarthur, and Jennifer Shaw, eds., *Music's Immanent Future: The Deleuzian Turn in Music Studies*.

25. For recent writings on Bloch and music, see Benjamin M. Korstvedt, *Listening for Utopia in Ernst Bloch's Musical Philosophy* (Cambridge University Press, 2010); Ruth Levitas, "Singing Summons the Existence of the Fountain: Bloch, Music, and Utopia," in Peter Thompson and Slavoj Žižek, eds., *The Privatization of Hope: Ernst Bloch and the Future of Utopia*, 219–45; Adrian Daub, "'An All-Too-Secret Wagner': Ernst Bloch the Wagnerian," *Opera Quarterly* 30, no. 2–3: 188–204; Beth Snyder, "Composing a German Utopia: Aesthetic Discourse and Musical Practices in Postwar East Germany (1949–1961)," PhD dissertation, New York University, 2016. On Jankélévitch's writings on music, see "Vladimir Jankélévitch's Philosophy of Music," *Journal of the American Musicological Society* 65, no. 1 (Spring 2012): 215–56; Stephen

Rumph, "Fauré and the Effable: Theatricality, Reflection, and Semiosis in the *Melodies*," *Journal of the American Musicological Society* 68, no. 3 (Fall 2015): 497–558; and Carolyn Abbate, "Ineffability," in *Oxford Handbook of Western Music and Philosophy* (forthcoming, 2017).

26. See Georgina Born, "For a Relational Musicology: Music and Interdisciplinarity, beyond the Practice Turn," *Journal of the Royal Musical Association* 135, no. 2 (2010); Benjamin Piekut, "Actor Networks in Music History: Clarifications and Critiques," *Twentieth Century Music* 11, no. 2 (September 2014); John Tresch and Emily I. Dolan. "Toward a New Organology: Instruments of Music and Science," *Osiris* 28 (2013): 278–98.

27. James Currie, "Music after All," *Journal of the American Musicological Society* 62, no. 1 (Spring 2009): 145–203.

28. Nicholas Mathew, "Reviews: Music and the Politics of Negation," *Journal of the American Musicological Society* 67, no. 3 (Fall 2014): 828–33.

29. Currie, 184.

30. Carolyn Abbate, "Music—Drastic or Gnostic?" *Critical Inquiry* 30, no. 3 (Spring 2004): 505–36.

31. Karol Berger, "Musicology according to Don Giovanni; or, Should We Get Drastic?" *Journal of Musicology* 22, no. 3 (Summer 2005); Michael Puri, "Review: Programming the Absolute: Nineteenth-century German Music and the Hermeneutics of the Moment, by Berthold Hoeckner," *Journal of the American Musicological Society* 59, no. 2 (Summer 2006); Lawrence Kramer, *The Thought of Music*.

32. Hans Ulrich Gumbrecht, *The Production of Presence: What Meaning Cannot Convey*.

33. See James Hepokoski, "Ineffable Immersion: Contextualizing the Call for Silence," *Journal of the American Musicological Society* 65, no. 1 (2012): 223–30. See also Judith Lochhead, "The Sublime, The Ineffable, and Other Dangerous Aesthetics," *Women and Music* 12 (2008): 63–74.

34. Michael Gallope, "Why Was This Music Desirable? On A Critical Explanation of the Avant-Garde," *Journal of Musicology* 31, no. 2 (Spring 2014): 199–230.

35. Clement Greenberg, "Towards a Newer Laocoön," *Partisan Review* 7 (July–August 1940): 296–310.

36. Deleuze, *Difference and Repetition*, 314.

37. Gaston Bachelard's 1936 book *Dialectique de la durée* argues that Bergson's *durée* is not continuous; it must be dialectically mediated by consciousness, structures, conventions, and languages. The book also argues that a passing melody is very far from a simple passing now; rather, it is exemplary of the complex and dialectical passage of lived time. Bachelard's book was an important influence on Deleuze and Guattari's theory of rhythm and *la ritournelle* as a punctuated, contrapuntal form of *durée*, as well as Henri Lefebvre's *Rhythmanalysis*.

38. On Deleuze's dialectic, see Deleuze, *Difference and Repetition*, 26, 76, 164, 178–79, and 182.

39. See Andrew Cole, *The Birth of Theory*; Karen Houle and Jim Vernon, eds., *Hegel and Deleuze: Together Again for the First Time*; Henry Somers-Hall, *Hegel, Deleuze, and the Critique of Representation: Dialectics of Negation and Difference*; and Eleanor Kaufman, *Deleuze: The Dark Precursor: Dialectic, Structure, Being*.

40. See Jacques Derrida, *Of Grammatology*. For Deleuze's review of Hyppolite's book, see "Appendix: Review of Jean Hyppolite, *Logique et existence*," in Hyppolite, *Logic and Existence*.

41. See M. L. West, *Ancient Greek Music*' and Penelope Murray and Peter Wilson, eds., *Music and the Muses: The Culture of 'Mousike in the Classical Athenian City*.

42. In the *Politics,* Aristotle writes: "It is clear, then, that there are certain things one must learn and be trained in with a view to the conduct [*diag g*] of leisure, and that these objects of training and instruction exist for their own sake." Barker, ed., 172.

43. Pythagorean metaphysics lived on throughout the dissemination of Renaissance Neoplatonism, and it persisted long into twentieth-century modernism through the metaphysics of number associated with the just intonation movement, numerology, and various strains of structural mysticism. See Alexander Rehding and Suzannah Clark, eds., *Music and Natural Order*. For the standard Pythagorean source book in European history, see Jocelyn Goodwin, *The Harmony of the Spheres: The Pythagorean Tradition in Music*.

44. Plotinus, *The Enneads*, 380–81.

45. Saint Augustine, *Enarrationes in Psalmos*, In Psalmum 32 *Enarratio* II, sermo I, 8 in v. 3. Translation by Oliver Nicholson via personal correspondence, June 3, 2016. Quoted in Bonds, 44. Augustine's Latin reads:

> *In iubilatione* cane: hoc est enim bene canere Deo, in iubilatione cantare. Quid est in iubilatione canere? Intellegere, verbis explicare non posse quod canitur corde. Etenim illi qui cantant, sive in messe, sive in vinea, sive in aliquo opere ferventi, cum coeperint in verbis canticorum exsultare laetitia, veluti impleti tanta laetitia, ut eam verbis explicare non possint, avertunt se a syllabis verborum, et eunt in sonum iubilationis. Iubilum sonus quidam est significans cor parturire quod dicere non potest. Et quem decet ista iubilatio, nisi ineffabilem Deum? Ineffabilis enim est, quem fari non potes: et si eum fari non potes, et tacere non debes, quid restat nisi ut iubiles; ut gaudeat cor sine verbis, et immensa latitudo gaudiorum metas non habeat syllabarum? *Bene cantate ei in iubilatione*.

46. Charlton T. Lewis and and Charles Short, "Jubilium," in *A Latin Dictionary*.

47. Oliver Nicholson, personal correspondence, June 3, 2016.

48. Augustine, *De musica,* trans. R. C. Taliafero (New York, 1947).

49. See Holly Watkins, *Metaphors of Depth in German Musical Thought*; and Mark Evan Bonds, "Disclosiveness," in *Absolute Music: A History of an Idea*, 112–26.

50. For an account of this historical change, see Bellamy Hosler, *Changing Aesthetic Views of Instrumental Music in 18th-Century Germany*; and John Neubauer,

The Emancipation of Music from Language: Departure from Mimesis in Eighteenth-Century Aesthetics. See also George J. Buelow, "Johann Mattheson and the Invention of the Affektenlehre," in *New Mattheson Studies*, ed. George Buelow and Hans Jochim Marx, 393–407; Stephen Halliwell, *The Aesthetics of Mimesis: Ancient Texts and Modern Problems*, and "Autonomy" in Bonds, 2014.

51. M. H. Abrahms, *The Mirror and the Lamp*, 92.

52. On Forkel's anticipation of the Romantic theme of music's ineffability, see Hosler, 177–88.

53. Johann Nikolaus Forkel, "Einzelne von allen übrigen abgesonderte Leidenschaft," in *Musikalische-Kritische Bibliotek* (Gotha, 1778–79; reprinted Hildesheim, 1964), ii, 65–67. Translation in Hosler, 181.

54. Lessing similarly writes of music's nonspecificity of emotion: "Now we are melting with woefulness, and all of a sudden we are supposed to rage. How so? Why? Against whom? Against the very one for whom our soul was just full of sympathy? Or against another? All these things music cannot specify; it leaves us in uncertainty and confusion; we have feelings, but without perceiving in them a correct sequence; we feel as in a dream; and all these disorderly feelings are more exhausting than delightful." Gotthold Ephraim Lessing, *Hamburgische Dramaturgie*, in *Gesammelte Werke*, ed. Wolfgang Stammler, vol. 2, Stück 27, 444. Translation in Hosler, 5.

55. Wilhelm Heinrich Wackenroder, *Confessions and Fantasies*, 191.

56. *E. T. A. Hoffmann's Musical Writings: Kreisleriana, the Poet and the Composer, Music Criticism*, ed. David Charlton (Cambridge: Cambridge University Press, 1989), 96.

57. Johann Gottfried Herder, *Selected Writings on Aesthetics*, 251.

58. At the hands of eighteenth- and nineteenth-century European writers, the sensuous inconsistency of music was not only cast as an ineffable longing or a transcendent art of feeling. It was occasionally linked to more serious failings of reason: the limits of the self, a crisis of the faculties, even psychological insanity. On music's linkages to the sublime and to madness, see Kiene Brillenburg Wurth, *Musically Sublime* (Fordham University Press, 2009); and John Hamilton, *Music, Madness, and the Unworking of Language*.

59. For recent accounts of the complex relations between German philosophy and music, see Lydia Goehr, *The Quest for Voice: Music, Politics, and the Limits of Philosophy*; Gary Tomlinson, *Metaphysical Song: An Essay on Opera, Sound Figures of Modernity*, ed. Jost Hermand and Gerhard Richter; Andrew Bowie, *Music, Philosophy, and Modernity*, *Music and German Philosophy*, ed. Oliver Furbeth; Julian Johnson, *Out of Time: Music and the Making of Modernity*.

60. In addition to Pedersen 2009 and Bonds 2015, on the emergence of absolute music, see Carl Dahlhaus, *The Idea of Absolute Music*.

61. See Deleuze, "The Image of Thought," *Difference and Repetition*, 129–67.

62. Gabriel Marcel, *Music and Philosophy*.

63. Clement Rosset, *Joyful Cruelty: Towards a Philosophy of the Real*.

64. Jacques Attali, *Noise: The Political Economy of Music*.
65. Henri Lefebvre, *Rhythmanalysis*.

PRELUDE

1. See Daniel Chua, *Absolute Music and the Construction of Meaning*; Susan McClary, *Conventional Wisdom: The Content of Musical Form*; Berthold Hoeckner, *Programming the Absolute: Nineteenth-Century German Music and the Hermeneutics of the Moment*.
2. Roger Scruton, "Effing the Ineffable," http://www.catholiceducation.org/en/religion-and-philosophy/apologetics/effing-the-ineffable.html, accessed May 25, 2015.
3. Theodor Adorno, "Music, Language, Composition," 116.
4. Arthur Schopenhauer, *The World as Will and Representation Vol.* 1, 256, translation modified.
5. Schopenhauer, *The World as Will and Representation Vol.* 1, 256.
6. Schopenhauer, *The World as Will and Representation Vol.* 1, 256.
7. On this topic, see Schopenhauer, *The World as Will and Representation Vol.* 1, 108–9.
8. Schopenhauer, *The World as Will and Representation Vol.* 1, 114.
9. Schopenhauer, *The World as Will and Representation Vol.* 1, 115.
10. Schopenhauer, *The World as Will and Representation Vol.* 1, 128.
11. Schopenhauer, *The World as Will and Representation Vol.* 1, 259.
12. On this point, Wagner was deeply influenced by Schopenhauer. See Brian Magee, *The Tristan Chord: Wagner and Philosophy*.
13. Schopenhauer, *The World as Will and Representation Vol.* 1, 260. Pages later, Schopenhauer writes of music's "secret" powers in relationship to narrative and pictures: "This close relation that music has to the true nature of all things can also explain the fact that, when music suitable to any scene, action, event, or environment is played, it seems to disclose to us its most secret meaning, and appears to be the most accurate and distinct commentary on it." And slightly later: ". . . music makes every picture, indeed every scene from real life and from the world, at once appear in enhanced significance, and this is, of course, all the greater, the more analogous its melody is to the inner spirit of the given phenomenon." (262–63).
14. Schopenhauer, *The World as Will and Representation Vol.* 1, 185.
15. Schopenhauer, *The World as Will and Representation Vol.* 1, 185.
16. For two roughly contemporaneous philosophical receptions of Pythagorean thinking, see Friedrich Wilhelm Joseph Schelling, *The Philosophy of Art*, 116–17; and George Wilhelm Friedrich Hegel, *Philosophy of Nature*, addendum to §301, and the *Lectures on Aesthetics*, 924.
17. See Bonds, 2014; "Hanslick the Ambivalent" in *Absolute Music*, 183–209.
18. Schopenhauer, *The World as Will and Representation Vol.* 1, 257, translation modified.
19. Schopenhauer, *The World as Will and Representation Vol.* 1, 262.

20. Schopenhauer, *The World as Will and Representation* Vol. 2, 448.

21. "For this reason the effect of music is so very much more powerful and penetrating than is that of the other arts, for these others speak only of the shadow, but music of the essence." Schopenhauer, *The World as Will and Representation* Vol. 1, 257.

22. Schopenhauer, *The World as Will and Representation* Vol. 1, 185.

23. Schopenhauer's metaphysics of music may avail itself of Pythagoreanism and Platonism, but it would be wrong to weave it into the historical concept of absolute music, as Carl Dahlhaus has done. For Schopenhauer, any recourse to Platonic abstractions is infused with the emotionally complex texture of the will. Emotions are central to music for Schopenhauer, which is why his ideas were so influential for Wagner, who himself coined the term "absolute music" only to polemicize against it. Schopenhauer's Platonism is there to manage philosophical paradoxes, not to purify musical form from its relationship to emotions.

24. Schopenhauer, *The World as Will and Representation* Vol. 1, 256, translation modified.

25. Schopenhauer, *The World as Will and Representation* Vol. 1, 257, translation modified.

26. Schopenhauer, *The World as Will and Representation* Vol. 1, 259, translation modified.

27. Schopenhauer, *The World as Will and Representation* Vol. 1, 264, translation modified.

28. In Schopenhauer's philosophy, this appears to be less of problem for the other arts, which make explicit their need to be mediated, to be indirect. As alluded to earlier, these participate in a process of representation or *Darstellung* in ways that are routed through more "indirect" objectifications of Platonic Ideas. He writes: "The (Platonic) Ideas are the adequate objectification of the will. To stimulate the knowledge of these by depicting [*Darstellung*] individual things (for works of art are themselves always such) is the aim of all the other arts (and is possible with a corresponding change in the knowing subject). Hence all of them objectify the will only indirectly, in other words, by means of the Ideas."

29. Schopenhauer, *The World as Will and Representation* Vol. 1, 261.

30. Schopenhauer, *The World as Will and Representation* Vol. 1, 262.

31. Schopenhauer offers as evidence of music's exceptionalism its strange lack of predictable mimesis in many cases; this is a symptom of the kind of deeper intensity that retains a certain distance from all that is conceptually mediated. In this way, Schopenhauer's position is a Romantic one that confounds the heretofore popular Aristotelian mimetic theory of music, which was highly dominant in the seventeenth and eighteenth centuries, up through the Enlightenment.

32. Schopenhauer, *The World as Will and Representation* Vol. 2, 448.

33. "Everywhere music expresses only the quintessence of life and of its events, never these themselves, and therefore their differences do not always influence it." Schopenhauer, *The World as Will and Representation* Vol. 1, 261.

34. Schopenhauer, *The World as Will and Representation Vol.* 2, 456.

35. See Schopenhauer, *The World as Will and Representation Vol.* 1, 260–61.

36. Schopenhauer, *The World as Will and Representation Vol.* 2, 406.

37. Schopenhauer writes: "That in some sense music must be related to the world as the depiction to the thing depicted, as the copy to the original, we can infer from the analogy with the remaining arts, to all of which this character is peculiar. . . ." *The World as Will and Representation Vol.* 1, 256.

38. Schopenhauer, *The World as Will and Representation Vol.* 1, 257–58, translation modified.

39. For a classic intellectual history of the chain of being, see Arthur O. Lovejoy, *The Great Chain of Being*. On Robert Fludd in particular, a key figure from the English Renaissance who anticipated Schopenhauer's Pythagorean treatment of the frequency spectrum as a chain of being, see Josceyln Goodwin, *Robert Fludd: Hermetic Philosopher and Surveyor of Two Worlds*.

40. Schopenhauer, *The World as Will and Representation Vol.* 1, 259.

41. Schopenhauer, *The World as Will and Representation Vol.* 1, 258.

42. See Güther Zöller, "Schopenhauer" in *Music and German Philosophy*, 129.

43. Schopenhauer, *The World as Will and Representation Vol.* 1, 256.

44. Schopenhauer, *The World as Will and Representation Vol.* 1, 256–57.

45. Schopenhauer, *The World as Will and Representation Vol.* 1, 257.

46. Schopenhauer, *The World as Will and Representation Vol.* 1, 257.

47. Nietzsche is critical of Schopenhauer's attempt to resolve the paradox of the ineffable, but he considers his own book to be a fitting extension of the spirit of Schopenhauer's thinking. In his words: "Schopenhauer, who did not conceal from himself the difficulty which the lyric poet posed for the philosophical view of art, believed that he had found a way out of the impasse, one along which I cannot follow him. Yet it was into his hands alone that the means were given to deal decisively with this difficulty, in the form of his profound metaphysics of music: and here I believe I had accomplished this task in his spirit and in his honor." Nietzsche, *The Birth of Tragedy*, 36–37.

48. Here Nietzsche endorses music's ineffability, and insists on both its unique specificity and its exceptionalism in relation to poetry and visual art:

> . . . music itself, in its full unrestricted form, has no *need* for the image and the concept, but rather only *tolerates* their proximity. Lyric poetry can express nothing which was not already present at the highest level of universality and validity in the music which compelled it to speak in images. The world symbolism of music utterly exceeds the grasp of language, because it refers symbolically to the original contradiction and pain at the heart of the original Unity, and therefore symbolizes a sphere which exists over and above all phenomena. In comparison with this, all phenomena are merely allegories: so *language,* as organ and symbol of phenomena, can never reveal the innermost depths of music, and as soon as it engages in the imitation of music, can only ever skim the sur-

face, while even the most eloquent lyric poetry is powerless to bring the deepest meaning of music as much as one step closer to us.

Nietzsche, *The Birth of Tragedy*, 42.

49. As Nietzsche says: "The optimistic dialectic drives music out of tragedy with the whip of its syllogisms: that is, it destroys the essence of tragedy, which can only be interpreted as a manifestation and transformation into images of Dionysian states, as visible symbolization of music, as the dream-world of a Dionysian intoxication." Nietzsche, *The Birth of Tragedy*, 79.

50. See Laura Odello, "Waiting for the Death Knell," in *Speaking of Music: Addressing the Sonorous*, ed. Keith Chapin and Andrew W. Clark (New York: Fordham University Press, 2013), 39–48.

51. Nietzsche says of a "music making Socrates" that he would be attuned precisely do that what exceeded the powers of reason: "[Socrates] must have asked himself the following question—perhaps whatever is not intelligible to me is not necessarily immediately unintelligent? Perhaps there is a domain of wisdom which excludes the logician? Perhaps art is even a necessary correlative of an supplement to science?"

52. Ernst Bloch, *The Spirit of Utopia*, 151–52, translation modified.

53. In an earlier German edition of Bloch's Giest der Utopie, there appears a fascinating passage comparing Schopenhauer with Hegel and Marx that existed in a 1923 revision, but did not survive into the third volume of the 1964 Werkausgabe that served as the foundation for all the English translations of Bloch's work:

> Aber die Objektsironie selber, die restaurative Umdrehung der Subjektsironie gegen die Welt zu einer Objectsironie, schließlich zu einer Ironie des Absoluten gegen die Subjekte, mit einem Wort: der reaktionäre, dialektisch ausspielende Absolutismus ist methodologisch auch bei Schopenhauer vorhanden und nicht wesentlich anders beschaffen als bei Hegel, dessen Individuen zwar mehr als nur die Fortpflanzung besorgen, aber dafür der gleichen Heterogenität der Zwecke, der List der Vernunft unterliegen; dessen Absolutum weiterhin zwar nicht Wille heißt, aber als Idee sich selber das gleiche Weltschauspiel vorführt. Ja zuletzt hat der Gott der umgeschlagenen Ironie, der Ironie von der anderen Seite, sogar noch im alldeduktiven "Produktionsprozess" des Marxismus einen Thron erlangt; —kurz, Wille, Idee und auch noch Produktionsprozess sind letzthin nur verschiedene Hypostasen des gleichen okkasionalistisch absoluten Urwesens.

Bloch, *Geist der Utopie*, 182 (Berlin: Paul Cassirer Verlag A.-G., 1923).

54. Bloch, *The Spirit of Utopia*, 154–55.

55. Theodor Adorno, *Mahler*, 70, translation modified. The term *Entwirklichung* (derealization, devaluation) similarly denoted a paradox in Marx's thinking whereby accomplished labor becomes unreal, as the object of one's labor becomes alienated and estranged from the work of the laborer.

56. Elsewhere with respect to Wagner, Adorno wrote similarly about Schopenhauer that his philosophy of music was a metaphysical romanticism that ignored his-

tory and objectivity: "... the sensuous musical context of Wagner's works can be seen to be essentially identical with the blind, circular, and profoundly ahistorical poetic content of Schopenhauer's philosophy, in which blind will becomes individuated, but only to devour the individual once again." Adorno, "Criteria of New Music," in *Sound Figures*, 163.

57. Adorno, *Mahler*, 71.
58. Adorno, *Mahler*, 153, translation modified.
59. Adorno, Aesthetic Theory, 137, translation of first sentence modified to remain more literal. The original reads: "Schopenhauer's principia individuationis, Raum, Zeit, Kausalität, treten in der Kunst, dem Bereich des bis zum Äußersten Individuierten, ein zweites Mal auf, jedoch gebrochen, und solche Brechung, erzwungen durch den Scheincharakter, verleiht der Kunst den Aspekt von Freiheit." A few pages prior, Adorno writes similarly of the paradoxical ontology of the artwork:

> Artworks have the absolute and they do not have it. In their movement toward truth artworks are in need of that concept that for the sake of their truth they keep at a distance. It is not up to art to decide whether its negativity is its limit or truth. Artworks are a priori negative by the law of their objectivation: They kill what they objectify by tearing it away from the immediacy of its life. Their own life preys on death. This defines the qualitative threshold to modern art. Modern works relinquish themselves mimetically to reification, their principle of death.

Adorno, *Aesthetic Theory*, 133.

60. Vladimir Jankélévitch, *Liszt: Rhapsodie et Improvisation*, ed. Francoise Schwab, 1998, 113–14, translation mine. The Greek phrase is taken from Anaxagoras, the pre-Socratic philosopher.

61. Jankélévitch's treatment of Schopenhauer in *Music and the Ineffable* is largely critical. He writes: "Schopenhauer's 'metaphysics of music' has often been criticized, sometimes at the cost of overlooking its complex and original intuitions. It is critical to point out, however, that all such *metamusic*: music thus romanticized, is at once arbitrary and metaphorical. It is arbitrary because one cannot see exactly what justifies taking the acoustic universe and privileging and promoting it to this degree above all others." Yet it is instructive to note that, early in his career, Jankélévitch ventured many comparisons between Schopenhauer and Bergson. This is particularly the case in Jankélévitch's 1931 monograph *Bergson*, in which Schopenhauer serves as a consistent point of reference. Later in his career, in some nonmusical contexts Jankélévitch cites Schopenhauer's philosophy in broad outlines, often approvingly. See his book *Will of Desire* (1957; substantial revision 1980), volume 3 of the triology *Le Je-ne-sais-quoi et le Presque-rien* (1980).

62. Jankélévitch, *Music and the Ineffable*, 12.
63. Jankélévitch, *Music and the Ineffable*, 14–15.
64. Jankélévitch continues:

But only an awareness that a way of speaking is, simply, a way of speaking can keep us honest. A metaphysics of music that claims to transmit messages from the other world retraces the incantatory action of enchantment upon the enchanted in the form of an illicit relocation of the here-and-now to the Beyond. Sophism gets extended by means of a swindle.... I would conclude, therefore, that music is not above the laws and not exempt from the limitations and servitude inherent in the human condition. And, finally, that if "ethics" of music is a verbal mirage, "meta-physics" of music is closer to being a mere rhetorical figure.

Jankélévitch, *Music and the Ineffable*, 15.

65. Gilles Deleuze, *The Logic of Sense*, 106.

66. Deleuze, *Difference and Repetition*, 276–77, translation modified.

67. Deleuze, *Difference and Repetition*, 277.

CHAPTER 1

1. Anthony Nassar's translator's notes for *The Spirit of Utopia* state that *an* is a causal preposition. In this way, the opening sentence could mean: "I exist or come into because of myself." See *The Spirit of Utopia*, 284, n. 1.

2. Bloch, *The Spirit of Utopia*, 3.

3. Bloch's commentary on Williams James's theory of "psychological life as a stream" can be found in *The Principle of Hope*, 291.

4. Benjamin Korstvedt's *Listening for Utopian in Ernst Bloch's Musical Philosophy* devotes substantial attention to Bloch's relationship with Lukács. In particular, he explores the metaphor of the *Teppich*, a concept Bloch borrows from Lukács. Also, in this regard see *Aesthetics and Politics*, and Martin Jay, "Bloch and Extension of Marxist Holism," in *Marxism and Totality*, 174–95, for a comprehensive overview of Bloch's philosophy that foregrounds the axis of his disagreements with Lukács.

5. Bloch, *The Spirit of Utopia*, 32.

6. Bloch, *The Spirit of Utopia*, 34, translation modified.

7. Bloch, *The Spirit of Utopia*, 163.

8. Bloch, *The Spirit of Utopia*, 163.

9. Bloch, *The Spirit of Utopia*, 101.

10. Bloch, *The Spirit of Utopia*, 101–3. Here Bloch's observations closely follow those of Schopenhauer, who remarks in *The World as Will and Representation*: "This close relation that music has to the true nature of all things can explain the fact that, when music suitable to any scene, action, event, or environment is played, it seems to disclose to us its most secret meaning, and appears to be the most accurate and distinct commentary on it." *The World as Will and Representation*, vol. 1, 261–62.

11. Bloch, *The Spirit of Utopia*, 103, translation modified.

12. As recounted briefly in the prelude to this book, despite his sympathy for certain aspects of Schopenhauer's thinking, on a metaphysical level Bloch does not agree with Schopenhauer's pessimistic view of reality, and in general fears that Schopenhau-

er's philosophy leaves subjects excessively passive in the face of the "tyranny" of the will's blind striving. Musically, Bloch fears that Schopenhauer venerates music to such an extent that it could essentially exist *without* the world altogether, and that there are consequently no genuinely dialectical, historically determined criteria for exemplary forms by which to judge or even assess musical expression. For Bloch's critical views of Schopenhauer's metaphysics of music see *The Spirit of Utopia*, 148–49, 153–55.

13. Bloch, *The Spirit of Utopia*, 100.

14. Bloch, *The Spirit of Utopia*, 146; see also Korstvedt, 39.

15. Henry George Liddell and Robert Scott, *A Greek-English Lexicon* (1940), "Tonos," http://www.perseus.tufts.edu/hopper/text?doc=Perseus%3Atext%3A1999. 04.0057%3Aalphabetic+letter%3D*t%3Aentry+group%3D44%3Aentry%3Dto%2F nos, accessed June 12, 2014.

16. Ibid.

17. The Greeks also had a second word for musical tones, one that denoted a "clear and distinct sound" that could be either vocal or instrumental: *phthoggos*. See Henry George Liddell, Robert Scott, *A Greek-English Lexicon* (1940), http://www.perseus. tufts.edu/hopper/morph?l=fqo%2Fggos&la=greek&can=fqo%2Fggos0&prior=h(&d =Perseus:text:1999.04.0057:alphabetic%20letter=*f:entry%20group=15:entry=fqoggh /&i=1#lexicon, accessed June 12, 2014. Aristoxenus defined it as "a falling of the voice on one pitch," and adds that it requires linkages to some kind of compositional assembly: ". . . It appears to be a *phthoggos* as such because it is ordered in a *melos* and stands harmonically on a single pitch." (Da Rios, 20.16–19). Quoted in Thomas Mathiesen, *Apollo's Lyre: Greek Music and Music Theory in Antiquity and the Middle Ages* (Lincoln: University of Nebraska Press, 1999), 306. Aristoxenus also likely associated *tonoi* with "positions of the voice." See Mathiesen, 302. *Tonoi* could be combined into systems of *harmonioi*, which for Plato and Aristotle alike a denoted a "full complex of musical elements," a proper fitting together of sonic multiplicities. See Mathiesen, 127. Gaudentius somewhat later elaborates on Aristoxenus ever so slightly: "A *phthoggos* is the falling of the voice upon one pitch; pitch is a tarrying and standing of the voice; whenever the voice seems to stop on one pitch, we say that the voice is a note that can be ordered in a melos." Gaudentius, "Harmonic Introduction," in Strunk, ed., *Source Readings in Music History*, 68.

18. David Hiley and Alex Lingas, "Tonus," *The Oxford Companion to Music*, http://www.oxfordreference.com.ezp2.lib.umn.edu/view/10.1093/ acref/9780199579037.001.0001/acref-9780199579037-e-6845?rskey=aEKner&result=6, accessed June 12, 2014.

19. Anthony Nassar's translation of *Spirit of Utopia* translates *Ton* as "note." Peter Palmer does the same in his translation of Bloch's collected *Philosophy of Music*. T. M. Knox likewise translated Hegel's *Lectures on Aesthetics* translates *Ton* variously as sound, note, and tone, depending on the context.

20. Johann Georg Sulzer, *Allgemeine Theorie der Schönen Künste*, available online at http://www.textlog.de/sulzer.html, accessed July 18, 2014.

21. Johann Georg Sulzer, *Allgemeine Theorie der Schönen Künste*, "Ton."(Musik): "Dieses Wort wird selbst in der Musik, wo es seine eigentliche Bedeutung vorzüglich behält, dennoch von ganz verschiedenen Dingen genommen."

22. Wilhelm Heinrich Wackenroder, *Herzensergießungen eines kunstliebenden Klosterbruders*, "Das merkwürdige musikalische Leben des Tonkünstlers Joseph Berglinger In zwei Hauptstücken," translation mine.

23. See the opening paragraph of Wackenroder's 1799 essay "Das eigentümliche innere Wesen der Tonkunst, und die Seelenlehre der heutigen Instrumentalmusik" in Wackenroder, *Confessions and Fantasies*, trans. Schubert, 188–94.

24. Bonds remarks on the intellectual lineage of this distinction: "Hanslick identifies *Ton* as the most basic element of music, and he places great importance on the distinction between tone, a quintessentially human product, and sound [*Schall* or *Klang*], a product of nature. This was a long-standing distinction found in commentaries by a wide range of writers that included Rousseau, Forkel, Krause, Mundt, and Kahlert." Bonds, *Absolute Music*, 146. See also Johann Gottfried Herder, who developed a rich contrast between *Schall* and *Ton* in "Critical Forests: Fourth Grove, on Riedel's Theory of the Beaux Arts" (1846) in Herder, *Selected Writings on Aesthetics*.

25. Holly Watkins quotes the following sentence from Wackenroder's *Joseph Berglinger*: "In the mirror of tones the human heart gets to know itself. Through them we learn to feel emotion; they give living consciousness to many spirits dreaming in hidden recesses of the soul, and they enrich the feeling of our interior with entirely new magical spirits." See *Metaphors of Depth in German Musical Thought*.

26. E. T. A. Hoffmann, "Beethoven's Instrumentalmusik." "In Wahrheit, der Meister, an Besonnenheit Haydn und Mozart ganz an die Seite zu stellen, trennt sein Ich von dem Innern Reich der Töne und gebietet darüber als unumschränkter Herr. Ästhetische Meßkünstler haben oft im Shakespeare über gänzlichen Mangel innerer Einheit und inneren Zusammenhanges geklagt, indem dem tieferen Blick ein schöner Baum, Blätter, Blüten und Früchte, aus einem Keim treibend, erwächst; so entfaltet sich auch nur durch ein sehr tiefes Eingehen in Beethovens Instrumentalmusik die hohe Besonnenheit, welche vom wahren Genie unzertrennlich ist und von dem Studium der Kunst genährt wird." See *E. T. A. Hoffmann's Musical Writings: Kreisleriana, The Poet and the Composer, Music Criticism*.

27. Frauke Otto, *Robert Schumann als Jean Paul Leser*.

28. John Daverio, *Robert Schumann: Herald of a New Poetic Age*, 46–47.

29. Stumpf's experimental approach focused almost exclusively on the experience of tones (in order to create a sufficiently reduced situation for experimentation), but was criticized as being "too elemental" to be useful to musicians. See Green and Butler, "From Acoustics to *Tonpsychologie*," in which the authors argue that Stumpf and Helmholtz did not teach us much about music because of the atomistic attention to tones, but did demystify some practical inheritances in the Western pedagogy of harmony, counterpoint, and composition, and gave us courage to apply empirical and experimental methodologies to music.

30. Benjamin Steege, *Helmholtz and the Modern Listener*. Steege's Foucaultian approach to Helmholtz argues that his innovations should be understood in light of a rich network of knowledge transformation in the mid- to late nineteenth century. Steege places particular emphasis on the constructivist power of discursive frames and "epistemic objects" even when guided by the telos of a rigorous empiricism. On Carl Stumpf, see *The Origins of Music*.

31. Erica Mugglestone, "Guido Adler's 'The Scope, Method, and Aim of Musicology' (1885): An English Translation with an Historical-Analytical Commentary," *Yearbook for Traditional Music* 13 (1981), no. 5. Also see Kevin Karnes, *Music, Criticism, and the Challenge of History: Shaping Modern Musical Thought in Late Nineteenth-Century Vienna*.

32. See Carl Dahlhaus, *Foundations of Music History*, and Karol Berger, "The Ends of Music History, or: The Old Masters in the Supermarket of Cultures" *Journal of Musicology* 31, no. 2 (Spring 2014): 186–98.

33. Heinrich Schenker, *Harmonielehre* (1906), 3. Schenker writes: "We immediately know which aspect of nature is indicated by word, which by color, and which by sculptured form. Only music is different. Intrinsically, there is no unambivalent association of ideas between music and nature. This lack probably provides the only satisfactory explanation for the fact that the music of primitive peoples never developed beyond a certain rudimentary stage.... It seems that without the aid of association of ideas human activity can unfold either in comprehension or in creation."

34. Schenker continues: "The motif, and the motif alone, creates the possibility of associating ideas, the only one of which music is capable. The motif is a primordial and intrinsic association of ideas. The motif thus substitutes for the ageless and powerful associations of ideas from patterns in nature, on which the other arts are thriving." Schenker, *Harmonielehre*, 4.

35. See Matthew Arndt, "Schenker and Schoenberg on the Will of the Tone," *Journal of Music Theory* 55, no. 1 (Spring 2011): 89–146.

36. Schoenberg, *Harmonielehre*, 314.

37. Schoenberg, *Harmonielehre*, 314.

38. Curiously, when Hegel discusses harmony, he concludes that no merely phenomenological or subjective account of harmony can be given; it must be mediated by the "objective determinateness" of number.

39. For more on the ideological afterlife of abstraction as an enduring issue for music theory, see David Cohen's deconstructive analysis of how a Platonic metaphysics of unity dominated early theories of consonance just as practical problems like seconds and thirds were subject to suppressions or strange justifications by the Enchiriadis authors. See "Metaphysics, Ideology, Discipline: Consonance, Dissonance, and the Foundations of Western Polyphony," *Theoria* 7 (1993): 1–85. See also Karl D. Braunschweig, "Disciplining Knowledge in Music Theory: Abstraction and the Recovery of Dialectics," *GAMUT: Online Journal of the Music Theory Society of the Mid-Atlantic* 5, no. 1 (2012).

40. Lee Rothfarb has adopted this term in his entry "Energetics" in the *Cambridge History of Western Music Theory*, and notes that it was a term coined by Rudolf Schäfke in *Geschichte der Musikästhetik* (1934). Ernst Kurth's *Grundlagen des linearen Kontrapunkts* (1917) seems to have been influential on Bloch, as was August Halm's *Von zwei Kulturen der Musik* (1913). Rothfarb has published translations and commentary of Kurth's writings, as well as a recent monograph on Halm's writings. See Lee Rothfarb, ed., *Ernst Kurth's Selected Writings*; and Lee Rothfarb, *August Halm: A Critical and Creative Life in Music*. Halm's *Von zwei Kulturen* was recently translated by Laura Lyn Kelly in "August Halm's 'Von zwei Kulturen der Musik,' Translation and an Introductory Essay," PhD dissertation, University of Texas, 2007.

41. Francesca Vidal writes similarly that for Bloch, "the suprahistorical aspect of music is seen as located in the *Ton*, with which the new is not described or depicted but adumbrated in sound [*anklingt*]. Tone is music's material. It enables music to say more than language can. This is meant as an explicit expression of the possibility for human beings to find themselves. Music is the medium of encounter with oneself." Francesca Vidal, "Bloch," in Stefan Lorenz Sorgner, Oliver Furbeth, and Susan H. Gillespie, eds., *Music in German Philosophy: An Introduction*, 172.

42. In the *Zusatz* to §301, Hegel describes an empirical example of the distinction between *Klang* and *Ton*.

43. As Hegel puts it in the *Zusatz* of §300 of the *Encyclopedia*: "*Klang* belongs to the sphere of mechanism since it is associated with heavy matter. Form, as wresting itself from heavy matter but as still attached to it, is for that reason still conditioned: it is the free physical utterance of ideality still linked to the mechanical sphere—the freedom *from* heavy matter which is at the same time *in* heavy matter."

44. Hegel, *Encyclopedia*, §299, translation modified.

45. Hegel, *Encyclopedia*, §300, Zusatz, translation modified.

46. Hegel, *Encyclopedia*, §299, translation modified.

47. Hegel, *Encyclopedia*, §300, Zusatz, translation modified: "The origin of *Klanges* is hard to grasp. *Klang* is the emergence [*hervortretend*] of the specific inner being freed [*geschieden*] from gravity; it is the *Klage* [action, claim, charge, accusation] of the ideal in the violence of otherness, but also its triumph over the latter since it preserves itself therein." He continues: "*Klang*, properly speaking, is reverberation [*Nachhallen*], the unhindered inner vibration [*inner Schwingen*] of a body which is freely determined by the nature of its cohesion."

48. Hegel, *Lectures on Aesthetics*, 890.

49. Hegel, *Lectures on Aesthetics*, 890, translation modified.

50. Hegel, *Lectures on Aesthetics*, 890, translation modified.

51. Hegel, *Lectures on Aesthetics*, 890-1, translation modified.

52. This move is presaged in Hegel's *Naturphilosophie* when the voice is distinguished from mere physical sound: "There is also a third form [of sound], in which the external stimulation and the sound emitted by the body are alike, i.e. human song. It is in the voice that this subjectivity or independence of form first occurs, and this

purely tremulous motion consequently possesses something which is in conformity with spirit." *Encyclopedia, Part II*, §301.

53. For Hegel, the voice has interiority, a certain subjective resonance, something Derrida will eventually critique as a closed circuit of metaphysical phonocentrism: "There is still a third form where the outer excitation and the sound emitted by the body [*das Schallen des Körpers*] are like in kind, and that is the singing voice of man. It is in the voice that we first have this subjectivity or independence of form; this merely vibratory movement thus has something spiritual about it."

54. Bloch, *The Spirit of Utopia*, 236.

55. I read this section of *The Spirit of Utopia* as a cryptic exploration of Marx's commodity fetish. See Karl Marx, *Das Kapital*, volume 1, part 1, section 4, "The Fetishism of the Commodity and Its Secret."

56. Bloch, *The Spirit of Utopia*, 8.

57. Hegel, *Introductory Lectures on Aesthetics*, 35.

58. Hegel, *Introductory Lectures on Aesthetics*, 35–36.

59. Bloch paraphrases the outline of Hegel's argument in the *Lectures on Aesthetics* in *The Spirit of Utopia* in Bloch, *The Spirit of Utopia*, 18.

60. Hegel, *Introductory Lectures on Aesthetics*, 36.

61. Bloch, *The Spirit of Utopia*, 35.

62. Bloch, *The Spirit of Utopia*, 34.

63. Bloch, "Magic Rattle, Human Harp," in *Essays on the Philosophy of Music*, 140.

64. Bloch, "Magic Rattle, Human Harp," in *Essays on the Philosophy of Music*, 140.

65. Bloch, "Magic Rattle, Human Harp," in *Essays on the Philosophy of Music*, 140.

66. Bloch, "Magic Rattle, Human Harp," in *Essays on the Philosophy of Music*, 140.

67. Bloch, "Magic Rattle, Human Harp," in *Essays on the Philosophy of Music*, 141, translation modified.

68. Bloch, "Magic Rattle, Human Harp," in *Essays on the Philosophy of Music*, 140.

69. Bloch, "Magic Rattle, Human Harp," in *Essays on the Philosophy of Music*, 141, translation modified.

70. Bloch, "Magic Rattle, Human Harp," in *Essays on the Philosophy of Music,* 140.

71. Bloch, *The Principle of Hope*, 1058.

72. The negation of painting into the infinity of music parallels, in broad outlines, the way music sublates the spatiality of painting into a realm of inner spirituality in Hegel's *Introductory Lectures on Aesthetics*. See, in particular, chapter 5.

73. Bloch positions the tone's potentiality, its "fiery eruption," once reflected in the virtuous self-maintenance of Hegel's *Erzittern des Körpers*, as the "final material moment" of music. This affirmation of potentiality has parallels with Bloch's "left Aristotelianism." See Bloch, *Avicenna und die Aristotelische Linke*.

74. Bloch, *The Spirit of Utopia*, 120.

75. Bloch, *The Principle of Hope*, 1072, translation modified.

76. Bloch, *The Principle of Hope*, 1080, translation modified.

77. When it comes to Hegel's understanding of music, he was generally subjectiv-

ist as opposed to formalist; he held that its basic ontological property was its capacity to externalize subjective inner life—to "make this inwardly veiled life and energy echo on its own account in tones" (*Aesthetics*, 1991, 2:902). Contrary to Hanslick, for Hegel, who loved attending performances of Rossini's operas in Vienna but had little interest in Beethoven (so far as we know), absolute music would unleash an undesirable outcome; it would "lose general human interest" because it would become formally introverted, made only for specialists. Hegel's rejection of formalism was drawn off the suspicions that it was both empirically inaccessible and metaphysically empty. Since music was suited to the expressive of subjective states, it should busy itself principally with the exteriorization of subjective interiors.

78. Hegel, *Lectures on Aesthetics*, 894.

79. For Bloch, *der Tonfall* (attack, inflection) marks the way the tone is implicated in an ontological self-encounter, or embodied auto-affection, centered in the larynx. Song presupposes inflection, tone, and intonation, releases it "as the most fleeting and yet most powerful thing . . . and gathers it into a continuous, compact construct." Bloch, *The Spirit of Utopia*, 96.

80. Bloch, *The Spirit of Utopia*, 180.

81. Bloch, *The Spirit of Utopia*, 112. See also Bloch, "The Exceeding of Limits and the World of Man at its Most Richly Intense in Music," in *Essays on the Philosophy of Music*, 207–8.

82. See Bloch, "On the Mathematical and Dialectical Character in Music." See also Bloch, *The Spirit of Utopia*, 148.

83. Bloch, *The Spirit of Utopia*, 113.

84. Bloch, *The Principle of Hope*, 1080.

85. Theodor W. Adorno, "Music and Language: A Fragment," in *Quasi una Fantasia: Essays on Modern Music* (New York: Verso, 1998), 1–8.

86. Bloch, *The Spirit of Utopia*, 144. Original: "Sicherlich, wie hier endgültig besprechbar wird, ist es nicht zufällig, daß gerade der Ton, wohlverstanden, der von Menschen begrauchte, radikal umgebrochene Ton, musikalisch einschlägt, daß gerade dieser zarte, durchsichtige Leib zum Träger musikalischer Zustände erwählt wird." Translation mine.

87. Bloch, *The Spirit of Utopia*, 160–61.

88. Bloch, *The Spirit of Utopia*, 160.

89. Bloch, *The Spirit of Utopia*, 58.

90. See also Bloch, *PH*, 1088, in particular the "incognito of the now."

91. Bloch, *The Spirit of Utopia*, 23.

92. Bloch, *The Spirit of Utopia*, 17.

93. Bloch, *The Spirit of Utopia*, 24.

94. For Bloch's complete discussions of Mozart and J. S. Bach as the twin characters of the second schema, see Bloch, *The Spirit of Utopia*, 48–55.

95. Bloch, *The Spirit of Utopia*, 55.

96. Bloch, *The Spirit of Utopia*, 56.

97. Bloch, *The Spirit of Utopia*, 56.
98. Bloch, *The Spirit of Utopia*, 57.
99. Bloch, *The Spirit of Utopia*, 142. Bloch writes: "In this way the tone pushes forward by itself, and a movement inherent in it reaches toward other notes by cadential compulsion."
100. Bloch, *The Spirit of Utopia*, 142.
101. For a critical survey of abstraction as a key factor in the history of tonal theory, see Braunschweig, "Disciplining Knowledge in Music Theory," 39–97.
102. Bloch, *The Principle of Hope*, 1074.
103. See "Philippe de Vitry's *Ars Nova*," trans. Leon Plantinga, *Journal of Music Theory* 5 (November 1961): 204–20; Jacques de Liège, *Speculum Musicae*, ed. Roger Bragard. *Corpus Scriptorum de Musica* 3, 7 vols. (Rome: American Institute of Musicology, 1955–73).
104. Bloch, *The Principle of Hope*, 1079.
105. Bloch, *The Spirit of Utopia*, 48.
106. Bloch, *The Spirit of Utopia*, 42.
107. Bloch, *The Spirit of Utopia*, 37.
108. Bloch, *The Spirit of Utopia*, 38.
109. Bloch, *The Spirit of Utopia*, 38.
110. Bloch, *The Principle of Hope*, 1075.
111. Bloch, *The Principle of Hope*, 1075–76.
112. Bloch, *The Spirit of Utopia*, 42.
113. See Bloch, *The Spirit of Utopia*, 94.
114. Though this passage of *The Principle of Hope* has no references to any other sources on music, I concur with Benjamin Korstvedt that Bloch likely developed his interpretation of the fugue and sonata in dialogue with August Halm's *Von zwei Kulturen der Musik*.
115. Bloch, *The Principle of Hope*, 1095. See Jean-Paul Sartre's interpretation of J. S. Bach's fugues in "The Artist and His Conscience," trans. Chris Turner, in *Portraits: Situations IV*, 15.
116. Bloch, *The Principle of Hope*, 1095.
117. Bloch, *The Principle of Hope*, 1095.
118. Bloch, *The Principle of Hope*, 1092.
119. Bloch, *The Principle of Hope*, 1095.
120. Bloch, *The Principle of Hope*, 1095.
121. Bloch writes: "The *granting or being-here of music*, as represented by *architectonic counterpoint*, remains and has primacy." Bloch, *The Principle of Hope*, 1095–96, translation modified, emphasis in original.
122. Bloch, *The Principle of Hope*, 1093.
123. Bloch, *The Principle of Hope*, 1093.
124. Bloch, *The Principle of Hope*, 1093.
125. Bloch, *The Principle of Hope*, 1096.

126. Bloch, *The Principle of Hope*, 1092.
127. Bloch, *The Principle of Hope*, 1092, translation modified.
128. Bloch, *The Spirit of Utopia*, 100.
129. Bloch, *The Spirit of Utopia*, 100.
130. Bloch, *The Spirit of Utopia*, 99–100.

CHAPTER 2

1. Ernst Bloch and Theodor Adorno, "Something's Missing: A Discussion between Ernst Bloch and Theodor W. Adorno on the Contradictions of Utopian Longing," in *Ernst Bloch: The Utopian Function of Art and Literature: Selected Essays*.
2. Ernst Bloch and Theodor Adorno, "Something's Missing: A Discussion between Ernst Bloch and Theodor W. Adorno on the Contradictions of Utopian Longing," 10.
3. Ernst Bloch and Theodor Adorno, "Something's Missing: A Discussion between Ernst Bloch and Theodor W. Adorno on the Contradictions of Utopian Longing," 12.
4. Adorno, "Bloch's 'Traces,' The Philosophy of Kitsch," 56.
5. Adorno, "Bloch's 'Traces,' The Philosophy of Kitsch," 57.
6. Adorno, "Bloch's 'Traces,' The Philosophy of Kitsch," 60.
7. Adorno, "Bloch's 'Traces,' The Philosophy of Kitsch," 53.
8. Adorno, "Bloch's 'Traces,' The Philosophy of Kitsch," 52, translation modified. Adorno's original reads: "Naïve Philosophie wählt das Inkognito des Schwandroneurs, des Wirtschausspielers mit falschen Bässen, der, arm, verkannt, den Staunenden, die ihm das Glas Bier bezahlen, weismacht, eigentlich ware er der Paderewski."
9. Adorno, "Bloch's 'Traces,' The Philosophy of Kitsch," 53, translation modified. An orchestrion is an automatic musical instrument such as a barrel organ, typically one that simulates a variety of instruments. Orchestrions were first developed in the late eighteenth century, and evolved throughout the nineteenth. Livingstone's translation of the term as "jukebox" is an apt point of reference, since orchestrions built in the early twentieth century similarly had coin slots that allowed customers to pick from several different songs. Adorno's original reads: "Es wird von Bloch entsühnt. Er wetteifert mit dem Schreier des unvergessenen Jahrmarkts, dröhnt wie ein Orchestrion aus der noch leeren Gaststätte, die auf die Gäste wartet."
10. Adorno, "Bloch's 'Traces,' The Philosophy of Kitsch," 51.
11. Adorno, *Towards a Theory of Musical Reproduction*, 167–68.
12. In *Aesthetic Theory*, Adorno states that such an ancient mimesis is intrinsic to the primitive impulses of human life and historically preceded intellectually self-conscious practices of artistic production. At the same time, this ancient "mimetic comportment"—also described as "the assimilation of the self to its other"— formed the basis for the emergence of modern rationalization: "By virtue of its basic material, music is the art in which the pre-rational, mimetic impulses ineluctably find their voice,

even as they enter into a pact with the processes leading to the progressive domination of matter and nature." Adorno, "Some Ideas on the Sociology of Music," 6.

13. Adorno, "Some Ideas on the Sociology of Music," 6. Adorno, *Towards a Theory of Musical Reproduction,* 52–53.

14. Adorno, *Towards a Theory of Musical Reproduction,* 52.

15. Adorno writes: "Every written note is the image of a beat: objectification of music, the conversion of the temporal flow into a spatial one, is not only formally a spatialization, but according to its original *content,* namely the spatialization of experience for the purpose of controlling it." *Towards a Theory of Musical Reproduction,* 53.

16. Adorno, "Music, Language, and Composition." The title of the German original is "Musik, Sprache und ihr Verhältnis im gegenwärtigen Komponieren." Translation modified.

17. Heidegger's *Dasein* is unlikely to have been intended here. See Martin Heidegger, *Being and Time.* By this point in Adorno's career, he had explicitly critiqued Heidegger's philosophy as a form of regressive idealism.

18. Hegel, *The Science of Logic,* 103.

19. Thomas Christensen, "Four-Hand Piano Transcriptions and Geographies of Nineteenth-Century Musical Reception," *Journal of the American Musicological Society* 52, no. 2 (Summer 1999): 255–98. See also Adrian Daub, *Four Handed Monsters: Four-Handed Piano Playing and Nineteenth Century Culture.*

20. This is reflected as well in Ernst Kurth's position that, in Christensen's words, "a well-performed piano arrangement was ... infinitely preferable to a badly executed orchestral performance led by a conductor with no empathy for the music." Christensen, "Four-Hand Piano Transcriptions," 264, n. 29.

21. Adorno, "Vierhändig, noch einmal," 142, quoted in Christensen, 262.

22. Adorno, "Motifs," 13.

23. Adorno, "Motifs," 14.

24. Adorno, "On the Fetish Character and the Regression of Listening," *Culture Industry Essays,* 53.

25. Adorno, "Music and Technique," 205.

26. Adorno, "Music and Technique," 206.

27. Adorno, "Vers un musique informelle," in *Quasi una fantasia,* 297–98, emphasis mine. In a late article comparing music and painting, Adorno writes similarly: "It suffices to recall that the act of notation is essential to art music, not incidental. Without writing [there can be] no highly organized music; the historical distinction between improvisation and composed music coincides qualitatively with that between laxness and musical articulation. This qualitative relationship of music to its visible insignia, without which it could neither possess nor construct or duration, points clearly to space as a condition of its objectification." Adorno, "On Some Relationships Between Music and Painting," trans. Susan Gillespie, *Musical Quarterly* 79 (1995), no. 1: 70; originally "Uber einige Relationen zwischen Musik und Malerei," first published in a *Festshrift* for the art patron Daniel-Henry Kahnweiler, 33–42, translation slightly modified.

28. Adorno, *Aesthetic Theory*, 118.

29. Adorno extensively describes in this lecture how the tone should not be reified as the central unit of music, but should be taken dialectically with other shapes and aggregates: "Dies zum Moment relativierte Unmittelbare in der Musik indessen wäre nicht der Ton sondern die an ihrer Zeitstelle als einigermaßen Plastisches, von Kontrast und Fortschritt Unterschiedenes, distinkt aufzufassende Einzelgestalt. Im musikalischen Phänomen sind ihr gegenüber die Töne abstrakt, erst herauszuschneiden; primär wären sie allenfalls akustisch nicht im kompositorischen Bezirk. Ce n'est pas le ton qui fait la musique." Adorno, *Gestammelte Schriften*, vol. 16, 520. The final sentence in French is Adorno's negative play on an old French proverb, "C'est le ton qui fait la musique," which means that one should be careful about the tone in which something is said, not just what is said. Adorno's meaning is quite different, of course. He repurposes the meaning of tone, for to his ears it means not the tone of one's spoken expression, but the normative unit of musical expression.

30. On Adorno's adoption of the term *art informel*, see Max Paddison, "Introduction: Contemporary Music: Theory, Aesthetics, Critical Theory," in *Contemporary Music: Theoretical and Philosophical Perspectives*, 5–6.

31. Adorno, *Philosophy of New Music*, 18.

32. Likewise, in "Some Ideas on the Sociology of Music," Adorno writes: "The compositional subject is no individual thing, but a collective one. All music, however individual it may be in stylistic terms, possesses an inalienable collective substance: every sound says 'we.'" In *Sound Figures*, 9.

33. Adorno, *Aesthetic Theory*, 78.

34. "If the language of nature is mute, art seeks to make this muteness eloquent [speak the unspeakable/utopia]; art thus exposes itself to failure through the insurmountable contradiction between the idea of making the mute eloquent, which demands a desperate effort, and the idea of what this effort would amount to, the idea of what cannot in any way be willed [non-intentional whole]." *Aesthetic Theory*, 78. For Adorno on a transfigured form of ugliness, see Peter Uwe Hohendahl's *The Feeling Promise of Art: Adorno's Aesthetic Theory Revisited*. The conviction that resistant art speaks in the form of an unreadable inscription—a hieroglyph, seismograph, or cipher—is a key metaphor for Adorno's writings from his early essay on Schubert to his late writings on fireworks in *Aesthetic Theory*. See Adorno, "Schubert," in *Night Music: Essays on Music 1928–62*, and *Aesthetic Theory*, 81.

35. See Martin Jay, *Marxism and Totality*.

36. Adorno and Horkheimer, *Dialectic of Enlightenment*, xvii.

37. Hegel, *Phenomenology of Spirit*, 11; and Adorno, *Minima Moralia*, 50.

38. Adorno, *Negative Dialectics*, 320.

39. For an assessment of the distinction between transcendent and immanent critique in the Marxist tradition, see Andrew Buchwalter, "Hegel, Adorno, and the Concept of Transcendent Critique," in *The Frankfurt School: Critical Assessments*, volume 3, 177–93.

40. Adorno, *Aesthetic Theory*, 78.

41. See Andrew Arato, "Esthetic Criticism and Cultural Criticism," in Andrew Arato and Eike Gebhardt, *The Essential Frankfurt School Reader*, 207–19.

42. Adorno, "Cultural Criticism and Society," in Theodor W. Adorno and Brian O'Connor, *The Adorno Reader*, 207.

43. Thinking can be no exception to the curse of making specific false claims. Hampered by its excessive preference for reflection on existence (rather than altering existence), the mind's activity inevitably produces contradictions that cannot be downplayed. "At the same time, however, immanent criticism holds in evidence the fact that the mind has always been under a spell. On its own it is unable to resolve the contradictions under which it labours. Even the most radical reflection of the mind on its own failure is limited by the fact that it remains only reflection, without altering the existence to which its failure bears witness." Adorno, "Cultural Criticism and Society," 208.

44. Adorno, "Cultural Criticism and Society," 208.

45. Adorno, "Cultural Criticism and Society," 207.

46. Adorno, "Cultural Criticism and Society," 208.

47. Adorno, "Cultural Criticism and Society," 208.

48. Of all his books, *The Dialectic of Enlightenment* (coauthored with Max Horkheimer) has very little (if any) orientation to utopia, and thus strongly corresponds to the "transcendent critique"—a condemnation of the society totality as the wrong world and a diagnosis of the irrational foundation of the Enlightenment project.

49. Adorno, "Cultural Criticism and Society," 207.

50. Adorno, "On the Contemporary Relationship between Philosophy and Music," 141.

51. Adorno, *Philosophy of New Music*, 31.

52. Adorno, *Aesthetic Theory* (Continuum Edition), 174.

53. Franz Brendel, *Geschichte der Musik in Italien, Deutschland und Frankreich* (1852). For an excellent overview of Brendel's indebtedness to Hegel, see Golan Gur, "Music and 'Weltanschauung': Franz Brendel and the Claims of Universal History," *Music & Letter* 92, no. 3 (2012). Here, Gur mentions other examples of important metanarratives of music history which include Johannes Forkel's *Allgemeine Geschichte der Musik* (1788); Raphael Kiesewetter, *Geschichte der europäisch-abendländlischen oder unserer heutigen Musik* (1834); F. J. Fétis, *Bibliographie universelle des musiciens et bibliographie générale de la musique* (1834–35); and August Wilhelm Ambros, *Geschichte der Musik* (1862–78).

54. Alois Riegl, *Stilfragen* (1893); and Heinrich Wölfflin, *Principles of Art History* (1915).

55. Adorno, "Some Ideas on the Sociology of Music," in *Sound Figures*, 5. "Sie hatte Stufen wie die Guidonische Reform, die Einführung der Mensuralnotation, die Erfindung des Generalbasses, der temperierten Stimmung, schließenlich die seit Bach unaufhaltsame, heute zum Extreme gediehene Tendenz zur integralen musikalischen Konstruktion."

56. Max Weber's *The Rational and Social Foundations of Music*, which was first published as *Die rationalen und soziologischen Grundlagen der Musik*. Given that Weber was not a specialist in music, it is instructive to consider his own sources for the *Grundlagen*. When surveying Weber's references, one is immediately struck by how much emphasis is placed on non-Western music that was studied by the comparative musicologists. Weber's footnotes cite works by Jean-Philippe Rameau, Moritz Hauptmann, Hermann Helmholtz, Frances Densmore, Curt Sachs, and Carl Stumpf, among many others.

57. Leslie Blasius, "Mapping the Terrain," in *The Cambridge Western History of Music Theory*, 27–45. For Adorno, since the *Tendenz des Materials* is only a product of social history, its workings can often be nonlinear: "The internal development of music, whose social implications have to be uncovered in each particular instance, is anything but self-contained. Music develops in accordance with its own internal laws ... it can also be moved and deflected directly by social force fields. To that extent it does not exhibit a seamless stylistic progression, a continuum." Adorno, "Some Ideas on the Sociology of Music," in *Sound Figures*, 11.

58. Bekker, *A Story of Music*, 59.

59. Adorno, *The Philosophy of New Music*, 99.

60. It was characteristic of Adorno's dialectic, however, that all emancipations and gestures toward autonomy retained their material and historical basis; individual technical decisions were never subsumed by the idealized teleology of artistic materials. In 1934, Adorno wrote a review of musicologist Rudolf Schäfke's 1934 compendium *Geschichte der Musikästhetik in Umrissen*, in which he expressed dismay at Schäfke's overreliance on the work of aestheticians, to the apparent neglect of writings and technical innovations of composers themselves. His opinion of Schäfke's *Geschichte* echoes a key attribute of the *Tendenz des Materials*: Adorno's conception was not a history of musical aesthetics, and still less a cultural history of music, but rather a speculative history of practical, used, compositional innovations. See Adorno, "Eine Geschichte der Musikästhetik" (1934), *Gestammelte Schriften*, vol. 19, 362.

61. Adorno, "The Relationship of Philosophy and Music," 145.

62. Adorno, *The Philosophy of New Music*, 31.

63. Adorno, "Music, Language, Composition," 113, translation modified. "Sprachähnlich ist sie als zeitliche Folge artikulierter Laute, die mehr sind als bloß Laut. Sie sagen etwas, oft ein Menschliches. Sie sagen es desto nachdrücklicher, je höher die Musik geartet ist. Die Folge der Laute ist der Logik verwandt: es gibt Richtig und Falsch. Aber das Gesagte lässt von der Musik nicht sich ablösen. Sie bildet kein System aus Zeichen."

64. Adorno, "On the Contemporary Relationship of Philosophy and Music," p. 145. "In becoming linguistic, music has asserted itself as an organ of imitation, but now, in contrast to its early gestural and mimetic impulses of subjectively mediated and reflected imitation, [as] an imitation of the things that transpire inside human

beings. The process of music's turn toward language [*Versprachlichung*] means its simultaneous transformation into convention and into expression."

65. Adorno, "On the Contemporary Relationship of Philosophy and Music," 145.

66. Beyond the parameters of tonal harmony, this conception of music's *Versprachlichung* might include Haydn's codification of sonata allegro form vis-à-vis tonal grammar in the late eighteenth century. See Kofi Agawu, *Playing With Signs: A Semiotic Interpretation of Classic Music*.

67. "On the Contemporary Relationship of Philosophy to Music," 137. Adorno states that "it is impossible to determine in any comprehensive way the meaning of music" and that "there is something enigmatic that is apparent in all music."

68. Adorno, "Music, Language, and Composition," 116.

69. Adorno, "Music, Language, and Composition," 114.

70. Adorno, "Music, Language, and Composition," 114.

71. Adorno, "Music, Language, and Composition," 116.

72. Adorno, "Music, Language, and Composition," 116.

73. Walter Benjamin, "On Language as Such and on the Language of Man," *Selected Writings, Vol. 1*, 1913–26, 62. In *Minima Moralia*, Adorno makes the connection himself: "Just as, according to Benjamin, painting and sculpture translate the mute language of things into a higher but similar one, so it might be supposed that music rescues name as pure sound, but at the cost of severing it from things." *Minima Moralia*, 222–23.

74. Benjamin, "On Language as Such and on the Language of Man," 62.

75. Benjamin, "On Language as Such and on the Language of Man," 73.

76. Benjamin, "On Language as Such and on the Language of Man," 74.

77. Benjamin, "On Language as Such and on the Language of Man," 74.

78. Benjamin, "On Language as Such and on the Language of Man," 73.

79. Adorno, "Music, Language, Composition," 122.

80. In *Aesthetic Theory*, Adorno describes the meaning of an artwork in these nonconceptual, nonintentional, and mimetic terms: *Sosein* ["thusness" or "like-so-ness"]; *So-und-nicht-anders-Sein*; *So ist es*; *Wie ist es*." In each case there is an effort to describe the work of art as mimetic of the way things are in general, but in a particular way that triggers a critical reflection of existence rather than a bounded, domineering representation. The mimesis here is named with an adverb: *so* ("so" or "thus" in English, indicating both consequence and an imitative "in this way") or, similarly, *wie* ("how," "the way in which"). See Jonathan Ullyot, "Adorno's *Comment c'est*," *Comparative Literature* 61, no. 4 (2009): 416–31.

81. Adorno, "Music, Language, Composition," 114; Adorno, *Aesthetic Theory*, 78.

82. Adorno, "On the Contemporary Relationship of Philosophy and Music," 140.

83. Adorno, "On the Contemporary Relationship of Philosophy and Music," 140.

84. Adorno, "On the Contemporary Relationship of Philosophy and Music," 142.

85. Adorno, "On the Contemporary Relationship of Philosophy and Music," 139.

86. Bloch, *The Spirit of Utopia*, 158.

87. In this essay, Adorno claims that in visual art and literature, by contrast, "this enigmatic character is hidden." Though his assessment of the other arts is less categorical elsewhere, it is instructive to see how Adorno claims here, from a comparative point of view, that language is too transparent to cognition, communication, and comprehension. Visual art is comparatively Apollonian. It is too objective, too external, too amenable to concrete associations, even when it comes to abstraction. In fact, as literature and visual art are better at concealing their irrational and enigmatic character, they may actually reproduce irrationality by concealing it. By contrast, since music makes irrational and enigmatic nature explicit—"immediately within the phenomenon itself"—it may then "also offer a point of departure for overcoming [immediacy]." Like Bloch's conception of the tone, language-like music for Adorno provides an exemplary case of the dialectic: its enigmatic sensuousness is immediate, but it is also the most technically mediated and ideologically disciplined of the arts.

88. Adorno, "Punctuation Marks," 300. Adorno's proposal of a mimesis between music and language has an important medieval precedent in the work of Johannes Cotto, *De Musica* (1100) in Claude Palisca, *Hucbald, Guido, and John on Music*, 116–17. Cited in Bonds, 54.

89. Adorno, "Punctuation Marks," 301.

90. Adorno, "On the Contemporary Relationship of Philosophy and Music," 138. "Sagt Musik, nach Schönbergs Wort, in der Tat ein nur durch Musik Sagbares aus, so nimmt sie damit ein Abgründiges und zugleich im emphatischen Sinn Zufälliges an."

91. Adorno, *The Philosophy of New Music*, 34.

92. Schoenberg, *Harmonielehre*, 238.

93. Charles Rosen, *Beethoven Piano Sonatas: A Short Companion*, Vol. 1, 4.

94. Adorno, *Minima Moralia*, 19. The quotation is an epigraph by Ferdinand Kürnberger.

95. Adorno, "On the Social Situation of Music," 403.

96. Adorno, "On the Social Situation of Music," 407.

97. See Allen Forte, "Sets and Non-Sets in Schoenberg's Atonal Music," *Perspectives of New Music* (Fall-Winter 1972), 58. Forte argues that Schoenberg's atonal period can be described as structural assemblages of sets, especially hexachords. Forte's strict formalism would have displeased Adorno the dialectician, who found great interest in remnants of tonal triads. Forte was dismissive of all that Adorno would have found rich: "About the diverging 'chordal streams' in m. 2 [of the *Five Orchestral Pieces*, op. 16], it can be said, without qualification, that (once again) the 'augmented triads,' 'minor triads,' and 'chromatic lines' so congenial to the amateur analyst are of no significance in themselves."

98. On Schoenberg's contrapuntal inheritance of the *Tendenz des Materials*, see J. Peter Burkholder, "Schoenberg the Reactionary," in *Schoenberg and His World*, for a study of the principles of developing variation and continuity with classical traditions from Schoenberg's early works through the late twelve-tone work, the String Quartet no. 4.

99. Adorno, "Why is the New Art so Hard to Understand?" in *Essays on Music*, 127–34.

100. Arnold Schoenberg, "The Relationship to the Text," 144.

101. See Lydia Goehr, "Adorno, Schoenberg, and the 'Totentanz der Prinzipien'—in Thirteen Steps," *Journal of the American Musicological Society* 56, no. 3 (2003): 595–636, for a discussion of the underlying philosophical parallel of *schweben* or a floating between two dialectical extremes shared by both composer and philosopher.

102. For a study of the complex relationship between Schoenberg and Adolf Loos's aesthetics that argues in a complementary fashion that Schoenberg's music is full of ornamentation, decoration, dialectical linkages to mimesis—all that exceeds the austerity of form alone—see Holly Watkins, "Schoenberg's Interior Designs," *Journal of the American Musicological Society* 61, no. 1 (2008): 123–206.

103. Adorno, "On the Social Situation of Music," 409.

104. Adorno, "The Function of Counterpoint in the New Music," 130.

105. See Bryan Simms, *The Atonal Music of Arnold Schoenberg 1908–1923*, 113–19; and Ethan Haimo, *Schoenberg's Transformations of Musical Language*. For an analysis of Schoenberg's early atonality through the perspective of transformational theory, see Michael Siciliano, "Toggling Cycles, Hexatonic Systems, and Some Analysis of Early Atonal Music," *Music Theory Spectrum* 27 (2005): 221–48; Alfred Cramer's review of Haimo's book in *The Journal of the American Musicological Society* 62, no. 2 (Summer 2009): 482–88; and Joshua Banks Mailman, "Schoenberg's Chordal Experimentalism Revealed through Representational Hierarchy Association Models (RHAMs), Contour Motives, and Binary-State Switching," *Music Theory Spectrum* 37, no. 2: 2015.

106. On Schoenberg's dialectical practice of composition, see Michael Cherlin, "Dialectical Opposition in Schoenberg's Music and Thought," *Schoenberg's Musical Imagination*. See also Walter Frisch, *The Early Works of Arnold Schoenberg, 1893–1908*.

107. See Shierry Weber Nicholsen, *Exact Imagination, Late Work, on Adorno's Aesthetics*, 19.

108. Adorno, *Mahler*, 6.

109. Adorno, *Mahler*, 20.

110. Adorno, *Philosophy of New Music*, 37–40.

111. Adorno, *Mahler*, 147.

112. Adorno, *Mahler*, 20.

113. Adorno, *Mahler*, 20.

114. Adorno, *Mahler*, 20–21.

115. Adorno, *Mahler*, 23.

116. Adorno, *Mahler*, 35.

117. Adorno, *Mahler*, 31.

118. For a detailed engagement with Adorno's book *Mahler* and its possibilities for musical analysis, see Seth Monahan, *Mahler's Symphonic Sonatas*.

119. Adorno, *Mahler*, 51. In this way Mahler's music retains its dialectical character. It is "a script prescribing its own interpretation," a monad with a certain *Erkenntnischarakter*, that is at once autonomous (monadic) and heteronomous (structurally linked to historical cognition and interpretation).

120. Adorno, *Mahler*, 147.
121. Adorno, *Mahler*, 47.
122. Adorno, *Mahler*, 58.
123. Adorno, *Mahler*, 32.
124. Adorno, *Mahler*, 39.
125. Adorno, *Mahler*, 33.
126. Adorno, *Mahler*, 39.
127. Adorno, *Mahler*, 61.
128. Peter Uwe Hohendahl, "Reality, Realism, and Representation," in *The Fleeting Promise of Art: Adorno's Aesthetic Theory Revisited*, 103–28.
129. Hohendahl, "Reality, Realism, and Representation," 114–15.
130. Adorno, *Mahler*, 129.
131. Adorno, *Mahler*, 25.
132. Adorno, *Mahler*, 27.
133. Reprinted in Schoenberg, *Style and Idea*, 462.
134. Adorno, *Mahler*, 35.
135. Adorno, *Mahler*, 146.
136. Adorno, *Mahler*, 25.
137. Adorno, *Mahler*, 147.
138. One could argue that Jankélévitch might agree about the reification of harmony, but one would have to acknowledge that he reads it contrariwise as artifice, as a tool of sober distancing and aestheticized play.
139. Adorno, *Mahler*, 154.
140. Adorno, "The Form of the Phonograph Record," 279–80, trans. Thomas Y. Levin. *Gestammelte Schriften*, band 19, "Die Form der Schallplatte," 533. "Waren aber die Noten noch ihre bloßen Zeichen, dann nähert sie durch die Nadelkurven der Schallplatten ihrem wahren Schriftcharakter entscheidend sich an. Entscheidend, weil dieses Schrift als echte Sprache zu erkennen ist, indem sie ihres bloßen Zeichenwesens sich begibt: unablösich verschworen dem Klang, *der dieser und keiner anderen Schall-Rinne innewohnt.*"
141. See Jacques Derrida, *Of Grammatology*, "The End of the Book and the Beginning of Writing," 6–26.
142. In *Of Grammatology*, Derrida asserts that this generalized notion of writing is an incessantly variable spatialization of time and temporalization of space. For Derrida's deconstructive method, recognizing *écriture* as a general condition enables one to deconstruct the ethnocentrism of philosophy, theology, or the authority of any other logocentric text that claims to be moored by a "transcendental signified"; to tap into a sense of infinite hospitality to the other; or to remain open for a utopian "democracy-to-come."

143. Adorno, "The Form of the Phonograph Record," 280.
144. Adorno, "The Form of the Phonograph Record." "Ist in den Schallplatten die musikalische Produktivkraft erloschen; haben sie keine Form mehr mit ihrer Technik gestiftet, so verwandeln sie dafür den jüngsten Klang alter Gefühle in einen archaischen Text kommender Erkenntnis." *Gestammelte Schriften*, vol. 19, 533.
145. There is a more forgiving take on Stravinsky that is offered in *Minima Moralia*, where Adorno seems to soften his tone.
146. Adorno, "The Form of the Phonograph Record," 280. "Am Ende sind die Schallplatten—keine Kunstwerke—die schwarzen Siegel auf den Briefen, die im Verkehr mit der Technik allenthalben uns ereilen: Briefen, deren Formeln die Laute der Schöpfung verschließen, die ersten und letzten, Urteil übers Leben und Botschaft dessen, was danach sein kann." *Gestammelte Schriften*, vol. 19, 534. Translation modified.
147. See Kittler, *Gramophone, Film, Typewriter*.
148. Adorno, "Radio Physiognomics," in *Current of Music*, 90.
149. Adorno, "Radio Physiognomics," 90.

INTERLUDE

1. "Die musikalischen Themen sind in gewissem Sinne Satze. Die Kenntnis des Wesens der Logik wird deshalb zur Kenntnis des Wesens der Musik führen." Ludwig Wittgenstein, *Notebooks* (7.2.15), translation mine.
2. For a succinct take on Wittgenstein's musical biography, see Bela Szabados, "Wittgenstein the Musical: Notes towards an Appreciation," in *Canadian Aesthetics Journal/Revue canadienne d'esthétique* 10 (Fall 2004), available online at http://www.uqtr.ca/AE/Vol_10/wittgenstein/szabados.htm, accessed October 6, 2012.
3. See Brian McGuiness, *Wittgenstein: A Life*, 34.
4. "Extracts from the diary of David Pinsent," in *Portraits of Wittgenstein*, 200, 204, 205.
5. See David Ferris, *Schumann's Eichendorff Liederkreis and the Genre of the Romantic Cycle*; Beate Perry, *Schumann's Dicterliebe and Early Romantic Poetics: Fragmentation of Desire*; Berthold Hoeckner, "Paths through *Dichterliebe*," *Nineteenth-Century Music* 30, no. 1: 65–80.
6. Paul Engelmann, *Letters from Ludwig Wittgenstein with a Memoir*.
7. Wittgenstein, *Culture and Value*, trans. Peter Winch, 62.
8. Stanley Cavell, "Music Discomposed," in *Must We Mean What We Say?* 200–202.
9. Later Anglo-American academic philosophers would adopt Wittgenstein's isolated musical observations and link them back up with more developed branches of his thought in order to produce a fuller Wittgenstinian "philosophy" of music. See, for example, Jerrold Levinson, "Musical Thinking," *Journal of Music and Meaning* 1, no. 2 (Fall 2003), http://www.musicandmeaning.net/issues/showArticle.php?artID=1.2, accessed November 14, 2012.

CHAPTER 3

1. Roland Barthes, "Listening," in *Responsibility of Forms: Critical Essays on Music, Art and Representation*, trans. Richard Howard.

2. See Roland Barthes, "The Grain of the Voice," and "Musica Practica," in *Image-Music-Text*, trans. Stephen Heath (Hill & Wang, 1977). For a broadly Heideggerian perspective on listening as asymbolic, nonintentional, or consonant with alterity, see Jean-Luc Nancy, *Listening*, trans. Charlotte Mandel.

3. Barthes remarked suggestively: "To find practical music in the West, one has to look to another public, another repertoire, another instrument (the young generation, vocal music, the guitar)." Roland Barthes, "Musica Practica," 149.

4. Barthes, "Grain of the Voice," 179.

5. On a more general level, neither Hegel nor the term "dialectic" was the polarizing term it would become in the wake of French post-structuralism in the late 1960s. Jankélévitch worked as colleagues at the Sorbonne with Jean Hyppolite, the famous Hegel expositor and translator of *The Phenomenology of Spirit*, whose teaching and writings on Hegel would be a tremendous influence on structuralism and post-structuralism during the postwar years. Jankélévitch and Hyppolite would serve on thesis committees together and work together as colleagues in the Sorbonne's philosophy department from 1949 until 1954, when Hyppolite accepted a post at the École normale supérieur.

6. Adorno, "The Relationship between Philosophy and Music," 139. In *Minima Moralia*, Adorno remarks similarly: "In the end indignation over kitsch is anger at its shameless reveling in the joy of imitation, now placed under taboo, while the power of works of art still continues to be secretly nourished by imitation." Slightly earlier, he writes: "The human is indissolubly linked with imitation: a human being only becomes human at all by imitating other human beings. In such behavior, the primal form of love, the priests of authenticity scent traces of the utopia which could shake the structure of domination." *Minima Moralia*, 225, 154. For Adorno, art remains the Hegelian sensuous embodiment of the idea; it never leaves behind sensuous appearance and particularity, audience reactions, or fetishistic attachments to materiality.

7. Adorno, "The Relationship between Philosophy and Music," 115. Elsewhere, he wrote: "The only person who can solve the riddle of music is the one who plays it correctly, as something whole."

8. Adorno, "The Relationship between Philosophy and Music," 139.

9. Adorno, "The Form of the Phonograph Record," 280.

10. In addition to serving has his mentor, Bergson was a significant intellectual influence on Jankélévitch throughout his career. Their first meeting occurred at the École normale supérieur in 1923 when Jankélévitch was an undergraduate, leading Jankélévitch to leave behind his old advisor, the idealist philosopher and cofounder of the *Revue de métaphysique et de morale*, Léon Brunschvicg. Taking up study with Bergson, Jankélévitch published his first article on the philosopher in 1924 while completing an MA thesis on Plotinus. He produced two more ("Prolegomena to Bergsonism"

and "Bergsonism and Biology"), in 1928 and 1929 respectively, while completing a doctoral thesis on Schelling, which he published in 1933. In 1931, Alcan Press published Jankélévitch's full-length monograph *Bergson*, a book that would go on to become the definitive prewar Francophone study of the philosopher.

11. Gilles Deleuze, *Kant's Critical Philosophy*, 8.
12. Immanuel Kant, *Critique of Pure Reason*, B351.
13. Kant, *Critique of Pure Reason*, B351.
14. Henri Bergson, *Matter and Memory*, 185.
15. Bergson, *Matter and Memory*, 185.
16. Deleuze, *Bergsonism*, 15–21.
17. Bergson, *Creative Evolution*, 267.
18. See Brian Kane, "Excavating Lewin's 'Phenomenology,'" *Music Theory Spectrum* 33, no. 1 (Spring 2011): 27–36; and Mayram Moshaver, "*Telos* and Temporality: Phenomenology and the Experience of Time in Lewin's Study of Perception," *Journal of the American Musicological Society* 65, no. 1 (Spring 2012): 179–214. See also *David Lewin's Morgengruß: Text, Context, Commentary*, ed. David Bard-Schwartz and Richard Cohn (Oxford, UK: Oxford University Press, 2015).
19. In Lewin's article, after he has concluded his detailed analysis of the sonority in measure 14, he instructively mimics the multiplicities of musical *durée* with a rhapsodic series of fanciful associations. See David Lewin, "Music Theory, Phenomenology, and Modes of Perception," *Music Perception* 3, no. 4 (Summer 1986): 327–92.
20. Jankélévitch, *Music and the Ineffable*, 93.
21. Alain Badiou, *The Adventure of French Philosophy*.
22. Bergson, *Time and Free Will: An Essay on the Immediate Data of Consciousness*, 129.
23. Jankélévitch, *Philosophie première*, 2. "On peut dire que la première manifestation du *sérieux* métaphysique a été l'acceptation du *tout-autre-ordre* et le refus de réduire à des différences de degré—diminutions ou augmentations—l'absolue différence de nature, l'hétérogénéité fondamentale de cet ordre-ci et de 'l'autre.'"
24. For an example of an openly mystical effort to access intuition, see Bergson's collection of lectures published in English under the title *The Creative Mind*.
25. Vladimir Jankélévitch and Louis Beauduc, *Une vie en toutes lettres*, ed. Françoise Schwab, 140. Letter from Vladimir Jankélévitch to Louis Beauduc, dated Oct 31, 1927, translation mine.
26. Emmanuel Lévinas, *Outside the Subject*, 84. Incidentally, Lévinas, like Jankélévitch, was also strongly influenced by Bergson. For Lévinas, the other was infinitely unknowable to an individual subject. Thus, one might say that for Lévinas, quoddity resided not immanently in the subject but transcendently in the other, obliging us to a metaphysical hospitality toward her or him, since they lived a past we did not live. On Bergson's influence on Lévinas, see Samuel Moyn, *Origins of the Other: Emmanuel Levinas between Revelation and Ethics* (Ithaca, NY: Cornell University Press, 2005). Catherine Clément also comments with regard to Jankélévitch's unique virtuosity to

write about music without succumbing to "shoddy lyricism." See Catherine Clément, *Syncope: The Philosophy of Rapture*, 4.

27. Lévinas, *Outside the Subject*, 84.

28. Vladimir Jankélévitch, interview with Vera Feyder, originally published 1985. Reprinted in Suarès, ed., *Vladimir Jankélévitch (Qui suis-je?)*, 67.

29. Jankélévitch, *Liszt: Rhapsodie et improvisation*, xx.

30. Jankélévitch, *Philosophie première*, 175, emphasis in original. Jankélévitch's "parousian" references the Greek *parousia*—a word that means an arrival, a coming, or a presence, and which is often used to indicate a communion with the divine. In the New Testament the word is used to indicate the second "coming" of Christ.

31. Jankélévitch, *Philosophie première*, 186.

32. Jankélévitch, *Philosophie première*, 175. Emphasis mine. "Il y a une improvisation-éternelle qui ne se réduit ni à la "primauté" l'anthropomorphisme créationniste.—La créature elle-même, qui est tout entière positivité posée, et posée dans la continuation la créature n'est jamais contemporaine de la position primordiale; jamais personne n'est témoin de l'instant créateur en cours d'intervalle, la connaissance prospective ou rétrospective, prévoyante ou retardataire arrivant toujours, tant elle est épaisse, avant ou après, mais jamais pendant ni sur le fait."

33. Bloch, *The Spirit of Utopia*, 200–201.

34. Hegel, *Encyclopedia*, §300, Zusatz, translation modified.

35. Jankélévitch, *Philosophie première*, 186. "C'est pourquoi la creature est le mixte d'une operation surnaturelle et d'une rélaité constituée: en elle-même, elle éprouve à la fois la recurrence infinie de la conscience et de la liberté, qui est perpetual report au delà, et l'inclination réifiante qui la fait digerer ses propres initiatives."

36. For a historical study of the semantic range of the French term *je-ne-sais-quoi*, see Richard Scholar, *The Je-ne-sais-quoi in Early Modern Europe: Encounters with a Certain Something* (Oxford, UK: Oxford University Press 2005).

37. Jankélévitch, *Forgiveness*, 6.

38. Jankélévitch, *Forgiveness*, 4.

39. Jankélévitch, *Forgiveness*, 5.

40. Jankélévitch, *Philosophie première*, 99.

41. Adorno, "Music, Language, Composition," 116.

42. Vladimir Jankélévitch, interview with Brigitte Massin and Jacques Chancel, in Guy Suarès, ed., *Vladimir Jankélévitch (Qui suis-je?)*, 77, translation mine.

43. Steven Rings, "Talking and Listening with Jankélévitch," *Journal of the American Musicological Society* 65, no. 1: 218–23. The term "deixsis" is a term that indicates a move beyond meaning toward the presence of lived experience (*Erlebnis*) in Gumbrecht, *Production of Presence: What Meaning Cannot Convey*.

44. Jankélévitch, *De la musique au silence: Faure et l'inexprimable*, 345, translation mine. "Quelque nature qu'on lui assigne (par exemple la grâce, le naturel ou la simplicité), il est toujours autre chose, pour la bonne raison qu'il n'est pas "chose," Res. En soi il n'est rien, et même il n'Est pas: fait de rien, comme on dit, il est lui-même un pur Rien."

45. Jankélévitch, *Music and the Ineffable*, 96.
46. Jankélévitch, *Music and the Ineffable*, 96.
47. Jankélévitch, *Music and the Ineffable*, 96.
48. Jankélévitch, *Music and the Ineffable*, 83.
49. Jankélévitch, *Music and the Ineffable*, 18.
50. Jankélévitch, *Music and the Ineffable*, 17.
51. See David Beveridge, "Dvořák's 'Dumka' and the Concept of Nationalism in Music Historiography," *Journal of Musicological Research* 12, no. 4 (1993).
52. Letter of November 28, 1890 (during the period of composition), *Antonín Dvořák to His Closest Friend*, ed. Milan Kuna (Prague: Nadační fond Pražský podzim, 2000), 45. Original in Czech; quoted in Dvořák, *Dumky: Klaviertrio op. 90*, version for piano, four hands, ed. Klaus Döge (Munich: G. Henle Verlag, 2008), 303–25.
53. Jankélévitch, *Music and the Ineffable*, 17.
54. Jankélévitch, *Music and the Ineffable*, 22.
55. Jankélévitch, *Music and the Ineffable*, 22. The original reads: "C'est qu'entre la première fois et la deuxième un intervalle de temps s'est écoulé qui rend l'itération novatrice, qui fait de l'insistance une incantation, de la monotonie une magie, de la répétition stationnaire un progrès."
56. Jankélévitch, *Music and the Ineffable*, 20.
57. Jankélévitch, *Music and the Ineffable*, 21.
58. Jankélévitch, *Music and the Ineffable*, 52.
59. Jankélévitch, *Music and the Ineffable*, 47.
60. Jankélévitch, *Music and the Ineffable*, 47.
61. Jankélévitch, *Music and the Ineffable*, 48.
62. Jankélévitch, *Music and the Ineffable*, 51.
63. Jankélévitch, *Music and the Ineffable*, 48.
64. Jankélévitch, *Music and the Ineffable*, 36.
65. Jankélévitch, *Music and the Ineffable*, 53.
66. Jankélévitch, *Music and the Ineffable*, 104–5.
67. Jankélévitch, *Music and the Ineffable*, 127.
68. Jankélévitch, *Music and the Ineffable*, 127.
69. Jankélévitch, *Music and the Ineffable*, 81.
70. Jankélévitch, *Music and the Ineffable*, 85.
71. Jankélévitch, *Music and the Ineffable*, 84.
72. Jankélévitch, *Bergson*, 9.
73. Jankélévitch, *Bergson*, 9.
74. Jankélévitch, *Bergson*, 9.
75. See Bergson, *Time and Free Will*, "The Intensity of Psychic States," 13–14.
76. Jankélévitch, *Bergson*, 9.
77. On Debussy's *Pelléas et Mélisande*, see *Debussy's Pelléas et Mélisande: Cambridge Opera Handbooks*, ed. Roger Nichols and Richard Langham Smith (Cambridge,

UK: Cambridge University Press, 1989). On the leitmotifs themselves, see Smith's chapter, "Motives and Symbols," 78–107.

78. Jankélévitch, *Bergson*, 9.
79. Jankélévitch, *Music and the Ineffable*, 131.
80. Jankélévitch, *Music and the Ineffable*, 131.
81. Jankélévitch, *Music and the Ineffable*, 132.
82. Jankélévitch, *Music and the Ineffable*, 135.
83. Jankélévitch, *Music and the Ineffable*, 139.
84. Jankélévitch, *Music and the Ineffable*, 151.
85. For Clément's writings on Jankélévitch, see Catherine Clément, "Au rhapsode," *Écrit pour Vladimir Jankélécvitch*, 107–15.
86. Catherine Clément, *Syncope: Towards a Philosophy of Rapture*, 5.
87. Jankélévitch, *Music and the Ineffable*, 28.
88. Jankélévitch, *Music and the Ineffable*, 77.
89. James Currie, "Where Jankélévitch Cannot Speak," *Journal of the American Musicological Society* 65, no. 1 (Spring 2012): 247–50.
90. Jankélévitch, *Music and the Ineffable*, 108.
91. Ranciére, *The Politics of Aesthetics*, 12–19.

CHAPTER 4

1. See Gilles Deleuze, *Cinema 2: The Time-Image*, 22–23. In the opening chapter, he writes of the time-image as a modern epoch of cinema that moves beyond representation and reveals the metaphysical machinery of time.
2. Deleuze and Guattari, *What Is Philosophy?* 165–66.
3. Deleuze and Guattari, *What Is Philosophy?*, 173.
4. Deleuze and Guattari, *What Is Philosophy?*, 168.
5. Andrew Hicks makes a consonant argument about Uexküll, Deleuze, and Guattari's proximity to Neoplatonic views of music in the introduction and conclusion to his book *Composing the World: Harmony in the Medieval Platonic Cosmos*, 11–15 and 247–54.
6. Deleuze, *Bergsonism*, 87.
7. Deleuze, *Difference and Repetition*, 217.
8. Deleuze, *Difference and Repetition*, 21, emphasis in original.
9. Deleuze, *Difference and Repetition*, 21.
10. Michael Gallope, "The Time of Repeating Life: Metaphysics and Ethics in Deleuze's Philosophy of Music," in Radical *Difference: Gilles Deleuze and the Theory and Philosophy of Music*.
11. Stéphane Mallarmé, *Un coup de dés jamais n'abolira le hazard*, in *Collected Poems and Other Verse*, 139–181.
12. Deleuze, *Nietzsche and Philosophy*, 27.
13. Deleuze, *Nietzsche and Philosophy*, 27.
14. Deleuze, *The Logic of Sense*, 125.

15. See Manuel DeLanda, *Intensive Science and Virtual Philosophy*, for a sustained development of Deleuze's ontology of dynamic matter into the realm of science.
16. Deleuze, *The Logic of Sense*, 124–25.
17. Deleuze, *The Logic of Sense*, 125.
18. For Deleuze, "Even the frontier is *not a separation*, but rather the element of an articulation, so that sense is presented both as that (1) which happens to bodies and (2) that which insists in propositions." For Lacan, who is developing speculative registers of the talking cure, the linguistic turn is a fully articulated position, where language and the body are part of the same substance: "Speech is in fact a gift of language, and language is not immaterial. It is a subtle body, but body it is. Words are caught up in all the body images that captivate the subject; they may 'knock up' the hysteric, be identified with the object of Penisneid, represent the urinary flow of urethral ambition, or represent the feces retained in avaricious jouissance." Jacques Lacan, "Function and Field of Speech and Language in Psychoanalysis" (1953) in *Ecrit: A Selection*, 95.
19. This definition of Deleuze's sense owes much to Gottlob Frege's "Sense and Reference," an article that was an important influence on Deleuze's thinking.
20. Deleuze, *The Logic of Sense*, 186.
21. Deleuze, *The Logic of Sense*, 189. Here, Deleuze is referencing the work of Melanie Klein.
22. See also Deleuze, "He Stuttered," in *Essays Critical and Clinical*, 107–14.
23. Deleuze, *The Logic of Sense*, 155.
24. Deleuze, *The Logic of Sense*, 155.
25. Deleuze, *Difference and Repetition*, 293.
26. Deleuze, *The Logic of Sense*, 248.
27. Deleuze, *The Logic of Sense*, 249.
28. Deleuze's recourse to thunder and lightning may be an oblique reference to Heraclitus's fragments on thunder, which, as they were reported by Hyppolitus of Rome in the *Refutation of All Heresies* (early third century CE), state that "thunderbolt steers all things." In *The Texts of Early Greek Philosophy*, Vol. 1, 157.
29. Deleuze and Guattari, *A Thousand Plateaus*, 342.
30. Deleuze and Guattari, *A Thousand Plateaus*, 348. In the previous chapter, "1730: Becoming-Intense, Becoming-Animal . . . ." the authors twice refer to the reterritorializing powers of music as potentially "fascist" and "reactionary," and as the force that induces a sense of "collective fascination." Similarly, in *Musica Ficta: Figures of Wagner*, Phillipe Lacoue-Labarthe refers to this aspect of music as "musicolatry."
31. See Deleuze, *Francis Bacon: The Logic of Sensation*.
32. Deleuze and Guattari, *A Thousand Plateaus*, 348.
33. Deleuze and Guattari, *Kafka: Toward a Minor Literature*.
34. Félix Guattari, diary entry; August 29, 1971. Curiously, Guattari continues to associate music with the infinite, recapitulating a traditional romantic theme most famously articulated by E. T. A. Hoffmann: "The collective assemblage of musical machines holds any anxieties of finitude at arm's length. Inasmuch as you can say of lan-

guage that it doubles all things related to death, you can think of music as condemning death itself to death." Nine years later, by the time of Deleuze and Guattari's *A Thousand Plateaus*, the authors place less emphasis on music as a radical tool for for *jouissance* and Dionysian intoxication, and (at least with respect to Schumann) take up traditionally Romantic themes of finitude, death, existential angst, and the ineffable.

35. Guattari, *Anti-Oedipus Papers*, 310.

36. Guattari, *Glossary of Schizoanalysis*. Written at the request of the English editors of *La Révolution moléculaire: Molecular Revolution, Psychiatry and Politics*, trans. Rosemary Sheed and introduced by David Cooper (Penguin Books, 1984). Published in Félix Guattari, *Les années d'hiver* 1980-85, 287-95.

37. See also Guattari, "The Role of the Signifier in the Institution," in *Molecular Revolution, Psychiatry and Politics*, 73-81.

38. For a comparative assessment of the mathematical bases of Deleuze and Badiou's ontologies, see Daniel W. Smith, "Mathematics and the Theory of Multiplicities: Badiou and Deleuze Revisited," *Southern Journal of Philosophy* 41 (2003): 411-49.

39. For a comprehensive survey of Pythagoreanism in Western musical thought up through the turn of the twentieth century, see Joscelyn Godwin, ed., *The Harmony of the Spheres: A Sourcebook of the Pythagorean Tradition in Music*.

40. Plato, *Timaeus*, 34b-37c.

41. See Goodwin, *Harmony of the Spheres*.

42. Other key Neoplatonic treatises that reflect ideas in the *Timaeus* include Augustine's *De musica*, which reflects the Pythagorean metaphysics of number, but as applied to poetic meter, away from the materiality of sound and towards the eternity of abstract truth and a knowledge of God. Augustine, of course, remained an advocate of secular learning. See also Calvin M. Bower, "The Transmission of Ancient Music Theory into the Middle Ages" in *Cambridge History of Western Music Theory*, 142. See also Hicks, *Composing the World: Harmony in the Medieval Platonic Cosmos*.

43. The Ikhwan al-Safa' (Brethren of Purity), "The Four Strings of the Lute and Their Parallels" (tenth century), in Goodwin, *Harmony of the Spheres*.

44. As a component of the *quadrivium*, music was not principally or even practically sonic; it focused on the study of intervallic proportions and harmonics on a monochord.

45. On Deleuze's reversal of Platonism, see Miguel de Beistegui, "The Deleuzian Reversal of Platonism," in *The Cambridge Companion to Deleuze*, ed. Daniel W. Smith and Henry Somers-Hall, 56-81.

46. Deleuze, *The Logic of Sense*, 176, translation modified.

47. Deleuze, *The Logic of Sense*, 179.

48. Konrad Lorenz, *On Aggression*, 28. Incidentally, Lorenz was himself influenced by Uexküll's innovative work in biosemiotics.

49. Biologists have historically disagreed about whether this display has a precise utility, though it is now commonly agreed that the leaf display involves attracting a female mate. For Deleuze and Guattari, the "display court" is an example of how expressive life is: relational, contrapuntal, and based in activities already at work in simpler

forms of life. It is instructive to note that even in his foundational solo work, Deleuze emphasizes that aesthetics and repetition are not simply products of expressive works of art, but are already at work in the rhythms of ordinary, everyday life. In *Difference and Repetition* he writes: "Even the most mechanical, the most banal, the most habitual and the most stereotyped repetition finds a place in works of art, it is always displaced in relation to other repetitions, and it is subject to the condition that a difference may be extracted from it for these other repetitions. For there is no other aesthetic problem than that of the insertion of art into everyday life." *Difference and Repetition*, 293.

50. Nagel writes: "There are facts that do not consist in the truth of propositions expressible in a human language. We can be compelled to recognize the existence of such facts without being able to state or comprehend them." Of course, Nagel would not agree with Uexküll's metaphorical "musical" vision of natural life. He dismisses it with an appeal to common sense: "The loose intermodal analogies—for example, 'Red is like the sound of a trumpet'—which crop up in discussions of this subject are of little use. That should be clear to anyone who has both heard a trumpet and seen red." Thomas Nagel, "What Is It Like to Be a Bat?" *Philosophical Review* 83, no. 4 (October 1974): 435–50.

51. Uexküll sought to develop speculative thinking about creaturely life that was derived from experiments, which he conducted primarily on invertebrates. His theories are broadly seen as progenitors of the cybernetic theory subsequently developed by Norbert Weiner in the 1940s. As with Guattari, the structural, flexible, and relational nature of Uexküll's *Funktionskreis* (operative in plant, animal, human, and microbial organisms alike) seems to have inspired him to turn to music as an apt metaphor for its interior operations.

52. Uexküll's protocybernetic view of life is likewise reflected in W. H. Thorpe's *Learning and Instinct in Animals* (1956), another book from Deleuze and Guattari's library. Thorpe writes, early on in his book: "As far as we know, everything that goes on in the bodies of living organisms, all transformations of energy that result in work being done, are due to arrangements which *in certain respects* are comparable to man-made machines."

53. Rhythmic recombination of counterpoint keeps creaturely movement alive through a "diagonal" interactivity of harmony and melody, or interpenetrating vertical and horizontal elements. See Deleuze and Guattari "1730: Becoming-Intense, Becoming-Animal . . . ," in *A Thousand Plateaus,* 295. This passage appears to summarize Boulez's own discussion of "diagonals," to which the authors make explicit reference just a page later.

54. While Uexküll frequently appeals to musical metaphors, he also offers amazingly vivid descriptions of the interior life of creatures. In my view, the frequent recourse to music allows him to posit an appealing metaphysical space beyond the empirical limits of the behaviorist who will cannot and will not speculate about that which he or she cannot observe directly.

55. See Deleuze and Guattari, *What Is Philosophy?* 68, 106; and Deleuze and Guattari, "7000 B.C.: Apparatus of Capture," in *A Thousand Plateaus*, 424–73. Many thanks

are due to Cesare Casarino for his help in pointing out this important commonality with Bloch and Adorno.

56. For Deleuze and Guattari's proposal that an ethical work of art is resistant, and akin to Adorno's conception of utopia, see Deleuze and Guattari, *What Is Philosophy?* 110. They write: ". . . Books of philosophy and works of art also contain their sum of unimaginable sufferings that forewarn of the advent of a people. They have resistance in common—their resistance to death, to servitude, to the intolerable, to shame, and to the present."

57. Deleuze and Guattari, *A Thousand Plateaus*, 350.

58. Deleuze and Guattari, *A Thousand Plateaus*, 349–50, translation and punctuation modified. The "little phrase of the cosmos" is likely a reference to Vinteuil's five-note violin phrase from Marcel Proust's *In Search of Lost Time* (1913–27).

59. Though curiously, eleven years later in *What Is Philosophy?* they offer a more open view of Cage's music. See Deleuze and Guattari, *What Is Philosophy?* 195.

60. Deleuze and Guattari, *A Thousand Plateaus*, 344.

61. Deleuze and Guattari, *What Is Philosophy?* 164.

62. This broadening compass has led to a growing "Deleuze and music" scholarship that seeks a broader canon of modernist inclusion. Most recently, see Edward Campbell, *Music after Deleuze*.

63. Roland-Manuel, *Histoire de la musique*, Vol. 2, 879. "Les musiciens qu'on vient de nommer [Bizet, Chabrier] ont ainsi retrouvé la tradition la plus exigeante et la plus sûre, avec le secret de cet empirisme sensualiste que les luthistes de Louis XIII avaient transmis aux praticiens du clavecin; secret perdu depuis le XVIII siècle et les froides lumières de son déclin. C'est l'ascèse janséniste détournée de ses fins pour ne s'appliquer plus qu'aux sciences du plaisir, haussant la délectation sensible à la dignité d'un régal de l'intelligence. A subtiliser sur le magistère harmonique, Chabrier, frère spirituel d'Édouard Manet, trahit la même race et le même esprit que no casuistes de la gastronomie et de la préciosité galante."

64. Guattari writes of hierarchy in musical institutions: "One has here to contrast the abstract machines of music (perhaps the most non-signifying and de-territorializing of all) with the whole musical caste system—its conservatories, its educational traditions, its rules for correct composition, its stress on the impresario and so on. It becomes clear that the collectivity of musical production is so organized as to hamper and delay the force of de-territorialization inherent in music as such. We may think here of the history of the church's relationship with music, which goes back to the origin of polyphony. For instance, the church always tried to block the machinic expansion of instrumental music, and to allow only singing. It tried to set dogmatic limits to composition, and to impose particular styles and forms." Félix Guattari, *La Révolution moléculaire: Molecular Revolution, Psychiatry and Politics*, 107.

65. Deleuze and Guattari, *A Thousand Plateaus*, 304.

66. Roland Barthes, "Loving Schumann," in *The Responsibility of Forms*, 293–94.

67. Deleuze and Guattari, *A Thousand Plateaus*, 340.

68. Deleuze and Guattari, *A Thousand Plateaus*, 299.
69. Deleuze, *The Logic of Sensation*, 36.
70. Deleuze and Guattari, *What Is Philosophy?* 173.
71. Deleuze, *Cinema 2: The Time Image*, 261.
72. Deleuze, *Cinema 2: The Time Image*, 260.
73. Deleuze, *Cinema 2: The Time Image*, 260.
74. Deleuze and Guattari, *What Is Philosophy?* 175–76.
75. Deleuze, *Cinema 2: The Time Image*, 271.
76. In *The Logic of Sense,* Deleuze foreshadows the themes of intertwining counterpoint and connective affects in the concept of "a coupled Figure." See Deleuze, *The Logic of Sense*, 72–73.
77. Deleuze and Guattari, *What Is Philosophy?* 176.
78. Deleuze and Guattari, *What Is Philosophy?* 173.
79. Deleuze and Guattari, *What Is Philosophy?* 176.

CONCLUSION

1. Theodor Adorno, "Some Ideas on the Sociology of Music," in *Sound Figures*, translation modified. The German original reads: "Durch ihr pures material ist Musik die Kunst, in der die vorrationalen, mimetischen Impulse unabdigbar sich behaupten und zugleich in Konstellation treten mit den Zügen fortschreitender Natur und Materialbeherrschung. Dem dankt sie jene Transzendenz über den Betrieb bloßer Selbsterhaltung, die Schopenhauer dazu veranlaßte, sie in der Hierarchie der Künste als unmittelbare Objektivation des Willens am höchsten zu stellen. Wenn irgendwo, dann reicht sie in der Tat dadurch über die bloße Wiederholung dessen, was ohnehin geschieht, hinaus. Zugleich aber wird sie eben dadurch auch tauglich zur stetigen Reproduktion der Dummheit. Wodurch sie her ist als Ideologie, ist ihrem ideologischen Unwesen am nächsten." Adorno, *Gesammelte Schriften*, band 16, 14.
2. Deleuze, *The Logic of Sense*, 248.
3. Jacques Derrida and Ornette Coleman, "The Other's Language: Jacques Derrida Interviews Ornette Coleman, 23 June 1997," trans. Timothy S. Murphy, in *Genre: Forms of Discourse and Culture* 37, no. 2 (2004): 323.
4. On a "general semiology" beyond language, see Ferdinand de Saussure, "The Object of Linguistics," in *Course in General Linguistics*, 16.
5. Richard Rorty, ed., *The Lingusitic Turn*. See Richard Rorty, "Introduction: Metaphysical Difficulties of Linguistic Philosophy," 1–39.
6. Jean Hyppolite, *Logic and Existence*.
7. Jacques Lacan, "The Function and Field of Speech and Language in Psychoanalysis," in *Écrits: The First Complete Edition in English*.
8. Gary Gutting, "The Hegelian Challenge," in *Thinking the Impossible: French Philosophy Since 1960*, 24–45.
9. Jacques Attali, *Noise: The Political Economy of Music*, 4.

SELECT BIBLIOGRAPHY

PRIMARY SOURCES

Adorno, Theodor. *Aesthetic Theory*. Trans. Robert Hullot-Kentor. Minneapolis: University of Minnesota Press, 1997.

———. *Alban Berg: Master of the Smallest Link*. Translation of *Alban Berg: Der Meister des kleinsten Übergangs*. Trans. Julian Brand and Christopher Hailey. Cambridge, UK: Cambridge University Press, 1991.

———. "Bloch's 'Traces': The Philosophy of Kitsch." Trans. Xavier Ribas. *New Left Review* 1, no. 121 (1980).

———. "Cultural Criticism and Society." In Theodor W. Adorno and Brian O'Connor, *The Adorno Reader*. Malden, MA: Wiley-Blackwell, 2000.

———. *Current of Music*. Trans. Robert Hullot-Kentor. Oxford, UK: Polity Press, 2009.

———. *Dialectic of Enlightenment: Philosophical Fragments*. Translation of *Dialektik der Aufklärung: Philosophische Fragmente*. Trans. Edmund Jephcott. Ed. Gunzelin Schmid Noerr. Stanford, CA: Stanford University Press, 2002.

———. *Essays on Music*. Trans. Susan H. Gillepsie and others. Ed. Richard Leppert. Berkeley: University of California Press, 2003.

———. *Gesammelte Schriften*. Ed. Rolf Diedemann, with the collaboration of Gretel Adorno, Susan Buck-Morss, and Klaus Schultz. 20 vols. Frankfurt am Main: Suhrkamp, 1970–.

———. *In Search of Wagner*. Translation of *Versuch über Wagner*. Trans. Rodney Livingstone. London: New Left Books, 1981.

———. *Introduction to the Sociology of Music*. Translation of *Einleitung in die Musiksociologie*. Trans. E. B. Ashton. New York: Seabury Press, 1976.

———. *Mahler: A Musical Physiognomy*. Translation of *Mahler: Eine musikalische Physiognomik*. Trans. Edmund Jephcott. Chicago: University of Chicago Press, 1992.

———. *Minima Moralia: Reflections from Damaged Life*. Translation of *Minima Moralia: Reflexionen aus dem beschädigten Leben*. Trans. Edmund F. N. Jephcott. London: New Left Books, 1974.

———. *Negative Dialectics*. Translation of *Negative Dialektik: Jargon der Eigentlichkeit*. Trans. E B. Ashton. London: Routledge & Kegan Paul; New York: Seabury Press, 1973.

———. *Night Music*. Trans. Wieland Hoban. Ed. Rolf Tiedemann. New York: Seagull Books, 2009.

———. *Notes towards a Theory of Musical Reproduction*. Trans. Wieland Hoban. Oxford: Polity Press, 2006.

———. "On Some Relationships between Music and Painting." Trans. Susan Gillespie. *Musical Quarterly* 79, no. 1: 66–79.

———. *Philosophy of New Music*. Translation of *Philosophie der neuen Musik*. Trans. and ed. Robert Hullot-Kentor. Minneapolis: University of Minnesota Press, 2006.

———. *Quasi Una Fantasia: Essays on Modern Music*. Trans. Rodney Livingstone. London: Verso, 1992.

———. *Sound Figures*. Translation of *Klangfiguren*. Trans. Rodney Livingstone. Stanford, CA: Stanford University Press, 1999.

Adorno, Theodor, and Ernst Bloch. "Something's Missing: A Discussion between Ernst Bloch and Theodor W. Adorno on the Contradictions of Utopian Longing." In *The Utopian Function of Art and Literature: Selected Essays*. Trans. Jack Zipes and Franklin Mecklenburg. Cambridge, MA: MIT Press, 1988.

Adorno, Theodor, et al. *Aesthetics and Politics*. London: Verso, 1980.

Ambros, August Wilhelm. *Geschichte der Musik*. Breslau: 1862–78.

Augustine of Hippo. *Confessions*. Trans. Henry Chadwick. Oxford, UK: Oxford World's Classics, 1998.

———. *De musica*. Trans. R. C. Taliafero. New York: Fathers of the Church, 1947.

———. *Enarrationes in Psalmos*. Vienna: Verlag der Österreichischen Akademie der Wissenschaften, 2003.

Aristotle. *The Metaphysics*, Books 1–9. Loeb Classical Library. Trans. Hugh Tredennick and George Cyril Armstrong. Cambridge, MA: Harvard University Press, 1933.

———. *The Physics*. Loeb Classical Library. Trans. Philip H. Wicksteed and Francis M. Cornford. Cambridge, MA: Harvard University Press, 1933.

———. *The Poetics*. Loeb Classical Library. Trans. W. H. Fyfe. Cambridge, MA: Harvard University Press, 1995.

———. *The Politics*. Loeb Classical Library. Trans. H. Rackham. Cambridge, MA: Harvard University Press, 1944.

Attali, Jacques. *Noise: The Political Economy of Music*. Trans. Brian Massumi. Minneapolis: University of Minnesota Press, 1985.

Bachelard, Gaston. *Dialectique de la durée*. Paris: Alcan, 1936.

———. *Dialectic of Duration*. Trans. Mary McAllester Jones. Manchester, UK: Clinamen Press, 2000.

———. *Intuition of the Instant*. Trans. Eileen Rizo-Patron. Evanston, IL: Northwestern University Press, 2013.
Baker, Nancy Kovaleff, and Thomas Christensen, eds. *Aesthetics and the Art of Musical Composition in the German Enlightenment: Selected Writing of Johann Georg Sulzer and Heinrich Christoph Koch*. Cambridge: Cambridge University Press, 1995.
Barker, Andrew, ed. *Greek Musical Writings I: The Musician and his Art*. Cambridge: Cambridge University Press, 1984.
Barthes, Roland. "Listening" and "Loving Schumann." In *Responsibility of Forms: Critical Essays on Music, Art and Representation*. Trans. Richard Howard. Berkeley: University of California Press, 1991.
———. "Musica Practica" and "The Grain of the Voice." Trans. Stephen Heath. In *Image-Music-Text*. New York: Hill and Wang, 1978.
Bekker, Paul. *Beethoven*. Trans. M. M. Bozman. London and Toronto: J. M. Dent & Sons, 1932.
———. *The Story of Music: A Historical Sketch of the Changes in Musical Form*. Trans. M. D. Herter Norton and Alice Kortschak. New York: W. W. Norton, 1926.
Benjamin, Walter. "On Language as Such and on the Language of Man," *Selected Writings, Vol. 1, 1913–26*. Ed. Marcus Bullock and Michael W. Jennings. Cambridge, MA: Harvard University Press, 1996.
Bergson, Henri. *Creative Evolution*. Trans. Arthur Mitchell. New York: Holt and Company, 1914.
———. *The Creative Mind*. Trans. Mabelle L. Andison. New York: Dover Publications, 2010.
———. *Time and Free Will: An Essay on the Immediate Data of Consciousness*. Trans. Frank Lubecki Pogson. New York: Courier Dover Publications, 2001.
———. *The Two Sources of Morality and Religion*. Trans. R. Ashley Audra and Cloudesley Brereton. South Bend, IN: University of Notre Dame Press, 1963.
Bloch, Ernst. *Atheism in Christianity: The Religion of the Exodus and the Kingdom*. Translation of *Atheismus im Christentum: Zur Religion des Exodus und des Reichs*. Trans. J. T. Swann. New York: Herder & Herder, 1972.
———. *Essays on the Philosophy of Music*. Trans. P. Palmer. Cambridge: Cambridge University Press, 1985.
———. *Geist der Utopie*. Berlin: Paul Cassirer Verlag A.-G., 1923.
———. *Gesamtausgabe*. 17 vols. Frankfurt am Main: Shurkamp, 1961-85.
———. *Heritage of Our Times*. Translation of *Erbschaft dieser Zeit*. Trans. Neville Plaice and Stephen Plaice. Berkeley: University of California Press, 1991.
———. *Literary Essays*. Translation of *Literarische Aufsätze*. Trans. Andrew Joron and others. Stanford, CA: Stanford University Press, 1998.
———. *The Principle of Hope*. Translation of *Das Prinzip Hoffnung*. Trans. Neville Plaice, Stephen Plaice, and Paul Knight. 3 vols. Cambridge, MA: MIT Press, 1995.
———. *The Spirit of Utopia*. Translation of *Geist der Utopie*. Trans. Anthony A. Nassar. Stanford, CA: Stanford University Press, 2006.

Boulez, Pierre. *Boulez on Music Today*. Trans. Susan Bradshaw and Richard Rodney Bennett. Cambridge, MA: Harvard University Press, 1971.
———. *Orientations*. Trans. Martin Cooper. Ed. Jean-Jacques Nattiez. Cambridge, MA: Harvard University Press, 1990.
Brendel, Franz. *Geschichte der Musik in Italien, Deutschland und Frankreich*. Leipzig: 1852.
Cavell, Stanley. "Music Discomposed," *Must We Mean What We Say?*, 180–212. Cambridge: Cambridge University Press, 2002.
Chabanon, Michel Guy de. "Sur la musique" (1779). In Strunk and Treitler, eds., *Source Readings in Music History*. New York: W. W. Norton, 1998.
Charlton, David, ed. *E. T. A. Hoffmann's Musical Writings: Kreisleriana, The Poet and the Composer, Music Criticism*. Trans. Martyn Clarke. Cambridge: Cambridge University Press, 1989.
Chladni, Ernst Florens Friedrich. *Die Akoustik*. 2nd ed. Leipzig: Brietkopf und Härtel, 1830.
———. *Entdeckungen über die Theorie des Klanges*. Leipzig: Wiedmanns Erben und Reich, 1787.
———. *Traité d'acoustique*. Paris, 1809.
Clément, Catherine. *Syncope: The Philosophy of Rapture*. Minneapolis: University of Minnesota Press, 1994.
Deleuze, Gilles. *Bergsonism*. Trans. Hugh Tomlinson and Barbara Habberjam. New York: Zone Books, 1990.
———. *Le Bergsonisme*. Paris: PUF, 1966.
———. "Boulez, Proust, and Time: 'Occupying without Counting.'" With an introduction and translation by Timothy S. Murphy. *Angelaki: Journal of the Theoretical Humanities* 3, no. 2 (1998).
———. *Cinéma 1: L'Image-mouvement*. Paris: Minuit, 1983.
———. *Cinema 1: The Movement Image*. Trans. Hugh Tomlinson and Barbara Habberjam. Minneapolis: University of Minnesota Press, 2006.
———. *Cinéma 2: L'Image-temps*. Paris: Minuit, 1985.
———. *Cinema 2: The Time Image*. Trans. Hugh Tomlinson and Barbara Habberjam. Minneapolis: University of Minnesota Press, 2005.
———. *Desert Islands and Other Texts (1953-1974)*. Trans. Mike Taormina. Cambridge, MA: MIT Press, 2003.
———. *Dialogues II*. Trans. Hugh Tomlinson, Barbara Habberjam, and Eliot Ross Albert. New York: Continuum, 2002.
———. *Difference and Repetition*. Trans. Paul Patton. New York: Columbia University Press, 1994.
———. *Difference et repetition*. Paris: Presses universitaires de France, 1968.
———. *Essays Critical and Clinical*. Trans. Daniel W. Smith and Michael A. Greco. New York: Verso, 1998.

——. *Expressionism in Philosophy: Spinoza.* Trans. Martin Joughin. New York: Zone Books, 1992.

——. *The Fold: Leibniz and the Baroque.* Trans. Tom Conley. Minneapolis: University of Minnesota Press, 1993.

——. *Francis Bacon: The Logic of Sensation.* Trans. Daniel W. Smith; afterword by Tom Conley. Minneapolis: University of Minnesota Press, 2003.

——. *The Logic of Sense.* Ed. Constantin V. Boundas. Trans. Mark Lester and Charles Stivale. New York: Columbia University Press, 1990.

——. *Logique du sens.* Paris: Minuit, 1969.

——. "Metal, Metallurgy, Music, Husserl, Simondon" (Seminar Session: February 27, 1979). Trans. Timothy S. Murphy, http://www.webdeleuze.com/textes/186, accessed December 20, 2016.

——. *Negotiations 1972–1990.* Trans. Martin Joughin. New York: Columbia University Press, 1997.

——. *Nietzsche et la philosphie.* Paris: Presses universitaires de France, 1962.

——. *Nietzsche and Philosophy.* Trans. Hugh Tomlinson. Columbia University Press, 2002.

——. *Le Pli: Leibniz et le Baroque.* Paris: Minuit, 1988.

——. *Pure Immanence: Essays on a Life.* Trans. Anne Boyman. New York: Zone Books, 2001.

——. "Review of Gilbert Simondon's *L'individu et sa genese physico-biologique.*" (1966). Trans. Ivan Ramirez. *Pli: The Warwick Journal of Philosophy* 12 (2001): 43–49.

——. *Spinoza: Practical Philosophy.* Trans. Robert Hurley. San Francisco: City Lights Books, 1988.

——. *Spinoza et le problème de l'expression.* Paris: Minuit, 1968.

——. *Two Regimes of Madness: Texts and Interviews 1975–1995.* Trans. David Lapoujade and Mike Taormina. Cambridge, MA: MIT Press, 2006.

——. "Vincennes Seminar Session, May 3, 1977: On Music." *Discourse* 30, no. 1 (Fall 1998); 205–18.

Deleuze, Gilles, and Guattari, Félix. *Anti-Oedipus.* Trans. Robert Hurley, Mark Seem, and Helen R. Lane. Minneapolis: University of Minnesota Press, 1987.

——. *A Thousand Plateaus.* Trans. Brian Massumi. Minneapolis: University of Minnesota Press, 1987.

——. *What Is Philosophy?* Trans. Graham Burchill and Hugh Tomlinson. London: Verso, 1994.

Derrida, Jacques. *The Gift of Death.* Trans. David Wills. Chicago: University of Chicago Press, 1996.

——. *Marges de la philosophie.* Paris: Les éditions de minuit, 1972.

——. *Margins of Philosophy.* Trans. Alan Bass. Chicago: University of Chicago Press, 1990.

———. *Of Grammatology*. Trans. Gayatri Chakravorty Spivak. Baltimore: Johns Hopkins University Press, 1974.
Descartes, René. *Compendium of Music*. Trans. Walter Robert. Introduction and notes by Charles Kent. Middleton, WI: American Institute of Musicology, 1961.
———. *The Passions of the Soul and Other Late Philosophical Writings*. Trans. Michael Moriarty. Oxford, UK: Oxford World Classics, 2015.
Du Bois, W. E. B. *The Souls of Black Folk*. New York: Penguin Classics, 1989.
Dvořák, Antonín. *Dumky: Klavier trio*. Opus 90 version for piano, four hands, ed. by Klaus Döge. Munich: G. Henle Verlag, 2008.
Engelmann, Paul. *Letters from Ludwig Wittgenstein with a Memoir*. New York: Horizon Press, 1967.
Fétis, F. J. *Bibliographie universelle des musiciens et bibliographie générale de la musique*. 2nd ed. Paris: Firmin Didot, 1878.
Flowers, F. A. *Portraits of Wittgenstein*. Bristol, UK: Thoemmes Continuum, 1999.
Forkel, Johannes. *Allgemeine Geschichte der Musik*. 2 vols. Leipzig: Schwickert, 1788–1801.
———. *Musikalische-Kritische Bibliotek*. Gotha: 1778–79. Reprinted Hildesheim: 1964.
Gaudentius. "Harmonic Introduction." In Strunk and Treitler, eds., *Source Readings in Music History*, 68. New York: W. W. Norton, 1998.
Goodwin, Jocelyn. *The Harmony of the Spheres: The Pythagorean Tradition in Music*. Rochester, NY: Inner Traditions, 1993.
Graham, Daniel W. *The Texts of Early Greek Philosophy*. 2 vols. Cambridge: Cambridge University Press, 2010.
Guattari, Félix. *The Anti-Oedipus Papers*. New York: Semiotext(e), 2006.
———. *Chaosmose*. Paris: Galilée, 1992.
———. *Chaosmosis*. Trans. P. Bains and J. Pefanis. Bloomington: Indiana University Press, 1995.
———. *Chaosophy*. New York: Semiotext(e), 1995.
———. "Cracks in the Street." *Flash Art* 135 (1987).
———. *The Guattari Reader*. Ed. G. Genosko, Oxford, UK: Blackwell, 1996.
———. *Molecular Revolution: Psychiatry and Politics*. Trans. Rosemary Sheed. New York: Penguin, 1984.
———. "La revolution moleculaire." *Le monde*, December 7, 1990.
———. "Ritornellos and Existential Affects." Trans. Juliana Schiesari and Georges van den Abbeele, *Discourse* 12, no. 2 (1990): 66–81.
———. "Ritournelles et affects existentiels." *Chemières* 7 (1987).
———. "Ritournelles et affects existentiels (Discussion)." *Les séminaires de Félix Guattari*, May 5, 1987.
———. *Soft Subversions*. New York: Semiotext(e), 1995.
———. *The Three Ecologies*. Trans. Ian Pindar and Paul Sutton. London: Athlone Press, 2000.
———. "Tokyo, the Proud," *Deleuze Studies* 1, no. 2 (2007): 93–99.

Guattari, Félix, and Shin Takamatsu. "Singularization and Style." *Parallax* 7, no. 4 (2001): 131–37.

Halm, August. "August Halm's 'Von zwei Kulturen der Musik': Translation and an Introductory Essay." PhD dissertation, University of Texas, 2007.

———. *Von zwei Kulturen der Musick.* Munich: G. Müller, 1913.

Hanslick, Eduard. *On the Musically Beautiful: A Contribution towards the Revision of the Aesthetics of Music.* Trans. Geoffrey Payzant. Indianapolis: Hackett Publishing, 1986.

———. *Vom Musicalisch-Schönen: Ein Beitrag zur Revision der Ästhetik der Tonkunst.* Leipzig, 1854.

Hegel, Georg Wilhelm Friedrich. *Enzyklopädie der philosophischen Wissenschaften.* Frankfurt am Main: Suhrkamp Verlag, 1970.

———. *Introductory Lectures on Aesthetics.* Trans. Bernard Bosanquet. New York: Penguin Classics, 1993.

———. *Lectures on Aesthetics.* Trans. T. M. Knox. 2 vols. Oxford, UK: Clarendon Press, 1975.

———. *Phäenomenlogie des Geistes.* Vol. 3, *Werkasugabe.* Frankfurt am Main: Suhrkamp Verlag, 1970.

———. *The Phenomenology of Spirit.* Trans. A. V. Miller. Oxford, UK: Oxford University Press, 1977.

———. *Philosophy of Nature.* Trans. A. V. Miller. Oxford, UK: Oxford University Press, 1970.

———. *The Science of Logic.* Trans. A. V. Miller. New York: Humanities Press, 1969.

———. *Vorlesungen über die Ästhetik.* Frankfurt am Main: Suhrkamp Verlag, 1970.

Herder, Johann Gottfried. *Selected Writings on Aesthetics.* Trans. Gregory Moore. Princeton, NJ: Princeton University Press, 2006.

Henry, Michel. *Material Phenomenology.* New York: Fordham University Press, 2008.

Heidegger, Martin. *Being and Time.* Trans. Joan Stambaugh and Dennis J. Schmidt. Stony Brook: State University of New York Press, 2010.

Hoffmann, E. T. A. *E. T. A. Hoffmann's Musical Writings: Kreisleriana, The Poet and the Composer, Music Criticism.* Ed. David Charlton. Cambridge, UK: Cambridge University Press, 1989.

———. *Fantasiestücke in Callot's Manier.* Frankfurt am Main: Deutscher Klassiker Verlag: 1993.

———. *Fantasy Pieces in Callot's Manner: Pages from the Diary of a Traveling Romantic.* Trans. Joseph M. Hayse. Schenectady, NY: Union College Press, 1996.

Hyppolite, Jean. *Logic and Existence.* Trans. Leonard Lawlor and Amit Sen. Stony Brook: State University of New York Press, 1997.

Ikhwan Al-Safa. *Epistles of the Bretheren of Purity.* Ed. Owen Wright. *On Music: An Arabic Critical Edition and English Translation of Epistle 5.* Oxford, UK: Oxford University Press, 2011.K

Jankélévitch, Vladimir. *L'Austérite et la vie morale.* In *Philosophie morale.* Paris: Flammarion, 1998.

———. *Bad Conscience*. (Translation of *La mauvaise conscience*, in *Philosophie morale*, 32–202. Paris: Flammarion, 1998.) Trans. Andrew Kelley. Chicago: University of Chicago Press, 2014.

———. *De la musique au silence: Fauré et l'inexprimable*. Paris: Librairie Plon, 1974.

———. *L'esprit de résistance: Textes politiques 1943–1983*. Paris: Albin Michel, 2015.

———. *Forgiveness*. (Translation of *Le pardon*, in *Philosophie morale*, 993–1149. Paris: Flammarion, 1998.) Trans. Andrew Kelley. Chicago: University of Chicago Press, 2005.

———. *Henri Bergson*. (Republished in 1959 and 1999. 4th ed. Paris: Presses Universitaires de France, 2008. Trans. Nils F. Schott. Durham, NC: Duke University Press, 2015.

———. *Le je-ne-sais-quoi et le presque-rien*. Paris: Éditions du Seuil, 1980.

———. *Liszt: Rhapsodie et improvisation*. Paris: Flammarion, 1998.

———. *La mort*. Paris: Flammarion, 1977.

———. *Music and the Ineffable*. (Translation of *La musique et l'ineffable*. Paris: Éditions du Seuil, 1983.) Trans. Carolyn Abbate. Princeton, NJ: Princeton University Press, 2003.

———. *La musique et les heures*. Paris: Éditions du Seuil, 1988.

———. *L'odyssée de la conscience dans la dernière philosophie de Schelling*. 1933. 2nd ed. Paris: Editions L'Hartmattan, 2005.

———. *Le paradoxe de la morale*. Paris: Éditions du Seuil, 1981.

———. *Philosophie première: Introduction à la philosophie du presque*. Paris: Presses Universitaires de France, 1953.

———. "Should We Pardon Them?" Trans. Ann Hobart. *Critical Inquiry* 22, no. 3 (1996): 552–72. ("Pardonner?" In *L'imprescriptible*. Paris: Éditions du Seuil, 1986.)

———. *Traité des vertus*, vol. 2: *Les vertus et l'amour*. Paris: Flammarion, 1986.

———. *Traité des vertus*, vol. 3: *L'innocence et la méchanceté*. Paris: Bordas, 1972.

———. *La vie et la mort dans la musique de Debussy*. Editions de la Baconniéré, 1978.

Jankélévitch, Vladimir, and Louis Beauduc. *Une vie en toutes lettres*. Ed. Françoise Schwab. Paris: Lianna Levi, 1995.

Kant, Immanuel. *Critique of Judgment*. Trans. Werner S. Pluhar. Indianapolis: Hackett Publishing, 1987.

———. *Critique of Pure Reason*. Trans. Norman Kemp Smith. Rev. 2nd ed. Basingstoke, UK: Palgrave Macmillan, 2007.

Kant, Immanuel, and Hans Siegbert Reiss. *Kant: Political Writings*. Cambridge, UK: Cambridge University Press, 1991.

Kierkegaard, Søren. *Either/Or II*. Trans. Howard Hong and Edna Hong. Princeton, NJ: Princeton University Press, 1990.

———. *Fear and Trembling* and *Repetition*. Trans. Howard Hong and Edna Hong. Princeton, NJ: Princeton University Press, 1985.

Kiesewetter, Raphael. *History of the Modern Music of Western Europe, from the First Century of the Christian Era to the Present Day*. (Translation of *Geschichte der europäisch-abendländlischen oder unserer heutigen Musik*.) Leipzig: Breitkopf & Härtel, 1834.) Trans. Robert Mülller. London: T. C. Tenby, 1848.

Klee, Felix, ed. *The Diaries of Paul Klee 1891–1918*. Berkeley: University Of California Press, 1964.

Kurth, Ernst. *Grundlagen des linearen Kontrapunkts*. Bern: Drechsel, 1917.

———. *Selected Writings*. Ed. Lee Rothfarb. Cambridge, UK: Cambridge University Press, 1991.

Lacan, Jacques. "The Function and Field of Speech and Language in Psychoanalysis." In *Écrits: The First Complete Edition in English*. Trans. Bruce Fink. New York: W. W. Norton, 2006.

Le Huray, Peter, and James Day. *Music and Aesthetics in the Eighteenth and Early-Nineteenth Centuries*. Cambridge, UK: Cambridge University Press, 1981.

Lessing, Gotthold Ephraim. *Gesammelte Werke*. Ed. Wolfgang Stammler. Munich: Carl Hanser Verlag, 1959.

Levinas, Emmanuel. *Otherwise Than Being*. Trans. Alphonso Lingis. Pittsburgh: Duquesne University Press, 1998.

———. *Outside the Subject*. Trans. Michael B. Smith. Stanford, CA: Stanford University Press, 1994.

Lukaçs, György. *Soul and Form*. Trans. Anna Bostock. Ed. Katie Terezakis and John T. Sanders. New York: Columbia University Press, 2010.

Lorenz, Konrad. *On Aggression*. Trans. Marjorie Kerr Wilson. New York: Routledge, 2005.

Mallarmé, Stéphane. *Un coup de dés jamais n'abolira le hasard*. Paris: Gallimard, 1993.

———. *Collected Poems and Other Verse*. Trans. E. H. and A. M. Blackmore. Oxford, UK: Oxford University Press, 2006.

Marcel, Gabriel. *Music and Philosophy*. Trans. Stephen Maddux and Robert E. Wood. Milwaukee: Marquette University Press, 2005.

Marx, Karl. *Capital*. Trans. Ben Fowkes. 3 vols. New York: Penguin Classics, 1992.

Mazzini, Giuseppe. Excerpt from *Philosophy of Music* (1836). Trans. Yvonne Freccero, with Giovanna Bellesia and John Sessions. In *Source Readings in Music History*, ed. Strunk and Treitler, 1085–1094. New York: W. W. Norton, 1998.

Moltmann, Jürgen, *Theology of Hope: On the Ground and the Implications of a Christian Eschatology*. (Translation of *Theologie der Hoffnung: Untersuchungen zur Begründung und zu den Konsequenzen einer christlichen Eschatologie*. Munich: Kaiser Verlag, 1964.) Trans. James W. Leitch. London: SCM Press, 1967.

Nagel, Thomas. "What is It Like to Be a Bat?" *Philosophical Review* 83, no. 4 (1974): 435–50.

Nancy, Jean-Luc. *Listening*. Trans. Charlotte Mandel. New York: Fordham University Press, 2007.

Nietzsche, Friedrich. *The Birth of Tragedy and Other Writings*. (Translation of *Die Geburt der Tragödie aus dem Geiste der Musik*.) Trans. Ronald Spiers. Ed. Raymond Guess and Ronald Spiers. Cambridge: Cambridge University Press, 1999.

———. *The Case of Wagner.* In *The Birth of Tragedy; and the Case of Wagner.* Trans. Walter Kaufmann. New York: Vintage Books, 1967.

———. *On the Genealogy of Morality.* (Translation of *Zur Genealogie der Moral.*) Trans. Carol Diethe. Ed. Keith Ansell-Pearson. Cambridge: Cambridge University Press, 2007.

Plato. *Laws.* Loeb Classical Library. Trans. R. G. Bury. Cambridge, MA: Harvard University Press, 1926.

———. *Republic.* Ed. Giovanni R. F. Ferrari and Tom Griffith. Cambridge: Cambridge University Press, 2000.

———. *Republic.* Trans. C. D. C. Reeve. Indianapolis: Hackett Publishing, 2004.

———. *Timaeus and Critias.* Trans. Desmond Lee. New York: Penguin Classics, 2008.

Plotinus. *The Enneads.* Abridged edition. Trans. Stephen McKenna. New York: Penguin, 1991.

Proust, Marcel. *In Search of Lost Time.* Trans. C. K. Scott Mocreiff, Terrance Kilmartin, and Rev. D. J. Enright. New York: Modern Library, 2003.

Roland-Manuel, Alexis, ed. *Histoire de la musique.* 2 vols. Encyclopédie de la Pléiade. Paris: Gallimard, 1960–63.

Rorty, Richard, ed. *The Lingusitic Turn.* Chicago: University of Chicago Press, 1967.

Rosset, Clement. *Joyful Cruelty: Towards a Philosophy of the Real.* Trans. Daniel F. Bell. Oxford, UK: Oxford University Press, 1993.

Rothfarb, Lee, ed. *Ernst Kurth's Selected Writings.* Cambridge: Cambridge University Press, 2006.

Rousseau, Jean-Jacques. *Collected Writings of Rousseau Vol. 7: Essay on the Origin of Languages and Writings Related to Music.* Trans. John T. Scott. Hanover, NH: University Press of New England, 1998.

Sartre, Jean-Paul. *Being and Nothingness: A Phenomenological Essay on Ontology.* Trans. Hazel Barnes. New York: Washington Square Press, 1992.

Saussure, Ferdinand de. *Course in General Linguistics.* Trans. Wade Baskin. New York: McGraw-Hill, 1959.

Schäfke, Rudolf. *Geschichte der Musikästhetik in Umrissen.* Berlin: Max Hesse Verlag, 1934. 2nd ed., Tutzing: Hans Schneider Verlag, 1964.

Schelling, Friedrich Wilhelm Joseph. *Philosophie der Kunst.* Darmstadt: Wissenschaftliche Buchgesellschaft, 1976.

———. *The Philosophy of Art.* Trans. Douglas W. Stott. Minneapolis: University Of Minnesota Press, 1989.

Schenker, Heinrich. *Harmonielehre* (1906). Vienna: Universal Edition, 1978.

———. *Harmonielehre.* Trans. Elizabeth Borghese. Cambridge, MA: MIT Press, 1978.

Schoenberg, Arnold. *Harmonielehre.* Vienna: Universal Edition, 1911.

———. *The Musical Idea and the Logic, Technique, and Art of Its Presentation.* Trans. and ed. Patricia Carpenter and Severine Neff. Bloomington, IN: Indiana University Press, 2006.

———. *Style and Idea: Selected Writings of Arnold Schoenberg.* Trans. Leo Black. Ed.

Leonard Stein. Berkeley: University of California Press, 1984.

———. *Theory of Harmony.* Trans. Roy E. Carter. Berkeley: University of California Press, 1983.

Schopenhauer, Arthur. *Parerga and Paralipomena: Short Philosophical Essays.* Trans. Eric F. J. Payne. 2 vols. Oxford, UK: Clarendon Press, 1974.

———. *Sämtliche Werke.* Ed. Arthur Hübscher. 4th ed. 7 vols. Weisbaden: F. A. Brockhaus, 1988.

———. *The World as Will and Representation.* Trans. Eric F. J. Payne. 2 vols. New York: Dover Press, 1959.

Serres, Michel. *Musique.* Paris: Le Pommier, 2011.

Spinoza, Baruch. *Ethics: Treatise on the Emendation of the Intellect and Selected Letters.* Trans. Samuel Shirley. Ed. Seymour Feldman. Indianapolis: Hackett, 1992.

Stivale, Charles J. "Pragmatic/Machinic: A Discussion with Fèlix Guattari (March 19, 1985). http://topologicalmedialab.net/xinwei/classes/readings/Guattari/Pragmatic-Machinic_chat.html. Accessed June 12, 2015.

Strunk, Oliver, ed. *Source Readings in Music History.* Revised ed. New York: W. W. Norton, 1998.

Stumpf, Carl. *The Origins of Music.* Trans. and ed. David Trippett. Cambridge: Cambridge University Press, 2012.

Suarès, Guy. *Vladimir Jankélévitch: Qui suis-je?* Paris: La Manufacture, 1986.

Sulzer, Johann Georg. *Allgemeine Theorie der schönen Künste* (1771–74). 5 vols. 2nd ed. 1792–95. Reprint, Hildesheim: Georg Olms, 1967.

Thorpe, W. H. *Learning and Instinct in Animals.* Cambridge, MA: Harvard University Press, 1956.

Uexküll, Jakob von. *A Foray into the Worlds of Animals and Humans with a Theory of Meaning.* Trans. Joseph D. O'Neil. Introduction by Dorion Sagan. Minneapolis: University of Minnesota Press, 2010.

———. *Streifzüge durch die Umwelten von Tieren und Menschen.* Berlin: Verlag von Julius Springer, 1934.

Wackenroder, Wilhelm Heinrich, and Ludwig Tieck. *Herzensergießungen eines kunstliebenden Klosterbruders.* Leipzig: Eugen Diederichs, 1904.

———. *Wilhelm Heinrich Wackenroder's Confessions and Fantasies.* Trans. Mary H. Schubert. University Park: Pennsylvania State University Press, 1971.

Weber, Max. *The Rational and Social Foundations of Music.* Trans. and ed. Don Martindale, Johannes Riedel, and Gertrude Neuwirth. Carbondale, IL: Southern Illinois University Press, 1958.

———. *Die rationalen und soziologischen Grundlagen der Musik.* Munich: Drei Masken Verlag, 1921.

Wittgenstein, Ludwig. *Culture and Value.* Trans. Peter Winch. Chicago: University of Chicago Press, 1980.

———. *Notebooks* 1914–16, 2nd ed. Trans. and ed. G. E. M. Anscombe. Chicago: University of Chicago Press, 1979.

———. *Philosophical Investigations*. Trans. G. E. M. Anscombe. 3rd ed. New York: Pearson, 1973.
———. *Tractatus Logico-Philosophicus*. (In English and German.) Introduction by Bertrand Russell. New York: Routledge, 2005.

SECONDARY SOURCES

Abbate, Carolyn. *In Search of Opera*. Princeton, NJ: Princeton University Press, 2003.
———. "Music—Drastic or Gnostic? *Critical Inquiry* 30, no. 3 (2004): 505-36.
———. "Sound Object Lessons" *Journal of the American Musicological Society* 69, no. 3 (Fall 2016): 793-829.
———. *Unsung Voices: Opera and Musical Narrative in the Nineteenth Century*. Princeton, NJ: Princeton University Press, 1991.
Abrahms, M. H. *The Mirror and the Lamp*. Oxford, UK: Oxford University Press, 1953.
Adiren, Philippe. "L'improvisation." *Chimères*, no. 7 (June 1989).
Agawu, Kofi. *Playing with Signs: A Semiotic Interpretation of Classic Music*. Princeton, NJ: Princeton University Press, 1991.
Arato, Andrew and Eike Gebhardt, eds. *The Essential Frankfurt School Reader*. New York: Continuum International, 1978.
Arndt, Matthew. "Schenker and Schoenberg on the Will of the Tone." *Journal of Music Theory* 55, no. 1 (Spring 2011): 89-146.
Ashby, Arved. *Absolute Music, Mechanical Reproduction*. Berkeley: University of California Press, 2010.
Ayrey, Craig. "Jankélévtich the Obscure(d)." *Music Analysis* 25, no. 3 (2006): 341-57.
Badiou, Alain. *The Adventure of French Philosophy*. Trans. and ed. Bruno Bosteels.
———. *Five Lessons on Wagner*. Trans. Susan Spitzer, with an afterword by Slavoj Zizek. New York: Verso, 2010.
Bard-Schwartz, David and Richard Cohn, Eds. *David Lewin's Morgengruß: Text, Context, Commentary*. Oxford, UK: Oxford University Press, 2015.
Beistegui, Miguel de. "The Deleuzian Reversal of Platonism." In *The Cambridge Companion to Deleuze*, ed. Daniel W. Smith and Henry Somers-Hall. Cambridge: Cambridge University Press, 2012, 56-81.
Berger, Karol. "The Ends of Music History; or, The Old Masters in the Supermarket of Cultures." *Journal of Musicology* 31, no. 2 (2014): 186-98.
———. "Musicology According to Don Giovanni; or, Should We Get Drastic?" *Journal of Musicology* 22, no. 3 (2005): 490-501.
Beveridge, David. "Dvořák's 'Dumka' and the Concept of Nationalism in Music Historiography." *Journal of Musicological Research* 12, no. 4 (1993): 303-25.
Blasius, Leslie. "Mapping the Terrain." In *The Cambridge Western History of Music Theory*, ed. Thomas Christensen. Cambridge: Cambridge University Press, 27-45.
Boldyrev, Ivan. *Ernst Bloch and His Contemporaries*. London: Bloomsbury, 2014.
Bonds, Mark Evan. *Absolute Music: A History of an Idea*. Oxford, UK: Oxford University Press, 2014.

———. *Music as Thought: Listening to the Symphony in the Age of Beethoven*. Princeton, NJ: Princeton University Press, 2006.
Boretz, Benjamin. "Rainy Day Reflections." *Perspectives of New Music* 46, no. 2 (2008): 59–92.
Born, Georgina. "For a Relational Musicology: Music and Interdisciplinarity, beyond the Practice Turn." *Journal of the Royal Musical Association* 135, no. 2 (2010): 205–43.
Bower, Calvin M. "The Transmission of Ancient Music Theory into the Middle Ages." In *Cambridge History of Western Music Theory*, ed. Thomas Christensen. Cambridge: Cambridge University Press.
Bowie, Andrew. *Music, Philosophy, and Modernity*. Cambridge: Cambridge University Press, 2009.
Braunschweig, Karl D. "Disciplining Knowledge in Music Theory: Abstraction and the Recovery of Dialectics." *GAMUT* 5, no. 1 (2012).
Buchanan, Ian, and Marcel Swiboda, eds. *Deleuze and Music*. Edinburgh: Edinburgh University Press, 2004.
Buchwalter, Andrew. "Hegel, Adorno, and the Concept of Transcendent Critique." In *The Frankfurt School: Critical Assessments*, vol. 3, ed. J. M. Bernstein. New York: Taylor & Francis, 1994, 177–93.
Buck-Morss, Susan. *The Origin of Negative Dialectics: Theodor W. Adorno, Walter Benjamin, and the Frankfurt Institute*. Hassocks, UK: Harvester Press, 1977.
Buelow, George J., and Hans Joachim Marx, eds. *New Mattheson Studies*. Cambridge, UK: Cambridge University Press, 1983.
Burkholder, Peter J. "Schoenberg the Reactionary." In *Schoenberg and His World*. Princeton, NJ: Princeton University Press, 1999.
Bryant, Levi R. *Difference and Givenness: Deleuze's Transcendental Empiricism and the Ontology of Immanence*. Evanston, IL: Northwestern University Press, 2008.
Campbell, Edward. *Music after Deleuze*. London: Bloomsbury, 2013.
Cavarero, Adriana. *For More Than One Voice: Toward a Philosophy of Vocal Expression*. Stanford, CA: Stanford University Press, 2005.
Chapin, Keith, and Andrew H. Clark, eds. *Speaking of Music: Addressing the Sonorous*. New York: Fordham University Press, 2013.
Cherlin, Michael. *Schoenberg's Musical Imagination*. Cambridge: Cambridge University Press, 2007.
Christensen, Thomas. "Four-Hand Piano Transcriptions and Geographies of Nineteenth-Century Musical Reception." *Journal of the American Musicological Society* 52, no. 2 (1999): 255–98.
———. "Psophos, Sonus, and Klang: Towards a Genealogy of Sound Technology." In *Organized Sound: Sound and Perception in Twentieth- and Twenty-First Century Music*, ed. Christian Utz, 47–59. Saarbrücken, Germany: PFAU (2013).
Chua, Daniel. *Absolute Music and the Construction of Meaning*. Cambridge, UK: Cambridge University Press, 1999.

Claussen, Detlev. *Theodor W. Adorno: One Last Genius*. Trans. Rodney Livingstone. Cambridge, MA: Harvard University Press, 2008.

Clifton, Thomas. *Music as Heard: A Study in Phenomenology*. New Haven: Yale University Press, 1983.

———. "On Listening to Herzgewächse." *Perspectives of New Music* 11, no. 2 (1973): 87–103.

Cohen, David. "Metaphysics, Ideology, Discipline: Consonance, Dissonance, and the Foundations of Western Polyphony." *Theoria* 7 (1993): 1–85.

Corbett, John. "Out of Nowhere: Meditations on Deleuzian Music, Anti-cadential Strategies, and Endpoints in Improvisation." In Daniel Fischlin and Ajay Heble, eds., *The Other Side of Nowhere: Jazz, Improvisation, and Communities in Dialogue*. Middletown, CT: Wesleyan University Press, 2004, 387–98.

Couzinas, Costas, and Slavoj Zizek, eds., *The Idea of Communism*. Brooklyn, NY: Verso, 2010.

Cramer, Alfred. Review of Ethan Haimo's *Schoenberg's Transformations of Musical Language*. *Journal of the American Musicological Society* 62 (2009), no. 2: 482–88.

Currie, James. "Music after All." *Journal of the American Musicological Society* 62 (2009), no. 1: 145–203.

———. *Music and the Politics of Negation*. Bloomington: Indiana University Press, 2012.

———. "Where Jankélévitch Cannot Speak." *Journal of the American Musicological Society* 65 (2012), no. 1: 247–50.

Cusset, Francois. *French Theory: How Foucault, Derrida, Deleuze, & Co. Transformed the Intellectual Life of the United States*. Trans. Jeff Fort. Minneapolis: University of Minnesota Press, 2008.

Dahlhaus, Carl. *Esthetics of Music*. Trans. Mary Whittall. Berkeley: University of California Press, 1982.

———. *The Idea of Absolute Music*. Trans. Roger Lustig. Chicago: University of Chicago Press, 1989.

———. *Die Idee der absoluten Musik*. Kassel, Germany: Barenreiter, 1994.

Daniel, Jamie Owen, and Tom Moylan, eds. *Not Yet: Reconsidering Ernst Bloch*. New York: Verso, 1997.

Darcy, Warren. "Rotational Form, Teleological Genesis, and Fantasy-Projection in the Slow Movement of Mahler's Sixth Symphony." *19th Century Music* 25 (2001), no. 1: 49–71.

Daub, Adrian. "'An All-Too-Secret Wagner': Ernst Bloch the Wagnerian." *Opera Quarterly* 30 (2014), no. 2–3: 188–204.

———. *Four Handed Monsters: Four-Handed Piano Playing and Nineteenth Century Culture*. Oxford, UK: Oxford University Press, 2014.

Daughtry, J. Martin. *Listening to War: Sound, Music, Trauma, and Survival in Wartime Iraq*. New York: Oxford University Press, 2015.

Daverio, John. *Robert Schumann: Herald of a New Poetic Age*. Oxford, UK: Oxford University Press, 1997.

Davies, Stephen. *Musical Meaning and Expression*. Ithaca, NY: Cornell University Press, 1994.
Deathridge, John. "Wagner and the Post-Modern," *Cambridge Opera Journal* 4 (1992), no. 2: 143–61.
———. "Waiting for Wagner: Reluctant Musicology, Radical Philosophy, and the Rescue of a Fraught Legacy" *Opera Quarterly* 30 (2014), no. 2-3: 267–85.
De Landa, Manuel. *Intensive Science and Virtual Philosophy*. New York: Continuum, 2002.
De Nora, Tia. *After Adorno: Rethinking Music Sociology*. Cambridge: Cambridge University Press, 2003.
Denning, Michael. *Noise Uprising: The Audiopoetics of a Musical Revolution*. Brooklyn, NY: Verso, 2015.
Descombes, Vincent. *Modern French Philosophy*. Trans. L. Scott-Fox and J. M. Harding. Cambridge: Cambridge University Press, 1980.
Dolar, Mladen. *A Voice and Nothing More*. Cambridge, MA: MIT Press, 2006.
Dosse, François. *Gilles Deleuze and Félix Guattari: Intersecting Lives*. Trans. Deborah Glassman. New York: Columbia University Press, 2010.
Erlmann, Veit. *Reason and Resonance: A History of Modern Aurality*. New York: Zone Books, 2010.
Faulkner, Keith W. *Deleuze and the Three Syntheses of Time*. New York: Peter Lang, 2006.
Feldman, Martha. "Music and the Order of the Passions." In *Representing the Passions: Bodies, Visions, Texts*, ed. Richard Meyer, 37–67. Los Angeles: Getty Trust Publications, 2003.
Ferris, David. *Schumann's Eichendorff Liederkreis and the Genre of the Romantic Cycle*. New York: Oxford University Press, 2000.
Forte, Allen. "Sets and Nonsets in Schoenberg's Atonal Music," *Perspectives of New Music* 11 (1972): 43–64.
Frisch, Walter. *Brahms and the Principle of Developing Variation*. Berkeley: University of California Press, 1990.
———. *German Modernism: Music and the Arts*. Berkeley: University of California Press, 2005.
———. "Music and *Jugendstil*." *Critical Inquiry* 17, no. 1 (1990): 138–61.
Gallope, Michael. "Is There a Deleuzian Musical Work?" *Perspectives of New Music* 46, no. 2 (2008): 93–112.
———. "The Time of Repeating Life: Metaphysics and Ethics in Deleuze's Philosophy of Music." In *Radical Difference: Gilles Deleuze and the Theory and Philosophy of Music*, ed. Brian Hulse and Nick Nesbitt, 77–102. New York: Ashgate, 2010.
———. "Why Was This Music Desirable? On A Critical Explanation of the Avant-Garde," *Journal of Musicology* 31, no. 2 (2014): 199–230.
Geoghegen, Vincent. *Ernst Bloch*. New York: Routledge, 1996.
Geroulanos, Stefanos. *An Atheism That Is Not Humanist Emerges in French Thought*. Stanford, CA: Stanford University Press, 2010.

Goehr, Lydia. "Adorno, Schoenberg, and the 'Totentanz der Prinzipien'—In Thirteen Steps." *Journal of the American Musicological Society* 56 (2003), no. 3: 505–636.
———. *Elective Affinities: Musical Essays on the History of Aesthetic Theory*. New York: Columbia University Press, 2008.
———. *The Imaginary Museum of Musical Works: An Essay in the Philosophy of Music*. Oxford: Oxford University Press, 1992.
———. "Political Music and the Politics of Music." *The Journal of Aesthetics and Art Criticism,* 54 (1994), no. 1: 99–112.
———. *The Quest for Voice: On Music, Politics, and the Limits of Philosophy*. Oxford: Oxford University Press, 2002.
Gordon, Peter E. *Continental Divide: Heidegger, Cassirer, Davos*. Cambridge, MA: Harvard University Press, 2010.
Gracyk, Theodor, and Andrew Kania. *The Routledge Companion to Philosophy and Music*. New York: Routledge, 2011.
Green, Burdette, and David Butler, "From Acoustics to *Tonpsychologie*." In *The Cambridge Western History of Music Theory*, ed. Thomas Christensen. Cambridge: Cambridge University Press, 246–71.
Gur, Golan. "Music and 'Weltanschauung': Franz Brendel and the Claims of Universal History." *Music & Letters* 92 (2012), no. 3.
Gutting, Gary. *French Philosophy in the Twentieth Century*. Cambridge: Cambridge University Press, 2001.
———. "The Hegelian Challenge." In *Thinking the Impossible: French Philosophy since 1960*, 24–45. Oxford, UK: Oxford University Press, 2011.
Grimes, Nicole, Siobhán Donovan, and Wolfgang Marx, eds. *Rethinking Hanslick: Music, Formalism, and Expression*. Rochester, NY: University of Rochester Press, 2013.
Gumbrecht, Hans Ulrich. *The Production of Presence: What Meaning Cannot Convey*. Stanford, CA: Stanford University Press, 2004.
Hägglund, Martin. *Radical Atheism: Derrida and the Time of Life*. Stanford, CA: Stanford University Press, 2008.
Haimo, Ethan. *Schoenberg's Transformations of Musical Language*. Cambridge: Cambridge University Press, 2006.
Halliwell, Stephen. *The Aesthetics of Mimesis: Ancient Texts and Modern Problems*. Princeton, NJ: Princeton University Press, 2002.
Hallward, Peter. "The One or the Other: French Philosophy Today." *Angelaki: Theoretical Journal of the Humanities* 8 (2003), no. 2: 1–32.
———. *Out of this World: Deleuze and the Philosophy of Creation*. New York: Verso, 2006.
Hamilton, John. *Music, Madness, and the Unworking of Language*. New York: Columbia University Press, 2008.
Hansen, Miriam. "Mass Culture as Hieroglyphic Writing: Adorno, Derrida, Kracauer." In *Adorno: A Critical Reader*, Nigel Gibson and Andrew Rubin, eds., 57–85. Hoboken, NJ: Wiley-Blackwell, 2002.

Hardt, Michael, and Antonio Negri. *Labor of Dionysius: A Critique of State-Form*. Minneapolis: University of Minnesota Press, 1994.
Hasty, Christopher. "The Image of Thought and the Ideas of Music." In *Sounding the Virtual: Gilles Deleuze and the Theory and Philosophy of Music*. Farnham, UK: Ashgate, 2010.
Hatch, Christopher. "The Wondrous Trumpet Call in Beethoven's *Fidelio*." *Opera Quarterly* 15 (1999), no. 1: 5–17.
Heller-Roazen, Daniel. *The Fifth Hammer: Pythagoras and the Disharmony of the World*. New York: Zone Books, 2011.
Hepokoski, James. "Ineffable Immersion: Contextualizing the Call for Silence." *Journal of the American Musicological Society* 65 (2012), no. 1: 223–30.
Hermand, Jost, and Gerhard Richter, eds. *Sound Figures of Modernity*. Madison: University of Wisconsin Press, 2006.
Hicks, Andrew. *Composing the World: Harmony in the Medieval Platonic Cosmos*. Oxford, UK: Oxford University Press, 2017.
Higgins, Kathleen Marie. *Is Music a Universal Language?* Chicago: University of Chicago Press, 2012.
Hinton, Stephen. "Adorno's Unfinished Beethoven." *Beethoven Forum* 5 (1996).
Hoeckner, Berthold, ed. *Apparitions: New Perspectives on Adorno and Twentieth-Century Music*. New York: Routledge, 2006.
———. "Paths through *Dichterliebe*." *Nineteenth-Century Music* 30 (2006), no. 1: 65–80.
———. *Programming the Absolute: Nineteenth-Century German Music and the Hermeneutics of the Moment*. Princeton, NJ: Princeton University Press, 2002.
Hughes, Joe. *Deleuze and the Genesis of Representation*. London: Continuum, 2008.
Huhn, Tom. *Cambridge Companion to Adorno*. Cambridge: Cambridge University Press, 2004.
Howat, Roy. "Ravel at the Piano." In *The Cambridge Companion to Ravel*, ed. Deborah Mawer, 71–96. Cambridge: Cambridge University Press.
Hohendahl, Peter Uwe. *The Fleeting Promise of Art: Adorno's Aesthetic Theory Revisited*. Ithaca, NY: Cornell University Press, 2013.
Hosler, Bellamy. *Changing Aesthetic Views of Instrumental Music in 18th-century Germany*. Ann Arbor, MI: UMI Research Press, 1981.
Hudson, Wayne. *The Marxist Philosophy of Ernst Bloch*. London: Palgrave Macmillan; New York; St. Martin's Press, 1982.
Hullot-Kentor, Robert. *Things beyond Resemblance: Collected Essays on Theodor W. Adorno*. New York: Columbia University Press, 2006.
Huyssen, Andreas. "Adorno in Reverse: From Hollywood to Richard Wagner." In *Adorno: A Critical Reader*, Nigel Gibson and Andrew Rubin, eds. Hoboken, NJ: Wiley-Blackwell, 2002, 29–56.
Hyde, Martha. "Neoclassic and Anachronistic Impulses in Twentieth-Century Music." *Music Theory Spectrum* 18 (1996), no. 2: 200–235.
Hyppolite, Jean. *Genesis and Structure of Hegel's "Phenomenology of Spirit."* Trans.

Samuel Cherniak, John Heckman. Evanston, IL: Northwestern University Press, 1979.
Janicaud, Dominique, et al. *Phenomenology and the Theological Turn: The French Debate*. New York: Fordham University Press, 2001.
Janik, Allan, and Stephen Toulmin. *Wittgenstein's Vienna*. New York: Simon and Schuster, 1973.
Jarvis, Simon. *Adorno: A Critical Introduction*. New York: Routledge, 1998.
Jay, Martin. *The Dialectical Imagination: A History of the Frankfurt School and the Institute for Social Research 1923–1950*. Berkeley: University of California, 1973.
———. *Downcast Eyes: The Denigration of Vision in French Thought*. Berkeley: University of California Press, 1994.
———. *Marxism and Totality*. Berkeley: University of California Press, 1986.
Johnson, Julian. *Out of Time: Music and the Making of Modernity*. Oxford, UK: Oxford University Press, 2015.
———. "Review of *Music and the Ineffable*." *Music and Letters* 85 (2004), no. 4: 643–47.
Kaminsky, Peter. "Ravel's Late Music and the Problem of 'Polytonality.'" *Music Theory Spectrum* 26 (2004), no. 2: 237–64.
Kane, Brian. "Excavating Lewin's 'Phenomenology.'" *Music Theory Spectrum* 33 (2011), no. 1: 27–36.
———. *Sound Unseen: Acousmatic Sound in Theory and Practice*. Oxford, UK: Oxford University Press, 2014.
Karnes, Kevin. *Music, Criticism, and the Challenge of History: Shaping Modern Musical Thought in Late Nineteenth-Century Vienna*. Oxford, UK: Oxford University Press, 2008.
Katz, Mark. *Capturing Sound: How Technology Has Changed Music*. Berkeley: University of California Press, 2004.
Kaufman, Eleanor. *Deleuze: The Dark Precursor: Dialectic, Structure, Being*. Baltimore: Johns Hopkins University Press, 2012.
Kerslake, Christian. "The Vertigo of Philosophy: Deleuze and the Problem of Immanence." In *Radical Philosophy* 113 (2002): 10–23.
Kittler, Friedrich A. *Discourse Networks 1800/1900*. Trans. Michael Metteer and Chris Cullens. Stanford, CA: Stanford University Press, 1996.
———. *Gramophone, Film, Typewriter*. Trans. Geoffrey Winthrop-Young. Stanford, CA: Stanford University Press, 1999.
———. "Music als Medium." In *Wahrnehmung Und Geschichte: Markierungen Zur Aisthesis Materialis*, ed. Bernhard Dotzler and Ernst Martin Müller. Berlin: Akademie Verlag, 1995.
Kojève, Alexandre. *Introduction to the Reading of Hegel*. Trans. James H. Nichols. Ed. Raymond Queneau and Allan Bloom. Ithaca, NY: Cornell University Press, 1980.
Korstvedt, Benjamin. *Listening for Utopia in Ernst Bloch's Musical Philosophy*. Cambridge: Cambridge University Press, 2010.
Kosík, Karel. *Dialectics of the Concrete: A Study of Problem of Man and World*.

Trans. Karel Kovanda and James Schmidt. Dordrecht, Netherlands: D. Riedel, 1976.
Kutschke, Beate. "Music and Other Sign Systems," *Music Theory Online* 20 (2014), no. 4.
Kramer, Lawrence. *Expression and Truth: On the Music of Knowledge.* Berkeley: University of California Press, 2012.
———. *The Thought of Music.* Berkeley: University of California Press, 2016.
Lacoue-Labarthe, Phillipe. *Musica Ficta: Figures of Wagner.* Trans. Felicia McCarren. Stanford, CA: Stanford University Press, 1991.
Langer, Susanne. *Philosophy in a New Key: A Study in the Symbolism of Reason, Rite, and Art.* Cambridge, MA: Harvard University Press, 1942.
Latham, Alison. *The Oxford Companion to Music.* Oxford: Oxford University Press, 2011.
Lee, Sherry. "A Minstrel in a World without Minstrels: Adorno and the Case of Schreker." *Journal of the American Musicological Society* 58 (2005), no. 3: 637–94.
Leppert, Richard. *Aesthetic Technologies of Modernity, Subjectivity and Nature: Opera, Orchestra, Phonograph, Film.* Berkeley: University of California Press, 2015.
———. "Music 'Pushed to the Edge of Existence' (Adorno, Listening, and the Question of Hope)." *Cultural Critique* 60 (2005): 92–103.
Levinson, Jerrold. *Musical Concerns: Essays in the Philosophy of Music.* Oxford, UK: Oxford University Press, 2015.
———. "Musical Thinking." *Journal of Music and Meaning* 1 (2003), no. 2.
Lewin, David. "Behind the Beyond: A Response to Edward T. Cone." *Perspectives of New Music* 7 (1969): 59–69.
———. "Music Theory, Phenomenology, and Modes of Perception." *Music Perception* 3 (1986), no. 4: 327–92.
———. *Studies in Music with Text.* Oxford: Oxford University Press, 2006.
Liddell, Henry, and George Robert Scott, *A Greek-English Lexicon.* Oxford, UK: Oxford University Press, 1940.
Lippman, Edward A. *History of Western Musical Aesthetics.* Lincoln: University of Nebraska Press, 1992.
Looney, Aaron T. *Vladimir Jankélévitch: The Time of Forgiveness.* New York: Fordham University Press, 2015.
Lovejoy, Arthur O. *The Great Chain of Being.* Cambridge, MA: Harvard University Press, 1936.
Macherey, Pierre. *Hegel or Spinoza.* Trans. Susan M. Ruddick. Minneapolis: University of Minnesota Press, 2011.
Magee, Brian. *The Tristan Chord: Wagner and Philosophy.* New York: Macmillan, 2002.
Maas, Sander van, ed. *Thresholds of Listening: Sound, Technics, Space.* New York: Fordham University Press, 2015.
Mailman, Joshua Banks. "Schoenberg's Chordal Experimentalism Revealed through Representational Hierarchy Association (RHA), Contour Motives, and Binary State Switching." *Music Theory Spectrum* 37 (2015), no. 2: 224–52.

Mathew, Nicholas. "Reviews: Music and the Politics of Negation." *Journal of the American Musicological Society* 67 (2014), no. 3: 828–33.
Messing, Scott. *Neoclassicism in Music from the Genesis of the Concept through the Schoenberg/Stravinsky Polemic.* Rochester, NY: University of Rochester Press, 1996.
Matthesen, Thomas. *Apollo's Lyre: Greek Music and Music Theory in Antiquity and the Middle Ages.* Lincoln: University of Nebraska Press, 1999.
———. "Ethos and Harmonic in Ancient Greek Music Theory." *Journal of Musicology* 3 (1984): 264–79.
McClary, Susan. *Conventional Wisdom: The Content of Musical Form.* Berkeley: University of California Press, 2001.
McGuinness, Brian. *Wittgenstein: A Life.* Berkeley: University of California Press, 1988.
Monk, Ray. *Ludwig Wittgenstein: The Duty of Genius.* New York: Random House, 2012.
Moreno, Jairo. *Musical Representations, Subjects, Objects: The Construction of Musical Thought in Zarlino, Descartes, Rameau, and Weber.* Bloomington: Indiana University Press, 2004.
Moshaver, Maryam. "*Telos* and Temporality: Phenomenology and the Experience of Time in Lewin's Study of Perception," *Journal of the American Musicological Society* 65 (2012), no. 1: 179–214.
Moten, Fred. *In the Break: The Aesthetics of the Black Radical Tradition.* Minneapolis: University of Minnesota Press, 2003.
Moyn, Samuel. *Origins of the Other: Emmanuel Levinas between Revelation and Ethics.* Ithaca, NY: Cornell University Press, 2005.
Mugglestone, Erica. "Guido Adler's 'The Scope, Method, and Aim of Musicology' (1885)." *Yearbook for Traditional Music* 13 (1981): 1–21.
Muñoz, José Estseban. *Cruising Utopia: The Then and There of Queer Futurity.* New York: NYU Press, 2009.
Murray, Penelope, and Peter Wilson, eds., *Music and the Muses: The Culture of 'Mousike' in the Classical Athenian City.* Oxford, UK: Oxford University Press, 2004.
Neubauer, John. *The Emancipation of Music from Language: Departure from Mimesis in Eighteenth-Century Aesthetics.* New Haven: Yale University Press, 1985.
Nichols, Roger, and Richard Langham Smith, eds. *Debussy's Pelléas et Mélisande: Cambridge Opera Handbooks.* Cambridge: Cambridge University Press, 1989.
Nicholsen, Shierry Weber. *Exact Imagination, Late Work, On Adorno's Aesthetics.* Cambridge, MA: MIT Press, 1999.
Norris, Christopher. "Utopian Deconstruction: Ernst Bloch, Paul de Man and the Politics of Music." In *Music and the Politics of Culture,* ed. Christopher Norris, 305–47. London: Norris & Wishart. New York: St. Martin's Press, 1989.
Otto, Frauke. *Robert Schumann als Jean Paul Leser.* Frankfurt am Main: Haag & Herchen, 1984.
Paddison, Max. *Adorno, Modernism, and Mass Culture: Essays in Critical Theory and Music.* London: Kahn and Averill, 2004.

———. *Adorno's Aesthetics of Music*. Cambridge: Cambridge University Press, 1997.
———. "Music as Ideal: the Aesthetics of Autonomy." In *Cambridge Companion to Nineteenth Century Music*, ed. Jim Samson, 318–42. Cambridge: Cambridge University Press, 2001.
Palisca, Claude. *Hucbald, Guido, and John on Music*. New Haven: Yale University Press, 1978.
Parret, Herman. "Kant on Music and the Hierarchy of the Arts." *Journal of Aesthetics and Art Criticism* 56 (1998), no. 3: 251–64.
Peden, Knox. *Spinoza Contra Phenomenology: French Rationlism from Cavaillès to Deleuze*. Stanford, CA: Stanford University Press, 2014.
Pederson, Sanna. "Beethoven and Freedom: Historicizing the Political Connection." *Beethoven Forum* 12 (2005), no. 1: 1–12.
———. "Defining the Term 'Absolute Music' Historically." *Music and Letters* 90 (2009), no. 2: 240–62.
Perry, Beate. *Schumann's Dicterliebe and Early Romantic Poetics: Fragmentation of Desire*. Cambridge: Cambridge University Press, 2003.
Peters, Gary. *The Philosophy of Improvisation*. Chicago: University of Chicago Press, 2009.
Piekut, Benjamin. "Actor Networks in Music History: Clarifications and Critiques." *Twentieth Century Music* 11 (2014), no. 2: 191–215.
Prieto, Eric. *Listening In: Music, Mind, and the Modernist Narrative*. Lincoln: University of Nebraska Press, 2002.
Puri, Michael. "Dandy, Interrupted: Sublimation, Repression, and Self-Portraiture in Maurice Ravel's *Daphnis et Chloé* (1909–1912)" in *Journal of the American Musicological Society* 60 (2007), no. 2: 317–72.
———. "Review Essay: Hoeckner, Berthold: *Programming the Absolute: Nineteenth-Century German Music and the Hermeneutics of the Moment. Journal of the American Musicological Society* 59 (2006), no. 2: 488–501.
Rahn, John. "*Mille Plateaux*, You Tarzan: A Musicology of (an Anthropology of *A Thousand Plateaus*)." *Perspectives of New Music* 46 (2008), no. 2: 59–92.
Rosen, Charles. *Beethoven Piano Sonatas: A Short Companion, Vol. 1*. New Haven: Yale University Press, 2002.
Rancière, Jacques. *Aisthesis*. Trans. Zakir Paul. London: Verson, 2013.
———. *The Politics of Aesthetics*. Trans. Gabriel Rockhill. New York: Continuum, 2006.
Rehding, Alexander. *Hugo Riemann and the Birth of Modern Musical Thought*. Cambridge: Cambridge University Press, 2003.
———. "Wax Cylinder Revolutions," *Musical Quarterly*, 88 (2005), no. 1: 123–60.
Rehding, Alexander, and Suzannah Clark, eds. *Music and Natural Order*. Cambridge, UK: Cambridge University Press, 2001.
Richter, Gerhard, ed. *Language without Soil: Adorno and Late Philosophical Modernity*. New York: Fordham University Press, 2010.

Rings, Steven. "*Mystères limpides*: Time and Transformation in Debussy's *Des pas sur la neige*." *19th-Century Music* 32 (2008), no. 2: 178–208.

Rothfarb, Lee. August Halm: A Critical and *Creative Life in Music*. Rochester, NY: University of Rochester Press, 2009.

Scherzinger, Martin. "Music, Corporate Power, and Unending War." *Cultural Critique* 60 (2005): 23–67.

Scherzinger, Martin, ed. *Music in Contemporary Philosophy*. New York: Routledge, 2015.

———. "Musical Modernism in the Thought of 'Mille Plateaux' and Its Twofold Politics." *Perspectives of New Music* 46 (2008), no. 2: 130–58.

Schorske, Carl E. *Fin-de-Siécle Vienna*. Cambridge: Cambridge University Press, 1981.

Scruton, Roger *Aesthetics of Music*. Oxford, UK: Clarendon Press, 1999.

———. "Effing the Ineffable," http://www.catholiceducation.org/en/religion-and-philosophy/apologetics/effing-the-ineffable.html, accessed May 25, 2015.

Shaviro, Steven. *Without Criteria: Kant, Whitehead, Deleuze, and Aesthetics*. Cambridge, MA: MIT Press, 2009.

Shawn. Allen. *Arnold Schoenberg's Journey*. Cambridge, MA: Harvard University Press, 2003.

Shehadi, Fadlou. *Philosophies of Music in Medieval Islam*. Leiden, Netherlands: E. J. Brill, 1995.

Siciliano, Michael. "Toggling Cycles, Hexatonic Systems, and Some Analysis of Early Atonal Music." *Music Theory Spectrum* 27 (2005), no. 2: 221–47.

Simms, Bryan. *The Atonal Music of Arnold Schoenberg 1908–1923*. Oxford, UK: Oxford University Press, 2000.

Smith, Colin. *Contemporary French Philosophy: A Study in Norms and Values*. Westport, CT: Greenwood Press, 1964.

Smith, Daniel W. "Mathematics and the Theory of Multiplicities: Badiou and Deleuze Revisited." *Southern Journal of Philosophy* 41 (2003): 411–49.

Sorgner, Stefan Lorenz, Oliver Furbeth, and Susan H. Gillespie, eds. *Music in German Philosophy: An Introduction*. Chicago: University Of Chicago Press, 2011.

Spitzer, Michael. *Metaphor and Musical Thought*. Chicago: University of Chicago Press, 2004.

———. *Music as Philosophy: Adorno and Beethoven's Late Style*. Bloomington: Indiana University Press, 2006.

Stamatellos, Giannis. *Plotinus and the Presocratics: A Philosophical Study of Presocratic Influences on Plotinus' Enneads*. Albany, NY: SUNY Press, 2007.

Steege, Benjamin. *Helmholtz and the Modern Listener*. Cambridge: Cambridge University Press, 2011.

Steinberg, Michael. *Listening To Reason: Culture, Subjectivity, and Nineteenth-Century Music*. Princeton, NJ: Princeton University Press, 2006.

Sterne, Jonathan. *The Audible Past: Cultural Origins of Sound Reproduction*. Durham, NC: Duke University Press, 2003.

Strunk, William Oliver, and Leo Trietler, eds. *Source Readings in Music History*. New York: W. W. Norton, 1998.

Subotnik, Rose Rosengard. "Adorno's Diagnosis of Beethoven's Late Style: Early Symptom of a Fatal Condition. *Journal of the American Musicological Society* 29 (1976): 242–75.

———. *Deconstructive Variations: Music and Reason in Western Society*. Minneapolis: University of Minnesota Press, 1996.

———. *Developing Variations: Style and Ideology in Western Music*. Minneapolis: University of Minnesota Press, 1991.

———. "Why is Adorno's Music Criticism the Way It Is? Some Reflections on Twentieth-Century Criticism of Nineteenth-Century Music." *Musical Newsletter* 7 (1977), no. 4: 3–12.

Szabados, Bela. "Wittgenstein the Musical: Notes towards an Appreciation." *Canadian Aesthetics Journal/Revue canadienne d'esthétique* 10 (2004).

Taruskin, Richard. *The Oxford History of Western Music*. Oxford, UK: Oxford University Press, 2005.

———. "The Poietic Fallacy." *Musical Times* 145 (2004), no. 1886: 7–34.

Tassone, Giuseppe. "The Politics of Metaphysics: Adorno and Bloch on Utopia and Immortality." *The European Legacy* 9 (2004), no. 3: 357–67.

Taylor, Charles. *Hegel*. Cambridge: Cambridge University Press, 1975.

Toews, John Edward. *Hegelianism: The Path toward Dialectical Humanism, 1805–1841*. Cambridge: Cambridge University Press, 1980.

Tomlinson, Gary. *Metaphysical Song: An Essay on Opera*. Princeton, NJ: Princeton University Press, 1999.

———. "Musical Pasts and Postmodern Musicologies: A Response to Lawrence Kramer." *Current Musicology* 53 (1993): 18–24.

Tompson, Peter and Slavoj Žižek, eds. *The Privatization of Hope: Ernst Bloch and the Future of Utopia*. Durham, NC: Duke University Press, 2013.

Tresch, John, and Emily I. Dolan. "Toward a New Organology: Instruments of Music and Science." *Osiris* 28 (2013): 278–98.

Trietler, Leo. *Music and the Historical Imagination*. Cambridge, MA: Harvard University Press, 1990.

Trippett, David. *Wagner's Melodies: Aesthetics and Materialism in German Musical Identity*. Cambridge, UK: Cambridge University Press, 2013.

Udoff, Alan, Ed. *Vladimir Jankélévitch and the Question of Forgiveness*. Lanham, MD: Lexington Books, 2013.

Ullyot, Jonathan. "Adorno's *Comment c'est*." *Comparative Literature* 61 (2009), no. 4: 416–31.

Velema, Floris. "From Technique to Technology: A Reinterpretation of Adorno's Concept of Musical Material." *Soundscapes* 10 (2007).

Wallace, Robert W. *Reconstructing Damon: Music, Wisdom Teaching, and Politics in Perikles' Athens*. Oxford, UK: Oxford University Press, 2015.

Wasser, Audrey. *The Work of Difference: Modernism, Romanticism, and the Production of Literary Form.* New York: Fordham University Press, 2016.
Watkins, Holly. *Metaphors of Depth in German Musical Thought.* Cambridge: Cambridge University Press, 2011.
———. "Schoenberg's Interior Designs." *Journal of the American Musicological Society* 61 (2008), no. 1: 123–206.
Weheliye, Alexander G. *Phonographies: Grooves in Sonic Afro-Modernity.* Durham, NC: Duke University Press, 2005.
West, M. L. *Ancient Greek Music.* Oxford, UK: Oxford University Press, 1992.
Wiskus, Jessica. *The Rhythm of Thought: Art, Literature, and Music after Merleau-Ponty.* Chicago: University of Chicago Press, 2013.
Wurth, Kiene Brillenburg. *Musically Sublime.* New York: Fordham University Press, 2009.
Zangwell, Nick. *Music and Aesthetic Reality: Formalism and the Limits of Description.* New York: Routledge, 2015.
Ziarek, Kryzysztof. "Beyond Critique." In *Adorno and Heidegger*, ed. Iain Macdonald and Krzysztof Ziarek. Stanford, CA: Stanford University Press, 2008.
Žižek, Slavoj. *Organs without Bodies: On Deleuze and Consequences.* New York: Routledge, 2004.
Zöller, Günther. "Schopenhauer and the Self." In *The Cambridge Companion to Schopenhauer,* ed. Christopher Janeway, 18–43. Cambridge: Cambridge University Press, 1999.

INDEX

Abbate, Carolyn, and the "drastic," 15, 168
Abrams, M. H., on music and mimesis, 23
"absolute dissonance" (Adorno), 148
absolute music, 256; Hegel and, 277n77; metaphysical formalism of, 68; "no other music but absolute music" (Bloch), 87; overlap with music's ineffability, 30–31, 33–34, 130–31; and Schopenhauer's metaphysics, 268n23
abyss: of Romantic depth, 54; Schopenhauer's metaphysics as a language of the, 59; of Schopenhauer's will, 50; as what music "says" (Adorno), 129
actor-network theory, 253
Adler, Guido, 74–75, 83, 111, 133, 158
Adorno, Theodor W.: on the absolute, 34; critical views on Heidegger, 281n17; "demythologized prayer," 131, 194, 199, 202, 254; as "enemy," 13; repetition for, 243–44; rhythm for, 243–44; *Schriftcharakter*, 155, 166, 191; *Wahrheitsgehalt*, 108, 119, 192, 229, 241; "The whole is the false," 119
affective coextension, connective theory of (Deleuze and Guattari), 242
affective force, of sound/music, 205–6, 213–14, 216–18

affective taxonomy, 1
affect theory, 252
Affektenlehre, 1, 23, 39, 43, 46, 128, 189
amateurism: analyst, 286n97; composer (Cavell), 164; philosopher (Boulez), 262n16; pianist, 8–9, 46, 66, 160–61, 165–66, 236
Aquinas, Thomas, 21
architecture: in Bloch, 86, 92; the "cloister," 93; Egyptian architecture that preserves the dead, 91; Loos's push for function in, 143
Aristotle, 3–4, 20–21, 50, 111
ars nova, 95
Artaud, Antonin, 212
artworks: and the absolute (Adorno), 271n59; *Geist* in, 116; for Hegel, 241; imitating "an expression that would not be interpolated human intention" (Adorno), 120; as like a complete organism (Schoenberg), 142; as mimetic of the way things are, 285n80; as pure expression, 118; as pure presence (a "sensation in itself"), 28, 61, 206; repetition's place in (Deleuze), 296n49; similarity of life and, 198; society's relationship to, 133; without purpose, 247; yet to come, 214, 229, 234, 245

326 Index

atonality: onset of (Adorno), 110; of Schoenberg, 27, 143–44, 147–48, 231; of Webern, 118
Attali, Jacques, 31–32, 255
Augustine of Hippo, Saint: on jubilation (*jubilum*), 22–23; on secular learning, 296n42
automatism, in Wagner's music (Bloch), 54

Bach, J. S., 24, 93, 96, 99, 124, 129, 134, 217
Bachelard, Gaston: critique of Bergsonism, 28, 168, 264n37; and the term "dialectics," 18
Bacon, Francis, 210, 216, 234
Badiou, Alain, 173, 219, 238, 253
Barthes, Roland, 8, 201, 253–54; idealizing the intimacy of domestic music-making, 232; as influence on Jacques Attali's *Noise*, 31; on listening, 165–66; on music's usefulness to philosophical practice, 200; on Schumann, 232
Bartók, Béla, 189, 231
Beethoven, Ludwig van, 8, 15, 93; "Beethovenian blaze" (Bloch), 105; diminished seventh chord in, 134; expressive rage and fury of, 136; *Fidelio*, 236; fugato for (Bloch), 145; Hegel's (lack of) interest in, 277n77; "meta-musical" monuments by, 184; moral will of Beethoven's music, 54; resistance of the late style of (Adorno), 135; Schopenhauer's knowledge of, 46; Sonata no. 14 in C-sharp minor, "Quasi una fantasia," 134–36; Symphony no. 3, "Eroica," 99–103; Symphony no. 5, 24, 73
befuddlement: of Barthes, 165; from feelings, 25; as illumination, 4; of intellectuals, 249–50, 257; methodological (for Adorno), 158; of music's ontology, 252, 257; of Socrates, 2; of Wittgenstein, 164
Bekker, Paul, 125
Benjamin, Walter, 130
Berg, Alban, 102, 124, 160, 231
Bergson, Henri, 7, 17–18, 20, 28, 58, 195; *durée*, 168, 172–73, 178, 194, 207, 209, 265n37; as influence on Jankélévitch, 290n10; as influence on Lévinas, 291n26; "qualitative multiplicity," 171–74, 194
Berio, Luciano, 231
Berlioz, Hector, 93, 231
biosemiotics, 226, 228, 296n48
Bizet, Georges, 93, 231
blankness: of Bloch's tone, 245; of music, 17, 30, 32, 131, 201, 255–56; of musical form, 247; of the question "Why?," 238
Blasius, Leslie, 124–25
Bloch, Ernst: on the adagio, 103–4; conception of *Ton*/tone, 26, 63–106; conception of utopia, 53, 64–70, 84–93, 98–105, 107–14; critiqued by Adorno, 109–10; disagreements with Schopenhauer, 272n12; event-forms (*Ereignisformen*), 26, 91–98, 104, 106, 111, 136, 145, 229; *Geist*, 49, 81–84, 91–92, 96, 109; "Gothic line," 92–95, 98; "innermost heaven of fixed stars," 85, 95–96; "magic rattle," 81–84, 111–12, 117, 156; on modern art, 92; as utopia's rehabilitator, 105
body: effect of words on the (Deleuze), 212; and language, 211, 295n18; as the locus of form's organizations (Foucault), 249; relationship between the soul and the (Plato), 220; Schopenhauer on the experience of one's own, 35–36, 65
Boethius, *musica mundana*, 21, 219, 221
Bonds, Mark Evan, 23, 274n24
Born, Georgina, 14
Boulez, Pierre, 231; associations with Deleuze, 238, 262n16; attachment to the literate tradition, 263n22; in Deleuze and Guattari's writing, 11, 238, 240, 297n53
bowerbird, "display court" of the, 225–26, 233–34, 296n49
Brendel, Franz, 123
Bruckner, Anton, 93, 126

Cage, John, prepared piano, 230

Carroll, Lewis, 212
Cavell, Stanley, 164
Caverero, Adriana, as influence on field of sound studies, 15
Chabrier, Emmanuel, 231
chance, of the dice throw (Deleuze), 210, 213
Christensen, Thomas, 113
Chua, Daniel, 33
Cicero, 21
cinema. *See* film
Clément, Catherine, 31, 200–201
Coleman, Ornette, on repetition, 249
composer: as exemplary subject (Bloch), 95–97, 105, 114, 201; labor of (in the properly resistant musical work), 136; as "magnetic somnambulist" (Schopenhauer), 37; as merely an empirical occasion for the instance of a "minor literature" (Deleuze and Guattari), 217; as never an unflagging genius (Jankélévitch), 192
composition: Attali's prized practice of, 32; clichés in rule-based, 126; as a conversation with the material (Jankélévitch), 200; developed independently of their psychological and social functions into the realm of pure form, 91; ethical, 10, 203, 234, 240, 246; event-forms (*Ereignisformen*), 26, 91–98, 104, 106, 111, 136, 145, 229; modern, 117–18; the "paradigm of all true composition" (Adorno), 123–24; as recollection and discovery (Adorno), 114; resistant, 126–27, 133, 136–37, 158
confidence: Schopenhauer's, 48; Wittgenstein's, 161
continuo, 124
cosmos: cosmic harmony, 221–23; cosmic noise, 214; cosmic proportion(s), 86, 296n44; cosmic pulse of syncopation, 242; cosmic rhythm(s), 29, 209–11, 214, 234, 247; cosmic *ritournelle*, 215, 229–30, 232; cosmic structure(s), 205, 219; cosmic universality, 220

counterpoint: in Deleuze and Guattari (via Uexküll), 228, 237–40; imitative, 98; linear, 103, 137; logic vs., 97; in Schoenberg, 143–44; and the tone, 112
culture industry, 107, 126, 238, 251
Currie, James, 14–15, 201
cybernetics, 217–19, 226, 253, 297nn51–52

Dahlhaus, Carl, 268n23
Debussy, Claude, 231; *La mer*, 189; *Pelléas et Mélisande*, 11, 195–96
"deixsis," 292n43
Deleuze, Gilles: anti-Platonism of, 223–24; "crack" of, 213; dynamism of rhythm, 207–9; repetition, 208–15, 244–45, 249, 296n49; on sound in film, 235
Deleuze, Gilles, and Félix Guattari: "a-signifying semiotics," 61, 206, 218–19; opposition to any kind of *Versprachlichung*, 228; *la ritournelle*, 29, 205–7, 210, 214–17, 224–36, 240–41; "sensation in itself," 28, 202, 206, 241; (re-)territorialization, 216, 225, 229, 244–45; "time-image," 235–36, 294n1
Denning, Michael, 11
Derrida, Jacques: *archi-écriture*, 155; and Hegel (per Gutting), 254; and the linguistic turn, 18; notion of writing, 288n142
diagōgō, 20
dialectics, 17–20; contrapuntal dialectic (Deleuze and Guattari), 202, 208–9, 213, 224, 241; dialectical solutions to the paradox of the ineffable, 49–62; of the ineffable, 22–23, 31, 91; as "intransigence towards all reification" (Adorno), 122; as linked to the *Tendenz des Materials* (Adorno), 122–27; of loneliness (Schoenberg), 146; and music history, 95–98; "the pseudomorphosis of dialectics" (Adorno), 109; and the tone (Bloch), 73–74, 90, 94; unwoven dialectic (Jankélévitch), 28, 49–50, 59, 182–84, 190–91, 199–203, 208, 246–47

diminished seventh chord, 133–35; as the death of tonality, 231
divine: communion with the, 292n30; divine cause, 21; "divine creation" (Adorno), 120, 131, 192; divine futures, 156; divine harmony, 221; divine inconsistency (Jankélévitch), 193, 202, 254; divine language, 130; the "Divine Monochord," 220–22, 296n44; "divine name," 117, 194, 238; divine sense, 214; divine substance (thing-in-itself), 169, 257; music as an exemplary vehicle of the, 22
Dolan, Emily, 14
Dvořák, Antonín, 185–86

Eikhenbaum, Boris, 27
Eliot, T. S., 27, 132
Engelmann, Paul, 163
equal temperament, 76, 124
ethics, 10–11; Adorno's, 119, 245; Bergson's, 219; Bloch's, 245; Deleuze and Guattari's, 229–32, 245, 249; Jankélévitch's, 182–83, 191, 198, 242; modernist, 246; of modern music, 248; of musical composition, 246; non-normative, 257; of the twelve-tone method, 251; of the vernacular, 252; of "Warum?," 238; without criteria, 249
ethos doctrine, 1, 3, 6, 20, 111
exactitude: of Adorno's thinking, 105, 110, 245; "exact imagination" (Nicholsen), 155; of music, 37, 221, 245
expression: artworks' pure, 118; creaturely, 225; inexpressive, 184; instrumental, 5; musical, 49, 90, 233, 248; reverse, 187; sexual, 215

Feyder, Vera, 177
film: emotions in, 115; film music, 31, 134, 143, 145; film sound, 235; as having a privileged relationship to the machinery of lived time, 204; Mahler's epic sense of scale as cinematic, 150; as a mode of thought and being, 253; "time-image," 235–36, 294n1

Fludd, Robert, 221–23
forgiveness, 180, 192
Forkel, Johann Nikolaus, on music's ineffability, 24
formalism: for Abbate, 15; absolute music's metaphysical, 68; of Adorno, 12, 115–16, 151, 154, 168, 241, 243; blank formalism, 131; for Bloch, 88; for Deleuze and Guattari, 231, 241; entwinement with historicism and praxis, 126; of Forte, 286n97; of Hanslick, 75; for Hegel, 87, 277n77; of the ineffable (Adorno), 154; of Kant, 27; of the modern arts, 132; of music, 39, 251; in the paradox of the vernacular, 148; pathology of (Mann), 97; for Schoenberg, 142, 144–45; in the *Tendenz des Materials*, 136; vernacular formalism, 151; as a way of skirting the problems of the ineffable, 256
Foucault, Michel: on the body, 249; and Hegel (per Gutting), 254
Frege, Gottlob, 255
Freud, Sigmund, 7, 209; death drive, 216
fugato, 98–102, 145
fugue, 98–99, 102–3

Geist. See Hegel, G. W. F.
genius, 38, 96–98, 192, 201
Gershwin, George, 189
gods: challenging the power of, 5; a demiurge's mingling and re-differentiating the divisible and the indivisible, 220; gods of poetics, 87; Isis (Egyptian goddess), 99; pagan gods vs. the God of Abraham, 193–94; singing in jubilation for, 22; the voice of, 192, 205; the word of, 130
grace, 182, 190–93, 198
Greenberg, Clement: on abstraction across the arts, 16; on music, 19, 27
Guattari, Félix, 214–19. *See also* Deleuze, Gilles, and Félix Guattari
Guido of Arezzo, 123–25
Gumbrecht, Hans Ulrich, on gnostic meaning and drastic presence, 15

Gutting, Gary, 254

Halm, August, 76, 94, 103
Hanslick, Eduard, 88: as axiomatic for the Adorno's *Tendenz des Materials*, 125; conception of "tonally moving forms," 27, 68–69, 73–75; distinction between tone and sound, 274n24; and musical autonomy, 133; negative associations with music, 33; and Pythagorean speculations, 38; and the term "absolute music," 30
harmoniai (modes), banishment of, 1–2, 20
hearing and sight, hierarchy of, 67, 79–80, 86, 89
Hegel, G. W. F.: and absolute music, 277n77; art as "sensuous appearance of the Idea," 57, 147, 186, 202, 241; *Dasein*, 113; dialectics, 17–18, 168; double negation, 77–80, 90–91, 179, 233; *Geist*, 49, 57, 69, 81–84; on harmony and number, 275n38; on the ineffability of sense, 18; on *Klang*, 77–78, 133, 276n43, 276n47; on the tone, 69, 79–81, 84–91; "The true is the whole," 119; on the voice, 276n52, 277n53
Heidegger, Martin: Adorno's critique of, 281n17; "cult of death," 108; *Ereignis*, 212; as influence on field of sound studies, 15
Heine, Heinrich, 161–63
Helmholtz, Hermann von, 74, 274n29, 275n30
Hepokoski, James, on the ineffable and silence, 15
Heraclitus of Ephesus: the flowing river whose water is never the same at two different points, 172; on thunderbolts, 295n28
Herder, Johann Gottfried, on music's ineffability, 23–25
high art: vs. low art in Aristotle, 20; Mahler's music as, 149
historicism: for Abbate, 15; for Adorno, 156, 202, 232, 256; for Bloch, 202, 232; entwinement with formalism and praxis, 126; French historicism and Germanic death of tonality, 231; for Jankélévitch, 202, 219
Hjelmslev, Louis, 218
Hoeckner, Berthold, 33
Hoffmann, E. T. A., 6, 23–24, 31, 40, 68–69, 73–74, 217
Hofmann, Hans, 27
Hohendahl, Peter Uwe, 150
Hume, David, 209
humor, 188
Hyppolite, Jean, 17–18, 253–54; and Jankélévitch, 290n5

ignorance, pleas of, in Plato and Aristotle, 2, 4, 23
Ikhwan Al-Safa, 4, 10, 30, 48, 91, 199, 221, 261n9
immanent critique, 12, 17, 26, 27, 118–22, 126, 136–46, 153–58, 171, 245. *See also* transcendent critique
immediate copy. *See* paradox of the immediate/unmediated copy
immortality: desire for (Adorno), 108; listeners' expectation for, 192
Impressionism, 189
improvisation: for Attali, 32; for Cavell, 164; for Deleuze and Guattari, 11, 215, 241; for Jankélévitch, 57–58, 177–78, 181
infallibility, of music, 35, 39, 41, 50, 216
intention: in Adorno, 15, 118, 120, 129–31, 144, 168; allocution, 187; of an autonomous subject, 193; in Bloch's conception of the musical tone, 86, 94–95, 98, 109; and chordal impact, 128; in forgiveness (Jankélévitch), 180; in listening (Barthes), 165; in Mahler's music (Adorno), 148, 150; musical material as servant of, 200; nonintentional systems of the body, 36. *See also* will
Isis (Egyptian goddess), 99

Janáček, Leoš, 186
Janequin, Clément, 231

Jankélévitch, Vladimir: as "anti-Adorno" (Taruskin), 13; Bergson as mentor to, 290n10; *charme*, 182–84, 189–92, 199–202, 216; critical views on Schopenhauer, 271n61; "divine inconsistency," 193, 202, 254; and Hyppolite, 290n5; *La mort*, 175–76; listening as a practice, 181, 192–93; metaphysical speculations of, 193–99; music's "speculative multiplicity," 28, 165–68, 184, 190–91
jazz: for Adorno, 115, 145; free jazz (in Attali), 32
Judiasm, Mahler's and Schoenberg's, 146

Kafka, Franz, 150, 234
Kandinsky, Wassily, 27, 132, 142
Kant, Immanuel: *Critique of Pure Reason*, 169–70; on knowledge, 35, 169–70; "purposiveness without purpose," 27; on time, 172; and the "transcendental," 169–72, 236. *See also* thing-in-itself
Kierkegaard, Søren, 7, 209; and self-reflection, 87
kitsch: the deadening repetition of, 46; of the dominant seventh chord, 136; indignation over, 290n6; kitschy referentiality in *Herzgewächse*, 143–44; in Mahler, 147, 149, 154
Kittler, Friedrich, on the phonograph, 11, 156
Kivy, Peter, 116
Klang, 77–78, 133, 276n43, 276n47
Klee, Paul, 29, 231–32, 239, 240
knowledge: Enlightenment knowledge linked with the powers of technology (Adorno), 119; of the essence of logic leading to knowledge of music's essence (Wittgenstein), 161; as a form of recollection (Plato), 114; and instinct, 36; limits of, 178, 180; as mediated by the form of the concept (Kant), 35; musical objects as (Adorno), 136; production of (Kant), 169–70; value of nonconceptual and intuitive (Schopenhauer), 35

Kojève, Alexandre, 17, 167
Kraus, Karl, 143
Kristeva, Julia, 253
Kröger, Horst, 107
Kurth, Ernst, 76, 94, 281n20

Labor, Josef, 164
Lacan, Jacques, 212, 217, 219, 254, 295n18
Langer, Susanne, 27
language: acquisition of, 212–13; as fully real structuring of life (Deleuze), 212; as part of the same substance as the body (Lacan), 212, 295n18
Lassus, Orlando de, 96–97
Latour, Bruno, 253
law: Adorno's Apollonian, 166; "disintegration of the Law which prescribes direct, unique listening" (Barthes), 165; of exchange value, 107, 119; music as a meditation of law against the chilling hyperchaos of the universe (Jankélévitch), 198; music's lack of natural, 76, 86, 122, 243
Lefebvre, Henri, 32
Lévinas, Emmanuel, 175–77, 291n26
Lewin, David, 171, 182
Liège, Jacques de, 95
linguistic turn, 130, 155, 170, 243, 252–55, 295n18
Liszt, Franz: *Faust Symphony*, 195; improvisational compositional style of, 10, 177; *lassu/friss* structure, 186
literature: Adorno's writing on, 150, 286n97; a "minor literature" (Deleuze and Guattari), 217, 233, 238
logocentrism, 254
longing: affective, 25; in film (Adorno), 115; in instrumental music (Hoffmann), 24; object of art's, 123; in utopia (Bloch), 108; vernacular, 149
Loos, Adolf, 143, 287n102
Lorenz, Konrad, 225
low art, vs. high art in Aristotle, 20
Lukaçs, György, 150

Luther, Martin, 99

madness: music's ability to cause, 6, 266n58; music's inability to cause, 55–56; rhythm's ability to cause, 3; of Schumann, 230, 233; the sublime's link to, 266n58; *Wahrheitsgehalt*'s grounding in, 241
Maeterlinck, Maurice, 137–39
Mahler, Gustav, 93; Adorno's study of, 168; compositions as event-forms (Bloch), 26; *Das Lied von der Erde*, 104, 154, 231; reflected cry and laughter in (Adorno), 56; a "self-approaching" in (Bloch), 103–4; the "smell" of, 150–51; Symphony no. 1, 147; Symphony no. 9, 153; vernacular in, 10, 12, 145–59; Wittgenstein's distaste for, 160
Mallarmé, Stéphane, 132, 209–10
Mann, Thomas, 97
Marcel, Gabriel, 31
Marx, Karl, 7, 53, 55, 64, 86, 118, 229, 270n55
material turn, 252
Mathew, Nicholas, 15
McClary, Susan, 33
mechanical reproduction: as emancipatory, 156; as foreclosing positive access to music's utopian potentiality, 114; as a form of mediation, 11
Meillassoux, Quentin, 219
melancholy: in *Herzgewächse*, 137–39; of temporality, 184
melos doctrine, 5, 94, 273n17
memory: and Bergson's conception of spirit, 171; involuntary, Proustian recollections brought about by music, 188; knowledge as a form of recollection, 114; musical notation and, 112; remembrance, 123
Merleau-Ponty, Maurice, as influence on field of sound studies, 15
Messiaen, Olivier, 189, 231
Metallica, as "enforced" mode, 1
metaphor: Schopenhauer's metaphysics of music's dependence on, 58; Uexküll's use of musical, 227, 297n50

metaphysics: of the gestalt, 41; of music (Schopenhauer), 45–48, 55, 58–59, 224, 268n23, 269n47, 271n61, 271n64; of number, 21, 23, 220, 265n43, 296n42; Platonic, 53; Pythagorean, 37, 44–46, 221, 241–42, 265n43; of rhythm (Deleuze), 32, 50, 60–61, 207, 209, 218–19; Romantic, 32; of sound, 233; of subjective inwardness embodied by tones (Hegel), 84; transcendent, 88; of unity (Schenker), 76
mimesis: ancient (Adorno), 280n12; attempt to overcome a conventional conception of (Schopenhauer, Deleuze, and Guattari), 224; ethical and intellectual potential of, 21; between modern formalisms (Adorno), 132–23; between musical elements and social effects, 1–3, 111–12; between music and language, 127–36, 233, 284n64; negative, 120; as the prespiritual (in art), 116; of Schopenhauer, 39, 41, 43; as threat of a dangerous multiplicity (Plato), 61
modernism: Adorno on, 116–17; celebration of through caricature, 13; ethics of, 10, 19, 32, 158, 203, 217; fractured modernism, 127; high modernism, 11, 240; music's exceptionalism and, 17; Pythagorean metaphysics in, 265n43; resistant modernism, 117
monochord, 220–22, 296n44
More, Thomas, 107
Mörike, Eduard, 163
Mosolov, Alexander, 189
motif: in Debussy's *Pelleas et Melisande*, 195; in Deleuze and Guattari (via Uexküll), 228; Jankélévitchian leitmotif, 179; as the logos of music's ideal mediation (Schenker), 75, 275n34; Mahler's manipulation of, 148; in the *ritournelle*, 225; in Schumann's "Warum?," 237; Wagnerian leitmotif, 148, 238
Mozart, Wolfgang Amadeus, 15, 217, 231; in Bloch's conception of tone, 93, 96,

Mozart, Wolfgang Amadeus, (*continued*) 99–100; compositions as event-forms, 26; diminished seventh chord in, 134; for the education of children, 1; fugato for, 102, 145; *ritournelle* in, 231; Schopenhauer's knowledge of, 46; Wittgenstein's taste for, 160, 163

multiplicity: Being as a creative (Deleuze), 60; dangerous (mimesis), 61; of Jankélévitch's ethical modernism, 10–11; of languages, 130; polyphonic, 208; productive and inconsistent, 31; qualitative (Bergson), 171–74, 194; speculative, 168, 184, 190–91; of vernacular idioms in Mahler's music, 12, 153

music: as an art form that exemplifies structure rather than representation (Schopenhauer, Deleuze, and Guattari), 224; as an "a-signifying semiotics" (Deleuze and Guattari), 61, 206, 218–19, 241; as aspiring to disclose the ineffable (Bloch), 67; autonomous music as secretly critical of the society it reflects, 15; "as condemning death itself to death" (Hoffmann), 295n34; as the daughter of time (Jankélévitch), 181; as a dialectical riddle (Adorno), 129; as door to utopia (Adorno and Bloch), 110; as an ephemeral Pythagoreanism of the cosmos (Jankélévitch), 198; as exceptional, 21, 24–25, 27, 35, 38–41, 48–49, 57–58, 61, 66, 68, 105, 130, 154, 167, 221, 233, 242, 244, 255–56, 268n31; as (not) exceptional, 221; as (quietly) exceptional, 228, 255–56; as harboring an exclusive or privileged link to the lived movements of time (Jankélévitch), 204; as an immediate copy (Schopenhauer), 25–26, 29, 30, 36, 40, 51–55, 61–62, 68–69, 77, 86, 88–90, 106, 128, 152, 166, 181, 190, 202, 218–19, 224, 228, 238, 254; as an infinitely graded ineffability beyond the limits of a language of emotions (Forkel), 24; as integrated with visual and textual media (Deleuze), 205; as an "intensive root" of utopia (Bloch), 88; as a linkage between sonic sensation and abstract form (Greenberg), 19; as the machinic art form par excellence (Guattari), 218; as a magnet for philosophical conundrums, 10; naïve escapist music as an ecstatic mimesis of the emotional power of cinema, the flux of sexual excitement, and the powers of the commodity form (Adorno), 115; as a negation of the "peaceful separatedness" of visual arts in the form of a sonic flux that results in an oscillating vibration of a musical tone (Hegel), 79; as saying everything but defining nothing (Bloch), 104; as a silent respite from the noise of the cosmos, 197–98; slipperiness of, 15; as transcendent art of feeling, 6; as utopian (Adorno), 136; as like the voice of God (Jankélévitch), 192; as wallpaper (Jankélévitch), 30; as weapon, 5. *See also* absolute music

Nagel, Thomas, 226, 297n50

Nancy, Jean-Luc, as influence on field of sound studies, 15

negation: determinate negation, 108, 157; double negation (Hegel), 77–80, 90, 179; as essential to the processes of life (Bachelard), 168; historical negation of externalized matter mediated by *Geist* (Hegel and Bloch), 84; of ideology (Adorno), 200; of one medium to another (Hegel), 233; "the politics of negation" (Currie), 15; silence as a perpetually incomplete negation, 199; utopian negation, 119; of *Versprachlichung* in music (Jankélévitch and Adorno), 204

New German School, 123, 217

Nicholsen, Shierry Weber, 145, 155

Nicholson, Oliver, on Saint Augustine's use of the word *jubilum*, 22

Nietzsche, Friedrich, 7, 209; via Deleuze

Index   333

contra Hegel, 17–18, 214; as inspiration for Deleuze and Guattari's *ritournelle*, 205; as inspiration for Deleuze's anti-Platonism, 223; on lyric poetry, 269nn47–48; and music, 244, 246, 269n48, 270n49; realm of the Apollonian, 57, 208; and repetition, 209–10; in response to Schopenhauer, 50–52, 269n47; topology of (in Deleuze and Guattari), 61; and the unmediated copy, 25–26

noise: cosmic, 197, 214; creaturely, 240; inconsistency of, 230; music imitating, 189; pure, 198; "superficial noise of daily existence" (Jankélévitch), 199; unconscious noise of the real, 11

notation, musical: in Adorno, 112, 115–16, 123–24, 157–58, 168, 181, 281n15, 281n27; associated with *ars nova*, 95; in Bekker, 125; in Christensen, 113; in Jankélévitch, 184; in relation to *Ton*, 71

notation, rhythmic, 209

noumenon. *See* thing-in-itself

novel, and Mahler's form, 150

opera: in Bloch's writing, 93–94, 98–99; *Pelléas et Mélisande* (Debussy), 11, 195–96. *See also* Wagner, Richard

orchestrion, 109, 280n9

organisms, as bodies, 142, 194, 297nn51–52

Pachelbel, Johann, 99

paidia, 20

painting: abstraction in modern, 16; and Adorno, 281n27; Art Informel, 117; and Benjamin, 286n73; Deleuze's study of Francis Bacon, 210, 216, 234; and Hegel, 79, 84, 88, 102, 233, 277n72; and the tone (Sulzer), 71–72

Palestrina, Giovanni Pierluigi da, 97

Pandora (streaming music service), 1

panic, Dionysian, 165

paradox of a maximally ephemeral transcendence embodied by an ethical musical experience, 192

paradox of negativity (Jankélévitch), 180

paradox of the immediate/unmediated copy, 25–26, 29, 30, 36, 40, 51–55, 61–62, 68–69, 77, 86, 88–90, 106, 128, 152, 166, 181, 190, 202, 218–19, 224, 228, 238, 254

paradox of the ineffable, 10, 26, 30–31, 43–62, 90, 105–6, 118, 120, 128, 145, 173, 206, 219, 224, 233, 242, 246, 251–52, 269n47

paradox of the vernacular, 11–13, 27, 30, 110, 145–54, 243–58

Pater, Walter, 27

phonograph (record), 11; for Adorno, 155–59, 168, 191

phthoggos ("a clear and distinct sound"), 273n17

phylogenesis, 216–17, 234, 240

piano: abstract sounds of as potentially representational (Deleuze and Guattari), 238; arrangements for, 281; as a mirror of imaginary tones, a musical typewriter of extraordinary potentiality, sonic furniture, 113–14; as pedagogical tool (for Jankélévitch), 175–77; prepared, 230; in the *Tendenz des Materials*, 122–23; in Wittgenstein's life, 160–64

Piekut, Benjamin, 14

Pinsent, David, 161–63

Plato: in Deleuze, 60–61; doctrine of anamnesis, 123; *Meno*, 114; paranoid take on music from, 20; in Schopenhauer, 38–39, 42–49, 62, 242; Socrates's banishment of certain modes and rhythms, 1–3, 20; *Timaeus*, 21, 220

Plotinus, 21–23, 31, 34, 194

poetry: born of the *Geist* of music (Nietzsche), 51; Deleuzian artwork as a "poem without figures," 214; and Hegel, 92; of Heine (in Schumann's *Dichterliebe*), 161–63; Homeric, 20; independence from music, 38, 88; intertwining with music (Deleuze and Guattari), 233; mimetic relationship with music, 1, 20; Nietzsche on lyric poetry, 269nn47–48; "poem about

poetry (*continued*)
poetry" (Jankélévitch), 17; the poetic state, 184; "residue" of (Bloch), 107; in Schoenberg's formalism, 144; tension between procedure and, 104

polyphony: "alert polyphonic thinking" of Schoenberg (Adorno), 144; music's polyphonic character, 194–95; as an oblique afterimage of the social character of ancient mimesis (Adorno about Schoenberg's), 117–18; ontological, 246; vocal, 97, 125

popular music, 8, 11, 149, 243

present: in *charme*, 183–84; the creative instant (Jankélévitch), 178, 180; "darkness of the lived moment" (Bloch), 64, 90, 179; "privileged instants" (Deleuze), 208

Princeton Radio Project, 156

Prokofiev, Sergei, 189

Proust, Marcel, 134, 150, 209; *In Search of Lost Time*, 298n58

Ptolemy, 21

punctuation, 132–36, 139–41, 149

puns, 58

Pythagoras: Pythagorean comma, 45, 75–76, 124; Pythagorean cosmology, 21, 29, 39, 207, 219–23; Pythagorean metaphysics, 37, 44–46, 221, 241–42, 265n43; Pythagorean speculations (in Hanslick), 37

quadrivium, 21, 37, 95, 207, 221, 224, 241, 296n44

Quintilianus, Aristides, 221

quoddity, 173–84, 190–93, 199, 212; for Lévinas, 291n26

radio, 157

Rameau, Jean-Philippe, 232

Rancière, Jacques, "distribution of the sensible" in the arts, 11, 203, 263n21

Ravel, Maurice: *Le tombeau de Couperin*, 187–88; mechanical and neoclassical tropes in, 10

Reger, Max, 93

repetition: art's repetition of, 214; creative, 186–87; Deleuze's theory of, 208–10, 296n49; involuntary repetition of the vernacular in Mahler, 151; for Jankélévitch, 186–87; kitsch's deadening, 46; music reaching beyond mere (Adorno), 244; for Ornette Coleman, 249; a rhythm of difference and, 60–61; in Satie's *Vexations*, 187

resistance: of Beethoven's late style (Adorno), 135; creating genuinely resistant art, 54–55, 114–18, 229–30, 298n56; ethical, 10, 168, 244–45; fracture as a part of musical, 115; in language, 132; of literature, 150; in Mahler (Adorno), 12, 145–50, 157; musical form as the proper grounds for (Adorno), 247; of music to interpretive scrutiny and semantic decoding, 5; of music to the reasoned containers of language (Wackenroder), 24; in the paradox of the vernacular, 11, 252; political, 15; resistant modernism, 117; Schoenberg's, 143–45; utopia as a resistant falsehood, 108, 119

rhizomatic: fabric of social movements, 253; framings of music history, 14

Riegl, Alois, 123

Robbe-Grillet, Alain, 235

Rodin, Auguste, 240

Roland-Manuel, Alexis, 231–32

Rosen, Charles, 134–35

Rosset, Clement, 31

Rousseau, Jean-Jacques, 6, 50, 111

Rudaki, 5, 261n9

Russell, Bertrand, 255

Satie, Erik, 187–88

Saussure, Ferdinand de, 252, 254

Schall, 72–73, 77, 83, 156, 274n24

Schelling, Friedrich Wilhelm Joseph: admiration from Deleuze, 59; Pythagorean thinking in the music writing of, 37–38;

as subject of Jankélévitch's doctoral dissertation, 7, 17, 167, 189
Schenker, Heinrich, 74–76, 88, 125, 133, 186, 275nn33–34
Schoenberg, Arnold, 8, 27, 69, 93, 157, 160, 186; in Adorno's writing, 117–18, 122, 126, 128–29, 133, 152, 217, 231; "dialectics of loneliness," 146; *Herzgewächse*, 137–45; and historical contingency, 86; on Mahler, 151; and the tone, 74–76
Schopenhauer, Arthur: and absolute music, 268n23; Adorno on, 54–57; Bloch on, 53–54, 272n12; Deleuze on, 59–61; Jankélévitch on, 57–59, 271n61; on music, 25–26, 34–42; on music's relationship to narrative and pictures, 267n13; on the paradox around music's proximity to Kant's noumenal, 25; Plato in, 38–39, 42–49, 62; on reason and feeling, 35. *See also* paradox of the immediate/unmediated copy; paradox of the ineffable
Schubert, Franz, 93; *Die schöne Müllerin*, 171–72, 182; whistled by Wittgenstein, 161
Schumann, Robert, 21; admiration for (Adorno, Deleuze, Guattari, Wittgenstein, and Barthes), 8; in Deleuze and Guattari's writing, 230–38, 242; *Dichterliebe*, 162–63; on tones, 73; understood only through the praxis of performance (Barthes), 165; "Warum?," 29, 236–38; whistled by Wittgenstein, 161
Schütz, Heinrich, 99
science, art and (Nietzsche), 270n51
Scruton, Roger, 34, 116
Second Viennese School, 10, 248
self-encounter, Bloch's, 63–66, 81, 83, 87, 93, 114
"self-tone" (Uexküll), 227
semiotics, 252–55; "a-signifying semiotics," 61, 206, 218–19. *See also* biosemiotics
sense, and rhythm, 212
serialism: institutional, 164; integral, 8, 116, 124; total, 145, 164
Shklovsky, Victor, 27

Shostakovich, Dmitri, Symphony no. 11, 189
Siegel, 81–84, 89, 92, 98, 104, 156
signifier, radical elimination of the (Guattari), 218
silence: call for, 7, 16, 28, 34; cosmic, 191–99; of the God of Abraham, 193; of an inhuman modern condition, 105; making the mute elegant (Adorno), 282n34; of the musical experience, 183; music as, 198; music as in a temporal state between articulation and, 193; as a perpetually incomplete negation, 199; Wittgenstein's, 160–64
singing: for Bloch, 278n79; feeling-oneself-sing, 190; in jubilation, 22; singing-to-oneself, 82–83, 93, 111, 215
Slayer (band), as "enforced" mode, 1
song: bird song, 10; ecstatic song of the common vineyard worker, 23; linked to poetry and dance, 20; "natural song" (Adler), 75; protest songs, 98; shepherd's song (*jubilum*), 22; undeveloped song, 111; unformed song (Adler), 83; verses in, 93
Spinoza, Baruch, 204–5
Spotify, 1
Steege, Benjamin, 74, 275n30
Stockhausen, Karlheinz, 214, 231, 235
Strauss, Richard, 93, 102; Wittgenstein's distaste for, 160
Stravinsky, Igor, 231; primitivism of, 115, 149
structuralism, 18, 61, 166, 218–19, 223–24, 231, 242, 253–55
Stumpf, Carl, 74, 274n29
stupidity, the constant reproduction of (Adorno), 244
Subotnik, Rose Rosengard, 13
suffering, in Mahler, 146, 149
Sulzer, Johann George, 71–72
Sweelinck, Jan P., 99
syncope, 200. *See also* Clément, Catherine

Taruskin, Richard: forecasting the demise of musical literacy, 11, 263n22; labeling Jankélévitch "anti-Adorno," 13

Tchaikovsky, Pyotr Ilyich, 143
technique: archaic or outworn techniques in Bloch's event-forms, 95–97, 102–6; as the foundation of all art (Deleuze and Guattari), 248; musical material as a precise history of compositional (Adorno), 122
Tendenz des Materials, 122–27, 157, 231–32, 284n57; Mahler's compositions and the, 149, 152; and *la ritournelle*, 205; Schoenberg's compositions and the, 137, 144
thing-in-itself: craving for the, 54; hearing as privileged sense for accessing, 58; as inaccessible, 35, 43, 180–81, 191, 194; mathematics as able to access, 219; music's relation to, 25–26, 55, 68–69, 130, 194, 254; for Schopenhauer, 65; for speculative realists, 253
Thorpe, W. H., 297n52
Tieck, Ludwig, 6, 24, 40
time: for Bergson, 169–73; for Bloch, 64; consciousness of, 64; and film, 204, 235–36; the flow of lived (Deleuze and Guattari), 205–8; flux, 49, 91; inconsistency of musical (Jankélévitch), 49, 177–81, 191, 200; and Jankélévitch's *charme*, 183; for Kant, 172; musical notation's reorganization of musical (Adorno), 112, 116; music's exceptionalism and the passage of, 58; *syncope* (Clément), 200. *See* present
Tin Pan Alley, as naive escapism, 115, 145
Ton: as distinct from *Schall* or *Klang* (Hanslick), 274n24; as a modifier for compound nouns, 70; translation of, 71–72, 273n19. *See* Bloch, Ernst
topology, Nietzsche's, 51, 61
totality: Adorno's notion of, 118; appearance of (in Mahler's music), 151; Deleuze and Guattari's rejection of any governing logic of, 228; music's expression of an emotional, 40; organic, 189–94; social, 107–8, 122, 167, 190

transcendent critique, 120–26, 131, 136, 155, 171. *See also* immanent critique
translation: "the dark untranslatable core of materiality," 253; of "*Ich bin an mir*" (Bloch), 63; of instrumental music, 5; of lower language into higher language (Benjamin), 130; music as "prototype of untranslatability," 131; of music into words (Deleuze and Guattari), 233; of *la ritournelle*, 205; a supposed "perpetually inaccessible translator" (in Plato and Aristotle), 4; of the word *Ton*, 71

Uexküll, Jakob von, 225–28, 234, 237, 240, 297nn50–52, 297n54
unmediated copy. *See* paradox of the immediate/unmediated copy
utopia: for Adorno, 107–27, 157; for Bloch, 53, 64–70, 84–93, 98–105, 107–14; Bloch as rehabilitator of, 105; longing in (Bloch), 108; in Mahler's music, 146, 151; in modern art, 120; as a resistant falsehood, 108, 119; in Schoenberg's music, 145; visual (in Jankélévitch's marginal notes), 175–76

vagueness: as explanatory/illustrative, 9, 17; of music, 26, 28, 30, 88, 129, 187
Varèse, Edgard, 231
vernacular. *See* Mahler, Gustav; paradox of the vernacular
Versprachlichung (tonal language), 172; for Adorno, 7, 27, 105, 128, 131, 144, 166, 238, 284n64; for Bloch, 131; for Deleuze and Guattari, 216–17, 228, 232, 248; for Jankélévitch, 28, 181–82, 186, 190, 201–2, 204; in Mahler's music, 147, 149; and the *Tendenz des Materials*, 152, 155, 157; for Wittgenstein, 164
vibration: in Hegel, 77–81, 84, 87, 276n46; in modern painting (Greenberg), 16
Vitry, Philippe de, 95
Vitus, Saint, dance of, 115
voice: Being as, 223; in Berg's *Wozzeck*, 102;

for Bloch, 278n79; distinction between mere physical sound and the (Hegel), 276n52; of God, 192, 205; interiority of (Hegel), 87, 277n53; and *phthoggos*, 273n17; "unknown voice" (Jankélévitch), 199

Wackenroder, Wilhelm Heinrich, 6, 23–24, 40, 68–69, 72–74, 81, 83, 85, 91, 111
Wagner, Richard, 8, 30, 46, 68, 93–94, 96, 102, 132, 134, 184; and absolute music, 268n23; as balancer of Apollonian and the Dionysian drives, 51; as "confirming" and "affirming" the will (Bloch), 53–54; as "enforced" mode, 1; and leitmotif semantics, 148, 238; as restorer of excellence to the aesthetic sphere (in Nietzsche's view), 52; *Tristan* chord, 231
Wahl, Jean, 17, 167
"walk-up" music (for mound-approaching pitchers), as "enforced" mode, 1
Watkins, Holly, 23
Weber, Max, 95, 123–25, 134, 284n56
Webern, Anton, 117–18

Weiner, Norbert, 297n51
Whitehead, Alfred North, 253
whole: part as representative of, 38, 142; "The true is the whole" (Hegel), 119; "The whole is the false" (Adorno), 119. *See also* totality
will, 25, 30, 35–60, 67–68, 90, 106, 149, 173, 183, 197, 224, 227–28, 233, 242, 244, 247, 257
wine, as poetic fuel, 5
Wittgenstein, Ludwig, 28, 160–66, 170, 180, 183, 255
Wittgenstein, Paul, 160
Wölfflin, Heinrich, 123
Wolf, Hugo, 93

Young, La Monte, 231

Zarlino, Gioseffo, 221

www.ingramcontent.com/pod-product-compliance
Lightning Source LLC
Chambersburg PA
CBHW021933290426
44108CB00012B/822